Information Technology and Scholarship

Applications in the Humanities and Social Sciences

edited by
Terry Coppock

Published *for* THE BRITISH ACADEMY
by OXFORD UNIVERSITY PRESS

Oxford University Press, Great Clarendon Street, Oxford OX2 6DP

Oxford   New York
Athens Auckland Bangkok Bogota Bombay
Buenos Aires Calcutta Cape Town Dar es Salaam
Delhi Florence Hong Kong Istanbul Karachi
Kuala Lumpur Madras Madrid Melbourne
Mexico City Nairobi Paris Singapore
Taipei Tokyo Toronto Warsaw

and associated companies in
Berlin Ibadan

British Library Cataloguing in Publication Data
Data available

ISBN 0-19-726205-8

Typeset in England by the Alden Group, Oxford
Printed in Great Britain on acid-free paper by
Alden Press, Oxford

Contents

List of Contributors

Professor A. H. Anderson, Cognitive Engineering, Dept of Psychology, University of Glasgow, Glasgow, G12 8QQ.

Professor R. C. Beacham, Dept of Theatrical Studies, University of Warwick, Coventry, CV4 7AG.

Professor R. Blundell, Dept of Economics, University College London, Gower Street, London, WC1E 6BT.

Professor R. J. Bradley FBA, Dept of Archaeology, University of Reading, Whiteknights, PO Box 217, Reading, RG6 2AW.

Dr M. T. Bravo, Dept of Social Anthropology, University of Manchester, Roscoe Building, Manchester, M13 9PL.

Professor A. D. Cliff FBA, Dept of Geography, University of Cambridge, Downing Place, Cambridge, CB2 3EN.

Professor J. T. Coppock FBA, The Carnegie Trust for the Universities of Scotland, Cameron House, Abbey Park Place, Dunfermline, Fife KY12 7BUZZ.

Professor C. Crook, Dept of Human Resources, Loughborough University of Technology, Loughborough, LE11 3TU.

Dr I. Cross, Faculty of Music, University of Cambridge, West Road, Cambridge, CB3 9DP.

Dr J. A. Doornik, Nuffield College, Oxford, OX1 1NF.

Professor E. C. Fernie, Courtauld Institute of Art, Somerset House, Strand, London, WC2R 0RN.

Professor J.-P. Genet, Maitre de Conference l'Histoire Medievale, Paris, 147 Avenue Parmentier, 75010 Paris.

Professor G. N. Gilbert, Dept of Sociology, University of Surrey, Guildford, GU2 5XH.

Professor A. F. Heath FBA, Nuffield College, Oxford, OX1 1NF.

Professor D. F. Hendry FBA, Nuffield College, Oxford, OX1 1NF.

Dr E. Higgs, School of Historical, Political and Sociological Studies, University of Exeter, Exeter, EX4 4QJ.

Mr G. Judge, Dept of Economics, University of Portsmouth, Portsmouth, PO1 2UP.

Sir Anthony Kenny FBA, Rhodes House, Oxford, OX1 3RG.

Professor D. N. MacCormick FBA, Faculty of Law, University of Edinburgh, Old College, South Bridge, Edinburgh, EH8 9YL.

Dr A. A. Marsden, Dept of Music, University of Lancaster, Lancaster, LA1 4YN.

Professor R. J. Morris, Dept of Economic and Social History, University of Edinburgh, William Robertson Building, 50 George Square, Edinburgh, EH8 9JY.

Professor S. Openshaw, Centre for Computational Geography, University of Leeds, Leeds, LS2 9JT.

Dr A. Prescott, Dept of Manuscripts, The British Library, Euston Road, London, WC1B 3DG.

Dr S. Ross, Humanities Computing and Information Management, Faculty of Arts, University of Glasgow, Glasgow, G12 8QQ.

Professor T. Scaltsas, Dept of Philosophy, University of Edinburgh, David Hume Tower, George Square, Edinburgh, EH8 9JX.

Professor S. Shennan, Institute of Archaeology, University College London, 31-34 Gordon Square, London, WC1H 0PY.

Dr R. M. Smith FBA, Cambridge Group for the History of Population and Social Structure, University of Cambridge, 27 Trumpington Street, Cambridge, CB2 1QA.

Dr S. Smith, Institute of Historical Research, University of London, Senate House, Malet Street, London, WC1E 7HU.

Dr K. I. B. Spärck Jones FBA, Computer Laboratory, University of Cambridge, New Museums Site, Pembroke Street, Cambridge, CB2 3QG.

Professor P. R. Susskind, Centre for Law, Computers and Technology, University of Strathclyde, Glasgow, G1 1XQ.

Ms H. Sutherland, Dept of Applied Economics, University of Cambridge, Sidgwick Avenue, Cambridge, CB3 9DE.

Dr H. Thompson, Human Communications Research Centre, University of Edinburgh, 2 Buccleuch Place, Edinburgh, EH8 9LW.

Professor M. Twycross, Dept of English, University of Lancaster, Lancaster, LA1 4YW.

Professor W. Vaughan, Dept of History of Art, Birkbeck College, 43 Gordon Square, London, WC1H 0PD.

Professor A. G. Wilson FBA, Vice-Chancellor's Office, University of Leeds, Leeds, LS2 9JT.

Preface

In 1992 the British Academy and the British Library established a joint panel under my chairmanship to review Information Needs in the Humanities, with special reference to the use of information technology (IT). It reported in 1993 and a manuscript report has been deposited at the National Reference Library at Boston Spa; a summary illustrative document has also been published, entitled *Information Technology in Humanities Scholarship*. From the inquiry it seemed logical to take the study further by examining IT applications in all the major disciplines and, since the Academy has accepted responsibility for both the humanities and the social sciences, to extend such a study to include the major social science disciplines.

Accordingly, the Academy agreed to host a symposium which I convened at the Academy's offices on 18–19 October 1996, to examine the application of IT in research in the different disciplines, with particular reference to two questions: (i) 'to what extent had the advent of IT affected the scholar's choice of research topic – had it been more of the same or were completely new topics being investigated which were previously impracticable?', and (ii) 'had there been significant changes in the way in which these research topics were approached?'. It was clear that the ability to handle large quantities of data at high speed had affected the scale on which studies were undertaken and had certainly enabled some topics to be approached that were formerly considered too laborious and time-consuming. The importance of extending the area covered and the time dimensions should not be underestimated, but the more fundamental question was whether the advent of IT had led to the adoption of quite new approaches – in other words, had there been any kind of paradigm shift? Were we still in a situation comparable to that of the change from horse-ploughing to tractor-ploughing, where we simply did more of the same, but faster and better, or had completely new ideas been developed?

Having agreed the scope of the symposium, the next (and perhaps the most difficult) task was to identify potential contributors who had something significant to say and who were known to be undertaking work of this kind. Furthermore, they had to be willing to speak at the symposium and to contribute a scholarly paper for subsequent publication. This led to widespread consultation with senior figures in the different disciplines, but the level of expertise proved very variable. A further complication was the widening scope of IT. There had been a tendency to equate IT with computing and the handling of large quantities of numerical data, and computers do in fact play a key role. But there is a growing interest in the handling of text, especially in the humanities, and graphic representation – of maps, drawings, paintings and other artefacts – is of increasing importance, as the papers on theatre history, the history of art, and musical representation show.

In addition to giving some account of their own research, contributors were asked to provide a broad overview of developments in their field, in so far as these could be identified. Those who agreed to contribute were asked to prepare a draft paper, to make a short verbal presentation at the symposium, and to revise the paper in the light of the discussion for subsequent publication. It was intended that as much discussion as possible should occur at the symposium and, in part to facilitate this, a commentator was identified for each paper to open the discussion and subsequently to produce the written critiques which accompany the papers in this volume. In the event, not all who were invited to speak were subsequently willing to revise their papers to the required standards; but this provided an opportunity to fill some gaps and three papers which were not delivered at the symposium have been included, viz., on econometrics by David Hendry and Jurgen Doornik, on social anthropology by Michael Bravo and on philosophy by Theodore Scaltsas.

In the absence of any comprehensive survey, it cannot be claimed that the contributions are necessarily representative of the current situation in the different humanities and social science disciplines, or in those broad fields as a whole. The only common characteristic is variability. In some fields, such as linguistics in the humanities and econometrics in the social sciences, computer applications are now the norm; in others, such as theatre studies and the history of art, only a small minority is active in research using IT.

Sir Anthony Kenny, Past President of the Academy and a pioneer of applications of computers to critical analysis of classical texts, has contributed an introduction on scholarship and information technology, and Alan Wilson, Vice-Chancellor of Leeds University, has concentrated on the commonalities in approaches to IT in the social sciences. The remaining papers fall into the two groups, nine in the humanities and seven in the social sciences. To provide a link between the two, Seamus Ross has contributed a paper on networking, and the volume concludes with a overview of the symposium and of possible future developments.

Thanks are due to many people for their contributions to making the symposium a success. Rosemary Lambeth, an Assistant Secretary at the Academy, was the administrative linchpin, making the arrangements and corresponding with contributors both before and after the symposium. Chairmen of sessions, speakers and commentators all created the basis for lively discussions, and Sir Charles Chadwyck-Healey hosted a dinner for those with a formal role in the symposium. I must add a special word of thanks to Ann Law in Glasgow University and Theodore and Patricia Scaltas in Edinburgh University, who gave invaluable help when I was laid low for six months by a serious illness. I believe that this volume, though unavoidably delayed, will provide an important benchmark in a period of rapid change in the role of information technology in scholarship and teaching in the humanities and social sciences.

Terry Coppock

Scholarship and information technology

ANTHONY KENNY

Past President of The British Academy

The British Academy exists to foster scholarship in both the humanities and the social sciences. The impact of information technology on the two sets of academic disciplines has been very different. The research methods of social scientists have been transformed by the use of the computer; the humanities have been comparatively unaffected. Any reader of the present work will see ample evidence of the differing fortune of information technology in the two areas: what remains unclear is how far this divergence was predictable from the outset, and how far it is the result of contingent patterns of academic fashion.

Of course, there are many ways in which all scholars, in whatever discipline, have found their environment changed out of recognition since computers were invented. For all scholars a central part of the environment is the library. Before the age of the computer this was, for most scholars most of the time, their own University library, accessed through its local hard-copy catalogue. Nowadays all academic libraries have automated their current cataloguing, and most academic libraries have had their catalogues retrospectively converted. The networking of catalogues has meant that every major library has the catalogue of every other. The pooling of records has meant that the forty million titles of the great OCLC catalogue in the sky can be accessed by cataloguers world wide. Even those who regret the loss of the card catalogue, or mourn for the old guard books, of their own institution must find compensation in the ability to read others' catalogues without leaving their own library or indeed their own study. Not only have the old catalogues been networked but new kinds of catalogue (e.g., of incipits) and new kinds of search (e.g., by years of publications) have become possible.

Within the libraries not only the catalogues but also texts have been digitized. Most standard works of reference have now gone electronic, such as the national bibliographies , the Oxford English Dictionary, and the Dictionary of National Biography. A series of vast computerized concordances, beginning with the *Index Thomisticus*, was succeeded by the realization that word searches were nowadays best conducted by the individual user on full-text databases. Commercial and academic providers have now made available the entire output of the authors of ancient Greece and Rome, most of the classics of poetry and prose in English, the Old and New Testaments in several languages, the gigantic output of the Greek and Latin Fathers, the Dead Sea Scrolls and portions of Buddhist Scripture. One can say that the literary canon has been digitized: and also many deutero-canonical writers, such as neglected women authors, are now available in electronic form. Most current major newspapers, and long runs of previous ones are accessible digitally. So too are many collections of manuscripts, from Beowulf to the Wittgenstein *Nachlass*.

The digitization of texts is important for librarians because it brings great benefits of preservation – the Burney collection of eighteenth century newspapers in the British Library would long since have been worn out by consultation had it not been rescued by the advent first of microfilm and now of computerization. The computer offers new modes of access: the public, which could never see more than a single page of an illuminated manuscript on exhibition can now view digital facsimiles of all pages together – without even needing to click a mouse, now that page-turning has been realistically simulated.

There is no doubt that all of us who use libraries, whatever our discipline, have lived through a revolution. But now that the revolution is complete, where are we? It is here that humanists and social scientists give very different answers.

For the scholar who works on texts – in philosophy, classic, modern languages, biblical studies – the passage of the revolution has brought us not to 1793, or even 1805, but to 1816. The Bourbons and the Habsburgs are still there. The book has not died, and is not showing any signs of doing so: more and more monographs are produced each year. Even the print-on-paper academic journal, which has long been pronounced to be in terminal decline, is taking an unconscionable time dying. But what is most noticeable is how little change in the content of articles and books has been brought about by the advent of information technology. Several contributors to this book remark on the very meagre harvest reached by a literature search for scholarly work indebted to the computer. I have had the same experience: a search of recent issues of some fifty journals in theology, classics and English literature produced one review of the CD-Rom Index Thomisticus, and several references to e-mail discussion groups, and nothing else.

Introducing a symposium on computing in the humanities at Elvetham Hall in 1990, I said

> Between humdrum task performance and showpiece research, what the humanities scholarly community is really anxious to see is work which is both (a) respected as an original scholarly contribution within its own discipline and (b) could clearly not have been done without a computer. After thirty-odd years of this kind of research, there are embarrassingly few books and articles which can be confidently pointed out as passing both tests.

I expected this remark to be immediately challenged: I thought participants in the conference would quickly bring to my attention seminal works I had overlooked. This did not happen; and the material contained in this present volume does little to dispel the sense that the promise once held out by enthusiasts for computing in the humanities has been largely unfulfilled. Information technology has had little influence on linguistics; classicists find it hard to list new scholarly work whose nature has been profoundly changed by technology. Even in archaeology, which was one of the first humanities disciplines to be involved with information technology, and where electronic publishing gives enormously improved possibilities for the presenting of evidence, the actual nature of research has been remarkably little affected by the computer.

After 45 years of humanities computing why has IT had so little effect on scholarship? Several hypotheses can be put forward.

There are those who believe that all humanists are by nature Luddites who hate innovation of any kind. If there is any truth in this, it is unlikely to be the complete explanation. After all, the classicists, who might have been expected to be the most conservative of scholars, were the first to have their texts digitized in the *Thesaurus Linguae Graecae* and most of the early computer-assisted stylometric studies concerned texts in ancient Greek.

At the other extreme there are those who say that digitization has not yet provided humanists with the tools they really need for their research. Complaints are made about the early digitized texts; so Standardised General Mark-up Language (SGML) and the Text Encoding Initiative (TEI) are introduced. Then it is found that the software which was adequate to analyse the crude untagged texts is useless to exploit the new ones. We are told that the textual-research community is in need of a whole new generation of text analysis tools. This might be called the 'one more heave' school of explanation. But it is implausible to claim that the discipline of humanities computing is in its infancy, several decades after the appearance of some of the classics in the field. Where this thesis is most plausible is in the area of art history, where it is only recently that digitization has permitted the production of colour images at a resolution sufficient to satisfy the demands of scholars.

Much more plausible is the contention that computers have not been properly exploited in the humanities because there has been a shift in scholarly focus or paradigm. Some say that computers came just at the wrong time, when scholars' interests were moving from textual studies to critical theory, women's studies and the like. Computers were ill-qualified to answer the questions posed by Structuralist, Post Structuralist and Feminist critics. This is undoubtedly true, but one may wonder whether it is just a malign coincidence, or whether it has deeper causes. Perhaps humanists and scientists are different kinds of people with different kinds of tastes, and those who do not like mathematics may have been influenced by this in an early career choice. Now to their dismay they see quantification invading their own subject, whether it be English literature, Greek history, or New Testament theology. If these subjects no longer offer any escape from those wretched numbers, they might as well have become physicists or engineers. So now the more abstract, intuitive and ideological branches of the humanities become attractive to refugees from the relentless advance of technological rigour.

Another, quite different explanation is that the computer has become invisible. As Stephen Shennan points out, archaeologists in their fieldwork all make use of laptops but when publishing their results they do not mention this any more than they say they used trowels. Again, it has been pointed out that if a classicist, searching a database, hits the jackpot and finds a really interesting text, the resulting article will look exactly like a traditional article; but it would not have been there except for the digitized textual databank.

Others point out that while IT has had little visible effect on what has been written in literary subjects, it has had a substantial, and beneficial effect, on what has not been written. Dissertations that were essentially essays in vocabulary counting would not now be awarded doctorates. There was a certain kind of scholar who, editing a text by an author, would feel obliged to draw the reader's attention to all possible parallels to each passage of the text. An edition of a work by Cicero, for instance, would contain a few lines of text at the top of the page, followed by dense footnotes containing substantial portions of all Cicero's other works. The logical conclusion of this style of editing, of course, was a set of volumes of Cicero's complete works which differed from each other only in the lines in large print at the top. This type of scholarly editor has now been replaced by hypertext.

But even if information technology has had a substantial, if concealed, effect on humanities scholarship the impact can not be said to be comparable to the shift from oral to written culture, or to the introduction of printing. It has been more like the effect on *Biblioteksreise* of the switch from stage coach to railway, or the effect on scholarly communication of the introduction of the penny post. It has not so much changed patterns of scholarship as improved the life of the scholar, by freeing up a great deal of time from donkeywork for genuine research.

Matters are very different when we turn from the humanities to the social sciences. Here too it is not always easy to distinguish between developments which allow work to proceed faster from those that move research towards new paradigms. In the picturesque words of one of our contributors it may be that the computer has achieved nothing that could not have been done by a scholar working with a set of index cards, a shoe box, and about an hundred years to spare. But if this is true, it is surely an instance where a quantitative change turns into a qualitative change.

For instance, the capacity and rapid operation of super computers allow census data to be exploited, by geographers and sociologists, in ways never before dreamt of. The computer simulation of social processes allows the social sciences to mimic experimental procedures without the ethical problems of experimenting on real human beings. In economics the consequences of fiscal changes can be predicted with a scope and accuracy never before attainable. Indeed it can be claimed without hyperbole that a single suite of programs has changed the whole nature of econometrics.

The experience of IT within the discipline of history seems to have been midway between that of the humanities and the social sciences. Historians who base themselves principally on texts seem, like students of literature, to have made comparatively little use of the computer. On the other hand, those who deal with material which lends itself to tabulation, such as voting data and employment records, claim to have overturned many a cherished myth, such as the belief that the USA was a melting pot which provided a unique level of social mobility. Though even here, enthusiasts speak rather of standing on the edge of a breakthrough, rather than of a victory already accomplished.

In law the impact of IT on legal exposition and legal studies has so far been slight. The early availability of full text legal databases at first held out great hope for both academics and practitioners, but surprisingly little use seems to have been made of the retrieval systems, perhaps because keyword searching is an inadequate research tool. Like humanities scholars, lawyers passed from a period of optimism about IT to one of scepticism. But unlike humanities scholars, who have trimmed their expectations to a moderate realism, Richard Susskind remains an optimist. The disillusion, he claims, was due to the technology lag: that is to say, the gap between data processing and knowledge processing. 'It will be some years yet' he says 'before advanced enabling techniques such as conceptual retrieval, expert systems and hypertext are refined and applied successfully to help manage the difficulties which earlier technology has left as its legacy.' But later on 'systems will effortlessly guide hitherto perplexed users through the labyrinths of the law.' Indeed it is possible that they may do much of judges' work for them: 'it is possible for example that the information which will be accessible on the global highway will guide our social, domestic and working lives more directly than the primary sources (legislation and case law) themselves. In a sense this legal guidance may come to be regarded as the law itself and not just a representation of it.'

I turn finally to my own discipline of philosophy. In most areas of philosophy outside formal logic the impact of IT has been as modest as in any other text-based subject. The desire of philosophers and linguists to replace keyword-searching by concept-searching is still a long way from being adequately fulfilled. In the area of philosophical psychology, however, the computer has offered a set of metaphors and models of research which have fascinated philosophers of mind. Here it is not a matter of the computer being used as a tool to research the nature of mind; it is rather the claim that the mind, properly understood, is neither more nor less than a computer. The early ambitions of Artificial Intelligence to duplicate or simulate human understanding have largely been thwarted or abandoned. But the belief that behind perception, language and behaviour there are inner computational processes taking place in the mind survived the initial set backs. Indeed the belief was given a powerful stimulus by the development of parallel distributed processing. Cognitive scientists, at the point where the frontiers of philosophy, psychology, and linguistics meet, pin great hopes on the computer's power to simulate the neural processes of the human brain. Other philosophers are critical of talk of inner representations and processes as based on a misreading of the relationship between mind and brain.

I once used to hope that the use of computers and quantitative techniques in the study of the humanities would do something to bridge the gap between the two cultures lamented by the late C.P.Snow. In fact, what we have seen developing is a new culture gap: alongside the physical scientists there are, in the humanities and social sciences, computing academics and non-computing academics. The two groups still communicate, but with less and less comprehension of each other's work. We may be about to see the speciation of a third culture between Snow's original two.

Digital philosophical reasoning

THEODORE SCALTSAS

Department of Philosophy
University of Edinburgh

Abstract. Philosophy has been one of the pioneering disciplines with respect to the use of computers for searches of texts and of abstracts of publications. Current philosophical research involving use of computers centres on three areas. First, investigation is being undertaken on concept searches. These are sophisticated searches, for example of selected types of occurrence of clusters of terms, all of which express the same general concept. Second, extensive research is conducted on the generation of hypertext methods for displaying and relating arguments (expressed in natural language). The arguments are presented in formats and structures which reflect the philosophical elements between the arguments. Finally, the possibility of constructing philosophical expert systems is being explored. These are systems that will engage the user in argumentation at different levels of philosophical expertise.

A brief overview of the philosophical computer activity

We are now, at last, requiring our students to submit their essays in *printed* hard copies. Soon they will be submitting them on the Web. We email each other, access the library records from our desk, search electronic abstracts of publications in journals and read and search some of the main source-books on CD-ROM. Academics also cut and paste their own writings, and we let the computer prove challenging logical theorems for us. We also talk a lot about computers. In fact, models of the mind that draw their inspiration from the functioning of computers, or the structure of computers, or the networking within computers, have dominated the philosophy of mind in the past few decades, and continue to do so. Less so, but increasingly, talk of computers is entering political theory and action theory in relation to decision making (see Scaltsas 1990) Questions of how new methods of voting will change the fibre of the democratic process are taking centre stage as computers are becoming household items and interactive networks are spreading in society.

What next? Concept searches and argumentation. Concept searches will emerge as more complex word searches than we have seen so far. They will stem from a variety of methods of discovering and registering ways in which expressions cluster around concepts. At the same time, education will enjoy the next major wave of innovation of information technology, through the demystification of Artificial Intelligence (AI). Computer programs are being composed which will present the academic material in an interactive way to the user, at all educational levels. In philosophy this is already taking the form of programs which will engage the user in argumentation. Once such programs are developed, they will immediately and inevitably lead to the generation of knowledge bases which will contain philosophical expertise, and which will guide the philosophical researcher through complex structures of theory, articulated in the dialogical argumentation. Ongoing research on concept searches and 'expert philosophical systems' is the subject of a much of the present article. The reader will detect that it promotes the view that the impact of information technology in philosophical research is more radical than Anthony Kenny's appraisal of it in his Introduction to this volume.

The relevance of AI

The paper begins with the bad news – so as not to be accused of digital optimism – before computers-in-philosophy are given their due. The bad news is not catastrophic, but mostly of the 'not quite yet' type. It has to do with hopes the scientific community had for AI, which have not been realized yet, nor are they imminent, while some, the most ambitious ones, are being given up. At its most optimistic, AI aspired to the duplication of the human activity of understanding by the computer. In its more modest attire, it aimed for the simulation of human understanding. Putnam (1992: 11; 1994: 392-3) expresses serious scepticism regarding its success on either domain. He has reservations regarding the achievement of AI so far, without arguing against the possibility of receiving interesting results from it at some future date. (The distinction between duplicating and simulating is taken from Putnam.)

On the other hand, there is a brighter outlook about the model of the mind that computers have offered philosophy. This is a modular model, according to which, to use Dennett's description, one proceeds 'by analyzing a person into an organization of subsystems (organs, routines, nerves, faculties, components – even atoms) and attempting to explain the behaviour of the whole person as the outcome of the interaction of these subsystems' (Dennett 1981: 153). According to Dennett (125), 'AI has made a major contribution to philosophy and psychology by revealing a particular way in which simple cases of Hume's Problem can be solved', namely the problem of internal homunculi posited to explain how mental events of perception or understanding take place (p.122). Even if this attribution of originality to AI can be questioned, as it is by Putnam (1994:391 where he traces the origin of this conception of the mind to Alan Turing and computer science, which he distinguishes from AI.), nevertheless, the modular model of the mind sieved through to philosophy from AI through the communication bridge that was established between the two disciplines by Putnam's theory of functionalism.

The concern in this paper is to explore, not the contributions computers have made to philosophy as an object of study themselves, but their contribution as a philosophical tool. Even here, the discussion will be limited to some central areas which will not be covered by other contributions to this volume. Thus, the serious impact of computers on philosophical scholarship, as a result of the stylometric studies of the philosophical texts of philosophers will not be discussed. Such studies address questions of textual dating and textual authenticity, and therefore make a significant impact on questions of the intellectual development of particular philosophers, regarding the doctrines or beliefs that are to be attributed to them. Such, for example, has been the pioneering and influential work by Kenny (1978) on Aristotle's ethical books. Subsequent such studies have been by Ledger (1989), and also by Brandwood (1990), on Plato's dialogues.

The aim is to examine whether the impact of computers in philosophy has brought about a paradigm shift in the discipline. Are philosophers asking different questions than they asked before, owing to the use of computers in philosophy? Are they forming theories which are a result of research made possible by computers? Are they turning to directions which could not be envisaged without the use of computers? On the way towards answering these questions, further important influences that the computers are having on philosophy will be considered.

There is a fourfold division. One type comprises projects which use computers for tasks that could in principle be carried out without computers; at the opposite extreme are projects which use computers for tasks that could not be carried out without computers. Again, one type comprises projects which use computers to address conventional questions; at the opposite extreme are projects which, on account of the facility provided by computers, address questions that presuppose a paradigm shift in philosophical explanations. An example of a task which, though it could not be carried out without computers, nevertheless does not presuppose a paradigm shift, is the proof of an extremely complex logical formula by the computer.

The projects undertaken in philosophy and the achievements of each undertaking do not divide neatly into this fourfold division. The very same technological achievement might be used to ask conventional questions, or might spark off a paradigm shift; again, gradual advances along a traditional research path might reveal unsought for information which might lead to questions of an entirely novel kind. What follows is an examination of applications of computers to philosophy which fall within the region of tasks which would not be attempted without computers, and tasks which we would not have thought of without computers.

Concept searches

First consideration is given to the *Philosopher's Index* (Philosophy Documentation Centre, updated yearly) which has been in circulation for many years and publishes a compilation of abstracts of philosophical books and articles in the main philosophical journals. Interestingly, it started being published in book form, not electronically. The value in this publication is, of course, the search facility, which, in the beginning, was organized through a combination of the order in which the abstracts were published and the indexes. Presently, and for some years now, the *Index* has been made available in electronic form. This allows for much faster searches of the abstracts, according to many more keys. This in itself is a great advance and of much assistance to researchers in philosophy, but it does not constitute an advance from the point of view of the present concern. The questions that are being asked and answered in the electronic version of the *Philosopher's Index* are the same as those that were asked when it was published in hard copy only. Yet, much more is possible, and has in fact been realized in a different project on academic abstracts in chemistry, which has already achieved results from an approach that would be open to the *Philosopher's Index* to implement now.

The *Language Technology Group* in the Human Communications Research Centre (HCRC) of the University of Edinburgh has developed a program, SISTA (see website http://www.hcrc.ed.ac.uk/AnnualReport95/Text/hi4-www.html#hi4-Key2) which surveys abstracts of chemical papers written over several decades. The abstracts contain key technical terms, and the program is designed to observe which key terms cluster together in the abstracts. The program uses the information about the key terms by being in the position to inform the user that a topic is being discussed in an abstract, or in the corresponding paper, even when the key term for that topic is not mentioned in the abstract. The program achieves this by having charted the clusters of terms in the abstracts, and by calculating the probability of a particular topic *a* being discussed in a paper when the term '*a*' is not present in the abstract. This is attained on the basis of the fact that *a* is discussed in most cases when *b* and *c* are discussed, and in this case, the abstract does make mention of *b* and *c* though not of *a*. Thus the user may be alerted by the computer to the relevance of a paper for his/her research, even though the paper would not have been identified when the abstracts were searched for the desired subject *a*. Even more dynamically, *a* does not have to be a topic discussed in any of the abstracts, but the term '*a*' can be associated by the user with certain topics in the abstracts, so that it comes up when these topics come up. Thus a search of the abstracts may alert the user to any type of information relevant to the topic discussed in an abstract, even if that information is not found in the abstract.

While the operation works, it is not asking new questions and not generating a paradigm shift. This is true; but an entirely independent program to SISTA, yet related with respect to its operation, might make that difference. Such a program was presented at the annual conference of the Association for Computers and the Humanities at the Sorbonne in Paris in April 1994. The name of the Project is Arachne. What the program does is to scan large bodies of text and register groups of terms co-occurring in the text, within a specified proximity. Then it creates a statistical chart of the co-occurring terms, according to frequency of co-occurrence. A particular term could co-occur with other terms in different clusters, with different frequency.

What is interesting about Arachne is that it starts not with conceptual questions, but with statistical ones. It makes no presuppositions about which terms should or should not co-occur. Nor, very importantly, is it seeking any specific terms and their cooccurrence. Rather, it begins scanning the text in a 'free search', looking for co-occurrent terms of any kind. As a consequence, its results are entirely unpredictable and hence, potentially very valuable because, over a large corpus, co-occurrence would not be accidental. Although many of the clusters would be rather predictable, the method has the power to uncover relations between terms which had thus far gone unnoticed. Even more, it may bring to scholars' attention conceptual practices of which they are not aware, and which point to conceptual relations that hitherto have not been studied. Thus, it is possible for the method to uncover significant co-occurrences between terms which do not fall within any of the categories of related terms that are studied by philosophers, such as genus-species terms, being the definition of a term, being the opposite of a term, being synonyms, expressing necessary or sufficient conditions, and so on. Thus the method has the potential of alerting scholars to correlations between terms leading to discoveries about conceptual relations in our practices.

Related to the previous two projects is a current concern of Project Archelogos (see website http://www.archelogos.phil.ed.ac.uk/) for concept searches. This is described below, but it suffices, for the moment, to say that it comprises the creation of a database with philosophical arguments. Archelogos is currently investigating methods by which concept searches can be conducted by the computer. There is a fundamental difference between searching for terms and searching for concepts. Searching for a term in a text is an activity not bound by the meaning of the term; the computer will register all occurrences of the term. If semantic considerations are taken into account, then the occurrences of a term would have to be segregated into groups of synonymy. This would presuppose a method by which the computer could be alerted to changes of meaning between different occurrences of the same term. The alerting could be tied to a systematic feature of the context in which the term occurs, signalling which meaning the term has in that context, or, if such a systematic feature is not available, term-tagging that is introduced by the authors of the text. Either method would allow the computer to segregate different uses of the same term, corresponding to its various meanings.

Yet, this would still not constitute a concept search. That is so because the same concept could be expressed by different terms; not necessarily all occurrences of each of these terms but only some of each, under a specific usage of it, and so on Thus, concept searching is not only a matter of conducting complex Boolean searches (allowing one to search for the occurrence of alternative terms). Concept searching involves methods of distinguishing between sub-uses of terms, which normal Boolean searches do not segregate. Insofar as context can be one of the parameters in differentiating between the various uses of a term, methods such as the one described above in SISTA, or in Arachne, which are sensitive to the environment of the occurrence of a term, may prove to be innovative. (But, so as to curtail excessive optimism, reservations should be registered concerning the power of, at least formalist, computer languages, to capture context, as in Kime's (1997: 14) article, 'Reinventing the square wheel').

When advances are made with regard to concept searching, it will be possible to search for philosophical positions, expressed in sentences or phrases. This will allow users of databases such as Archelogos, or the *Philosopher's Index*, which contain many philosophical positions and arguments in them, to be searched for philosophical positions or theses found in the database in various lexical forms.

Symbolic reasoning

It is well known that one of the great successes in the application of computers is in the domain of logic. Many programs have been created to prove theorems on computer, and there are many, very successful on-going automated reasoning projects throughout the academic world. Furthermore, there is a very useful educational spin-off, with a multitude of logic instruction programs which are successfully being employed in first-year formal logic courses in universities.

But computability has not always been a winning strategy in the applications of computers in the sciences. In a book which is critical of the goals of artificial intelligence, entitled *What Computers Still Can't Do*, Dreyfus (1992) compares artificial intelligence to alchemy. The point of his comparison is to suggest that initially, the artificial intelligence programme set too high goals for itself, goals that, as it is transpiring, are untenable. What artificial intelligence sets out to achieve is to simulate human behaviour, so as to produce useful robots in different facets of human life. Dreyfus reports that 'we found, first, that the descriptive or phenomenological evidence, considered apart from traditional philosophical prejudices, suggests that non programmable human capacities are involved in all forms of intelligent behaviour' (285). In view of this problem, the program of the simulation of human behaviour is bound not to succeed completely. It is the latter qualification on which Dreyfus concentrates. Not succeeding completely still allows for several useful possibilities. One, in particular, which Dreyfus develops, seems very promising.

Dreyfus describes a trend in logic programs, whereby the computer and the user work together towards the resolution of a problem. In particular, he refers to SAM, Semi-Automated Mathematics, which is a program that has solved an open problem in lattice theory, and quotes its developers: 'Semi-automated mathematics is an approach to theorem-proving which seeks to combine automatic logic routines with ordinary proof procedures in such a manner that the resulting procedure is both efficient and subject to human intervention in the form of control and guidance' (Dreyfus; 301). This heuristic use of the computer, as a work-tool rather than as a worker itself, is the way that computers will be increasingly used in philosophy. The domain in which they will be so used is the domain of *argumentation*.

A straight-forward application of computers for aiding the user in understanding argumentation is a program called *Dialogue*. *Dialogue* is an educational program, targetted at undergraduates. It undertakes to present to the student the arguments in Plato's dialogue *The Euthyphro*. It operates by presenting the premises to the student, and asking them to choose one of a number of possible conclusions. If the student does not select the correct conclusion, *Dialogue* offers similar examples, trying to get the student to 'see' which conclusion follows in the original case.

A more ambitious but not yet realized endeavour is the program *Socrates*, by Project *Archelogos* (see website: http://www.archelogos.phil.ed.ac.uk). *Socrates* is a database containing a philosophical expert system called *Virtual Dialogue*. An expert system, as described by Fargues (1990; 272-4), in his article on 'Remarks on the interrelations between artificial intelligence, mathematical logic, and humanities', involves a database that contains knowledge of a specific domain, which is usually presented in the form of rules on a domain of objects. This applies to formalizable knowledge domains, as for instance, the criteria for dating archaeological artefacts.

Virtual Dialogue has two aspects. In one aspect it is characterized as a knowledge database, and in the other it is viewed as an expert system. As a knowledge database,

Virtual Dialogue organizes knowledge in the form of interrelated arguments. The arguments are the objects; the 'rules' are embodied in the interrelations of the arguments to one another. The arguments consist of premises and conclusions. The interrelations between the philosophical theses, whether premises or conclusions, may vary in kind. Thus, given a thesis, another thesis can be an objection to it (with supporting premises of its own); another thesis can be an amendment of the original one, in view of the objection; further, a thesis can be a synthesis of two other theses within the context of a criticism and so on. The computer prompts the user for a commitment to a thesis, and then gradually takes the user through objections, and amendments, or refinements, of the thesis, by prompting the user to choose at each step, and then confronting the user with more criticism and possibilities of responding to it constructively.

As an expert system, *Virtual Dialogue* will be a heuristic device for philosophical solutions. This pertains to the logic of the expert system, namely, the system having the power to perform logical operations on theses, according to various strategies employed in the database, and codified into rules. These strategies represent the ways in which philosophers tackle philosophical problems captured in relations between theses or arguments. The possibilities of automatic analyses of theses, and/or derivations of theses, is an exciting area of research, promising a heuristic device for philosophical innovation. It is here that the service of SAM to mathematics can be undertaken by a corresponding program for philosophy. The philosophical expert system would make alternative suggestions on the basis of trying out different codified tactics of analysing and relating theses to one another. The user would be involved in choosing between the alternatives, steering the computer in the direction that seemed most fruitful. A program such as *Socrates* is initially designed to instruct the expert, as well as the student. But it is the conviction of the researchers involved in its construction that it will also become a heuristic philosophical device, first for the student, and gradually for the practising philosopher.

A significant by-product of this research will be the generation of research in philosophical method. The strategy philosophers use in solving philosophical problems will be scrutinized. Students acquire solution-strategies in postgraduate seminars by 'osmosis'. The generation of philosophical expert systems requires that these heuristic tactics be identified, and codified into rules, as was done for mathematics. Their codification will enable the computer to apply the corresponding rules to the arguments and theses in a virtual dialogical exchange with the user, in order that alternative solutions be proposed to problems found. The achievement of mathematics, and of other sciences in which there already are such expert systems, in codifying their heuristic practices should be both an encouragement and an inspiration to philosophers to attempt the same in the domain of argumentation.

Graphical reasoning

Another aspect of reasoning that has generated new research in philosophy is graphical reasoning. By this is meant not only the use of shapes to represent reasoning, but also the manipulation of shapes to reason. The example *par excellence* is Hyperproof, the program developed by Barwise and Etchemendy (1992). Hyperproof provides training in formal logical reasoning through a system of visual (and linguistic) information about a situation. It prompts users to use that visual situation, manipulating the objects in it on the computer, in order to carry out specified reasoning tasks. Although the use of the program so far parallels the use of logic programs in university instruction, and in that respect it does not cover new philosophical territory, the value of the program lies in its heuristic utility.

The Human Communications Research Centre of Edinburgh University conducted an investigation, under the direction of Stenning, to determine the utility of teaching logic using visual representations (pers. communication). Their data were the performance of Stanford University students in logic, the students having been trained either on Hyperproof, or on a symbol-manipulation system. The results were interesting, and surprising. The investigators found out that about half the students did better using visual representation instruction than they did with symbolic representation. This realization does raise novel questions in philosophy regarding the mechanism of thinking, which can have profound implications for teaching as well as for theories of the representation of reasoning.

A further program that makes use of diagrammatic relations to represent logical entailment is Project Archelogos. Archelogos uses computer technology to store, organize and search the philosophical arguments that can be found in the ancient Greek philosophical texts. The analysis of the texts into arguments is carried out by experts in classical philosophy, who are authoring their own original analyses, while reporting and commenting on the most important analyses of the commentators of the past and present.

In Archelogos, the diagrams are formed not by lines but by text. Specifically, the shape of the text is meaningful, signalling logical relation. Thus, information is being passed on to the user both linguistically and visually. The diagrammatic format is applied to the way that the arguments are presented. An *argument* is understood as a thesis followed by a because-statement. Thus, indenting depicts the logical hierarchy between statements, where each (indented) level supports the non-indented premiss above it as a proof, or explanation, or evidence, or example, or other statement. Because-statements are placed under the conclusion and are indented. Since every one of the premisses supporting a conclusion can itself be the conclusion of further because-statements, and so on, the whole structure may result in a multi-layered sequence of arguments and sub-arguments. The result is that one can immediately 'perceive' the logical relation between theses, in argument structures that branch off in inverted tree-like forms. Furthermore, each (indented) level can be hidden away. As a consequence, a structure of multiple branchings-off, eight or nine levels deep, can be read in many visual formats: either isolating only the conclusion and the premisses of the main arguments (two or three levels deep), or expanding the argumentation into the desired depth of sub-arguments at will. This allows the reader to follow argument-threads, distilling away the clutter of sub-arguments that interrupt the flow of the argument in question, as arguments are given within the text. The Project Archelogos home page entry gives a sample structure of Archelogos argumentation. (http://www.archelogos.phil.ed.ac.uk/)

The Project is currently investigating, in conjunction with the Human Communications Research Centre of the University of Edinburgh, the possibilities of using HyperTextual organization of the text, with graphic-reasoning techniques, in order to maximise the division of comprehension-labour between the linguistic and the visual. It is also expected that this distribution of comprehension-labour will increase the heuristic value of the database.

Finally, an entirely different use of graphical reasoning is made in Project Hyper-Space, opening the way to new methods of problem-solving and philosophical heuristics. It is an instance of the 'case-method' in problem-solving. This is a general method of approaching a problem, not by classifying it under a principle and then following the reasoning prescribed by the theory, but rather, by placing the problem within a 'space of cases', which it is known how to handle, and by being guided for the solution of this problem by our actions in these cases. As a method it is more empirical, insofar as it proceeds by comparing case-tokens, rather than by moving to the level of theorems and principles.

HyperSpace in particular is an application of the case-method of problem solving to moral theory. It is a database constructed by Mostert *et al.* (1992). In their paper 'Learning ethical decision-making in a multi-dimensional problem space', they point out the advantages of their method of problem solving in the moral domain by comparison to the traditional deductive approach (pp 247-57). The first complaint is that as a decision-making system, the deductive method is cumbersome and complex insofar as incompatibilities between principles are resolved through the introduction of second, third, and higher order moral principles (pp 248-9). Secondly, they identify a problem concerning the 'transformation' of a case from a raw description into a problem that is subsumed under moral concepts and principles that has a well-defined structure. This transformation is required in order to place the case in the moral domain and to be guided towards its resolution. But, they point out that 'A deductive model does not offer an explanation and justification of this transformation. In other words, it does not help in performing one of the most complex tasks of ethical problem solving: the transformation of the 'raw description' of a case into a case in which all the relevant moral dimensions have become visible' (p 249).

How does the case-problem-solving method overcome these difficulties? With this method, a case that is given a raw description is evaluated with respect to certain coefficients. Thus, in a case where the question would be whether a person is happy, relevant coefficients would be such features as the person's health, financial situation, self-satisfaction. These coefficients represent the moral dimensions in which this case is defined. The moral dimensions determine the moral space that comprises the database. Evaluating the case in question along the dimensions that describe it allows one to give it a place within the multi-dimensional space of the database. This space contains in it what the authors of the HyperSpace database call 'clear cases' (p 250). These are cases where our intuitions are unwavering about their moral resolution. These cases occupy key positions in the moral space of the database, and are located in terms of their values along the dimensions that define them. Problematic cases are also placed in the moral space according to their values along the dimensions that determine them. Once they have a place in the moral space, their proximity to the clear cases, in which scholars know how to proceed, points the way as to how to proceed in the problematic ones.

The difficulties of the deductive method itemized above are overcome here because the theory provides a way of transforming the raw description of the case into one that places it within the moral domain. This is achieved through the determination of the values of a case along the dimensions defining it (e.g., the financial dimension, the health dimension, the self-satisfaction dimension). The determination of the course of action is much more intuitive, since it is derived not through the application of multiple antagonistic principles, but through their similarity to cases in which the moral agent knows how to proceed.

Mostert *et al.* (1992: 250) say that the method promotes the view that 'solving an ethical problem is comparing it with the decisions earlier made'. HyperSpace's case-method of problem solving illustrates an attempt to generate a program that operates along the principles of virtue ethics: learning from the clear cases, rather than from principles, and responding to new problematic cases by being guided by the way in which moral agents would be disposed to act in the proximate clear cases. The authors of HyperSpace further point out the heuristic value of their case-method. The user might have theoretical 'surprises' in instances where 'a hard case' ends up close to the 'morally admissible' cases, though the user intuitively tends to decide the case as describing an 'impermissible act' (p 252). The result would be either the reconsideration of the clear cases, or the enrichment of the moral space with new clear cases, or a novel moral dimension that had not been recognized before.

Conclusion

The impact of computer applications to philosophy has already been multi-faceted and in some cases radical in the changes it is bringing about. These applications are already facilitating intelligent searches over vast terrains of text, searches that go beyond the mere detection of the occurrence of a term in a text. Some of these searches may turn up unpredictable conceptual relations, not classifiable under the current philosophical categories. They provide the possibility of informative and instructive dialogue with the user on technical philosophical topics. These dialogues have the potential of becoming heuristic venues for the entertainment of alternative solutions to philosophical puzzles. Heuristic value also characterizes the applications which develop new methods of reasoning, exploiting the graphical representation of logical relations. Finally, new methods of moral problem-solving are being generated with the help of computer applications that have advantages over more traditional problem-solving methods. But most significantly, this is only the beginning of the exploitation of this technology in the philosophical domain. Philosophy entered this arena decades after sciences such as mathematics, where computer applications have been so valuable and successful. The proximity between philosophical and mathematical reasoning encourages, if not promises, extensive use of computers here too, with great expectations on the anticipated results.

Acknowledgement

I would like to thank the editor for the inspiration for this volume, and for inviting me to contribute to it. Project Archelogos is sponsored by the Greek Ministry of Education and the Leventis Foundation.

References

Barwise, R. and Etchemendy, R. (1992), 'Visual information and valid reasoning'. In Burkholder, L. (ed.) (1992) 160–82.

Brandwood, L. (1990), *The Chronology of Plato's Dialogues* (Cambridge).

Burkholder, L. (1992) (ed.), *Philosophy and the Computer* (Boulder).

Conant, J. (1994) (ed.), *Words and Life* (Cambridge, Mass.).

Dennett, D. (1981), *Brainstorms* (Brighton).

Dreyfus, H. L. (1992), *What Computers Still Can't Do: A Critique of Artificial Reason* (Cambridge, Mass.).

Fargues, J. (1990), 'Remarks on the interrelations between artificial intelligence, mathematical logic, and humanities'. In Ennals, R. and Gardin, J.-C. (eds.), *Interpretation in the Humanities: Perspectives from Artificial Intelligence*. In *Library and Information Research Report 7* (Wetherby).

Kenny, A. (1978), *The Aristotelian Ethics: A Study of the Relationship between the Eudemian and the Nicomachean Ethics of Aristotle* (Oxford).

Kime, P. (1997), '*Reinventing the square wheel*'. In O'Nuallain (1997).

Ledger, G. R. (1989), *Re-counting Plato: A Computer Analysis of Plato's Style* (Oxford).

Mostert, van Willigenburg P., T., and Fernhout F. (1992), 'Learning ethical decision-making in a multi-dimensional problem space'. In Burkholder, L. (ed.) 247–57.

O'Nuallain, S., Mc Kevitt, P., and Mac Aogain, E. (1997) (eds.), *Two Sciences of Mind* (Amsterdam).

Putnam, H. (1992), *Renewing Philosophy* (Cambridge, Mass.).

—— (1994), 'Artificial Intelligence: much ado about not very much'. In Conant (1994), chapter 20.

Scaltsas, T. (1990), 'Parallel governing', *Journal of Applied Philosophy*, 7(2): 153–8.

—— (1997), 'The representation of philosophical argumentation'. In Bynson, T. and Moor, J. (eds.) *The Digital Phoenix: How Computers are Changing Philosophy* (Oxford).

—— and Karasimanis, V., 'Argument-analysis as interpretation'. In Dragona-Monachou, M., and Roussopoulos, G. (eds.) *Ancient Greek Philosophy Today*, Fédération Internationale des Sociétés Philosophiques (FISP), (Athens) 389–409.

SISTA, *Language Technology Group* Human Communications Research Centre (HCRC) of the University of Edinburgh; website: http://www.hcrc.ed.ac. uk/AnnualReport95/Text/hi4-*www.html#hi4-Key2 Socrates*, Project *Archelogos*, based at the University of Edinburgh, website: http://www.archelogos.phil.ed.ac.uk/

Information technology in archaeology: theory and practice

STEPHEN J. SHENNAN

Institute of Archaeology
University College London

Abstract. The first use of computers in archaeology occurred in the 1960s and involved the application of statistical methods. It was associated with the emergence of new theoretical approaches to the study of prehistoric societies. From the early 1980s interest in the use of computer-based methods for academic archaeological research declined. This was the result of a growing disillusionment with the results achieved and of changing theoretical orientations within the discipline, which led to a rejection of what were perceived to be 'scientific' approaches. At the same time, the appearance of microcomputers made information technology (IT) techniques widely available for the first time to field archaeologists and other outside academic institutions. This led to a growth in the importance of mundane computer applications for recording excavations and post-excavation analysis. More recently there have been developments which have led to IT methods once again having a more central role in academic research. Geographic Information Systems provide new and more powerful way of performing traditional archaeological tasks, as well as new means of analysing spatial data. The use of multimedia techniques over the Internet has the potential to solve current major problems of research access to raw archaeological data. The creation of virtual reality reconstructions can offer new insights into experiencing the past. The renewed interest in computer-based modelling has begun to provide a rigorous way of looking at how micro-scale social and ecological processes give rise to complex and counter-intuitive outcomes.

The Early Years

The use of computers in archaeology began in the early 1960s and involved the application of the methods of numerical taxonomy and multivariate statistics. It was associated with the emergence of the so-called 'New Archaeology' (Caldwell 1959), the object of which was to develop a more rigorous and scientific approach to archaeology, in the context of a new understanding of the process of culture change. At this time the availability of the new computer-based methods had a significant impact on thinking within the discipline as a whole. To illustrate this point it is worth mentioning two classic examples from the period.

The first is Clarke's 'Matrix analysis of British beaker pottery' (Clarke 1962), which was an attempt to apply the methods of numerical taxonomy to a hallowed topic in British prehistory, the systematization of the form and decoration of Bell Beaker pottery, and put it on a more 'scientific' footing. It can be seen as the beginning of a direct attack by Clarke on the foundations of archaeology in in the United Kingdom (UK). When he published *Analytical Archaeology* a few years later (Clarke 1968), computer-based methods of quantitative and spatial analysis formed a major part of his project for the reconstruction of archaeology.

The second example is Lewis and Sally Binford's factor analysis of Mousterian Palaeolithic tool assemblages (Binford and Binford 1966). Like Clarke's work, this too addressed a key archaeological topic about which there was a well-established received view: why did the assemblages vary in their proportions of different types of stone tools? The traditional point of view was that they represented the assemblages of different tribes, who had different ways of doing things, including making and discarding stone tools, and who replaced one another in their occupation of particular sites and regions. This explanation was a classic example of the view of culture change which Lewis Binford and his colleagues were rejecting, in favour of a more complex approach which argued that change in the archaeological record could occur for many different reasons, including changes in the way people exploited their environment (see, e.g., Binford 1962). The Binfords carried out a factor analysis of a number of Mousterian assemblages and concluded from its results that the differences they could identify between the assemblages derived from the fact that they represented different tool kits of artefact types associated with different site functions, and not the characteristic assemblages of specific tribes. Accordingly, the traditional interpretation could be rejected in this particular case and doubt was cast on the whole traditional edifice of archaeological explanation.

Two other important aspects of processual archaeology, as it came to be called (e.g., Hodder, 1982a), were also closely linked with computer-based quantitative methods. The study of exchange was high on the agenda because the way in which exchange was organized was seen as closely linked to past forms of society in general, which archaeologists were now attempting to reconstruct. Exchange was something which archaeologists could identify from their material because the use of scientific methods to characterize artefacts was making it possible to identify the sources of lithic and ceramic artefacts on archaeological sites. In combination these developments led to an interest in analysing and interpreting regional distribution patterns of artefacts by means of the methods of quantitative spatial analysis recently developed by geographers (e.g., Hodder and Orton 1976); thus, the mechanisms of exchange and its social organization could be inferred.

Finally, it is important to mention another central topic in the archaeology of this period: the study of prehistoric cemeteries. Two classic studies (Binford 1971, Saxe 1970) had argued that burial rituals reflected key aspects of the organization of the societies which carried them out, so that the archaeological study of the remains of such rituals could, like the study of exchange patterns, help archaeologists in their efforts to make inferences about the nature of prehistoric societies. How was it possible to detect relevant patterning in data sets consisting sometimes of hundreds of graves with a wide range of artefacts present in different combinations? The answer was through the use of such computer-based quantitative techniques as factor and cluster analysis (e.g., S.E. Shennan 1975, Neustupny 1973).

In summary, it can be said that from the early 1960s to the late 1970s computer-based quantitative techniques were central to the archaeological research frontier, and indeed to the ideology of those who frequented it. The methods had a major impact on the research topics which were tackled and how they were approached, in a way that has not been true subsequently. Nor were these the only computer-based methods used, although they were by far the most important. The same period saw the first attempt at a cooperative regional research database, with archaeologists in the south-western United States agreeing to collect and share standard information concerning site locations and their local environments (Euler and Gumerman 1977). Finally, the first archaeological computer simulations provided a means of operationalizing the systemic models of culture change which were central to the whole processual approach (Hodder 1978, Renfrew and Cooke 1979).

Changing frameworks

These trends were not continued. One part of the reason for this is that the initial optimism with which the techniques were used and viewed faded. They did not offer some sort of direct path to the truth about the past after all. On the one hand, a given statistically-identified pattern could be produced by a variety of different processes (see, e.g., Renfrew 1977); on the other, many of the analyses which had been carried out, including the Binfords' factor analysis, turned out to be flawed in methodology and/or interpretation. So scepticism became the order of the day.

More important than this, however, was the fact that the research frontier in British academic archaeology moved on in a different direction. In the course of the 1980s processual archaeology, with its emphasis on systemic explanation, the development of generalizations, testing hypotheses and the relations between people and their environments, was rejected. In its place emerged so-called 'post-processual' archaeology, influenced by structuralism and critical theory and concerned with questions of meaning, ideology and human intentionality (e.g., Hodder 1986, Shanks and Tilley 1987*a*, 1987*b*). 'Science' was on the evil side of the binary oppositions, together with capitalism, colonialism, rationality, and white middle-class males. Computer applications were associated with science and were thus ideologically suspect; in any event they were assumed to be largely if not entirely irrelevant to the study of past meanings.

The result was that computer-based work disappeared from the theoretical cutting edge and became a rather minor technical province of interest to a limited number of people. Moreover, the publication of such work became ghettoized, in the UK at least, by becoming largely restricted to the proceedings of the annual Computer Applications in Archaeology conference, where the protagonists could talk to one another without much regard as to whether anyone else was listening. In fact, the conferences sometimes contained examples of innovative and interesting work which has had very little wider influence (e.g., Stutt 1988).

The history of this conference encapsulates the development of computer-based approaches to archaeology in the UK. It was started in the mid-1970s by computer scientists in Stafford and Birmingham who were interested in archaeology but were in no sense part of the academic archaeology mainstream, and was then taken over by archaeologists interested in computer methods in themselves, increasingly people whose work was in the 'public archaeology' sector.

These theoretical and other developments occurred in the early 1980s, at precisely the time of the emergence of micro-computers, which had the effect of widening the use of IT techniques and bringing them out of the university mainframe/research environment to which they had previously been restricted. In archaeology, once computer applications moved out of universities they became much more concerned than before with issues of data management at site, region and national level. The use of computer databases to store archaeological data at all these levels could have had a major impact on archaeological research in the UK, and may still do so, but as yet this has not happened. There are various reasons for this, in addition to the theoretical shift already noted.

At a national level there have been many problems in the setting up of an archaeological database and the information provided has been, understandably enough, at a very summary level indeed, heavily influencd by the nature of its long-standing manual predecessor, and of relatively little use for research purposes. At the next level down, computer-held data in County Sites and Monuments Records are required largely for planning purposes rather than research, and in general they are again insufficiently detailed for many if not most research purposes. Furthermore, the archaeological field units which collect the vast majority of the primary data in the UK (and elsewhere) do not have research as a primary goal. They obtain their funds largely by carrying out contracts for clients who need work done in advance of building developments. Completion of the contract involves the production of an archive satisfying basic standards, but those archives have been largely on paper and only minimally computer-based. The result is a vast amount of data which languishes in a fairly unusable state. To be fair, however, the situation is at least partly a result of the visual nature and complex structure of archaeological data from excavations. Special-purpose databases have been constructed but there are too few scholars and too little unanimity of aims for these to have become significant community resources employed to achieve common or related research goals.

At least until very recently the problems have been compounded, especially at field unit level, by a lack of expertise in database construction. It has been assumed that producing a database structure is simply a matter of putting a paper system onto a computer. Over the years there have been far too many archaeological examples of systems where the effort of getting the data out was at least as great as that of putting it in in the first place, going back to the British Academy Major Research Project on the Origins of Agriculture in the 1970s.

Databases, in fact, as they are currently used in archaeology for such purposes as excavation recording, represent one of the ways in which IT techniques have become everyday tools for archaeologists. At least ideally, such computer-based techniques provide an improved means of doing the routine tasks archaeologists have always done, especially in the field and in post-excavation work. Nowadays carrying out a geophysical survey of a site always involves computerized data logging followed by the use of image analysis software to clean up the results and produce the clearest possible picture. The use of specialized programs to produce site stratigraphic matrices enables inconsistencies in recording to be picked up, vital for the correct interpretation of the site (e.g., Herzog and Scollar 1991). At least one aspect of the use of CAD techniques in archaeology is as a new way of preparing the excavation plans which have always been at the heart of site recording (see, e.g., Beex 1995). The use of remote sensing (e.g., Ebert 1984, Farley *et al.* 1990) and the computer rectification of oblique aerial photographs fall into the same category, as does much archaeological science, where the analysis of instrumental results will usually involve some form of computer-based statistical or graphical analysis.

Clearly, in this sense IT-based techniques are highly relevant to the way archaeological research is carried out, even if not to the topics selected, but they are quite likely to be 'invisible'; few people report that their excavation involved the use of trowels. However, while some projects are at the forefront in their use of a wide range of IT-based tools which have effectively revolutionized the process of field data collection, in the majority of contract-funded fieldwork, which forms the vast bulk of archaeological fieldwork the world over, only the most basic of these tools are used. In summary then, by the early 1990s the use of IT techniques to perform the mundane tasks central to archaeological data collection was more widespread than ever before. Indeed, the bulk of IT applications had by this time moved outside the university sector altogether. At the cutting edge of research, on the other hand, in the development of new theory and of case-studies based on it, IT applications had more or less disappeared, for the reasons already given.

In the field of post-Palaeolithic European prehistory, that with which the present author is most familiar, there has been perhaps only a single influential contribution since the early 1980s in which the use of computer-based techniques has played a central role, beyond the mundane tool aspect already discussed (Mithen 1990). Similarly, a scan of the last five years of *Antiquity*, perhaps the single most influential archaeological journal published in the UK, with a world-wide coverage, produced only half a dozen papers in which computer-based methods played a significant role, and that in a journal which publishes 800 pages per year.

The example of *Antiquity*, in fact, suggests that it is not just the post-processual theoretical trends which are behind the decline in the centrality of computer-based methods from its late 1970s peak, since the influence of these trends has been much less marked outside the UK, especially in North America. This feeling is confirmed by an examination of the pages of the leading North American journal, *American Antiquity*, and of the Boston based *Journal of Field Archaeology*. Here too, apart from the 'tool' uses of computer-based techniques, they figure very little. The only difference is in the continued use of statistical methods in North America. These were always more important to American than British archaeologists and they would certainly ascribe their continued use of such techniques to a belief in the importance of empirically documenting their claims which they would see as lacking in much recent British academic archaeology.

It appears then that at any level beyond the collection of data in the field and outside the area of archaeological science, the vast majority of archaeologists, both in universities and outside them, and especially in the UK, feel that they can carry out their work perfectly satisfactorily without using their computers for anything more high-powered than word-processing, sending email or using the Internet, and this despite the array of novel techniques presented to them annually by the proceedings of the Computer Applications in Archaeology conferences and at less regular intervals by the Data Analysis and Computer Applications Commission of the International Union of Pre- and Protohistoric Sciences, which go largely unread outside the small circle of enthusiasts who attend them but which figure very significantly in the references of this paper.

However, there are signs that this situation is changing and in the remainder of this paper a number of areas of IT application which have emerged in recent years will be examined, together with the impact they are having, or may have, on archaeological research and the way it is approached.

Recent Developments

Geographic Information Systems

Geographic Information Systems (GIS) provide the methodological tools for the presentation and analysis of spatially-referenced data and have in many ways a natural fit with the kinds of things which archaeologists have always done, especially the preparation and interpretation of distribution maps (Green 1990). Since their introduction to archaeology a decade or so ago (see Kvamme 1989) they have become quite widely used as the software has become increasingly accessible, although this is still not reflected in the mainstream journals. Indeed, in the majority of cases their application has been no different from the traditional distribution map – they are an impressive way of presenting data. However, their potential for analysis has also been used, and this has had a particular impact on research connected with the field of so-called 'cultural resource management' (see, e.g., Renfrew and Bahn 1991: 470–480).

Planners and countryside managers are concerned to minimize the damage to archaeological sites caused by building developments and at the same time to minimize the costs to developers of the archaeological work required to mitigate the damage which they cause. This has led to considerable work in the field of spatial predictive modelling using GIS techniques, especially in North America (see, e.g., papers in Allen *et al.* 1990). The object is to use existing information about site locations, in terms of such features as topographic situation, soil type and distance from water to predict which areas will have a greater probability of containing archaeological sites. The success of such attempts at prediction has been variable and in any event they presuppose that the data available for building the predictive models are representative of the distribution and characteristics of the archaeological remains within the region. If not, the result will be misleading and potentially destructive self-fulfilling prophecies. From the management point of view the assumptions behind such work are not important so long as the predictions work, but from the substantive point of view of wishing to understand why people in the past located their activities where they did, the use of GIS technology has tended to encourage a rather naive and old-fashioned environmental determinism, as a number of people have pointed out (e.g., Gaffney *et al.* 1995); however, this situation has now begun to change (see, e.g., papers in Lock and Stancic 1995), as ways are found to use GIS tools in the context of new approaches.

It is certain that Geographic Information Systems are here to stay because of their practical use as spatial databases for a great variety of archaeological purposes, and some of their more interesting potentials will be noted below.

Multimedia

Like Geographic Information Systems, the use of multimedia techniques, in principle at least, fits in well with aspects of traditional archaeological work, in this case publication. The publication of excavations in particular has always involved the integration of a textual account with references to plans, section-drawings, lists of feature descriptions, counts of different kinds of finds, photographs and, in recent years, such things as video diaries. As publication costs have risen, it has become increasingly accepted that the published version should be little more than a relatively brief synthesis, while the bulk of the effort and the information goes into a properly documented archive stored in some recognized repository.

As noted already, the outcome of all this is that the bulk of archaeological data, in the UK at least, is becoming effectively inaccessible. Once the report has been written the raw data are rarely if ever looked at again because of the practical difficulties of using the archives. This is, or should be, a problem of some concern to the discipline, for two main reasons. On the one hand, it casts doubt on the justification for spending large amounts of public and private money on retrieving archaeological data. On the other, it is leading to a situation where the inferences drawn from the most basic archaeological information are never subjected to critical scrutiny. Since public critical scrutiny of ideas and information by a community of scholars is at the heart of any academic discipline, this is extremely worrying, regardless of the validity or otherwise of any particular fieldworker's inferences and interpretations. Moreover, in the few cases where repeated reinterpretation has gone on over the years, notably the mesolithic site of Starr Carr, excavated by Clark (Clark 1954, Legge and Rowley-Conwy 1988), the process has been enormously productive.

Experiments in the creation of multimedia excavation reports and archives have been going on for some years now (e.g., Rahtz *et al.* 1992, Wolle and Shennan 1996) and it is clear that the work of criticism and reassessment would be greatly aided by the preparation of excavation archives in this form and their availability over the Internet, because it would make the basic information more widely available and much easier to use in a critical fashion. Furthermore, the availability of open hypermedia systems means that there is no need for the data to be put into some special format. Even the most basic data organization is time-consuming, however, not to mention the need for such archives to be properly documented, and the characteristic problem arises that individuals, or individual organizations in this case, would be required to pay the cost of providing a public good with little if any benefit to themselves. It is difficult to see such a thing happening without some element of externally-derived incentive or compulsion. Nevertheless, in the UK initiatives are being taken in this area by the British Academy and others, in the form of the electronic journal Internet Archaeology and the Arts and Humanities Data Service which have recently been set up (see Ross, this volume). It will be extremely interesting to see how excavators and others respond to the requirements of these new publication and archiving possibilities and how successful the Data Service will be in creating tools for accessing archives stored in different ways on different systems (see http://ads.ahds.ac.uk/ahds/project/metadata/res_dev_wrkshp1.html).

Virtual reality

Reconstructions of one kind or another have always played a role in archaeological interpretation, perhaps most famously in the drawings of Alan Sorrell, with their lowering clouds and distant rainstorms sweeping the landscape, but in the immediate future it seems likely that they will take on a new significance as a result of a convergence between current theoretically-based interests and the availability of new technology (cf. Beacham, this volume).

The interest arises from recent developments in post-processual archaeology which emphazize such topics as the phenomenology of landscape (Tilley 1994) and the experience of life in the past. For example, it is suggested that the relevant view of neolithic monuments such as megalithic tombs is not that contained in the archaeologist's plan but involves conveying what it would have been like to approach and enter the monument through a contemporary landscape (see, e.g., Richards 1993). Unless we have some sense of past lived experience, the argument goes, we are unlikely to understand past meanings. The technology is now available to convey some of this by means of computers, through the use of virtual reality systems, based on information derived from GIS digital terrain models, CAD-produced plans and solid modelling. Examples of the such work have existed for some time, for example in the reconstruction of the Dresden Frauenkirche (Collins *et al.* 1995) or, in a more limited but more strictly archaeological context, the work of Chalmers and colleagues (1995) on the Malta Hypogeum (and see again Beacham, this volume). However, they are now beginning to be used much more extensively; for example, in the presentation and interpretation of the results of the current excavations at Catal Hoyuk (see http:// catal.arch.cam.ac.uk/catal/ catal.html).

Here then is a case, like the initial taking up of statistical analysis by the 'New Archaeologists', where a computer-based technology can play a significant role in the implementation of a new theoretical approach. Even if the technology does not dictate the research aims, without it the realization of those aims would be much more difficult. This link between theory and IT method may be contrasted with the 'atheoretical tool' uses of IT described above.

Modelling

The final topic to consider is that of computer-based modelling, by which is meant the dynamic modelling of human activities through time rather than the kind of static statistical predictive modelling referred to above. As noted already, this emerged in the 1970s as a feature of processual archaeology, and it was very much in keeping with its ethos, particularly its interest in systems theory. Such models and simulations peaked sharply in the late 1970s and then rapidly disappeared, rejected because of their intrinsic failings on the one hand and the theoretical shift against 'science' already described on the other. In the last few years there has been a renewed interest in such formal modelling as a result of the emergence of a new theoretical trend in archaeology concerned with the role of individual decision-making, the costs and benefits of such decisions and, perhaps most importantly, their unintended consequences. There are several extra-disciplinary sources for this interest, perhaps the most important of which is evolutionary ecology (Smith and Winterhalder 1992a, Winterhalder and Smith 1992). Unlike the previous generation of systems models then, the new formal models start at the micro-scale, with some notion of individual entities which can change their state; larger scale patterns emerge from interactions between these entities. Some of these models are relatively complex simulations generating outputs which may be compared with evidence from the archaeological record. Others are more in the nature of thought experiments developed to explore the implications of theoretical ideas (e.g., Neiman 1995). The justification for exploring ideas in this particular way is the realization that models and simulations provide a rigorous way of looking at outcomes, and outcomes may be complex and counter-intuitive.

One example of the first type of approach is Mithen's modelling of mesolithic hunting decisions on the basis of expectations derived from optimal foraging theory (Mithen 1990). In fact, he found that the archaeologically documented animal bone assemblages from his sites did not correspond in their composition to the outcomes of decisions based on minimizing risk or maximizing calorific intake. Rather, they made more sense if it was assumed that a key aim of hunting was the gaining of prestige.

Such models can be given a given spatial structure by locating social actors in a landscape provided by a GIS. An example is Kohler and van West's study (1995) of social cooperation and settlement aggregation in the south-western United States. This involved households taking decisions about whether to cooperate and share resources in the light of average local levels of subsistence production and their temporal and spatial variability, derived from spatial distributions of reconstructed values of the severity of drought.

More generically in the spatial domain is the development of cellular automaton models (see Gilbert in this volume). These are computer programs which define lattices of cells, each of which is characterized by some value; minimally there will be two such values but there can be more. The cells change their state according to rules specified by the program. The key aspect of the rules is that they take into account solely the existing state of the cell and those of its neighbours. Out of these local interactions all sorts of large-scale patterns can emerge as the program runs. Thus the models provide a sort of universal tool for starting at the level of the individual entity, or cell, and modelling interactions at differing spatial scales and their patterned outcomes (see, e.g., Sigmund 1993). One example is the work of Steele and his colleagues on modelling the human colonization of the Americas, where the generic cellular automaton starts to shade off into a raster GIS in terms of the different properties of the cells within the model (Steele *et al.* 1996).

In summary, modern modelling in archaeology, as in related disciplines, is not a matter of constructing lumbering systemic dinosaurs as it was in the 1970s, but rather of building tactical models to explore the outcomes of particular situations, specific or generic, in the belief that more often than not words alone are unequal to the task. Behind such models though lies a philosophy which is much more in keeping with processual archaeology than with subsequent developments in archaeological theory. While the New Archaeologists failed in their rather naive endeavour of discovering 'laws of culture process', what we may perhaps call 'neo-processualists' take the view that at the micro-level there are indeed regularities in human action, but the patterns which emerge from them are historically contingent and formal models provide the best, perhaps the only, means of exploring them. The formal model building and the theory are inextricably intertwined in a distinctive approach to archaeological research.

Summary and conclusion

Archaeology has quite a long and complex history of involvement with IT-based techniques, affected by theoretical, methodological, technical and institutional factors.

At the field recording and data presentation level, as well as in archaeological science, archaeology is now pervaded by the mundane use of such techniques, which have provided new tools for doing old jobs and are now indispensable, but the rest of archaeology has been relatively unaffected; quantitative data analysis, for example, has remained very much a minority interest. The development of multimedia archives available over the internet may change this situation because of its importance in providing the basic information about field projects to the scholarly community. It is hard to see how academic archaeology can maintain its credibility for long without access to this.

Three other areas where computer-based techniques have the potential to make a significant impact in archaeology deserve particular mention. GIS can be (and are being) incorporated in the same low-level but indispensable way that databases have been, but they also provide an important basis for two very different areas of work, virtual reality and dynamic space-time modelling, associated with very different, even opposed, theoretical perspectives. Nevertheless, both these perspectives have the potential to make computer-based techniques more relevant to the core research interests of the discipline than they have been for the past twenty years.

References

Allen, K., Green, S. W. and Zubrow, E. (1990) (eds.), *Interpreting Space: GIS and Archaeology* (London).

Beex, W. (1995), 'From excavation drawing to archaeological playground: CAD applications for excavations'. In Wilcock and Lockyear (eds.), 101–8.

Binford, L. R. (1962), 'Archaeology as anthropology', *American Antiquity* 28: 217–25.

—— (1971), 'Mortuary practices: their study and their potential', in Brown (ed.), 6–30.

—— and Binford, S. R. (1966), 'A preliminary analysis of functional variability in the Mousterian of Levallois Facies', *American Anthropologist* 68, pt. 2, no. 2: 238–95.

Brown, J. A. (1971) (ed.), *Approaches to the Social Dimensions of Mortuary Practices* (Memoir No. 25 of the Society for American Archaeology).

Caldwell, J. R. (1959), 'The new American archaeology', *Science* 129: 303–7.

Chalmers, A., Stoddart, S., Tidmus, J. and Miles, R. (1995), 'INSITE: an interactive visualisation system for archaeological sites'. In Huggett and Ryan (eds.), 225–8.

Clarke, D. L. (1962), 'Matrix analysis and archaeology with particular reference to British beaker pottery', *Proceedings of the Prehistoric Society*, 28: 371–83.

—— (1968), *Analytical Archaeology* (London).

Clark, J. G. D. (1954), *Excavations at Starr Carr* (Cambridge).

Collins, B., Williams, D., Haak, R., Trux, M., Herz, H., Genevriez, L., Nicot, P., Brault, P., Coyere, X., Krause, B., Kluckom, J. and Paffenholz, A. (1995), 'The Dresden Frauenkirche – rebuilding the past'. In Wilcock and Lockyear (eds.), 19–24.

Earle, T. and Ericson, J. E. (1977) (eds.), *Exchange Systems in Prehistory* (New York).

Ebert, J. (1984), 'Remote sensing applications in archaeology'. In Schiffer (ed.), 293–362.

Euler, R. and Gumerman, G. (1977), *Investigations of the Southwestern Anthropological Research Group: an Experiment in Archaeological Cooperation* (Flagstaff).

Farley, J. A., Limp, W. F. and Lockhart, J. (1990), 'The archaeologist's workbench: integrating GIS, remote sensing, EDA and database management'. In Allen *et al.* (eds.), 141–64.

Gaffney, V., Stancic, Z. and Watson, H. (1995), 'Moving from catchments to cognition: tentative steps towards a larger archaeological context for GIS', *Scottish Archaeological Review* 9/10: 41–64.

Green, S. W. (1990), 'Approaching archaeological space: an introduction to the volume'. In Allen *et al.* (eds.), 3–8.

Herzog, I. and Scollar, I. (1991), 'A new graph theoretic oriented program for Harris matrix analysis'. In Lockyear and Rahtz (eds.), 53–9.

Hodder, I. (1978) (ed.), *Simulation Studies in Archaeology* (Cambridge).

—— (1982a), 'Theoretical archaeology: a reactionary view'. In Hodder (1982b), 1–16.

—— (1982b), *Symbolic and Structural Archaeology* (Cambridge).

—— (1986), *Reading the Past* (Cambridge).

—— and Orton, C. R. (1976), *Spatial Analysis in Archaeology* (London).

Huggett, J. and Ryan, N. (1995) (eds.), *Computer Applications and Quantitative Methods in Archaeology 1994* (Oxford).

Kamermans, H. and Fennema, K. (1996) (eds.), *Interfacing the Past: Computer Applications and Quantitative Methods in Archaeology CAA95* Analecta Praehistorica Leidensia 28 (Leiden).

Kohler, T. and van West, C. (1995), 'The calculus of self-interest in the development of cooperation: socio-political development and risk among the Northern Anasazi'. In Tainter and Tainter (eds.), 119–37.

Kvamme, K. (1989), 'Geographic information systems in regional archaeological research and management'. In Schiffer (ed.), 139–203.

Legge, A. J. and Rowley-Conwy, P.A. (1988), *Star Carr Revisited* (London).

Lock, G. and Stancic, Z. (1995) (eds.), *Archaeology and Geographical Information Systems: a European Perspective* (London).

Lockyear, K. and Rahtz, S. P. Q. (1991) (eds.), *Computer Applications and Quantitative Methods in Archaeology 1990* (Oxford).

Mithen, S. (1990), *Thoughtful Foragers* (Cambridge).

Neiman, F. (1995), 'Stylistic variation in evolutionary perspective: inferences from decorative diversity and inter-assemblage distance in Illinois woodland ceramic assemblages', *American Antiquity* 60: 7–36

Neustupny, E. (1973), 'Factors determining the variability of the corded ware culture', in Renfrew (1973) 725–30.

Rahtz, S. P. Q. (1988) (ed.), *Computer and Quantitative Methods in Archaeology 1988* (Oxford).

—— Hall, W. and Allen, T. (1992), 'The development of dynamic archaeological publications'. In Reilly and Rahtz (eds.) 360–84.

Reilly, P. and Rahtz, S.P.Q. (1992) (eds.), *Archaeology and the Information Age: A Global Perspective* (London).

Renfrew, C. (1973) (ed.), *The Explanation of Culture Change* (London).

—— (1977), 'Alternative models for exchange and spatial distribution'. In Earle and Ericson (1977) 71–90.

—— and Bahn, P. (1991), *Archaeology: Theory, Methods and Practice* (London).

Renfrew, C. and Cooke, K. L. (1979) (eds.), *Transformations: Mathematical Approaches to Culture Change* (London).

Richards, C. (1993), 'Monumental choreography: architecture and spatial representation in late Neolithic Orkney'. In Tilley (1993) 143–78.

Saxe, A. (1970), 'Social Dimensions of Mortuary Practices', unpublished Ph.D. dissertation, Dept. of Anthropology, University of Michigan.

Schiffer, M. B. (1984) (ed.), *Advances in Archaeological Method and Theory*, volume 1 (New York).

—— (1989) (ed.), *Archaeological Method and Theory*, volume 1, (Tucson).

Shanks, M. and Tilley, C. (1987a), *Re-Constructing Archaeology* (Cambridge).

—— —— (1987b), *Social Theory and Archaeology* (Cambridge).

Shennan, S. E. (1975), 'The social organisation at Branc', *Antiquity* 49: 279–88.

Sigmund, K. (1993), *Games of Life* (London).

Smith, E. A. and Winterhalder, B. (1992a), 'Natural selection and decision making: some fundamental principles'. In Smith and Winterhalder (1992b) 25–60.

—— and Winterhalder, B. (1992b), *Evolutionary Ecology and Human Behaviour* (New York).

Steele, J., Sluckin, T. J., Denholm, D. and Gamble, C. S. (1996), 'Simulating hunter-gatherer colonisation of the Americas'. In Kamermans and Fennema (1996) 223–7.

Stutt, A. (1988), 'Expert systems, explanations, arguments and archaeology'. In Rahtz (eds.), 353–68.

Tainter, J. A. and Tainter, B. B. (1995) (eds.), *Evolving Complexity and Environmental Risk in the Prehistoric Southwest*, (Proceedings of the Santa Fe Institute 24) (Reading, MA).

Tilley, C. (1993) (ed.), *Interpretative Archaeology* (Oxford).

—— (1994), *A Phenomenology of Landscape: Places, Paths and Monuments* (Oxford).

Wilcock, J. and Lockyear, K. (1995) (eds.), *Computer Applications and Quantitative Methods in Archaeology 1993* (Oxford).

Winterhalder, B. and Smith, E. A. (1992), 'Evolutionary ecology and the social sciences'. In Smith and Winterhalder (1992b) 3–24.

Wolle, A. C. and Shennan, S. J. (1996), 'A tool for multimedia excavation reports – a prototype'. In Kamermans and Fennema (eds.) 489–95.

Commentary

RICHARD BRADLEY

Department of Archaeology
University of Reading

Professor Shennan has discussed the use of information technology in a historical framework, beginning with the 'New Archaeology' of thirty years ago. On one level the use of computers illustrates a model that will be familiar to the archaeologists themselves: a new kind of technology became available which provided an immediate way in which an elite could distinguish itself from the rest of the population. As these techniques became more widely available, they soon lost their distinctiveness and the elite looked for other media through which to display their special status. For some of them, post modernism provided a suitable alternative.

When the 'New Archaeology' first developed, it was criticized by traditionalists for its departure from humanistic values and for a wilful obscurity; in their eyes radical archaeology was defined by its approach to the computer. Above all, they saw this development as a retreat from the first hand acquaintance with archaeological data that was fundamental to the health of the discipline. Now that processual archaeology has lost its initial attraction, it is the same people who use information technology as a management tool, compiling even longer lists than they had done before. As anyone who has used Sites and Monuments Records will confirm, these lists lack much intellectual content. The amount of material available has increased out of an proportion to its scholarly significance.

Now that the archaeological community no longer resists the allure of the new technology, another small group of researchers, poorly funded and geographically dispersed, is making an attempt to put it to use as a means of theory building. Professor Shennan is right to say that this is an overdue but very welcome development. After a generation of machine-based pedantry there are signs of a fresh creativity at work, and this results from attempts to simulate the complex patterns of human behaviour in the past. It avoids the over-abstraction that characterized so much of the New Archaeology and finds some common ground with the critics of that approach by focusing far more closely on the local and the contingent. The human actor has replaced the system as the central point of analysis. This is as true of attempts to recreate the experience of living in prehistoric buildings or moving across ancient landscapes as it is of studies of such major topics as the organization of food production or even the extinction of the mammoth (Mithen 1990, 1993). At its best this work does justice to the real complexity of archaeological data.

A final point is perhaps more contentious. This symposium is concerned with Information Technology yet archaeologists are more concerned with *data* than they are with information. Unlike other subjects in the humanities, archaeology is prone to destroy its own raw material. That is the nature of excavation, which lies at the very heart of the discipline. This has placed a unique obligation on the fieldworker to provide a record of his or her observations so comprehensive that the original material could be replaced in the ground. Of course this is quite impossible, but it does mean that archaeological interpretations – the true business of research – become obscured by a mass of detailed description that would be unthinkable in other fields. The computer has allowed this to be better organized and easier to distribute, but it also allows the quantity of data to increase even more. It would not be a healthy move if this body of undigested description were to be disseminated as it stands. One danger of making excavation records available through the new technology is that it defers any attempt to define the intellectually important results of a project. Another is that the continued availability of these data depends entirely on upgrading the available technology so that it is still accessible. That is not true of printed texts. One of the largest field projects to use the new technology took place in the late 1980s. Less than ten years later the data collected at the time are inaccessible (Ackerly 1995). It is vital to avoid the same predicament. There is endless scope for experiments with new media, but, whatever the means at their disposal, the duty of archaeologists remains what it always was. They must synthesize their observations and interpret them before they set them free.

References

Ackerly, N. (1995), '"This does not compute": the All-American Pipeline Project revisited', *Antiquity*, 69: 596–601.

Larsen Peterkin, G., Bricker, H. and Mellars, P. (1990) (eds.), *Hunting and Animal Exploitation In the Late Pleistocene and Mesolithic of Eurasia* (Washington)

Mithen, S. (1990), *Thoughtful Foragers: A Study of Prehistoric Decision Making* (Cambridge).

Mithen, S. (1993), 'Simulating mammoth hunting and extinctions. Implications for the Late Pleistocene of the Central Russian Plain'. In Larsen Peterkin, Bricker and Mellars (eds.), 163–78.

Computers and the concept of tonality

ALAN MARSDEN

Department of Music
Lancaster University

Abstract. This papers focuses on one kind of use of computers in music: as tools for the development of music theory, and in particular on computer-based research in tonal theory. Early work in formalizing tonal theory in quasi-axiomatic terms, and writing programs to test these formulations, has revealed that this approach, while producing creditable results, is unlikely to arrive at a flawless theory. Later work has used computers in statistical studies based on empirical psychological data, and in modelling putative brain processes using a neural-network paradigm. In both cases the notion of tonal axioms is abandoned in favour of a notion of listeners' sense of a potentially shifting and ambiguous 'tonal centre'. The latter part of the paper argues that the axiomatic approach should not be ignored, but that it should be reoriented so as to focus on the comparison of alternative theories and on the 'constructive' application of theoretical rules. In both, computers have the potential to be useful tools.

Computers and music

Music has always had a close connection with technology; in fact, except in the case of singing, music inhabits an interaction between people and technology in the form of musical instruments. It is no surprise, therefore, that the 'new technology' should have given rise to new instruments. Synthesizers are commonplace, but all kinds of more exotic instruments based on the new technology exist also. The word 'information' in 'information technology' suggests a special kind of technology, and, indeed, the capability of processing 'information', since music and sound can be taken as types of information, has given rise to 'instruments' which manipulate existing sounds rather than producing new ones. The most sophisticated of these 'instruments' are computer programs which operate on a digitized representation of sound, using the same principles of digital representation as are used for CD recordings. (The quantity of computer processing required means that the sound-processing is rarely real-time, i.e., the process of transformation typically takes longer than the sound lasts, so that the source sound and transformed sounds must be written to files which can then be 'played' to hear the sound.) These manipulations can involve changing the speed of a sound, or its pitch or tone quality, or more wholesale changes such as breaking the sound into tiny pieces (a process called 'granulation') which can then be put together in a different way to produce a sound which is new but recognizably related to the original. The advent of such sound-manipulating computer programs has given rise to a completely new kind of music, generally referred to as 'electro-acoustic' music, in which a composer creates a piece by working directly with the sound of the piece rather than writing a score for other musicians to perform. In this sense computer music is closer to sculpture and other visual arts in which the artist works directly with the medium. The design, implementation and use of sound-creating and sound-manipulating computer programs has become a major research field, spawning its own journals (e.g., *Computer Music Journal*), societies and conferences.

Manipulations of sound by computer can also be used for purposes other than composition, in particular in the editing of sound recordings. Recently there has been interest in 'restoring' old recordings by removing noise. Computers are also used in manipulating other kinds of musical information, but here an immediate difficulty arises in how music is to be represented in computational form. Although there are many different precise formats for digitized sound, all are based on similar principles and conversion between them is well understood. On the other hand, there is no agreement about the representation of musical notes. MIDI (Musical Instrument Digital Interface) is a very widely accepted standard for communication between synthesizers and between computers and synthesizers and related equipment, but it represents only a limited amount of musical information. For example, it does not distinguish between 'enharmonic' pitches, such as C sharp and D flat, which sound the same (on most instruments) but must be considered different for many musical purposes. Many different schemes for representing music exist, most translating symbols which appear in music notation into sequences of ASCII characters. However, it is only music which consists of a single melodic line, such as folksongs, for which the symbols of a score form a natural sequence. For more complex music, there are decisions to be made about how to handle the different 'dimensions' of the music, besides the fundamental decisions on precisely what information needs to be represented. The Humdrum toolkit (Huron 1994) recognizes that these decisions cannot be final, and so adopts a representation protocol into which new representations can be accommodated. There is also a proposed standard, called Structured Music Description Language (SMDL) based on SGML (ISO 1991). For details of musical representation schemes the reader is referred to Selfridge-Field (1997) and for discussion of the issues surrounding the representation of music to Marsden (1996). In the absence of an acceptable standard, most researchers needing to process musical information by computer use MIDI if it is adequate for their purpose, since this affords a simple means of input and output via a synthesizer, or design their own representation scheme and input information by hand. Input by scanning musical scores is a topic of intense research, but has yet to reach a level of reliability to make it practical.

Partly because of these difficulties in representation, and partly because musical processes are often difficult to define sufficiently precisely for implementation in a computer program, computers have had considerably less impact in musical research not concerned with composition and performance (Marsden 1993). Furthermore, musicology has not traditionally relied on the routine processing of large quantities of data, the kind of applications in which computers are most readily useful. Researchers have typically been concerned with single pieces or small corpuses of music. There are exceptions, however, such as the large number of manuscript sources of J.S. Bach's *Well-Tempered Clavier*, book II, studied with the aid of a computer database of all the variant readings of all the known sources (Tomita 1993, 1995). Furthermore, there certainly are questions in which musicologists are interested which would be best answered by systematic study of large quantities of data. For a fuller overview of musical applications of computers, concentrating on non-sound-processing applications, the reader is referred to Hewlett and Selfridge-Field (1985–1996), Haus (1993) and Marsden and Pople (1992).

The topic of this paper is in the area of music theory. Here the interest in computers is not so much due to their capacity for processing information as in the fact that they process information in a precisely specified way. Where the objective of research is to produce a precise description of some process or phenomenon, which is an objective of some branches of music theory, a computer can be a very useful tool in verifying the accuracy and adequacy of a theoretical description. Firstly, the computer (or at least the language used to program it) furnishes a formal basis in which to make a description precise. Secondly, it provides a means for testing the description by applying the resultant program to actual musical data and verifying that the results are in accordance with the process or phenomenon described. It cannot be said that computers have had a significant impact on music theory in general – in many uses of music theory the total precision of a computerized theory is unnecessary and burdensome – but some researchers find the formal approach fruitful, and there is a growing interest in this kind of research for what might be regarded as reasons of 'engineering': if computers are to perform useful musical tasks, then programmers must have a precise understanding of the tasks to be performed.

Tonality

A significant feature of most musics is an apparently systematic use of pitch. The physical means at musicians' disposal (instruments and the human voice) generally allow for a much greater range and combination of pitches than is commonly used. It is as if painters, who by paint and brush could paint any shape on their canvas, generally chose to paint only certain shapes. Historically, painters often chose to concentrate on certain shapes, of course, because their aim was to relate their paintings to the world in which they lived – such as the world of people and landscapes. A parallel argument of 'imitation of nature' does not so obviously apply in the case of music. Furthermore, this phenomenon of pitch organization, commonly called 'tonality' when referring to its manifestation in the music of Europe (and later America) from about 1650 to 1900 and beyond, is not only a matter of composers' practice. There is clear evidence that it is a part of listeners' culture also: even listeners with no formal training can detect 'wrong' pitches in a piece of music they have never heard before. The phenomenon has fascinated music theorists for centuries, and there have been many attempts at explanation – both in the sense of defining the organization of pitch which constitutes tonality, and in the sense of explaining why this organization should arise.

Since the advent of computers, researchers have been using them in the manner outlined above with the objective of achieving better explanations of tonality. Generally speaking, the objective has been to write computer programs which are capable of performing tasks which involve some knowledge of tonality (e.g., making an analysis of a piece of music, transcribing a piece into music notation, or composing a new piece or part of a piece). If the programs are successful, the formal definitions embodied in the programs can be taken to be explanations of tonality (in the sense of defining the organization of pitch).

It will become clear in the course of this paper, as many readers might guess already, that the programs written to date cannot be considered to be totally successful in the sense suggested above. Indeed, the author argues in his conclusion that the likely finding of this kind of research is that 'tonality' as commonly understood by musicians cannot be directly translated into a computational concept because it is too diffuse for the medium. However, to avoid having something too diffuse even for an academic paper, let me define somewhat more precisely what question music theorists are grappling with. Let us take this question here to be 'What does it mean to say that a passage of music is in the key of, say, C major?' (Note that by 'a passage of music' is meant either a complete piece of music or some continuous segment within a piece.)

Pre-computational tonal theories

Some account of theories of tonality before the advent of computers might be useful to the reader. It was indicated earlier that explanation of tonality had two aspects: definition of the organization of pitch which constitutes tonality, and explanation of why it should arise. These two aspects suggest two kinds of tonal theory: axiomatic theories and process theories. Explanations of the first kind attempt to state the properties of tonal organization so that, for example, one could distinguish a tonal piece of music from one that is not, because the former would have these properties while the latter would not. The second kind instead attempts to state a mechanism by which organization of pitch such as found in tonal pieces should arise. The two kinds often coexist in a single theory.

Early theories of pitch organization in Europe were indebted to Pythagoras's idea that pitch organization consisted of small-integer ratios between frequencies. Boethius, in the fifth century, even went so far as to call music 'number made audible'. This reflection of heavenly order – in the sense both of order as observed in the motion of the moon, planets and stars (the 'music of the spheres') and of divine perfection in such numerical relations – was taken as the basis for explaining the harmonious effect of the musical intervals formed by such frequency ratios. These are the perfect consonances octave, fifth and fourth, formed by the ratios 2:1, 3:2 and 4:3 respectively. Less harmonious, by this theory, are the imperfect consonances major third, minor third and their inversions, minor sixth and major sixth, formed by the ratios 5:4, 6:5, 8:5 and 5:3.

The fundamental unit of the theory promulgated by Rameau in the eighteenth century is not the interval but the triad, a combination of three pitch classes (an octave-generalization of pitch, i.e., middle C, the C an octave higher, and every other C are all of pitch class C) forming a pattern consisting of the intervals of a fifth, a major third and a minor third. Triads exist in two forms, major and minor, and there can be alterations of these also. A justification for the major triad as a fundamental unit was easily found in the acoustical properties of most resonant bodies, such as are used in the construction of musical instruments. In sounding a single note, an instrument generally produces not a single frequency but a number of frequencies related to each other in a manner described by the 'harmonic series'. The lowest six frequencies in such a series form, when taken as separate pitches, a major triad. This is a kind of empirical explanation – triads are observed in musical instruments – in contrast to the rationalist explanations based on frequency ratios. Justifications of the minor triad were similarly sought in acoustics.

Heinrich Schenker, in the early decades of the twentieth century, also sought to justify his tonal theory on the 'chord in nature' (*Der Klang in Natur*) (Schenker 1979), but there are other elements in the theory which are grounded on what a composer *does* with this natural chord. (It must be said, though, that Schenker emphatically sought to justify tonality on absolute, and not cultural, grounds.) His theory is about the relationship between actual notes in actual pieces of music, and not a theory of relations between abstract pitches.

While this quick survey of pre-computational tonal theories has been chronological, it is a mistake to infer a progression of tonal theories from axiomatic to empiricist to process. Theories of frequency ratios, for example, have always been popular, and are manifested in current interest in 'just intonation'. The group-theoretic ideas found in the work of Balzano (1982) might be regarded as similarly axiomatic.

Rule-based theories

Digital computers provide a means for 'implementing' axiomatic theories, i.e., for carrying out procedures which can at least be justified on the basis of the axioms. Furthermore, if the program is correctly written, the computer does not carry out procedures which are *not* justified by the axioms. One can be certain, therefore, that the behaviour of the computer program is determined by the axioms and only the axioms. This is in contrast to application of a theory by a human researcher. Often the researcher knows the phenomenon under investigation, and he or she has to be very careful not to take steps in processing some data (e.g., in determining the key of a passage of music) which are not justified by the axioms. In fact, the only way to be certain is to check each step of the processing, which is tedious and error-prone. A computer, on the other hand, has no prior knowledge of the domain and it cannot but act in accordance with its program. It is principally for this reason of 'cleanliness' and ignorance of the domain that computers are used in research in music theory. Another possible motivation is that computers could speed up testing of a theory so that it could be tested with a large sample of music, but to date the shortcomings of computer-implemented theories are often evident when applied to only a small sample of music!

One implementation of a tonal theory, expressed as a systemic grammar, was reported by Winograd (1968). Though one of the first such attempts, it can also be regarded as one of the most successful for reasons to be explained below. The 'networks' of Winograd's grammar essentially describe, in layers of increasing detail, the configurations possible in a piece of tonal music. The grammar is organized into five layers:

Composition, which obviously encompasses the entire piece; Tonality, which is a passage governed by a single key; Chord Group, which is a sequence of chords which functions as a single harmonic unit; Chord, which is a 'vertical slice' of the music during a particular time period when there is no change of notes sounding; and Note. A Composition is specified by the grammar to be a sequence of one or more Tonalities which are constrained to be in the tonic key and to be non-modulatory (i.e., to end with a cadence in that key). The second layer of the grammar specifies that a Tonality is made up of a sequence of Chord Groups and/or other Tonalities (which need not be in the tonic key), with various constraints on their features. The third layer, for purposes of illustration, is shown in Figure 1. This network specifies that a Chord Group must have a 'type' and a 'relative root', i.e., a harmonic function relative to the key of the Tonality in which it occurs. The type may be either 'direct' or 'indirect' (a distinction concerning whether or not a harmonic chord with some other root occurs as part of the group, used elsewhere in the grammar). The requirement that both features be present is indicated by the curly brace. The 'relative root' may be 'altered', in which case it is one of the harmonic functions specified there, or it is 'unaltered', in which case it is one of the harmonic functions numbered I to VII. (These functions are immediately meaningful to musicians.) The requirement that there be only one of each feature present is indicated by the square brace. The special notation ':*K* = min:' means that the function 'major III' is only possible when the key of the Tonality is minor. The two lower layers of the grammar

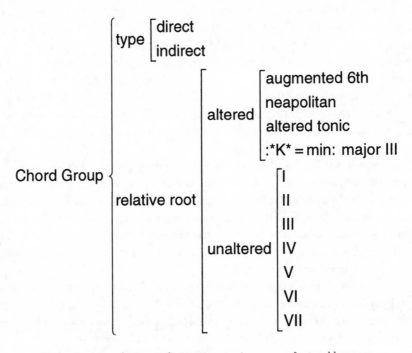

Fig. 1. A portion of Winograd's (1968) systemic grammar for tonal harmony

specify the various types of chord, including their inversion and completeness, and the possible notes ('C natural in the fourth octave', for example). Each layer of the grammar has two components not illustrated in Figure 1: a specification of 'realizations', i.e., how the structure (Composition, Tonality, Chord Group, Chord and Note) is realized in sequences of other constituents, according to its features; and a specification of what those constituents are in terms of structures defined at this or lower layers of the grammar.

This grammar was embodied by Winograd in a computer program, written in LISP, whose input represented pieces of music, and whose output was a parsing of the input in terms of the grammar. The objective of the computer program, therefore, was to discover how a piece could be accounted for in terms of the grammar. The output effectively also constituted a harmonic analysis of the piece, assigning a key to each passage and a harmonic function to each chord. In fact, many accounts are possible for most pieces using the grammar, so Winograd incorporated features in the program which were intended to find the 'best' account, meaning the one most likely to accord with a musician's harmonic analysis of the piece. This is a topic which will be returned to below. The results for three pieces of music are given in Winograd's paper. These indicate that the parser is capable of correctly interpreting key and harmony in many cases, but it also makes serious mistakes. Winograd does discuss how the parser and grammar could be improved to avoid such mistakes, but these were not implemented because, apparently, the cost of computer time in 1968 was prohibitive.

Other, more recent researches have followed this same paradigm: a tonal theory is expressed in some more or less formal way; a computer program is written to embody the theory; representations of pieces of music are given to the program to analyse; the results are judged by the closeness of their match with the analyses of the same pieces by musicians. Two particular projects of note are those of Maxwell (1992), whose objectives were very similar to those of Winograd, though his approach was different and he aimed to treat music of a more contrapuntal nature, and Longuet-Higgins and his co-workers (Longuet-Higgins 1978, Longuet-Higgins and Steedman 1971), whose objectives were rather different. Their program was designed to take input representing the keypresses on a piano or other keyboard instrument involved in performance of a piece of music, and to produce as output a representation of the piece in the form of music notation. This requires resolving various considerations of the temporal relationships of notes, which is a very lively topic of research but separate from the topic of this paper, and resolving the 'spelling' of pitches (e.g., is the 'black note' just above middle C to be written as C sharp or D flat?). To resolve this latter question also requires determination of the key of the passage of music.

A different kind of paradigm is adopted by Ebcioglu (1992), whose program is designed not to analyse existing music but to generate new music, in his case harmonizations of chorale melodies in the style of J.S. Bach. In principle this involves understanding the same underlying tonal theory as in the case of the work referred to above. Indeed, it would be possible to embody Winograd's grammar in a program different from his which was intended to perform precisely the task Ebcioglu sets out to achieve: the harmonization of melodies. Instead of the program starting from the music and determining which branches of the grammar network it must move *up* to explain the piece, the program would decide which branches to move *down* to generate appropriate Tonalities, then Chord Groups, then Chords, and finally Notes to accompany the melody provided. However, Ebcioglu's system is expressed in quite different terms, and in fact the theoretical possibility of a single theoretical account underlying both analysis and composition has not been realized. The theory underlying Ebcioglu's program is expressed in a large number of rules in a form closely related to predicate logic. Unlike the other systems referred to above, the relation of theory to program is very close, since the program was implemented in a logic programming language, designed and implemented by Ebcioglu himself, in which programming code and logical expression are almost one and the same. The output of the program is extremely successful, in that it produces harmonizations which would give credit to a music student, but they are nevertheless recognisably not in the true style of J.S. Bach.

Other projects which employed this paradigm of generation include Sundberg and Lindblom (1976, 1991), whose aim was to produce nursery tunes in the style of Tegner, Baroni *et al.* (1992) who had a number of projects connected with various aspects of generating melodies (Lutheran chorales, French eighteenth-century chansons, and Legrenzi arias), and Kippen and Bel (1992), whose concern was the *tabla* drumming of North India and whose program generated new variations on well-established patterns. All of these are repertoires without harmony, and while this does not mean that they did not have to concern themselves with tonality (Kippen and Bel did not), it does mean that the *tonal* theory of the projects was less sophisticated than in the examples discussed above.

Statistical theories

In the examples of rule-based theories described above, and in many others, the researchers recognize that their programs do not function perfectly. Winograd's program produced analyses which a musical expert would not. Ebcioglu's program produced harmonizations which were recognisably different in style from those of Bach. The researchers conclude that while the program makes mistakes, it could be improved by refinement. However, these refinements are not reported, and their absence could be interpreted as indicating that such improvement through refinement is impossible, and that the programs and others like them will always make mistakes. (This question is returned to below.) One response to this is to accept that there will be mistakes, but to aim for some measure of confidence in the program's results.

On a rather simple view, for a piece of music to be in a certain key means that it will use certain pitches and not others. The simplest pieces in C major, for example, use only the white keys on a piano. A simple approach to determining the key of a passage of music, therefore, is to determine which key is satisfied by the collection of pitches the passage uses. However, a passage can be clearly in a particular key even if the collection of pitches used is not unique to that key. Furthermore, the collection of notes used in a passage of music frequently belongs to no single key (in the sense mentioned above), even though the passage may be clearly in a single key. (Some notes would be recognized by a musician as not belonging to the key and be described as 'chromatic'.) Thus the simplistic approach is far from adequate.

The idea is not without value, however. A more sophisticated development of this approach counts the frequency of occurrence of each pitch class (which, as the reader will recall, is an octave generalization of pitch) or, better still, the total duration occupied by each pitch class. This yields a frequency or duration profile for each of the twelve pitch classes. Research which has done such counts on actual pieces has found that, when normalized for key (i.e., effectively transposing every piece to the same key), the pitch profiles for pieces in major keys on the one hand and minor keys on the other are remarkably consistent. The tonic pitch class occupies the greatest duration, the fifth the next greatest duration, and so on, largely matching the importance afforded each scale degree in traditional tonal theory. Furthermore, the data correlate closely with empirical results from experiments on listeners' judgements of the 'fittingness' of pitches in a tonal context. Krumhansl and Kessler (1982; Krumhansl 1990) played various kinds of musical sequence to listeners to establish an unambiguous context, followed by a single 'probe tone'. The listeners had to rate how well the tone fitted into the tonal context of the previous sequence. Again, the tonic was found to fit best, the fifth next best, and so on. (The correlation is even closer than this suggests.) The pitch profile for a major key (in this case C major) is shown in Figure 2. Krumhansl (1990: 75–76) suggests that the experimental results show that listeners have a consistent sense of hierarchy of pitches within a key, and she hypothesizes that this comes about by listeners internalizing the patterns of pitch distribution heard in actual pieces of music.

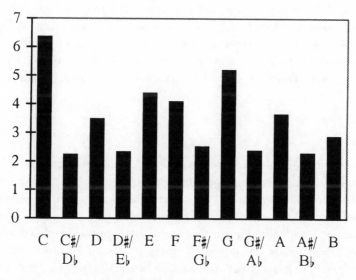

Fig. 2. The pitch profile of C Major

Krumhansl proposes a key-finding algorithm based on this research. The pitch profile of a passage of music is determined by summing the durations of all the notes of each pitch class occurring in the passage (i.e., all the Cs, all the C sharps/D flats, etc.), a task easily performed by a computer program. (For this purpose MIDI data are satisfactory since MIDI represents the start and end times of each note, and for this application distinctions of different enharmonic pitches are not necessary.) The computer program can then calculate the correlation of the observed profile with the ideal profiles of each key, derived from the experimental data mentioned above. The most closely correlating key can be taken to be the tonic, with the degree of correlation taken as a measure of confidence in the result. The algorithm has been tested on a number of pieces and while the most closely correlating key is not always the actual tonic, the algorithm performs as well as the other key-finding algorithms with which it is compared (viz., Longuet-Higgins and Steedman 1971, Holtzman 1977, Krumhansl 1990: 89–96). The algorithm is adopted in the most well-developed software tool kit for musicologists, Humdrum (Huron 1994: 328).

This is a different kind of theory and a different kind of use of computers from the rule-based research discussed above. The arithmetic business of determining pitch profiles and correlations does not need the 'cleanness' and detachment from the domain that is required for proper testing of rule-based theories. Instead, the role of the computer is simply to act as a rapid calculator, taking the tedium out of counting pitches, removing the error from calculations of correlation, and doing all this much faster than a person could, so allowing a larger quantity of data to be examined. As for the kind of theory, a comparison with pre-computational theories is instructive. While rule-based or grammatical theories like Winograd's are axiomatic, in the manner of the small-integer theories of the ancients, this kind of profile theory has, like Rameau's theory, a more empirical basis. The relationship of the theory to the concept of tonality (defined in cultural or cognitive terms) is also different. Here the function which the program computes is absolutely clear, and there is no question of mistakes. Where there is uncertainty, however, is in the relevance of the results for musicians. On the one hand is a musician's concept of the key of a piece, on the other hand is the entirely systematic output of the program, and between the two there is a putative probabilistic relationship, but no more.

Process theories

Both the rule-based and statistical theories reviewed here rely on computers for practical reasons only. Winograd's grammar could have been tested by hand, though the process would have been time-consuming and error-prone. Pitch-class duration profiles can also be determined by hand, though the process is not only time-consuming and error-prone but tedious as well. A different kind of theory altogether, best exemplified in the work of Leman (1994, 1995), would be impossible without computers, since the quantity of computation required is so great. Leman uses an artificial-neural-net paradigm of computing and aims explicitly to model brain activity in response to music. Just as the theory of Schenker referred to above is concerned with actual notes in actual music, Leman's theory is concerned with actual responses (taken to be analogues of brain responses) to actual music. Furthermore, Schenker's theory was seen to be derived from the interaction of acoustics and musicians' activities, and likewise Leman's theory places tonality as emerging from the interaction of acoustics with the functioning of the ear and brain.

Leman starts from a model of the ear and auditory nerve. Thus the initial part of the model converts from a simple representation of the frequencies present in the sound to a representation in which the acoustical relationships between these frequencies is also inherent. This is passed to a Kohonen net, which is a particular kind of artificial neural network in which response units are arranged in a lattice or 'map'. Every input unit is linked to every unit on the map, with varying degrees of strength. This is illustrated schematically in Figure 3, where units are indicated by squares, the strength of activation of a unit is indicated by the size of the circle in the square, connections are indicated by lines (the connections to only one unit on the map are illustrated), and the strength of a connection is indicated by the thickness of the line. As with other neural nets, the strengths of connections are adapted in response to the input in the course of 'training'. The training of Kohonen nets is referred to as 'unsupervised learning' or 'self-organization' because there is no corrective or supervisory input on the 'output' side of the network to indicate the desired pattern of response. The pattern of response emerges solely from the input data and the dynamics of adaptation. In simple terms, in a Kohonen net the unit on the map which responds most strongly to a particular pattern in the input units adapts the strength of its connections with the inputs so as to more closely match the input pattern. Furthermore, the connections of other units nearby on the map are similar adapted. At first the pattern of response to a given input is random (illustrated in the upper half of Figure 3). After training, a specific region of the map responds to that input, with the strengths of connections with the most responsive unit closely matching the strengths of activation in the input units. Furthermore, similar inputs (in the sense of having similar patterns of activation in the input units) will activate regions nearby on the map, while contrasting inputs will activate regions far away. Thus a kind of 'map' of the relationships in the input emerges in the lattice of response units.

The inputs to Leman's networks are, broadly speaking, the strength of different frequency bands in the sound, plus a kind of echo of the frequencies present in the recent past. (There is thus a strong relationship with the concept of pitch profile from Krumhansl's work.) The outputs broadly represent keys. The arrangements which emerge on the map through training with input representing sequences of music correspond to the classical relationship of keys known as the 'circle of fifths'. Recall that the pattern of response in the network which corresponds to the idea of key emerges from the data and the interaction of the components of the network without any other intervention. At no point is the key explicitly indicated to the network, nor is the network given any confirmation that its response is correct. Early phases of this research used a rather unrealistic kind of input – typical cadence patterns using 'Shepard tones' (i.e., tones which are constructed to behave like pitch classes rather than pitches; the register

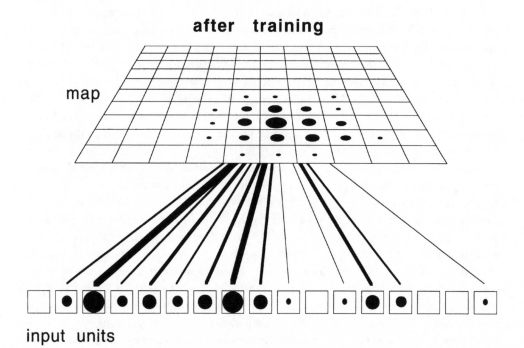

Fig. 3. Schematic diagram of a hypothetical Kohonen net

or octave of the tones is of little relevance). The computation involved in training a network is very intense. An extremely large number of calculations, none very complex in itself, is required for input representing even a short sequence of music. Recently, access to a supercomputer has allowed a test with a substantial quantity of real music – a commercial recording of J.S. Bach's *Well Tempered Clavier* on a clavichord – producing similar results, illustrated in Figure 4 (Leman and Carreras 1995). The map shows the unit which was most strongly activated, after training, by a cadential pattern in each key (upper case for major keys, lower case for minor keys). It must be read as a toroidal surface on which the top and bottom edges are connected, and the left and right edges also connected. The circle of fifths for major keys can thus begin at C at the bottom in the middle, and pass diagonally upwards through G, then over the right edge to the left to D, A, E, B, F sharp, once again over the edge to C sharp, A flat, E flat, B flat, then passing over the top right corner to the bottom left to F, and finally back to C. Furthermore, keys which are related by other means are close on the map, e.g., relative major and minor (such as C major and a minor), and parallel major and minor (such as A major and a minor).

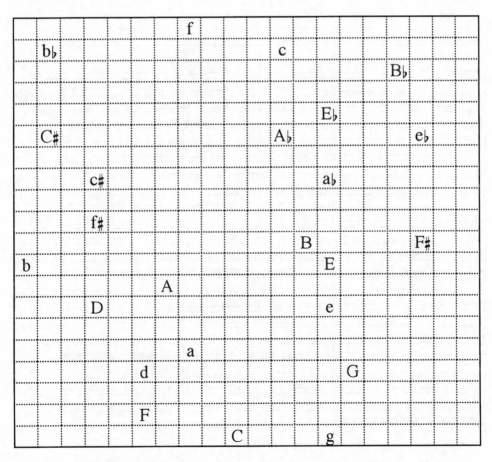

Fig. 4. map of response patterns obtained from training of a Leman's network with a recording

Leman also considers how, having been trained, a network would respond to a real piece of music. Once again, an actual recording is used for this analysis, which is extremely unusual in the literature of music analysis. The result is not a clear decision that one passage of the music is in one key, another in another key, and so on, but instead different tonal centres are activated to different degrees in different parts of the piece. This is illustrated in Figure 5, where the strength of activation of the unit for each key (again, upper case indicates major keys, lower case minor) is indicated by the height of the corresponding line. At each point the space under the line for the most strongly activated key is coloured black. Again, Leman's theory can be related to the profile-matching theory of Krumhansl in that the output is not a single key but a value for each possible key, but instead of the results being taken as probabilistic, as in Huron's adaptation of Krumhansl's algorithm, they are taken to represent the listener's shifting and ambiguous sense of tonal centre. This may well be closer to actual listeners' responses than the perhaps over-precise analyses of harmony of classical tonal theory.

Furthermore, a number of the philosophical problems of an axiomatic theory are

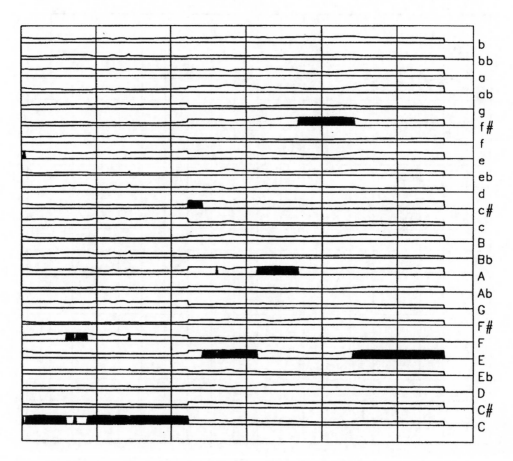

Fig. 5. Response of Leman's tonal model to a recording (Leman 1994: 196) © Swets & Zeitlinger

avoided in this approach (see Lischka 1991, Kaipainen 1996). However, the central concept of key is no longer directly represented in the theory (though it underlies assumptions made in its development – the extent to which these determine the resulting theory is worthy of investigation). Instead key becomes an emergent property of the functioning of the network, and as such requires interpretation of the network's behaviour. Again a parallel can be drawn with Schenker's theory in that changes of key, in the Schenkerian view, emerge from details of the voice leading.

New directions for axiomatic theories

Where has nearly thirty years of implementing tonal theory by computer brought us? Certainly it has not brought a software machine which could be considered to ascribe keys to passages of music with reliability and accuracy. Every implementation and theory has shortcomings. In retrospect, we can see that these shortcomings are inherent in tonal theory even in non-computational form, at least in so far as it is taken to be a quasi-mathematical theory. While tonal theory was expressed in words, and applications of it were carried out by musicians who could use their judgement, the problems only appeared to be at the periphery, in early music and music which approached the breakdown of tonality witnessed in the twentieth century. Once attempts were made to implement tonal theory by computer, there was no place for human judgement in its application, and the lack of formal rigour became apparent. As mentioned above, researchers have expressed the view that refinements to their programs could overcome these difficulties, and that a satisfactory computer implementation of tonal theory is possible. The fact that this has not been achieved in thirty years of research suggests, on the contrary, that it is not possible, though one cannot claim that this has been proven. Instead more recent work has moved tonal theory out of the sphere of modelling and placed it either in a probabilistic relationship to the computer's output or at the level of the emergent properties of the interaction of sound with an ear-and-brain model.

Nevertheless, axiomatic theories still have an important role to play, but their status needs to be rethought. Firstly, computer programs are, perforce, a kind of embodiment of axiomatic theories, and if one is to write successful computer programs, an understanding of the task at hand in axiomatic terms is highly desirable. Secondly, axiomatic theories have a clear role in pedagogy. In fact, classical tonal theory has its historical origins in pedagogical texts, dating as far back as Guido d'Arezzo in the eleventh century. While a teacher's expectation is that students will eventually transcend the rules they are taught, the rules themselves have an important guiding role in the early stages when students' musical intuitions are undeveloped. Since research is a kind of pedagogy of oneself and one's colleagues, axiomatic theory has a role in research also. The axiomatic approach does not need to be overturned, but rather reoriented on two grounds.

The first ground is a quasi-mathematical one. The test of adequacy for an analytical tonal theory implemented in a computer program is, as mentioned above, that the program produce analyses of passages of music in agreement with those of a musical expert. For example, if the expert states that a passage is in the key of F major, the computer program's output should ascribe the key of F major to the same passage. If the domain of music to which the theory is to apply is finite, e.g., the theory might apply specifically to the chorale harmonizations of J.S. Bach, and if the key of every passage of music in this domain is known, then a computer program whose output is totally accurate is possible, at least in principle. The program could simply recognize the passage input and output the appropriate key, using a table which associated each passage with its key. However, such a program would not normally be considered to embody a *theory*, since it would involve no generalization. A theory should properly be smaller than the data to which it applies. The discussion above suggested that a proper theory of tonality which is totally accurate might not be possible, on the grounds that it has not been achieved despite researchers' efforts, but that such not-quite-accurate theories have been found to be nonetheless useful in, for example, pedagogy. Teachers, at least, have been prepared to sacrifice total accuracy for the conciseness of a generalizing theory. There would appear often to be a relation between the size of a theory and its accuracy. Winograd's theory consists of five networks, which range in depth from three to seven levels, their associated realizations, and two tables. Maxwell's, which would probably perform more accurately, consists of fifty-five rules, some of which are quite complex. The most accurate system to date, though of a different kind, is Ebcioglu's, which has approximately 350 rules, constraints and heuristics (1992: 312). A measure of other factors, such as clarity, might also be useful. Winograd's theory was described as successful because, for its rate of success, it is both concise and, largely as a result of its hierarchical organization, clear. What one would consider an acceptable balance between size, accuracy, clarity and other factors would depend on one's intended use for a theory. (Discussion of the role of pragmatics in computational research in music from a different perspective can be found in Marsden 1995.)

A tonal theory which is totally accurate appears thus to be an inappropriate objective. In fact if one moves away from the domain of a fixed repertoire of music with fixed key for each passage to a more natural one in which the possibility that different musicians will ascribe different keys to the same passage, or in which the repertoire is infinite, or at least not fully known in advance, then the objective of a theory known to be totally accurate becomes impossible. Even if the key ascribed by a computer program embodying the theory to each passage considered so far has been in agreement with experts' ascriptions, one can never be certain that this will be so for the next passage considered or for the next expert consulted. The methods of proof which mathematicians use to establish that a theory is true for an infinite domain are not applicable here, and the domain does not have the consistency which enables physicists to believe that the theories they derive from limited observation will apply in all appropriate circumstances.

The appropriate objective for research in axiomatic tonal theory, then, is not a totally accurate theory but a theory which balances accuracy, size, and possibly other factors in a manner appropriate to the task at hand. This has been true for tonal theory in the past. The distinct advantage of the computational approach now available to us is that it affords a means for the assessment of alternative theories. Firstly, the formal representation of theory required for representation in computational form means that comparisons of size become meaningful and practical. If two theories are represented in the same manner, one can realistically compare the size of one with the size of another. The rough comparisons above suggest, for example, counting the number of rules, but much more sophisticated and precise measures are possible. (For this kind of application of a formal grammar, see Marsden 1991.) Secondly, the implementation of a theory by computer allows its proper testing, so that one can gather reliable data about the accuracy of a theory. In fact, given the right sort of formal representation, it would be possible to draw other conclusions about the power and effectiveness of a theory. For example, would a theory be able to ascribe a key to any passage of music, or are there passages of music which the theory would recognize as having no key? Would a theory ascribe with certainty one key to any passage of music, or would it suggest a number of possible keys with varying degrees of certainty?

The second consideration in reorienting the axiomatic approach to tonal theory, approached already in the last two questions, is an epistemological one. Tonality is a different kind of phenomenon from the mathematical properties which the axiomatic approach was designed to describe. To describe a number as prime, for example, is to state a timeless property of the number. We can define an axiomatic theory of prime numbers, and apply this theory to determine unequivocally in each case whether or not a number is prime. In the physical world, one cannot talk of timeless properties for real objects, but still objects can be considered unequivocally to possess properties, e.g., that the temperature of something is 20°C. A device can be constructed to report the temperature of an object unequivocally, and the behaviour of this device can be described in axiomatic terms. When a musician states that a particular passage is in C major, on the other hand, it is erroneous to consider her or him to be simply reporting a property of the music rather like the temperature of an object. Different musicians can ascribe different keys to the same passage of music, and even a single musician can be aware that alternative ascriptions of key are possible. The conclusion of key is an *interpretation* which would appear to depend not only on the details of the passage of music, but upon things the musician brings to the music also, such as the context of the passage and the musician's past experience. The process of ascription of key, as with all music-analytical processes, is a *constructive* one.

This is recognized to a degree in classical tonal theory, and even in a computational implementation like Winograd's. The 'rules' of tonality describe what is possible and acceptable. The details of any particular analysis will depend on the musician's application of the rules, which is subject to variation. Winograd's computer system consisted of two distinct parts: the grammar, which specified the interpretations possible; and a parser which determined a particular interpretation for a passage. Winograd explicitly recognized that alternative interpretations were possible, and the parser was designed to seek the 'best' interpretation using a numerical means of assessment. Maxwell's system similarly used a numerical preference measure, but it was not clearly separated from the rules. The two-part division can be found in other systems also. Kippen and Bel's Bol Processor (1992), for example, has a grammar to define the possible sequences, and an interpreter which employs the differing weights of rules to determine the sequences actually produced. Lerdahl and Jackendoff's theory (1983) contains 'preference rules' whose application depends on their interaction in a way not fully specified in the theory.

The essential distinction is between rules and their interpretation or application, and it is found also, of course, in classical tonal theory. While the procedure of application or interpretation is generally not described, it is often considered to be goal-oriented. In the early stages of learning about harmony, for example, students are generally taught the basic rules governing which kinds of pitch combinations and sequences are possible. These rules allow considerable freedom in the selection of actual pitches in a task such as chorale harmonization, so students are usually advised to aim for smooth movement of the inner parts, i.e., that the intervals between successive notes in the alto and tenor voices should be small. This guidance does not constitute a procedure to adopt in harmonizing a chorale, however. Selection of the smallest possible interval at one point may force a large interval in another part or later in the same part. Students must learn how to resolve such conflicts, and that they produce different harmonizations shows that they adopt different implicit procedures. The goal of smooth movement of the parts, however, remains the same. Winograd's parser was designed to achieve the goal of finding 'strong' harmonic progressions. Maxwell's system was directed at a different goal: maintaining the current key until such point as the progressions interpreted became too 'weak'. The advantage of the computational approach here is that it affords a means of making the interpretation or application process explicit. Furthermore, with an appropriate design of system, the goal-orientation can also be made explicit. Traditionally, tonal theory has focused on the 'rules' of tonality. The variability of tonal analyses from one musician to another, however, and indeed the whole constructive nature of tonal analysis, implies that the other half of tonal theory, the mechanism for applying the rules, is just as important. The computational approach affords a means of investigating this.

Conclusion

In summary, two significant contributions of computers to research in tonal theory can be identified. Firstly, the difficulties of treating tonality as a quasi-mathematical phenomenon have been laid bare. Secondly, computers have engendered an alternative and novel kind of approach to tonality which avoids these difficulties and instead models the interaction of music and brain. Axiomatic approaches to tonal theory, however, are not redundant, and there are two potential contributions of computers in the reorientation of this kind of research. Firstly, the proper comparison of alternative tonal theories is facilitated through their expression in formal terms and their testing through computer implementation. Secondly, the design of algorithms, parsers, heuristics, search strategies, and the like enables the investigation of the application of the 'rules' of tonal theory.

The computer's contribution in music theory, therefore, is not one of providing a machine for ready and reliable answers to old questions, like some kind of musical calculator. Instead, the application of computers forces a reformulation of the question on firmer assumptions and reorients it towards novel areas of research. There are parallels here with other musical applications of computers. As mentioned above, computers have had little impact in traditional musicology, but they are beginning to be used in novel kinds of musicological research. In composition, the advent of computers and software capable of processing sound in previously unimagined ways has given rise to a completely new kind of music.

References

Balaban, M., Ebcioglu, K. and Laske, O. (1992) (eds.), *Understanding Music with AI: Perspectives on Music Cognition* (Cambridge, Mass.).

Balzano, G. J. (1982), 'The pitch set as a level of description for studying musical pitch perception'. In Clynes (ed.) 321–51.

Baroni, M., Dalmonte, R. & Jacoboni, C. (1992) 'Theory and analysis of european melody'. In Marsden and Pople (eds.) 187–205.

Clynes, M. (1982) (ed.), *Music, Mind and Brain* (New York).

Ebciolgu, K. (1992), 'An expert system for harmonizing chorales in the style of J. S. Bach'. In Balaban *et al.* (eds.) 292–333.

Haus, G. (1993), *Music Processing* (Oxford).

Hewlett, W. B. and Selfridge-Field, E. (1985–1996) (eds.), *Computing in Musicology* v1–10, (almost annual) (v. 1–4 named *Directory of Computer Assisted Research in Musicology*), Menlo Park, Ca.: Centre for Computer Assisted Research in the Humanities.

Holtzman, S. R. (1977), 'A program for key determination', *Interface*, 6: 29–56.

Howell, P., West, R. and Cross, I. (1991) (eds.), *Representing Musical Structure* (London).

Huron, D. (1994), *The Humdrum Toolkit; Reference Manual*, Distributed by the *Centre for Computer Assisted Research in the Humanities*, Stanford University, CA, USA. (Humdrum is available by *ftp* from archive.uwaterloo.ca in directory uw-data/humdrum, or from the Centre for Computer Assisted Research in the Humanities.)

ISO (International Standards Organization) (1991), Committee Draft International Standard 'Information Technology – Standard Music Description Language' (ISO/IEC CD 10743, 1991).

Kaipainen, M. (1996), 'Representing and remotivating musical processes: modelling a recurrent musical ecology', *Journal of New Music Research*, 25: 150–78.

Kippen, J. and Bel, B. (1992), 'Modelling music with grammars: formal language representation in the Bol Processor'. In Marsden and Pople (eds.) 207–38.

Krumhansl, C. L. (1990), *Cognitive Foundations of Musical Pitch* (New York & Oxford).

—— and Kessler, E. J. (1982), 'Tracing the dynamic changes in perceived tonal organization in a spatial representation of musical keys', *Psychological Review*, 89: 334–68.

Leman, M. (1994), 'Schema-based tone centre recognition of musical signals', *Journal of New Music Research*, 23: 169–204.

—— (1995), *Music and Schema Theory – Cognitive Foundations of Systematic Musicology* (Berlin).

—— and Carreras, F. (1995) 'Simulation of listening to Bach's *Wohltemperiertes Klavier*', Proceedings XI *Colloquio di Informatica Musicale* (Bologna) 173–6.

Lerdahl, F. and Jackendoff, R. (1983), *A Generative Theory of Tonal Music* (Cambridge, Mass.).

Lischka, C. (1991), 'On music making', Proceedings IX *Colloquio di Informatica Musicale* (Genoa) 80–4.

Longuet-Higgins, H.C. (1978), 'The perception of music', Interdisciplinary Science Reviews, 3: 148–56.

—— and Steedman, M. J. (1971), 'On interpreting Bach', Machine Intelligence, 6: 221–41.

Marsden, A. (1991), 'Musical abstractions and composers' practice', Proceedings IX Colloquio di Informatica Musicale, (Genoa) 40–54.

—— (1993), 'Musical informatics: an emerging discipline?' Revue. Informatique et Statistique dans les Sciences Humaines, 29: 77–90.

—— (1995), 'Musical pragmatics and computer modelling'. In Tarasti (1995) 335–48.

—— (1996), 'Symbolic representation for music'. In Mullings, Kenna, Deegan & Ross (eds.).

—— and Pople, A. (1992), Computer Representations and Models in Music (London).

Maxwell, H.J. (1992), 'An expert system for harmonic analysis of tonal music'. In Balaban et al. (eds.) 335–53.

Mullings, C., Deegan, M., Ross, S. and Kenna, S. (1996) (eds.), New Technologies for the Humanities (East Grinstead) 115–137.

Selfridge-Field, E. 1997, Beyond MIDI: The Handbook of Musical Codes (Cambridge, Mass.).

Schenker, H. (1979), Free Composition, Der freie Satz (New York).

Sundberg, J. and Lindblom, B. (1976), 'Generative theories in language and music descriptions', Cognition, 4: 99–122.

—— (1991), 'Generative theories for describing musical structure'. In Howell et al. (eds.) 245–72.

Tarasti, E. (1995) (ed.), Musical Signification: Essays in the Semiotic Theory and Analysis of Music (Berlin & New York).

Tomita, Y. (1993, 1995), J.S. Bach's Well-Tempered Clavier, Book II: A Critical Commentary (2 vols.) (Leeds).

Winograd, T. (1968), 'Linguistics and the computer analysis of tonal harmony', Journal of Music Theory, 12: 2–49.

Commentary

IAN CROSS
Faculty of Music
University of Cambridge

There appears to be numerous prospective roles for Information Technology in music scholarship, at least as many as in respect of the study of literature and language. However, while we have a variety of calculi whereby we can represent and manipulate significant features of language on computer we seem to lack these for music. It can be argued that this is because theories about music's organizing principles, and the epistemological status of these principles, are less developed and hence less computationally specific than is the case for language, and the mutability of the concept of 'tonality' – one of the cure concepts of Western music theory of the last three centuries – provides strong evidence for this assertion.

Tonality is a complex and dynamic concept that provides scholars of music with the most powerful way of rendering comprehensible much music in the Western tradition, yet it is surprisingly ill-defined even within conventional music theory. Dailies (in Groves Dictionary, 1980) offers no fewer than seven differing definitions of tonality of varying degrees of generality; some definitions apply only to a subset of pieces of music within the Western common-practice period (roughly, 1600–1900), while some appear applicable to the music of virtually any culture or time.

This imprecision within music theory sets constraints on any attempt to characterize tonality in computational terms, whether the products of these attempts are 'axiomatic' or 'distributed' systems. As Dr Marsden has ably pointed out, all current attempts to produce algorithmic devices that operate on tonal musical pitch relations have failed to some extent. This failure is typically manifested in one or both of two ways: as a level of performance that is simply too poor to be compared with that of even untutored human judgement, or as an incompleteness or lack of specificity in the computational processes that are employed or proposed.

I agree strongly with him that tonality is an 'emergent property', but I would differentiate out the factors that contribute to its emergence as being historical process, physical fact, psychoacoustical sensibility and cognitive capability. Physical fact seems immutable, and hence one might expect that its consequences for the formal representation of tonality would also be invariant and predictable; but when these physical facts are 'filtered' through our highly mutable psychoacoustical sensibilities and cognitive capabilities the picture is not so clear. For example, there is now good empirical evidence that the cognitive processes employed by a listener – consciously or unconsciously – in making judgements about tonal pitch relations are dependent on the nature of their mode of engagement with the music. Hence the cognitive context of the music – from the poesic (compositional) or the aesthosic (perceptual) perspective – must be considered to play a role in defining the functional (and hence, computable) characteristics of tonality.

Similarly, the historical dimension poses problems for the formalization of tonality; is the tonality of Lully that of Corelli? Can the scholar of Schubert's music who wishes to employ computational tools to elucidate that music employ the same formal representation as the scholar of Beethoven? All the evidence suggests that the existence of particularities of tonal usage in the music of a given composer – even of one who can be regarded as squarely within the canon of Western common tonal practice – implies that there will be specificities in the formal representation of that 'tonality' that limit the applicability of that formal representation to the music of others, and are perhaps sufficient to prevent the formulation of a general theory of tonality in computational terms.

If we wish to be in a position to employ computers most fruitfully within music scholarship it is vital to continue with research that elucidates the dynamics of tonality in perception and production. However, given the fluidity that tonality displays not only within music theory but also in our musical perceptions and judgements, perhaps the best way forward is to accept that the most that we can do in attempting to employ computational means of manipulating tonal musics is to develop pragmatic or heuristically-based computational accounts that adequately encapsulate the operational characteristics of tonal organization for piece(s) or genres that are the current foci of research, while continuing to recognize the provisional nature of the definitions employed. In other words, perhaps we should seek to develop computational representations and tools that have instrumental utility while at the same time striving to ensure that the primary features of these representations are commensurate with what is known – and with what can be discovered – of tonality as it appears and has appeared in our perceptions and productions.

Cultural history with a computer: measuring dynamics

JEAN-PHILLIPE GENET

Histoire Medievale
University of Paris

Abstract. Some of the reasons for the limited use of information technology by historians are discussed. For his research on medieval and sixteenth century English political ideas, the author has developed both a prosopographical database of more than 2000 authors dealing with history and politics, giving information on their local origin, training, profession and textual production, and a corpus of machine-readable political texts of this period. Two examples of the application of factor analysis, one to the population of authors and the other to a sample of speeches in the English Parliament, are provided. The author's analysis began with punched cards and a main frame computer, and the problems caused by the rapid changes in technology are described. The computer has been used of necessity to investigate aspects not amenable to traditional historical research. It has provided a key, but to use it the historian has had to become part archivist, part social scientist.

Introduction

Some questions are so obvious that they make you feel uncomfortable: as the first President of the young International Association for History and Computing, it has so often been my duty to produce two conflicting strands of discourse that a question such as 'Has information technology fostered a shift in the focus of research activity within – in this case – historical science?' is a painful reminder of unresolved contradictions. On the one hand, it was necessary to be optimistic, to convince fellow historians, including even the most stubborn opponents of screens and keyboards – not to mention the intermediary components – that computers were to bring swift and momentous changes in their work as historians at surprisingly low costs either in money or in time; and on the other, one had to stress how badly historians needed financial and technological assistance to help them to do this by reaching the 'next step', the one which would bring relief to all in the form of results convincing enough to sweep away all procrastination and opposition, whether from within the profession or from other areas.

The trouble is that, as is well known, new steps never stopped appearing, even though we had not yet recovered our balance after mounting the previous 'new step', launching us in an acrobatic race on what could best be described as Escher's stairs: stairs which, depending upon the perspective, ascend and descend at the same time. We had not yet mastered mainframes and punched cards, with their nice queuing for recovering batch work, FORTRAN programming and job control language, when we discovered the personal computer and the many packages which were devised to help us (after having learned how to use them, of course) master databasing, statistics, cartography, word and text processing. Then, both personal computers and packages became more powerful and more efficient, offering practically each year new opportunities which made what we had just done and completed at great pain look like amateurish, already outdated attempts. Then, there was the artificial intelligence craze, the CD-Rom boom and now he who has no e-mail and no discussion forum going on through the Internet is considered by some as irretrievably lost to civilization and scientific progress as Jonas shut up in his whale.

Technical progress is not in question (although it is the active subject of the question which is put to us), as if historians were all to react as one man to information technology and its evolution. True, they have to some extent reacted in the same way to the technical challenges as such: many colleagues – but by no mean all – are able to hand over their paper on a diskette written according to a given format, to operate an email, even to start a bibliographical search on the Internet to compare the wealth of references offered by the Library of Congress or the British Library with those available in their own university library. But, apart from adapting which is little more than surviving, what have we done, we historians, with information technology – and not information technology alone – to bring a change in the focus of historical research? To answer this question, we have to turn to the activity of the historians themselves; to follow a suggestion put forward by the organizer of the Symposium, my personal experience will be used, as a sort of 'ego-history'. This means that cultural history will be on the fore, a limitation which the papers of Smith and Morris in this volume will make more acceptable.

Historians and the computer

But it might be useful to start with some sort of comment on the question formulated by Sir Anthony Kenny in introducing this Symposium 'Why has information technology had so little current effect on humanities?'. First of all, most historians would basically agree with him, regarding their own discipline, and Morris may have been a little too optimistic in his own comment, even though he does not consider things from the same angle. After all, Robert Fogel is not a plain historian, but he took great pains to establish the specificity of his own trade as the 'new economic history'. It won him a Nobel Prize, but it is not sure that even this spared him the sarcastic comments his 'contrafactual history' drew from many historians. There is only one book which can be fairly recommended as one which could not have been written without a computer and which has set a new scientific standard for all historians: it is the study of the Florentine Catasto of 1427 by Klapisch and Herlihy (1978), and the two authors were so exhausted by their endeavour, however successful it proved to be, that they have apparently withdrawn from the arena of great computerized enquiries. Scientific journals such as *Histoire & Mesure*, *Quantum*, *History and Computing* and its national offsprings (*Mémoire Vive in France*), even *Historical Methods Newsletter*, however fascinating their content, are to a certain extent ghettoized. And obvious institutional reasons explain such a situation: historians do not work from collections of sources provided by specialized bodies, as economists, sociologists, and geographers apparently do; they do not work from examples like linguists either; even if they can work on models, it is only at a limited extent, and after having gathered an enormous set of data, as Smith said about the experience of the Cambridge Group for the History of Population. Historians spend a proportionately very large amounts of time reading and transcribing their sources, and the duration allotted for the completion of a thesis is so short that comparatively few will invest enough time in building and documenting an important database or learning sophisticated statistical techniques. After the thesis, historical work remains predominantly source-based and individual, and this counteracts the influence of information technology, as long as no sources are directly available and easy to handle in digitized form. The only optimistic touch may come from teaching, and although the United Kingdom is clearly here in an excellent position (to refer to what is done in Glasgow by Trainor and Spaeth, in London by Denley and Davies, and in Southampton by Coulson, to name but a few), the situation in France is now also improving.

The computer has not been used either because it was tempting or even because it was available. It has been used because it was needed. In the present case, the starting point was a study of Fortescue's political tracts. After reading Fortescue's writings and what had been written about them, it was felt that whatever their virtues, Chrimes and Ferguson, and Skeel and Gilbert, to mention some of the authors whose papers and books were then available, were leaving something aside. Not Fortescue's ideas, which they perfectly expounded and summarized, although it can be objected that in reformulating them in our own present language they were probably altering them to some extent. But what was missing was precisely the language of the times, all the connotations that the use of any individual word could arouse in the mind of a reader (or hearer) in, say, 1471. Now it all depends on how scholars see the language itself. There is at least one interpretation of language which describes it as being the most complex and comprehensive of social institutions, since in a given society it is the chief means of communication between its individual members, and it implies a certain degree of stability and accepted conventions to make this communication possible. And there is some irony in the fact that historians are willing to spend considerable energy in unravelling the functioning of an obscure governemental office which they see as a task for historians – while often neglecting the most obvious and the richest of their sources for the knowledge of medieval society, for that is the linguist's job.

Preparation of a prosographical database

The first step was to make a survey of Fortescue's lexical practice, which implied compiling a dictionary of the vocabulary he used in his works with a frequency list. In 1970, we started to write a program (called ALINE) which was supposed to do precisely this, while taking into account the lack of regular orthography which is an unhappy feature of medieval texts. This done, it appeared that to know Fortescue's vocabulary would be of little help if one was not able to point out its singularities by comparing it with the language of other authors of the same period. A systematic search for other political texts of the same period was started, and this led to the editing of four of the last of these unedited texts (Genet 1977). In some 25 years, a digitized library of English political texts whose vocabulary can be automatically handled has thus been created, which simply means that for each of those texts it is now possible to get an alphabetical list of words and a count of these words, and to generate the contexts which are the starting points of any semantic study.

Obviously, it is not all as simple as it may sound. For instance, the texts have not been recorded using the Text Encoding Initiative – Standardised General Mark-up Language (TEI-SGML) system which is nowadays advocated by linguists (see Hockey: 1992, 87–8); it did not exist when this work was started, and even now it still takes too much time since most of the texts are entered without external help. Earlier on, the Centre National de la Recherche Scientifique did provide some money for this, but it was then a most time-consuming process, which had to be done on punched-cards; and most of these early texts still have to be reworked, for instance to differentiate upper and lower case letters and to introduce the system of references most modern lexical software expects. However, it is possible to select from this library texts which can be rearranged in different corpuses, for instance according to their literary genre or chronological relationship, so as to discover the most telling differences or similarities between the various texts constituting the corpus. At the moment, this library contains all parliamentary texts which can be described as speeches from the origin to 1509, long poetical texts such as Piers Plowman (B and C), book VII of the Confessio Amantis, Richard the Redeless and Mum of the Sothsegger, as well as the shorter poems of John Lydgate and of Russell Hope Robins's collection of political poems, and a series of prose political tracts, ranging from a selection of Wycliffite texts to a group of early sixteenth century texts of Dudley, Eliott (The Governor) and Starkey, through Fortescue's tracts and some others.

But this was not enough. In the course of building this library, it was discovered that two other connected problems had to be solved, and that this solution was an indispensable prerequisite to the construction of any serious database. The first one was, 'What is a political text?' and the second was, 'Who are the authors of these texts?', i.e., where in the English society of their time do they speak from? This second question includes the word 'author', and indeed its answer presupposes at least a working definition of what an author is. The French poet Paul Valéry (Valéry, 1957 edn.) once remarked that it was a complicated thing to be an author, except for those who had no personal experience of such a task ('... *la notion d'auteur n'est pas simple; elle ne l'est qu'au regard des tiers.*'), but to the historian it is even more complicated than he thought. Those three questions, taken together, imply the development of a theory of text production for the late medieval period, which has been elaborated with the help of the writings of critics and social scientists as different as Pierre Bourdieu and Hans-Robert Jauss, himself a medievalist. As with all theories, there is no doubt that this one will be challenged, and any medievalist who will enter this field will be led to elaborate his own theory; the need for clarification and the categorization it induces is probably the greatest virtue of information technology.

Thanks to this theoretical approach, it was possible to delineate with some precision two 'fields' of political and historical text production which appeared to be so closely linked that they had to be studied together. It was also possible to attribute to these two fields all the texts which were found, though the actual knowledge of many of these was often restricted to their bare title (for instance, the many works mentioned by John Leland and John Bale which have not survived the dissolution of monasteries). For these texts, or at least for most of them, it was possible to name 'authors', or 'actors' as it is preferable to call them: some are simply authors in the modern sense, but other wrote texts without 'authorial' intention, for instance as part of their normal day-to-day business. Others were translators, editors, commentators or even scribes who, on some occasion, by selecting a given text or by devising a new arrangement, modified the textual history of a given work. The next step was therefore to compile a bio-bibliographical database on the 'actors' in the historical and political fields for a period which it was thought convenient to make longer than the one to which the texts belonged. Although the text library is confined to the medieval period and the early sixteenth century, the prosopographical study of the authors active in England was devised for a period ranging from 1300 to 1600; it would have been appropriate to go a little further, until 1640 at least, but the increase in the number of the authors from the middle of the sixteenth century made it impossible.

For this study, all the available data have been entered in a prosopographical dictionary. Since this dictionary was intended to be easy to access and use, it has been written in a standard text format, though not with a word-processor, but with an editor, to safeguard possibilities of later transfer. This prosopographical dictionary now contains data about 2100 individuals, and it is accompanied by three subsidiary dictionaries, one for untraced or controversial 'authors' (e.g., John Mandeville), a second one for Welsh authors and a third one for Irish authors, since their language was different. The format and structuring in paragraphs marked by a label have made it possible to generate semi-automatically two d-Base databases from it, one summarizing the information about authors (HP), the other containing data on the some 12,000 texts these men wrote, of which ca. 3900 may be described as 'historical' and ca. 2200 as 'political' (the remaining texts being those written by these same authors but concerning other fields). These two databases are far from satisfactory, since the identity of some of these authors is either dubious or shadowy, and since the genetic link between the two types of databases means that anonymous texts have had to be left aside for the time being, although they represent for some categories (e.g., the political poems or the cartularies) the majority of the texts produced during the period under scrutiny. Nevertheless, they provide some sort of starting- point. The relations between these databases have been summarised in Table 1.

Exploring the data

But how to explore and exploit this enormous quantity of data? There are here two distinct problems: the first is a problem of information retrieval, which is, at this stage,

Table. 1. Databases and their relations

TEXT   : internal information (**MEDITEXT**)
      dictionary   word lists
           word frequencies
           contexts
           semantic graphs (vicinities per word)
    : external information (**OPUS.DFF**)
        status : private and uncirculated, private but circulated with or without the "author's"
           consent
           public but unedited or edited
           working paper, draft, fair copy, printer's copy, manuscript edition, printed
           edition
           [each of these may be known in a number of different versions]
        nature : original new text, translation, comments, extracts from another text etc...
        AUTHOR (or translator, editor, commentator, illustrator...)
        chronological circumstances of writing and circulation.
        media of circulation : *MANUSCRIPT*
                : printed edition
        written for..., at the request of..., in reply to..., presented to...

AUTHOR (**HP??.DIC**) : text format;
        social origins and connexions
        education
        career (lay or ecclesiastical)
        political and religious affiliations
        travels
        writings arranged by fields : external information on texts.
     (**NP.DBF**) : summary in dBase format, excluding informations on texts (see OPUS.DBF).

MANUSCRIPT (**MS**):
        shelfmark and present location
        scribe, patron
        dates and location of writing
        dates and location of ownership(s)
        "quantity" of writing (nature of handwriting, size and spacing of letters, layout...)
        illuminations, decorations
        other texts present in the manuscript.

The chief content of each of the three databases is in italic; its actual name in heavy type; the database MS is not (and probably will never be) completed. OPUS and HP are connected and in a dBase format; both are issued from the HP files in PROSOP format, which contains all basic information in text format, including some of the texts (e.g. the parliamentary speeches), the majority of which, however, exists as independent entities.

rather simple since these databases are being dealt with as a group of independent entities, related one to the other, but not to the external world. In fact, with the fast-growing development of other databases or electronic catalogues in related fields, they could become related to other, external, entities. For instance, would it be possible to establish an automatic search link with an on-line Short Title Catalogue (STC), if it exists one day for the period prior to 1640, through the numbers which are entered in the database? Will it be possible to establish an automatic link with the new Dictionary of

National Biography? Or with the catalogue of incipits of the Institut de Recherche et d'Histoire des Textes (In principio)? Or, even more simply, with the catalogues of the British Library or the Bibliothèque Nationale in Paris, both now computerized? This seems at first sight ridiculous, such is the disproportion between these enormous collective enterprises and the limits which an individual experience such as the author's had to accept: but try to consider the relation the other way round. The reader in the great electronic library of the future, if he gets access to HP, MEDITEXT and their likes through the library catalogue, will be able (although only for the period and the fields covered by it) to start from one text he knows, and ask questions such as 'which other texts on this subject have been produced by English authors between 1375 and 1400?'; once the answer is given as a list of titles and authors, the reader can ask more about the authors or, if the texts are entered in MEDITEXT, and if he is doing research on a certain concept, he will then scan the dictionary of the words contained in the works previously listed and control their meaning in examining the contexts in which they are to be found.

But more immediate is the second problem: how to explore and to analyse the structures and the flows which are extant in the data? And this is where the title of this paper – 'measuring dynamics' – comes in. Much may be learnt by getting answers to questions, or simply by counting people. But it is simply impossible to explore in detail all the possible interrelations between the information contained in the data, especially taking into account all the changes introduced by time. After all, the job of the historian is precisely to understand how things change with time, and to do so the tool he would need ideally would be a method to compare strictly the same structure at two given moments, and to measure precisely what has changed. With very complex sets of data such as those we find in cultural history, this is difficult, maybe impossible (not least because 'same structures' simply do not exist). To avoid this difficulty, time has to be considered as a variable among others, and introduced in the system of data as such. By so doing, we can get an exact idea of the chronological dynamics; that is, once we have transformed all our data, which appear at first sight to be non-quantitative, into numerical data on which we can do measures: a step which, too often, would seem unnatural to cultural historians. This done, we have to rely on a statistical approach, and with it comes the greatest advantage the computer brings with it, the possibility to use measurement. There are many statistical methods available, but the one which has been favoured is factor analysis – *analyse factorielle des correspondances* in French – (see Cibois 1983 for a clear description of the method, see also Benzécri and Benzécri 1980, Bastin *et al.* 1980 and Benzécri *et al.* 1981 for examples of applications, Millet 1982 and Guerreau 1980 and 1981 for specific applications to medieval history), which is as much a measure of the quality of the distribution of the data as a measure of their correlation, and which has the advantage of offering results in two forms: the first one visually charts the structure which has been discovered; the other is a table of numbers, which gives a precise and detailed evaluation of the relations of the data between themselves. The method has been applied to prosopographical data (for an early example of application, see Millet 1982), that is, information on the lives of the authors, as well as to lexical data. Two examples of the factor analysis will be briefly discussed.

Factor analysis of the prosopographical and lexical data

Let us take, for example, the basic sociological facts about the 2100 authors existing in the
HP database: social and geographical origin, training, profession, religion. The structure
which emerges and is clearly visible on the graph (Figure 1) has nothing to surprise us at

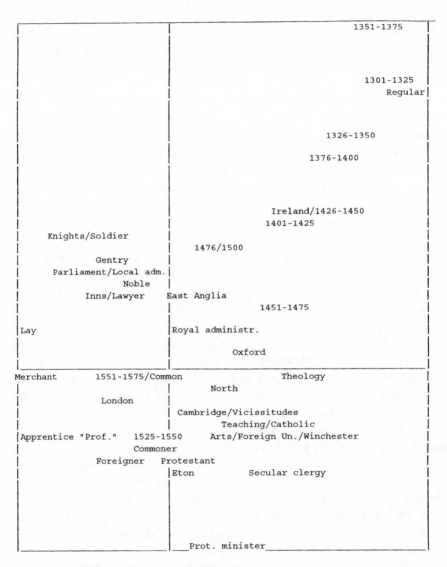

First axis : horizontal, 14,5 % of the total variance
Second axis : vertical, 7,8% of the total variance

Software : TRI-DEUX Version 2.2, PLANFA ("Représentation de plans factoriels" - september 1994);
informations : Philippe Cibois, UFR Sciences sociales Paris V, 12 rue Cujas, 75005, Paris.

Fig. 1. Factorial analysis of 2100 'authors' in history and politics, active 1300–1600

first sight; indeed, the 'discoveries' which factor analysis offers are usually not on the first two axis representing factor 1 and factor 2, since these two factors expressing the strongest 'differences' – to use a simple word – existing in the system of data (here 22% of the total variance) show things which are pretty obvious; but if the structure as such is not entirely new, it is here established with an unprecedented precision. A rough chronological ordering may be read from right (medieval) to left (modern), the medieval periods being themselves clearly identified on the second axis from top (early fourteenth century) to centre (late fifteenth century). On this sort of mapping or charting of the data, four main groupings can be seen: the medieval periods, closely linked with the regular clergy, Irish and East Anglian origins, are to be found on the north-east corner – the geographical metaphor has the advantage of suppressing the + and – signs, which are here but to express an Opposition. The only profession which is to be found in this corner is 'royal administration', a category which here confuses civil servants and members of the court or of the royal household. Oxford University makes a bridge to the next period, on the south-east corner, where are variables which are equidistant from the late medieval and from the sixteenth century. There are to be found Cambridge University, Winchester College or (already pointing to the west of the chart) Eton, foreign universities, a University degree in arts or theology, secular clergy education and a degree in theology or in arts. The 'catholics', in itself a sixteenth century category, are there, while the protestant ministers stand quite apart from the other variables, at the south of the table. On the western side are variables firmly associated with the sixteenth century: in the north-western quarter, the gentry and the nobility are close to members of Parliament, sailors and/or soldiers, lawyers and the local administration (such as sheriffs and justices of the peace); in the south-eastern quarter are other variables, people born in London, merchants, 'professionals', and commoners. At that stage, it is possible to order a new table, with the third and fourth axis, for instance, and analyse new sets of opposition.

Moreover, in Table 2, there are measures telling us which variables have real weight. On axis 1, the main opposition is in fact an opposition between the laity on the western (negative) side with 11.6 per cent of the variance expressed by the first factor, and the regular clergy, on the eastern side, with 14.1 per cent of the variance. Associated with 'laity', other variables on the western side play an important part, soldiers and sailors (5.5%), Members of Parliament (4.4%), knights (3.7%), local administrators (3.5%), members of the Inns of Courts (3.3%) and merchants (2.9%). With the regular clergy, on the eastern side, are theologians (9.5%), Oxford (3.9%), and teachers (3.2%). The chronological variables appear much lower, with only 2.1% for the two most important, 1551–1575 for the western side, and 1376–1400 for the eastern side. All the other variables are, in a way, determined by what is in fact their similarity in overall distribution with this core of dominant variables. On the second factor, another structure is revealed: the regular clergy (24.4% of the variance expressed by this factor) associated with the four fourteenth century periods (9.1% for the period 1351–1375) is opposed to the secular clergy, the protestants and arts degrees. The third factor will highlight the importance of the relation between the following variables: born in London, commoner, apprentice and merchant, opposed to practically everything else.

Table 2. Factorial analysis of 2100 'Authors' in History and Politics: Measures

NAME	INERTIA	CF	CPF	CF	CPF	CF	CPF	CF	CPF	CF	CPF
1301–1325	39	1190	18	1400	47	440	6	3788	703	−68	0
1326–1350	33	1051	15	1098	30	161	1	−634	20	−687	23
1351–1375	41	1113	18	1808	91	571	11	−712	28	3088	524
1376–1400	31	881	21	1002	51	113	1	−436	19	−202	4
1401–1425	31	658	11	557	15	−70	0	−498	25	−718	51
1426–1450	31	829	14	583	13	269	4	−495	19	−743	42
1451–1475	26	577	8	199	2	68	0	−99	1	−519	25
1476–1500	32	133	0	463	5	1135	41	−1032	54	−1035	53
1501–1525	21	262	2	−67	0	69	0	−226	5	−116	1
1526–1550	17	−151	2	−137	3	−61	1	−118	4	245	19
1551–1575	16	−161	3	−280	19	139	6	16	0	90	4
1576–1600	19	−324	21	−62	1	121	7	119	11	52	2
after 1600	13	−171	4	−13	0	−32	0	62	2	−68	2
South-South-West	14	−33	0	117	2	−79	1	113	3	−265	16
South-South-East	11	32	0	−40	0	−173	4	27	0	−55	1
Center	13	−69	0	20	0	−184	3	209	6	−103	2
East Anglia	16	−380	9	−165	3	667	63	95	2	−136	4
London	15	−40	0	242	8	71	1	−84	2	129	4
West Midlands	14	39	0	−123	2	−28	0	5	0	−61	1
North-East Midlands	14	136	1	192	3	−131	2	305	18	231	10
North	13	265	5	−90	1	−137	3	−23	0	95	3
Wales	14	−81	0	8	0	−277	5	−153	2	−130	2
Ireland	25	631	6	528	8	448	7	−211	3	−351	7
Foreign	25	−220	1	−383	8	827	47	−516	30	410	18
Commons	15	−141	2	−306	20	640	113	45	1	−29	0
Gentry	10	−81	1	−2	0	−148	10	52	2	−58	2
Knight	16	−678	37	510	39	−337	22	−34	0	60	1
Noble	14	−489	6	331	6	−374	9	−160	3	66	0
Apprentice	22	−906	9	−324	2	2205	124	75	0	−278	3
Household	12	−461	3	204	1	−289	3	−90	0	184	2
Grammar/Public Sch.	9	−55	0	−172	2	−59	0	28	0	42	0
Winchester	9	392	5	−279	5	−137	1	28	0	−277	9
London Schools	9	−26	0	−305	4	208	2	116	1	−120	1
Eton	9	4	0	−331	5	−236	3	−48	0	27	0
Oxford	11	283	39	46	1	−59	2	−2	0	−124	15
Cambridge	10	80	1	−202	15	−125	7	−8	0	136	13
Foreign Un.	11	442	19	−278	14	20	0	38	1	106	4
Inns of C.	12	−560	33	236	11	−284	20	18	0	−95	4
Arts	10	268	18	−295	42	−134	11	29	1	6	0
Théologie	18	801	95	−34	0	−8	0	−13	0	−2	0
Law/Medic.	10	207	3	−157	4	−101	2	−116	4	−150	7
Teaching	10	375	32	−234	24	−87	4	−15	0	−17	0
Lawyer	12	−399	19	210	10	−166	8	−51	1	−180	15
"Profession"	24	−433	14	−290	12	800	111	−167	8	12	0
Royal service	8	−165	5	133	7	−176	15	−45	1	−13	0
Local admin.	13	−536	35	358	29	−382	42	−60	2	−11	0
Merchant	29	−905	29	−14	0	1340	154	293	12	−162	3
Sold/sailor	22	−758	55	471	40	−118	3	18	0	142	7
Lay	21	−539	116	131	13	140	19	−2	0	−9	0
Secular	18	533	64	−348	51	−112	7	−7	0	−35	1
Regular	48	1370	141	1316	244	563	56	−32	0	7	0
Reformed	17	159	0	−871	18	96	0	93	0	925	40
Catholic	12	293	8	−225	9	−26	0	79	2	69	2
"Protestant"	12	41	0	−383	25	−72	1	−1	0	328	37
Parliament	13	−586	44	313	24	−337	35	−2	0	−45	1
Vicissitudes	8	113	3	−178	12	−27	0	31	1	132	13

Software : TRI-DEUX Version 2.2, ANECAR ("Analyse des écarts à l'indépendance" – September 1994); informations : Philippe Cibois, as note above.

NAME : name of the variable; CF : co-ordinates of the variable on the axis; CPF = contribution of the variable to the factor (/1000).

This method enables the historian to explore the enormous sets of data that computers bring on his desk, since it offers an efficient tool for measuring, especially for non-numerical data. But it does not offer historical results as such: it measures dynamics, true, but the historian still has to go back to the primary facts with two tasks. First to control his data – an example of this later – in order to be sure that his data are adequate, and then to interpret the results he has obtained. It must be stressed that the results of a factorial analysis are not stable results; this is a notable difference with other statistical methods, such as correlation analysis. Two variables are correlated or not, and this correlation can be adequately measured. Here, each time a new variable is introduced this entirely changes the results: the new variable may introduce a strong opposition which will reduce a hitherto important difference between variables. On a set of data such as the one used here, it is impossible to restrict the research to one decisive factorial analysis: it is necessary to do scores of new analyses, and to the set of sociological variables which has been used, it will now be possible to add, for instance, variables linked with the work of these men: in which field (religion, law, philosophy, history, politics) have they produced literary works, which literary form are they using (prose, drama, poetry...), in which language (Latin, French, English...), what kind of political work, what kind of historical work and so on.

The same method may be applied to the study of language. As an example, the reports of the Speakers' speeches which have been printed in the Rolls of Parliament from 1376 to 1407 (for a complete study, see Genet 1997) have been used. It is true that these are not the speeches really delivered by the Speakers: we have a French text, a report made by the Clerk of Parliament, whereas the Speakers spoke in English, and some of the texts have probably been very much abbreviated, sometime reduced to a bare abstract. Nonetheless, the specificity of these speeches is preserved; an analysis of the inertia (that is the variance) brought in by the most frequent words in the Speakers' speeches compared with that brought in by the most frequent words in the Chancellors' speeches is quite illuminating (Table 3). The two lists of words with the highest frequency in the speeches reveal that the vocabulary used by Chancellors and Speakers is very much the same: fourteen words in a list of twenty. The same may be said of the two lists concerning the Speakers: again, fourteen words out of twenty are common to the two lists. What does this mean? It means that the vocabulary on which oppositions, differences and similarities are to be analysed – because these are the words through which the speeches are mainly differentiated – is the basic working vocabulary of the Parliament; what we could call the 'political vocabulary' of the English Parliament, as transformed by its being recorded in French. If we examine the vocabulary of the sermons delivered by the Chancellors, we see on the reverse that only one word is common to the two lists: '*Dieu*' (they are all bishops, after all). This highlights the fact that the Chancellors' speeches, at this particular time at least, are primarily sermons. To each speech is therefore attached a number of words which are derived from the Biblical texts which have been chosen by the Chancellor preaching. Each Biblical text is different, and there are therefore broad differences in the vocabulary which are linked to the choice of the Biblical text, obliterating all other differences. What has been called before 'political vocabulary' is

Table 3. Frequencies and inertial in French Recording of Chancellors' and
Speakers' speeches

(a) Frequencies

Sermons 1377–1410		Speakers' speeches 1376–1397	
1 dire	143	roi	168
2 roi/s	130	seigneur	118
3 faire	103	dire	113
4 seigneur	85	commune/s	105
5 roialme	78	roialme	91
6 dieu	65	faire	81
7 parlement	53	seigneurs	59
8 bien/s	53	grand/e	54
9 grand/e	52	pouvoir	52
10 bon	48	parlement	52
11 pouvoir	45	bon	41
12 vouloir	44	Dieu	40
13 seigneurs	43	bien/s	36
14 commune/s	39	**personne/s**	35
15 **Saint**	38	**charges**	31
16 **temps**	36	**prier**	30
17 **cause/s**	31	vouloir	30
18 **Esglise**	30	**plaire**	27
19 **venir**	29	**montrer**	22
20 **manière**	25	**conseil**	20

(b) Inertia

Sermons 1377–1410		Speaker's speeches 1376–1397	
1 honorer	65	roialme	53
2 **Dieu**	32	roi	48
3 Vessel	30	seigneur	47
4 grace	25	grande/e	41
5 escripture	21	parlement	33
6 rejoier	21	seigneurs	32
7 ami	21	commune/s	30
8 salver	20	*corps*	25
9 gens	19	*heir*	25
10 etat/s	18	*saint*	24
11 entendre	16	personne/s	23
12 venir	14	charges	22
13 novelle/s	14	dire	22
14 loi	14	pouvoir	22
15 volonté	14	*sommes*	20
16 Citée	13	bon	17
17 predecessours	13	*Monseigneur*	17
18 especial	12	faire	15
19 necessaire	12	montrer	15
20 rebelle	12	*matière*	15

still a sort of common language (high frequencies), but which remains very much in the shadow of the religious vocabulary (low inertia).

The mapping for the Speakers' speeches (Figure 2) has some sort of chronological structure, as is to be expected in the case of political discourse; but it is far from obvious, since the most salient structure is the position of the speech of 1406, standing alone on the Western side of the graph and bringing with it 75 per cent of the variance expressed by the first factor, the fifteenth century texts being situated in the north-eastern part, the sixteenth century speeches being in the south-eastern one. If this graph has been chosen among many, it is precisely to show how the analysis itself must interfere with the composition of the corpus. In 1406, the speech of Sir John Tiptoft is not the ordinary opening speech of the Speaker: it occurs during the session, and it is a speech in which the Speaker conveys the approval by the Commons of the proclamation by the new Lancastrian power of the principles regulating the transmission of the crown. It is therefore different both in nature and in subject from the traditional (since Peter de la Mare) opening speech designed to convey the mood of the Commons to the King and to the Lords. The first factor is simply an exposure of the heterogeneity of its corpus, and the speech of 1406 is here opposed mainly to what we could characterize as the basic vocabulary of all the other speeches, which we could term 'the redress of grievances vocabulary', which is especially prominent in the fourteenth century, notably in 1381. The vocabulary associated with each of these speeches on factor 1 and factor 2 is shown in Table 4.

However, the most revealing opposition is the one which may be discovered on the second factor, opposing the two speeches of Sir Peter de la Mare in 1376 and Sir James Pickering in 1378 (north), to the three speeches of Sir Arnold Savage in 1401 and 1404 (south). De la Mare's speech in 1376 is the founding speech of the institution, so to speak: its impact has been enormous, as the many reports we have in the chronicles prove. The Parliamentary report is not particularly violent, but speaks frankly against the clique accused of ruining England, the *Privez autour le Roi* responsible for the heavy debts, the *sommes* very *grandes* which they have appropriated for their *singulier profit*, making impossible the *amendment* of Calais and the kingdom and the financing of the *guerres*. This vocabulary linked with the problems of finances, war and subsidies, is found again in Pickering's 1378 speech and in the other late fourteenth century speech. In opposition, Sir Arnold Savage's speeches evoke a very different atmosphere. In the wake of the Lancastrian Revolution, which left a King courting the Commons for support, Savage seizes the opportunity to develop his own ideas – though they might have been shared by other Lancastrian knights – on the new cooperation which is to take place between the Parliament and the Crown after the failure of Ricardian absolutism. Savage's speeches are ambitious, and some time this lay soldier and administrator is not far from delivering a sermon, especially in that well-known passage where he compares a Parliament's session with a mass. His first speech is a miniature Fürstenspiegel in which he shows (*montre*) that three things are necessary to the good governance of a kingdom, sense, humanity and wealth, the greatest wealth being for a king to have the heart of his people. Here too we have measures (tabulated in Table 4); and factorial analysis proves

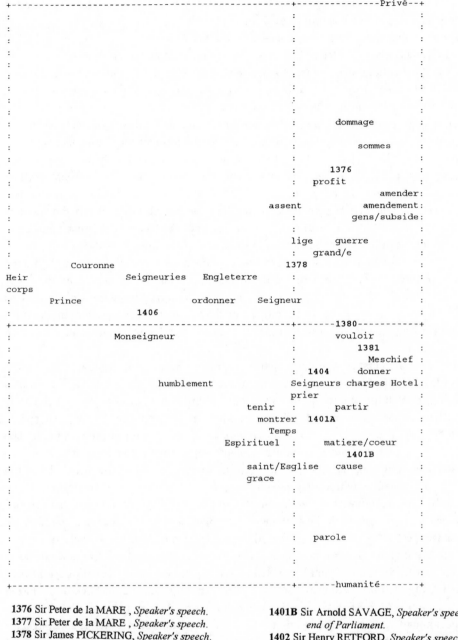

1376 Sir Peter de la MARE , *Speaker's speech.*
1377 Sir Peter de la MARE , *Speaker's speech.*
1378 Sir James PICKERING, *Speaker's speech.*
1380 Sir John de GILDESBURGH, *Speaker's speech.*
1381 Sir Richard WALDEGRAVE, *Speaker's speech.*
1382 Sir James PICKERING, *Speaker's speech.*
1401A Sir Arnold SAVAGE, *Speaker's speech.*

1401B Sir Arnold SAVAGE, *Speaker's speech at end of Parliament.*
1402 Sir Henry RETFORD, *Speaker's speech.*
1406 Sir John TIPTOFT, *Speech on the inheritance of the Crown.*
1407 Thomas CHAUCER, *Speaker's speech.*

Fig. 2. Speaker's speeches 1376–1407

Table 4. Speakers' speeches, factor 1 and 2

Factor 1 (persentage of the total variance = 18.4%)

Speeches

West (−)		East (+)	
1406	75%	1381	10.2%
1402	3.6%	1376	3.2%

Words

Heir/s	15.9%	charges	1.6%
corps	14.9%	sommes	1.4%
Couronne	7.6%	Hôtel	1.3%
Prince	7.5%	Meschief/s	1.2%
Monseigneur	7.2%	vouloir	1.1%
Seigneuries	4%	donner	1%
ordonnance	3.3%		
humblement	1.7%		
Seigneur	1.5%		
Engleterre	1.3%		
Conseil	1%		
Espirituel	1%		

Factor 2 (percentage of the total variance = 14.2%)

Speeches

South (−)		North (+)	
1401B	26.5%	1376	42.4%
1401A	12.6%	1378	8.6%
1404	6.4%		

Words

humanité	5.7%	Privé/s	12.2%
parole	4.2%	sommes	6.8%
saint	4%	profit	3.7%
matière	3.3%	grande/s	3.2%
grace	2.8%	dommage/s	2.8%
Esglise	2.5%	sembler	1.7%
montrer	2.3%	assent	1.5%
cause	2.3%	subside	1.4%
Seigneurs	1.9%	guerre	1.4%
prier	1.8%	lige	1.4%
coeur	1.7%	gens	1.4%
Temporel	1.7%	amender	1.3%
charges	1.5%	amendement	1.2%
partie/s	1.5%	chose/s	1.1%
tenuz/tenir	1.3%		
Espirituel	1.3%		
personne	1%		

to be a useful statistical tool for the exploration of political texts as well as for socio-cultural data.

The impact of computing on the work of historians

To summarize on the basis of this experience how the use of the computer has modified the historian's work, the first point which has to be stressed is that the computer has been used as a key. This key has opened doors which used to remain closed to the historian; and it has done this by enabling the historian to link together hitherto separated different types of activities. At the first stage, characterized by the accumulation of data, the historian has now to work as an archivist and a librarian, because he has to start from an inventory of his data. At the second stage, when he is confronted with the task of structuring and organizing his data, naming his variables and building strict definitions of the categories he will be using, he has to become a social scientist, using anthropology, sociology and literary criticism to produce a working theory of his field of study. At the third stage, when he has to embark upon an analysis of the now structured sets of data he has built, he has to use the specific methods of data analysis which are adapted to the sort of data he has been collecting. These approaches require new capacities from the historian, but these, obviously, must not be acquired at the expense of his traditional techniques, though it is to be admitted that there is here a real difficulty, since the time available to us for research is only too limited.

On two other levels, the computer and information technologies modify the work of an historian; so far, they have been left in the background. With new technologies such as CD-Rom and the Internet, the communication and diffusion of historical data and of historical literature, we are on the verge of a revolution, as everyone knows; the other level is that of teaching. Both levels are important, and would deserve a complete enquiry. But it is not certain that the processes which would have been discovered would prove to be very different from those taking place in other disciplines of the humanities; that is why it has been preferred to remain within the limits of what appears to be at the very core of the historical method itself.

But the trouble, and here it is necessary to come back to Anthony Kenny's opening remarks, is that these changes are unrecognized. If source editing has won some recognition from the profession, databasing, and corpus building are still clandestine activities, not worth mentioning in a bibliography or a curriculum vitae. They are even felt as dangerous: databasing makes the historian close to the archivist or the librarian, while for the necessary theorization involved by the definition of variables he behaves like any social scientist, sociologist or political scientist; computing is therefore a threat to the historian's identity, while it fails to convince because of unremarkable achievements. By and large, the explanation for these is clear enough. Wilson (in this volume) has told us that one of the great problems for computing and the social sciences was that they were not funded as 'big sciences': it is therefore no surprise that there should be no 'big results', which explains why computing is very low on the agenda for the professional needs of the historian. There should therefore be no surprise that there should be no 'big results' in the humanities. There is a lack of pressure on funding bodies, hence low funding, hence poor results and so on.

Conclusion

It is not until professional historians set up new methodological demands and new goals for their own discipline, history, that this vicious circle will be broken. The emergence of the electronic library, whether in situ or through the Internet, is one of the major challenges of our time: the organization of the vast quantities of texts which are the heritage of human civilizations and the free availability of these to all scholars is an urgent and enormous task, to which historians may or even must contribute. Their contribution will be essential to determine the social and cultural conditions of text production, the birth of the author in the modern sense, in relation to religious and political evolutions, and the transformations of the communication system of historical societies. Europe, and especially England, in which a specific and strikingly influential relation between the individual, the state and religion has developed from the XVth to the end of the XVIIth century, lies at the very root of these fundamental evolutions of European history. And no one will object that this is not 'big science'.

References

Benzécri, J. P., and Benzécri, F. (1980), *Pratique de l'analvse des données. 1. Analvse des correspondances., exposé élémentaire* (Paris).

Bastin, Ch., Benzécri, J. P., Bourgarit, Ch., Cazes, P. (1980), *Pratique de l'analyse des données. 2. Abrégé théorique. Etudes de cas modèles* (Paris).

Benzécri, J. P., forty other authors (1981), *Pratique de l'analyse des données. 3. Linguistique et lexicologie*, Paris. Cibois, Ph. (1980), La representation factorielle des tableaux croisés et des données d'enquête: étude de méthodologie sociologique, Thèse de doctorat, Université Paris V.

Cibois, Ph. (1983), *L'Analyse Factorielle* (Paris).

Genet, J. P. (1996), 'Un corpus de textes politiques: les textes parlementaires anglais 1376–1410'. In Ruggiero, A. (ed.), Histoire et Informatique. *Actes du IIIe Colloque National de l'Association Française pour l'Histoire et l'Informatique*, Université de Nice Sophia–Antipolis, June 1995, Special Issue of Cahiers de la Méditerranée, 53: 123–48.

—— (1977), (ed.), *Four English Political Tracts of the Later Middle Age*, Camden Fourth Series, XVIII, London (Royal Historical Society).

Guerreau, A. (1980), 'Douze doyennés clunisiens au milieu du XIIe siècle', *Annales de Bourgogne*, LII, 83–128.

—— (1981), 'Analyse factorielle et analyses statistiques classiques: le cas des ordres mendiants dans la France médiévale', *Annales Economies, Sociétés, Civilisations)*, XXXVII (5): 869–912.

Hockey, S. (1992), 'Linguistics, literature and philology'. In Genet, J. P. and Zampolli, A., (eds.), *Computers and the Humanities* (Aldershot) 1–18 and 83–94.

Klapisch, Ch. and Herlihy, D. (1978), *Les Toscans et leurs familles. Une étude du Catasto Florentin de 1421*, (Paris).

Millet, H. (1987), *Les Chanoines du Chapitre Cathédral de Laon. 1272–1412*, (Collection de l'Ecole Française de Rome, 56) (Rome).

Valéry, P. (1957 edn.), 'Au sujet du cimètiere marin'. In Hytier J. (ed.), *Mémoires du Poète*, Oeuvres, (Paris), p.1499.

Commentary

ANDREW PRESCOTT
Department of Manuscripts
The British Library

In introducing this symposium, Sir Anthony Kenny threw down a considerable challenge, asking us to explain why humanities computing has so far failed to deliver the
great changes in humanities scholarship which it has been promising for so many years.
Some of the surveys, particularly these on archaeology and art history, have suggested a
surprising answer to this, namely that computing has been associated with a highly
empiricist, almost pseudo-scientific, approach to the humanities, while the theoretical
concerns of humanities scholars have moved in a different direction, towards a much
more reflective view of their disciplines. It may seem that this is less of an issue in history,
which, it is widely agreed, is one of these disciplines where the advent of computers has
led to the development of new methodologies and the exploration of new types of
research material. However, I would like to suggest that the position is not as simple as it
seems at first glance.

The impact that computing has made on historical studies is reflected in the
appearance of a number of introductions to computing specifically aimed at historians,
one of the most distinguished of which is Greenstein's *Historians Guide to Computing*
(1994). Greenstein states that one of the aims of his book is to show that the use of the
computer 'neither makes nor requires a quantitative or "number-crunching" historian'
(1994: 1). Yet, in seeking to counter the most common objections to the use of computers
in historical studies, one of Greenstein's chief arguments is that historians frequently
make quantitative judgements and that computers allow such measurements to be made
more quickly and accurately (1994: 6–15). Like all the other similar guides, Greenstein's
book is devoted chiefly to quantitative techniques, grounded in the use of databases and
spreadsheets. Professor Morris has already indicated how historians have responded to
methods for the automated handling of text with less enthusiasm than their colleagues in
literary studies. Historical texts still remain largely subject to 'the careful and conventional assessment of the pencil-using historian'.

Professor Morris suggests that one reason for the lack of enthusiasm among
historians for electronic texts is that historians use text in a different way to literary
scholars. This is not entirely convincing – Professor Morris's diagrammatic illustration of
the 'extensive reading' model used by historians looks, after all, remarkably like a
representation of a hypertextual network. In seeking to explain why computing in
historical studies has been so intimately linked with quantitative techniques, it is more
fruitful to look at the preoccupations of the discipline itself. One reason is perhaps the
influence of the *Annales* school and its successor, the New History, the most eminent and
widely imitated school of historical thought this century.

The fascination of the New Historians with statistics is one of their most distinctive characteristics, reaching its apotheosis in P. & H. Chaunu's 3,729 page 'Statistical Part' which forms the first four volumes of their *Séville et l'Atlantique* (1956–60). Many of the criticisms of the New History have focused on this concern with what Le Roy Ladurie (1973: 301) called 'the silent and mathematical resurrection of the past'. François Dosse (1994: 160) complained that at present 'Clio is garbed in computers, in statistics and mathematical rigour'. He argues that this approach has dehumanized history by marginalizing the individual who represents a variable that cannot be accommodated within the statistical arrays. The computer, in his view, encourages this process by causing the historian to concentrate on the search for regular patterns in which the event, as a rupture or split in the pattern, is put to one side. From a different angle, Philippe Carrard (1995: 173) has also emphasized how 'New Historians, when they have processed their material electronically, never fail to mention it in their theoretical introductions ... or self-reflective conclusions'. Carrard sees the statistical arrays of the New History as a means of giving a scientific patina to historical research.

The criticisms of Dosse and Carrard form part of a general reaction to the New History which Laurence Stone (1979) has seen as representing perhaps a return to narrative, but which is perhaps more accurately seen as an attempt to rediscover the human dimension to history, particularly by concentrating on these marginal figures such as the heretics of Montaillou who cannot be easily accommodated within the regular patterns of statistical tables. There is a danger that, as part of this reaction against a serial history, the computer will be stigmatized as an instrument of dehumanization, and the practitioners of historical informatics will find themselves in the same impasse as the New Archaeologists. It is, of course, an oversimplification to see historical computing as exclusively concerned with quantification. Databases do not automatically mean statistics. The most influential tool in historical computing, Manfred Thaller's (1993) *Kleio* package, uses sophisticated semantic techniques to try and ensure that the historical text can be subjected to automated analysis without being placed in an anachronistic straightjacket. *Kleio* is firmly rooted in an awareness of, and concern for, the capricious fluctuations in the structure of historical texts. Nevertheless, there still remains a stubborn prejudice in the historical profession at large which equates the computer with quantitative techniques. Thus, in the volume on *New Perspectives in Historical Writing* edited by Peter Burke (1991), which provides a handbook on the New History for English-speaking readers, there is no reference to computing in the index. The few references to the use of computers by historians are subsumed under the heading of 'quantitative techniques'.

Professor Morris has shown how the availability of databases encouraged the use of neglected types of historical records such as poll books. There is an interesting contrast here with literary studies. The first fruits of literary computing have been electronic versions of canonical texts, such as *The Canterbury Tales* or *Piers Plowman*. These projects have sought to use computers to establish the author's 'original' text, thereby supporting a rather outmoded view of textual studies. For example, the proposal by Peter Robinson (1996) for an electronic 'Millenium Editions' project seems to use new technology to hark back to the heroic age of the Victorian great edition. By contrast, in historical studies the canonical texts such as parliamentary debates, chronicles, diaries or royal letters, have by and large not been prime candidates for production in electronic form. The focus has been on records containing large quantities of information which cannot readily be analysed using manual techniques. However, parliamentary debates, chronicles, letters and the like still remain of fundamental importance to historical research. The great value of Professor Genet's paper is that it reminds us that these texts are too important to remain the exclusive province of the pencil-wielding historian.

Professor Genet's paper illustrates that the old adage of Langlois and Seignebos (1898: 1), 'L'histoire se fait avec documents' (or, as it might be expressed now, 'L'histoire se fait avec textes') still holds true in an electronic environment. Professor Genet has attempted to build a bridge between quantitative techniques and documentary studies by seeking to apply statistical analysis to texts and showing how changes in texts can be measured through movement in time or linked to variables like social class. The historical text is, however, a very complex object, and my immediate reaction is to feel a doubt as to how far quantitative techniques can convey this complexity.

The 'political texts' which form the focus of one of the projects described by Professor Genet vary widely in their character, means of dissemination, language and authorship. Although there is a large literature from late medieval England dealing with political ideas and issues, it is very diverse in character. The political texts of England range from vernacular poems to legal treatises and more formal essays on the nature of kingship. In using a computer to analyse these texts, the challenge is to ensure that the methods used do not obscure their diversity. A computer can easily rob a text of its multi-faceted and multi-dimensional character and encourage a tendency to treat it as an isolated object. To emphasise the importance of this issue, it is worth looking more closely at some of these texts.

In 1393, in response to serious disturbances in the Midlands and northern England, the court of King's Bench held sessions at York and Derbyshire. Among the indictments taken by the court at York was one against over thirty people, mostly from Cottingham, near Hull, who were alleged to have belonged to a group of over a hundred people who had sworn together to support each other in lawsuits (Powell and Trevelyan 1899: 19–20, Robbins 1959: 60–1, Sayles 1971: 83–5). For at least eight years, they had made it impossible for any royal official to intervene in their locality. The indictment against them transcribes five verses in English which they were said to have publicly recited at Beverley and Hull in 1392. These declared their determination to resist any wicked people coming into their locality, to cover up for each other and to maintain their neighbours through thick and thin. However, the indictment does not make the author-ship of these verses clear. Were they composed by just one of those named in the indictment or by a group of them? Or were they well known verses taken up by the insurgents? How accurate was the copy in the indictments? In using an electronic text of these verses, one might wish to compare them with other insurgent literature, such as the letters ascribed to the rebels of 1381 copied by the chroniclers Knighton and Walsing-ham. These apparently stem from a differend social situation to the Yorkshire verses, but in some respects there appear to be comparisons, particularly in their expression of a neighbourly determination to support one another against the perceived injustices of royal officials. Alternatively, the researcher might wish to compare the language and imagery of the poem with other literature referring to livery and maintenance (Strohm 1992: 180–2). Even the metrical structure of the poem might be of interest – it has been pointed out that it uses a metre and rhyme scheme parodied by Chaucer in one of the Canterbury Tales (Strohm 1992: 1820).

The Yorkshire verses are at one end of the spectrum of political texts. At the other end might be Phillippe de Mézières' celebrated *Letter to Richard II* of 1395 (Coopland 1975), which urges the establishment of a lasting peace between England and France. Instead of an anonymous scrap of verse of mysterious origin, this is an extended literary piece by a well-connected and sophisticated literary figure, who reveals a great deal about himself. Mézières puts forward elaborate political proposals such as the project for an Order of the Passion to provide the mechanism for a new assault on the infidels. He develops his argument by the use of complex allegories and parables. He provides a shewd commentary on the economic and social consequences of the war between England and France. The questions which one would want to investigate with an electronic version of Mézières' texts are different to those raised by the Yorkshire song. One might want to explore the use of particular imagery or draw together and compare the treatment of different themes in different parts of the text. And of course one would wish to see how these components of Mézières' text compare with other works produced by him.

Between these two extrmes lie a variety of documents which again differ in their origins, audience and purpose, such as the 'Record & Process del Renunciation', an officially sponsored document justifying Henry IV's usurpation which was copied into the parliament roll and widely circulated in French and English (Wilkinson 1939, Strohm 1992: 75–94). This text was one of the series of examples which V. H. Galbraith (1964: 13) used to remind aspiring students of history that official records 'can no more be taken at their face value than chronicles' and indeed from time to time have an almost bogus character. He points out that 'The facts regarding the deposition of Richard II in 1399 were obscured by too simple reliance upon the 'official' Rolls of Parliament, which at this moment are a partisan compilation intended to justify his successor, Henry IV'. In the case of the 'Record & Proces', the value of an electronic text might be in investigating the way in which the account of the succession was mainpulated to justify the Lancastrian usurpation and the means by which this early propaganda was disseminated.

The concept of the author in this context is particularly difficult. It is not only that it can be difficult to define the 'author' of these texts. The relationship of the author to a particular text can change as the function of the text alters. This is illustrated by the case of Thomas Usk, the author of *The Testament of Love*, a scrivener who was secretary to the London mayor John of Northampton in the 1380s then switched his allegiance to Northampton's bitterest enemy, Nicholas Brembre. Usk denounced Northampton in an appeal which he wrote 'with myn owne [honde]'. This was very much a literary production in which Usk was, to use Professor Genet's term, the central 'actor'. This formed the basis of indictments against Northampton, but as Usk's appeal was successively redrafted, it ceased to become a personal denunciation by Usk and he was gradually moved off-stage, so that the 'authorial voice' changes (Strohm 1992: 145–60).

It may seem that the new technologies cannot assist in exploring such issues, but in fact they provide a powerful tool for examining textual shifts of this kind. When they are in digital form, the different states of these texts can be more readily compared. For example, a hyperlink provides a more expressive representation than is possible in a printed edition of the relationship between a file copy of an administrative or legal document and its enrolled version. A hypertextual edition of the documents relating to Usk's appeal would make the progressive transformation of his accusations more readily apparent and offer new perspectives on the relationship of these texts. Above all, links can be provided to images of the documents, so that a sense of its original archival context can be retained. And, of course, quantification of the type that Professor Genet has undertaken would still be possible.

Professor Genet's discussion of parliamentary reports of the speeches by the speaker and the chancellor is timely, given the recent announcement by the Public Record Office of the new electronic edition of the *Rotuli Parliamentorum*. Of all the major editions of medieval historical records, none is perhaps more deceptive than the eighteenth-century edition of the *Rotuli Parliamentorum* in the way in which it bundles together many heterogeneous records without distinction (Richardson and Sayles 1929, 1935, 1981, Roskell 1965). The *Rotuli Parliamentorum* encapsulate the dangers of print technology – the way in which it can subsume various materials into a continuous undifferentiated sequence, leaving the user with the impression that he is dealing with a mechanized transcript of a single continuous source.

However, much the same effect can be created with a computer, particularly if very varied records are subjected to a quantitative analysis. Reports of the speaker's activities during the reigns of Richard II and Henry IV are very patchy. The parliament rolls were by no means the 'minutes' of parliamentary discussion that might be imagined. Peter de la Mare is not even mentioned in the parliament roll of 1376; his speeches are known from chronicle evidence (Roskell 1965, Holmes 1975). The speaker's protestation is not always recorded; and of course the report is filtered through the clerk who summarized it for the parliament roll (Roskell 1965: 23–51). On one occasion, the clerk simply reported that the speaker made the protestation 'in customary fashion'. Occasionally other sources paint a different picture to that given in the official record, such as a newsletter of 1404 which makes it evident that the speaker used blunter words than the parliament roll suggests (Roskell 1965: 47–8).

The parliament rolls are very complex documents, and are only one of a series of texts describing what happened in the different parliaments, none of which records what was actually said. Both a printed edition and a purely quantitative analysis can tend to obscure these distinctions. However, an electronic edition using hypertext allows these different strands to be separated and explored, while still permitting quantitative and other forms of analysis. In attempting to retain the context of documents in this way, an archival understanding is vital, and Professor Genet's argument that historians must start to think more like archivists is consequently particularly pertinent.

In the curious book which must, I suppose, be regarded as Elton's historical testament, *Return to Essentials* (the title of which eerily prefigures the political slogan 'Back to Basics' coined shortly after the book appeared), Elton (1991: 41) denounces in characteristically vivid fashion the dangers posed to historical research by theoretical preconceptions and the 'cancerous radiation that comes from the forehead of Derrida and Foucault'. Elton's prescription against these dangers is a simple one: '*Ad fontes* remains the necessary war cry'. If this is expressed as an injunction to return to the analysis and criticism of texts, it seems curiously to echo the concerns of the very literary philosophers denounced by Elton. Nevertheless, Elton's motto is one that is very relevant to the position of historical computing.

If computer-aided history is seen as exclusively associated with quantitative techniques grounded in the use of databases and spreadsheets, it runs the risk of being seen as irrelevant to large swathes of historical research. An obvious way out of this impasse is through a greater use of the computer for textual analysis to show the plurality of meaning of texts, the way perceptions of them shift through time and the interconnections between them. Paul Strohm (1992) has urged that we must seek in historical texts 'a rich cacophony of voices where monovocality had formerly seemed to prevail' and encouraged us to view texts 'not as finalized sources but as argumentative and interpretative documents in their own right, as historical contestants and objects of contestation'. An electronic environment, which would permit a 'layering' of the textual evidence similar to that proposed for anthropological evidence, provides a better context for this kind of 'respectful interrogation' of the text than a printed edition. Historians are beginning to make some steps in this direction, such as the Hartlib Papers CD ROM produced by the University of Sheffield and Edward Ayer's project on the American civil war at the University of Virginia. We need to follow this lead, and move away from digits towards digitized texts.

In conclusion, I cannot resist referring to my favourite essay by a French historian, Lucien Febvre's A 'New Kind of History' of 1949 (1973). Febvre's wildly eclectic vision assumes a new relevance in the computer age. Febvre dreamt of a history which worked not only with texts but would use anything connected with mankind – crop distribution, paintings, the design of ships or bridles, the circulation of money, vernacular architecture, even eclipses of the moon. If he had been alive today, Febvre would have found Geographical Information Systems or multimedia irresistible. But the recurrent theme of Febvre's essay is that this vision cannot be achieved if we continue to work alone. Historical research needs to be conducted by teams of interdisciplinary researchers. Professor Genet has emphasized how time and money are the chief constraint on what can be achieved at the moment. Perhaps another reason why humanities computing has not yet achieved its full promise is that the tradition of the solitary scholar remains stubbornly persistent in much humanities research. If we are to realise the full potential of the new media, we need to start building these 'historical laboratories' Febvre dreamt of fifty years ago.

References

Burke, P. (1991) ed., *New Perspectives on Historical Writing* (London).

Currard, P. (1995), *Poetics of the New History: French Historical Discourse from Braudel to Chartier* (Baltimore).

Chaunu, P. and Chaunu, H. (1956–60), *Śeville et l'Atlantique entre 1504 et 1560*, 8 vols (Paris).

Coopland, G. (1975) ed. and trans., Phillipe de Mézières, *Letter to King Richard II. A Plea made in 1395 for Peace between England and France* (Liverpool).

Dosse, F. (1994), *New History in France: the Triumph of Annales*, trans. Conroy (Urbana).

Elton, G.R. (1991), *Return to Essentials* (Cambridge).

Febvre, L. (1973), *A New Kind of History from the Writings of Lucien Febvre*, ed., Burke, P. (London).

Fryde, E., and Miller, E. (1970). *Historical Studies of the English Parliament*, (Cambridge).

Galbraith, V. H. (1964). *An Introduction to the Study of History* (London).

Greenstein, D. (1994), *A Historian's Guide to Computing* (London).

Holmes, G. (1975), *The Good Parliament* (Oxford).

Langlois, C.-V. and Seignebos, C. (1898), *Introduction aux Etudes Historiques* (Paris).

Le Roy Ladurie, E. (1973), *Le Territoire de l'Historien* (Paris).

Powell, E., and Trevelyan, G. M. (1899), *The Peasants' Rising and the Lollards* (London).

Richardson, H. G., and Sayles, G. O. (1929). 'The Exchequer Parliament Rolls and Other Documents', *Bulletin of the Institute of Historical Research* (1929) 6: 129–55.

Richardson, H. G. and Sayles, G. O. (1935) eds., *Rotuli Parliamentorum Anglie Hactenus Inediti*, Camden Society, 3rd series, 51; reprinted In Richardson and Sayles (1981).

Richardson, H. G. and Sayles, G. O. (1981), *The English Parliament in the Middle Ages* (Hambledon).

Robbins, R. H. (1959), *Historical Poems of the XIVth and XVth Centuries* (New York).

Robinson, P. (1966), '... but what kind of electronic editions should we be making?' In ALLC-ACH 1996 Abstracts Bergen, 81–2.

Roskell, J. (1965), *The Commons and their Speakers in English Parliaments 1376-1525* (Manchester).

Sayles, G. O. (1971), *Select Cases in the Court of King's Bench*, vii (Richard II, Henry IV and Henry V), Selden Society, 88.

Stone, L. (1979), 'The revival of narrative: reflections on a new old history', *Past and Present*, 85: 3–24.

Strohm, P. (1992), *Hochon's Arrow: the Social Imagination of Fourteenth Centry Texts* (Princeton).

Thaller M. (1993), *Kleio: a database system*, Halbgrave Reihezur Historischen Fachtinformatith, B11 (Gottingen).

Wilkinson, B. (1939), 'The deposition of Richard and the accession of Henry IV', *English Historical Review*, 54: 215–39; reprinted In Fryde and Miller (1970).

Information Technology and social history: case studies of a subtle paradigm shift

BOB MORRIS

Economic and Social History
University of Edinburgh

Abstract. The historian is a story teller who endeavours to relate an understanding of the past to the culture of the present. The rule-based pattern-seeking abilities of modern information technology tend to intervene in the tension between the historian's respect for the particularity of time, place and person and the need to generalize in the face of the rich profusion of information. The historiography of the 1832 Parliamentary Reform Act reveals a move from an understanding based upon the speeches and diaries of participants to one based upon voters and the act of voting. Poll books, as a source, have exactly those features of regularity and repetition so suited to Information Technology (IT). Several issues were raised by the survey, notably the importance of nominal record linkage and of the coding and categorization of information (and hence of social science perspectives), the relative failure of historians to use text analysis, the dangers of the self sufficient universe of machine-readable data and the problems of presenting relatively complex results. It is important that all historians are able to evaluate the authority of computer-based results. IT has changed major features of historical understanding and, through Internet and CD Rom technology, is changing the way in which many will study, research and enjoy seeking knowledge of the past.

Historical practice and information technology

At heart all historians are story tellers who continually seek to establish and re-establish that relationship between past and present which is crucial in all cultures. Such stories may be called narratives, myths or even hypotheses according to need. In the past thirty years the practice and focus of the research and writing that has been directed towards this activity has been influenced by two major features. There has been the impact of the postmodern critique at its widest and most positive. This created a sense of the many 'stories' involved in the doing of history, a great sense of the 'text' as a rich and distorting intervention between past and present, and of the creative and value laden intervention of historians themselves (White 1973, 1978). Equally powerful in a direct and indirect sense has been information technology (IT). It is no accident that these influences should work together. Both are powerful aspects of the environment of all working historians, even of those who despise and pretend to ignore them. Both interact with each other. Information technology with its ability to fracture the relationship of time and space and transform the perception and substance of information of all kinds is indeed a postmodern technology which has claimed the attention of many cultural analysts (Lyotard 1984, Harvey 1984).

Like it or not, information technology has become a major form of authority in many historical accounts. Seminar papers, learned articles and major books now claim acceptance because of the 'database' and the manipulations of that database upon which their narratives are based. The database has the compelling authority which was once the monopoly of the footnote and the bibliography. It is as well to reflect on the nature of that authority. IT takes, transforms and filters 'texts' or what were once called sources, and creates data sets or 'meta sources' which are the object of further study.

This process has some analogies with the learned editions which emerged from the record series of the late nineteenth century but the process is more fundamental than that. Despite the great variety of applications available, information technology makes its major impact by manipulating large quantities of information at relatively high speed. But IT is above all a pattern-seeking, a pattern-responding and pattern imposing technology. Indeed, it demands patterns. The dominant forms of IT require data structured in fields and categories before the operations of IT have any meaning. The patterns may be little more than the key words of a search and sort operation or they may take the form of complex data structures and the manipulations of the neural network (Wilson and Blue 1992).

The historian, like many others, responds to this feature of the technology, without always reflecting upon the long-term impact which this has had upon historical practice in the last thirty years. There is a tension at the heart of historical practice between the historian's sense of the particularity of place, person and incident and the need to group, to generalize and to see regularities in the historian's attempt to handle the vast amount of information available about the past. IT tips the balance away from this sense of particularity.

This paper takes as a case study the impact of the 1832 Parliamentary Reform Act upon British political behaviour. This is a question which has been revisited by each generation of historians since the passage of the Act itself. The impact of information technology will be seen not so much in any revolutionary new technique but in a subtle shift of paradigm, in other words in the nature of, and the way in which, questions are asked. An area of the historical literature has deliberately been chosen within which information technology has not required sophisticated statistical and technological skills. There is little here that could not have been done by an historian working with a set of index cards, a shoe box and about an hundred years to spare. Such a disarming statement oversimplifies the issues facing all historians who would evaluate each other's work and communicate it to a wider audience. Handling larger and larger amounts of information at greater and greater speeds not only raises, directly or by implication, issues of statistical and social science theory but tends to do so in ways that are specific to historians.

Before the case study is examined some of the major and typical impacts which IT has had upon historical understanding in the last thirty years will be listed. In the United States (US), steam railways once took centre stage in the account of national development. Computer-assisted analysis and some careful econometric modelling reduced this position. Indeed, subsequent study suggested that the contribution of the railway to

British economic growth was far more substantial (Fogel 1964, Hawke 1970). Equally important to the American national myth has been the notion of the United States as the land of opportunity. A number of studies of social mobility in Europe and the US which were dependent upon IT showed that rates of social mobility were little different in the US from those in Europe, with the possible exception of unskilled labour. Studies such as the analysis of Philadelphia by Hershberg and his associates found little evidence of a 'melting pot' in American cities (Hershberg 1981, Kaeble 1981). In Ireland, historians such as Mokyr (1983) and O'Grada (1988) have used excellent area data in their studies of the famine period. Famine has been related to a wide range of socioeconomic features but especially to poverty. This example demonstrates the shift of focus which the use of IT can bring. The conclusions do not deny the importance of the attitudes and policies of British officials, but they do suggest that the Irish Famine might be usefully studied in the context of attitudes and policies relating to poverty as much has in a national narrative of British maltreatment of an oppressed people. In Great Britain, the 'industrial revolution' has always played a key part in the nation's understanding of itself. The notion of a sharp break in continuity has slowly been worn away by the national income historians whilst the history of population has itself been refocused on marriage and fertility, together with the assertion of a distinctive history of family and household structures (Crafts 1985, Wrigley and Scholfield 1981, Anderson 1971). This incomplete list indicates the ability of computer-based studies to assert complexity but above all to subvert a variety of dearly-held national narratives in ways which are both compelling and disturbing.

The historiography of the 1832 Parliamentary Reform Act and the computer.

A central part of the British national myth has been that of a great nation making progress towards prosperity and democracy; wealth for some, freedom and security for all. One key event in this history has been the passing of the Parliamentary Reform Act of 1832 and the events and developments associated with that change. The impact of IT on this historiography has been significant and highlights many of the impacts and problems associated with the powerful methodologies associated with the computer.

The meaning of the 1832 Parliamentary Reform Act has always been a contested one. Following earlier statements by Lord Grey and his Whig ministers, the constitutional lawyer Dicey expressed the matter directly and without any subtlety. The Act operated 'to diminish the power of the gentry and to transfer predominant authority to the middle classes' (Dicey 1885: 185).

Historians writing in the twentieth century under conditions of document-based scholarly history have made a variety of judgements but the basic elements were clear (Halevy 1927: 17 and 62; Woodward 1938: 84–88; Briggs 1950–52, 1956–57). Class analysis had a central place in an unresolved debate on gains and losses. There was a debate on the nature of change. Was it fundamental, gradual or non existent? There was an assumption, often little discussed, on the central place of party. There was a contested recognition of the danger of revolution and the degree to which this had been avoided.

There was curiosity over the nature of the agitation and the degree to which the working classes had been 'betrayed'. There was an assertion that 1832 had a key place in British progress to 'democracy'. The characteristic source materials were parliamentary speeches, pamphlets, newspaper reports of meetings and a series of political letters, diaries and memoirs. There were implicit theoretical assumptions about the link between agitation and change, and between socio-economic change and reform. By the 1960s, there were more explicit assumptions about links between local economic structures, the nature of local class structures and the reform agitation.

This situation was changed by a number of related developments. The first was the discovery of parliamentary poll books by Vincent (1967) and others. The second was the growing importance of survey-based election studies of voting. In Great Britain this was led by the series of Nuffield general election studies directed by Butler (Butler and Stokes 1969, Budge and O'Leary 1973). The influence of these developments on historians was reinforced by the impact of social science survey-based community studies of class, family and politics (Goldthorpe *et al.* 1969). As always, computer-based history was closely, though not exclusively, related to developments in social science.

The impact of these developments can be traced through a number of key works. Vincent (1967) made a careful tabulation of the information in those poll books which included information on occupation. He was amongst the first to show the very imperfect relationship between occupation and voting. One response to this observation was to link the evidence on voting behaviour from the poll books to other nominal records in order to increase the depth of knowledge of the socio-economic characteristics of individuals. Nossitor (1975: 172–3) linked Gateshead poll books to the rate books and the census manuscript. This strategy demonstrated a link between radical voting and low economic status. It also showed a dramatic age effect. The generation which came of age in the mid- and late-1820s were almost twice as likely to vote Whig as those who reached maturity under the Whig governments of the 1830s. Neale (1972: 69–73; 1981: 357–61) also made use of local rate books in Bath. He confirmed the link between radical voting and low socioeconomic status as well as demonstrating the lack of homogeneity of economic status within groups covered by specific occupational titles. Fraser (1976:229–31). made a detailed study of selected occupational groups in Leeds in the 1830s and showed that, although occupation overall was not a good predictor of voting, there were occupational groups which had a very strong bias such as the liberal-voting engineers and flax spinners. Like Hennock (1973) in an earlier study of municipal councillors and Woolley (1938) in his study of the House of Commons, Fraser laid great emphasis on the continuity of social structural features and the importance of party identity both in describing change and in predicting voting behaviour.

The technology of these studies was heroic and involved the 80-column punch card supplying data and instructions to SPSS (Statistical Package for the Social Sciences) in batch processing mode, the earlier Hollerith-type punch card with counter sorter, or even index cards. In many of these studies the computer was 'off stage'. The computer was responsible for creating the methods of social science survey and voting study which were driving the historians' curiosity. In other words, historians were asking questions and exploring methodologies which required the modern user-friendly, high storage capacity, interactive machines long before those machines were available. The primitive nature of the technology historians were using showed in the small sizes of population in many studies and the small cell totals in many of the tables.

Because historians needed to link records, they were not able to use the sampling strategies developed by social scientists. Typically historians do not require their computers to carry out very complex or sophisticated operations but they do require very large data sets to achieve record linkage and statistically-viable data sets. Such large data sets were difficult to handle within the technology of the 1970s. By the mid-1980s, these technological constraints were rapidly reducing (Morris 1995). Three studies illustrate the impact of the change. All three had one feature in common. They placed 'party' identity at the centre of their analysis. O'Gorman (1989a, 1989b). used a quantitative analysis of voter behaviour, paying especial attention to plumping. Phillips (1992), Phillips and Wetherell (1993) and Morris (1990a) used record linkage in a variety of ways. Phillips linked records from different poll books to create a dynamic history of an individual's involvement in a chosen constituency. His use of techniques of event history analysis showed the extent to which an individual's party voting could be predicted from votes in the previous election or elections, and more important, that the ability to predict a vote from previous vote(s) improved significantly after the 1832 Reform Act, thus suggesting that party identity did become more important after the Act and in this respect at least the Act marked a break in continuity. It provides a careful, measurable, quantifiable answer to an old question, did 1832 make any difference?

Morris (1990a) used a different strategy. The research design was based upon the familiar cross section in time but sought to link a wide variety of records. The poll book (Sims 1984) for the 1832 election was not only linked to that of an 1834 byelection but also to a trade directory (Shaw and Tripper 1988), to the membership lists of key voluntary societies, to subscription lists and to lists of pew rents from the key congregations in the town. This study also insisted upon a multi-dimensional coding for the occupational titles and an inference code to indicate the nature of the assumptions made when linking records. Such multi-dimensional codes enabled the flexibility offered by the computer to be used to explore further the complex link between occupational title and voting. The subscription lists and the codes provided two different measures of occupational status which showed that high status created a Tory bias in voting. The variety of nominal lists linked also showed that religious denomination was one of the best predictors of voting although its influence was often countered by occupational and community factors.

The historiography outlined above contained a movement from an emphasis on class to an emphasis on party. Party loyalty in turn has been linked to religion rather than to occupation. Attention has moved from the debates in parliament and the public meetings of the reform agitation and the election campaign to the act of voting itself. IT had an enabling role in this paradigm shift. The impact was incremental as the capacity and speed of machines increased. IT enabled historians to respond to the methodological and theoretical promptings of social science. In turn, it presented a variety of methodological problems for historians in forms which were more precise and acute. Record linkage, especially nominal record linkage and data categorization for occupational titles in particular, required an awareness of social science issues. Above all IT directed attention to a particular generic type of document.

Central to this process in terms of the case study has been the dominant part played by the poll book and associated methodologies. The poll book is an ideal document for the dominant forms of information technology available since the 1970s. For line after line and page after page the same structures appear – name, information regarding address, property and sometimes occupation together with details of voting. This information is ready-made for the cells of the spread sheet or the fields of the database. It was waiting to be coded and categorized for the statistical package. Thus historians have been attracted to those documents which respond to IT's thirst for regularity and repetition. The social relationships represented in such documents are the ones likely to attract attention, and accounts of them gain the authority that accompanies the well-analysed database. In the same way historians of the family have been drawn to the family as household (Wrigley 1973). The rich and complex census documents of the 19th century were important in this respect.

Why no text analysis?

In the literature surrounding the 1832 Reform Act, much less attention has been paid to the text of debates, speeches, diaries and letters. These are still picked over by the careful and conventional assessment of the pencil-using historian. The examination of such sources takes place despite the extensive use of text analysis in literary studies. Despite the urging of those involved in the text encoding initiative, historians have shown little desire to respond (Sperlberg McQueen and Burnard 1990, Burnard 1993). There are two reasons for this situation. Historians have been reluctant to conceptualize problems in a way which might respond to text analysis. For example, studies of authorship might well be brought to bear upon the parliamentary speeches involved in the reform debates of 1830–32. Were they written by Grey and Melbourne? Would it matter if analysis of authorship suggested that all the speeches involved in those debates were written by the same person, in other words that the intervention of the scribes involved in the creation of Hansard was very substantial?

Recent work on the language of politics and of social description has used the traditional strategy of careful and informed reading with little interest in a quantitative analysis of the language of the text or of matching language and content across texts (Wahrman 1992, 1995). Some of this reluctance comes from the way in which historians use text; they tend to be extensive rather than intensive users of text. Thus a study of the early writings of Samuel Smiles, author of *Self Help*, involved not only a reading of his books and his editorials in the radical *Leeds Times* but also references to Milton, the seventeenth century poet, Emerson and Channing, the American transcendental writers to Bentham and the utilitarians, as well as to the Bible culture of the Scotland of his childhood (Morris 1981). A machine readable database of the texts required was simply not available and is unlikely to be created even with current improvements in Optical

Character Recognition (OCR). More systematic attention to text of this sort is likely to be one of the future and productive developments in historical technique.

Nominal record linkage

The conclusions of many of these studies depend on the logic of nominal record linkage. This logic takes information from two or more records and 'links' them to form a new meta record on the basis that the records refer to the same place, event, household or, most important of all, the same individual. Nominal record linkage referring to individual people is central to the analysis of the poll books. Whatever rules a particular study adopts, there are two basic types of problem involved. The historian must avoid both making false links and failing to make true links. Problems are presented by common names and by name variations. Thus John Smith may occur in two lists but because it is a common name may refer to different people. The nineteenth century practice of naming sons after fathers creates a particular hazard for the unwary. On the other hand Mr John Smith and James Smyth Esq may well be the same person. Spelling variants are rare in Great Britain in the nineteenth century but were important in earlier centuries (Baskerville *et al.* 1992, Morris 1985). Such variants in spelling were more important in societies which crossed language barriers and in those which used systems of patronymic names (Kitts *et al.* 1990, Bouchard *et al.* 1981, Bouchard and Pouyez 1980). Various strategies have been adopted to reduce the chances of both these type of error. When records are chosen which are close together in time and place this reduces the chance of false links (Winchester 1970–71). If John Smith in an 1832 poll book is linked to John Smith in an 1835 list, the chance of one John Smith having left or died and been replaced by another of the same name is much less than a link between, say, 1832 and 1847. Historians also have a natural instinct to make maximum use of the information available. Thus the more features of a record which are in agreement, the more secure the link is held to be. Thus records with the same name and the same address or occupation are held to be more secure (Baskerville 1989, Elkit 1985). Morris (1982) took a slightly different approach and made distinction between the linkage of 'unique names', in other words those which are identical and occur only once in each list, and between linkages that used supplementary information (in the case of the poll books, addresses). Neither of these approaches to record linkage is without problems, but they all have a base in common sense and sound historical practice.

However, the very nature of record linkage produces unintended consequences. The methodology favours community studies limited to a discrete geographical area, such as a town, a parish or a county. It favours studies which are cross sections in time rather than longitudinal studies. This last problem can be overcome by using chains of records close together in time or by using the logic of demography and ageing to link records across time. Record linkage and list processing have done a great deal to rescue the lives of the poor. Through legal court records and the family reconstruction it has promoted 'history from below'. Despite this experience, record linkage as a methodology favours those of high status because historians in general have more information on those of higher status. Thus, it is easier to link male records than female records, not only because there are more of them but because many women changed their names on marriage and in general provided less information on any record they produced. Even amongst the male records there was a slight bias towards individuals of a higher economic/social status. For the Leeds Poll Book of 1832 it proved easier to link professional men and those of independent income. When the Leeds middle classes made a voluntary subscription for the relief of the poor during the cholera epidemic of that year, 59 per cent gave less than £1. When the subscription was linked to the poll book, the linked population contained 53 per cent who gave under £1. Thus record linkage directs attention to those of relatively high status and to the geographically, socially and economically stable. It directs attention to a geographical location. Thus it is easier to study stayers than goers. It is easier to study intra- than inter-community networks. In general nominal record linkage directs attention to relationships within communities rather than to the extensive networks which tend to be recorded in diaries and letters.

Data entry; optical character recognition and sampling

In many of the studies outlined here, storage capacity and speed of computing were major barriers in devising research strategies. By the 1990s, the major cost was not data storage or computing capacity but the cost of data input. Efforts to reduce this cost have centred upon sampling and in recent years upon optical character recognition (OCR). Recent improvements in OCR have been rapid. Initially, available scanners were limited to the reading of conventional late twentieth century type faces, but recent advances in software have provided 'teachable' OCR applications. These can 'learn' older type faces but they do require considerable consistency. The chipped type common before about 1880 and even the re-inking of a type face causing differential bleeding of ink around a seriphed type can cause confusion and chaos producing errors which require time-consuming manual correction. OCR for historians is still an art not a science. Skilled use can however provide limited improvements in the productivity of data input (van Horik 1993). Data input from manuscript sources will require skilled manual intervention for some time to come (Helsper *et al.* 1993).

Historians have considerable experience of sampling as a means of mediating their relationship with overwhelming quantities of data. Those prepared to use the strategies of random, stratified or other modes of sampling derived from experience of social science survey have very precise guidance as to the risks they are taking and the significance (in both the statistical and conventional meaning of the words) of the results they obtain (Schofield 1972). These strategies are valuable for historians who wish to use information from only one document source, such as a census household listing. For others the demands of record linkage mean that these strategies are of limited value. A 10 per cent random sample derived from two sources would produce a potential 1 per cent linkage population.

There are two means of overcoming this problem. The first is the community study in which 100 per cent of the population is taken from all documents. Data are derived from documents for which geographical and temporal contiguity make links likely. This is a productive strategy for the study of the geographically stable. The second is letter cluster sampling which has also been used as a means of providing potentially linkable data (Phillips 1992, Nenadic *et al.* 1992, Dupâquier and Kessler 1992). This method has made possible the production of some very rich data sets. The difficulty is that statistical theory provides very little guidance as to the risks and the significance of results. The problem arises in the many situations in which nominal data, especially surnames which are the major source of information for linking, are clearly not independent of variables under analysis such as occupation or voting behaviour. In many cases surnames are linked to intervening variables such as geographical location, family networks and ethnicity (Richardson 1994). The risks are probably limited in urban populations which are socially heterogeneous but lack sharp cultural differences. In populations dominated by specific surnames, or in which surnames are indicators of ethnicity or religion, letter cluster sampling carries major risks. Results from rural or county populations where family networks are influential and particular parishes were dominated by a few surnames show that letter cluster sampling is of limited value.

Information coding and categories

Many of the conclusions in these studies depend upon the coding and categorization of information, notably but not exclusively on occupation (Shürer and Diederiks 1993, Diederiks and Balkstein 1995). This dependence is inevitable given the huge amount of information involved. The Leeds Trade Directory of 1834 contained some 9,000 entries with over 2,000 different occupational titles. Some differences were trivial such as with 'shoe maker' and 'shoemaker', but this still left a mass of complex information which needed to be grouped in categories if comprehensible conclusions were to be drawn from them. Historians are no strangers to generalization but the computer demands explicit rule-based generalization. In general the tendency has been to turn to social science as the basis for the generalizations used. The principles of occupational categorization used by the Office of Population Censuses and Surveys (OPCS) provided a useful start. Others, notably in the BoothArmstrong classification, gain authority from using schemes of classification derived from the past in an attempt to avoid anachronism (Wrigley 1972). The problems involved go further than this. In the study of Leeds in the early 1830s information was linked from both a trade directory which gave occupational titles and a poll book with occupation titles. This information is an occupational title rather than a description of their occupation; such a title is an indicator of occupation made in the process of an attribution or assertion made by those involved in creating the document. The results of linking two documents with occupational titles were instructive. When the categories from the two documents were compared the divergence was striking (as shown in Table 1).

Some categories were more consistent than others but individual examples linked by unique names showed what was happening. The gentleman in the poll book became a lawyer in the trade directory, the cabinet maker became a second hand furniture broker,

Table 1. Comparison of the occupational status codes in the Poll Book and Directory for
Leeds 1834

Occupational group	Poll Book titles found in Equivalent category in the Directory (%)	Directory titles found in equivalent category in the Poll Book (%)
Retail and processing	86	73
Commerce	71	78
Banking and finance	91	91
Agents and travellers	58	52
Clerks and Bookkeepers	82	73
Manufacturing	65	69
Craft	75	80
Professional	84	70
Medical	96	94
Legal	98	93
Religion	100	100
Services	74	76
Construction	14	50
Independent income	80	81

Sources: Leeds Poll Book 1832; Leeds Trade Directory 1834.

the lawyer admitted he was also an insurance agent. The 'text' derived from these documents was part of what Morton has called ' the presentation of self in everyday documents', in other words each document represents a self presentation, a claim which has been accepted by the document maker (Morton 1994). Thus in the context of the election, individuals claimed status in the Weberian sense of 'social honour'. They used the title 'gentleman' to remind all that they had a property income or they used the title of the trade for which they served their time. In the business-seeking world of the trade directory they make clear the activities through which they earn their income as insurance agents and furniture brokers. Historians are used to statements such as 'merchants tended to vote Tory and manufacturers Whig'; perhaps these statements might also be 'Tories tended to call themselves merchants and Whigs admit they were manufacturers'. The tables from the analysis of the database seem very hard and authoritative but they conceal a process of inference which needs to be exposed more explicitly to the critique of labelling and categorization evident in the best of social science survey analysis as well as perhaps to the historian's sense of source criticism.

The self-sufficient universe of data

The final issue arising from this is the temptations of the self-sufficient universe of data which is offered by the methodology of the computer. However self-consciously the historian may battle against this temptation, it remains easier to manipulate information within the data set than to link it with information outwith that universe of data. Thus the poll book has encouraged the marginalization of class in the analysis of 1832. After all, the urban voting qualifications were devised to eliminate working-class people from the registers. Thus it is party politics which takes place within the universe of the poll book whilst class conflict is represented by the exclusion of 80 per cent of adult males from those lists. In the same way the study of the family has been directed to features of the household and the structures of life cycle events such as birth, marriage, birth of children rather than to links which are outwith such sources. Thus more attention has been paid to lodgers and servants than to the cousins, nephews and nieces made visible in letters and novels.

Why it matters to all historians

Thus the use of information technology has changed the focus and nature of practice amongst the small number of historians who use computers for more than word processing. Are the issues raised here of concern to more than this minority? There are two reasons why they should be. First, computer-using historians have made major changes to historical understanding which have affected the context in which all historians work. It seems important that those who never intend to engage in nominal record linkage or coding occupational titles should be able to assess the authority of the results coming from that process.

The second set of reasons arises from a series of current developments which propel all historians into an increasingly information-rich world which can be handled only through the rule-based regularities of IT. Historians of the recent past already face the issue of electronic data; in other words data which were created in and can be presented only in electronic form. These data will soon become a flood and cannot be assessed by conventional means. Government survey data such as the General Household Survey, the vast store of diplomatic and intelligence data which have been gathered in the past fifty years, and the huge quantity of data on retail sales collected from the bar codes that pass through the supermarket tills are only three examples. Historians of the social policy, diplomatic policy and consumer history of the past two decades will fail in their task if they cannot assess and use such sources. Few attempts seem to have been made to develop relevant strategies (Ross and Higgs 1993, Morris 1993, Zweig 1992). Some strategies will come from the experience of historians who have studied the population and voting history of the eighteen and nineteenth centuries; other strategies will come from raiding the methodologies of other disciplines.

Historians stand on the edge of a breakthrough in computer-based and networked teaching. The impact of the Internet will increase the density and complexity of information available at all levels of 'doing history' from the school pupil to the university professor. Bibliographical work is already more effective with on-line facilities. Electronic journals are developing in a way which not only mimics the journal on the shelf but is creating new forms of quasi-instant publication and multimedia. For example, articles can be published not only with footnotes but also with the data sets. This raises major issues of citation, versioning and scholarly control. It also changes the way in which historians will be able to react to each other's work. The methods of reviewing and reading books such as *Class, Sect and Party* (Morris 1990a) might be very different if the data could be accessed on line from Essex. This information universe is potentially immense. The computer not only enables historians to handle more information at greater speed, it also creates more information at greater speed. The skills required to search and evaluate such an information universe will be related to the skills of archive history as well as to the skills of social science, but the task of evaluating and specifying those skills has hardly begun.

References

Anderson, M. (1971), *Family Structure in Nineteenth Century Lancashire* (Cambridge).

Baskerville, S. W. (1989), 'Preferred Linkage and the analysis of voting behaviour in eighteeenth century England', *History and Computing*, 1: 112–20.

—— Hudson, P. and Morris, R. J. (1992) (eds.), 'Record linkage', *History and Computing*, Special Issue, 4.

Bouchard, G. and Pouyez, C. (1980), 'Name variations and computerized record linkage', *Historical Methods*, 13: 119–25.

—— Brard, P. and Lavoie, Y. (1981), 'Fonem: un code de transcription phonétique pour la reconstitution automatique des familles Saguenayenne's, *Population*, 36: 1085–104.

Briggs, A. (1950–52), 'The background of the Parliamentary Reform Movement in three English cities (1830–32)', *Cambridge Historical Journal*: 10, 293–317.

—— (1956–57), 'Middle class consciousness in English politics', 1780–1846', *Past and Present*, 9: 64–74.

Budge, I. and O'Leary, C. (1973), *Belfast: Approach to Crisis. A Study of Belfast Politics, 1613–1970* (London).

Burnard, L. (1993), 'The Text Encoding Initiative: towards a extensible standard for encoding texts'. In Ross, S. and Higgs, E. (eds.) (1993), *Electronic Information Resources and Historians: European Perspectives* (Gottingen).

Butler, D. and Stokes, D. E. (1969), *Political Change in Britain* (London).

Crafts, N. F. R. (1985), *British Economic Growth During the Industrial Revolution* (Oxford).

Dupâquier, J. and Kessler, D. (1992), *La Société Française au XIXe Siècle. Tradition, Transitions, Transformation* (Paris).

Elkit, J. (1985), 'Nominal record linkage and the study of non secret voting: a Danish case', *Journal of Interdisciplinary History*, 15: 419–43.

Fogel, R. W. (1964), *Railroads and American Economic Development* (Baltimore).

Fraser, D. (1976), *Urban Politics in Victorian England. The Structure of Politics in Victorian Cities* (Leicester).

Goldthorpe, J. H. , Lockwood, D. , Bechofer, F. and Platt, J. (1969), *The Affluent Worker in the Class Structure* (Cambridge).

Halevy, E. (1927), *The Triumph of Reform, 1789–1848* (London).

Harvey, D. (1989), *The Condition of Postmodernity* (Oxford).

Hawke, G. R. (1970), *Railways and Economic Growth in England and Wales, 1840–1870* (Oxford).

Helsper, E. L., Schomaker, L. R. and Grenon, M. (1993), 'Tools for the recognition of handwritten historical documents'. In Doorn, P. K. and van Horik, R. (eds.), 'Scanning and OCR', *History and Computing*, Special Issue, 5(2): 68–73.

Hennock, E.P. (1973), *Fit and Proper Persons. Ideal and Reality in Nineteenth Century Government* (London).

Hershberg, T. (1981) (ed.), *Philadelphia, Work, Space, Family and Group Experience in the 19th Century* (Oxford).

Kaeble, H. (1981), 'Social mobility in America and Europe: a comparison of nineteenth century cities, *Urban History Yearbook* (Leicester) 29–38

Kitts, A., Doulton, D. and Reis, E. (1990), *The Reconstitution of Viana do Castelo* (London).

Lyotard, J. F. (1984), *The Post Modern Condition: a Report on Knowledge* (Manchester).

Mokyr, J. (1983), *Why Ireland Starved: a Quantitative and Analytical History of the Irish Economy, 1800–1850* (London).

Morris, R. J. (1981), 'Samuel Smiles and the genesis of self help', *Historical Journal*, 24: 89–109.

—— (1985), 'Does nineteenth century nominal record linkage have lessons for the machine readable century'? *Journal of the Society of Archivists*, 7: 503–12.

—— (1990a), *Class, Sect and Party. The Making of the British Middle Class: Leeds, 1820–50* (Manchester).

—— (1990b), 'Petitions, meetings and class formation amongst the urban middle classes in Britain in the 1830s', *Tijdschrift voor Geschiedenis*, 103: 294–310.

—— (1993), 'Electronic documents and the history of the late 20th century black holes or warehouses'. In Ross, S. and Higgs, E. (eds) *Electronic Information Resources and Historians: European Perspectives* (Gottingen).

—— (1995), 'Computers and the subversion of British history', *Journal of British History*, 34: 503–28.

Morton, G. (1994), 'Presenting the self: record linkage and referring to ordinary historical persons', *History and Computing*, 6: 12–20.

Neale, R. S. (1972), *Class and Ideology in the Nineteenth Century* (London).

—— (1981), *Bath. A Social History 1680–1850* (London).

Nenadic, S., Morris, R. J., Smyth, J. and Rainger C. (1992), 'Record linkage and the small family firm: Edinburgh 1861–1891', *Bulletin of the John Rylands Library*, 74: 169–96.

Nossitor, T. (1975), *Influence, Opinion and Political Idioms in Reformed England. Case Studies from the North East, 1832–1874* (Brighton).

O'Gorman, F. (1989a), *Voters, Patrons and Parties: the Unreformed Electoral System in England, 1734–1932* (Oxford).

—— (1989b), 'Electoral behaviour in England, 1700–1872'. In Denley, P., Fogelvik, S. and Harvey, C. (eds.) *History and Computing II* (Manchester) 220–38.

O Gráda, C. (1988), *Ireland before and after the Famine. Explorations in Economic History, 1800–1925* (Manchester).

Phillips, J. (1992), *The Great Reform Bill in the Boroughs. English Electoral Behaviour, 1881–1841* (Oxford).

—— and Wetherell, C. (1993), 'Probability and political behaviour: a case study of the Municipal Corporations Act of 1835', *History and Computing*, 5: 135–53.

Richardson, S. (1994). 'Letter cluster sampling and nominal record linkage', *History and Computing*, 6: 168–76.

Ross, S. and Higgs, E. (1993) (eds.), *Electronic Information Resources and Historians: European Perspectives* (Göttingen).

Schofield, R. (1972), 'Sampling in historical research'. In Wrigley, E. A. (ed.), *Nineteenth Century Society* (Cambridge) 146–90.

Shaw, G. and Tipper, A. (1988), *British Directories: a Bibliography and Guide to Directories Published in England and Wales (1850–1950) and Scotland (1773-1950)* (Leicester).

Shürer, K. and Diederiks, H. (1993) (eds.), *The Use of Occupations in Historical Analysis* (Göttingen).

Sims, J. (1984) (ed.), *A Handlist of British Parliamentary Poll Books* (Leicester and Riverside).

Sperberg McQueen, C. M. and Burnard, L. (1990), *Guidelines for the Encoding and Interchange of Machine Readable Texts* (Chicago and Oxford).

Van Horick, R., (1993), 'Recent progress in the automatic reading of printed historical documents'. In Doorn, P. and Van Horick, R. (eds), 'Scanning and OCR', *History and Computing*, Special Issues, 5: 68–73.

Vincent, J. (1967), *Pollbooks. How Victorians Voted* (Cambridge).

Wahrman, D. (1992), 'Virtual representation: parliamentary reporting and languages of class in the 1790s', *Past and Present*, 136: 83–113.

—— (1995), *Imagining the Middle Class. The Political Representation of Class in Britain, c.1780–1840* (Cambridge).

White, H. (1971), *Metahistory: The Historical Imagination in Nineteenth Century Europe* (Baltimore).

—— (1978), *Tropics of Discourse* (Baltimore).

Wilson, C. L. and Blue, J. L. (1992), 'Neural network methods applied to character recognition', *Social Science Computer Review*, 10: 173–95.

Winchester, I. (1970–71), 'The linkage of historical records by man and computer: techniques and problems', *Journal of InterDisciplinary History*, 1: 107–24.

Woodward, E. L. (1938), *The Age of Reform, 1815–1870* (Oxford).

Wrigley, E. A. (1972), (ed.), *Nineteenth Century Society. Essays in the Use of Quantitative Methods for the Study of Social Data* (Cambridge).

—— (1973), *Identifying People in the Past* (London).

—— and Schofield, R. S. (1981), *The Population History of England, 1541–1871* (London).

Zweig, R. (1992), 'Virtual records and real history', *History and Computing*, 4: 174–82.

Commentary

STEVEN SMITH

Institute of Historical Research
University of London

Professor Morris has persuasively set out the advantages and disadvantages of computer-based historical studies and their future. Three aspects might be briefly reviewed by way of comment: the nature of technology; methodology or the nature of historical research; and the question of authority and the strategic advantages of computers.

Technology

Intrinsically, technology has no direction; it is neither progressive nor regressive. It is neutral. Technology is developed by a society in particular directions at specific moments, often being subject to both push and pull factors. The pull factors which Professor Morris ascribes to technology include its speed in searching and pattern seeking of greater amount of information. Positivist and statistical approaches to history benefit disproportionately from the new technology. In addition, there are other pull factors, such as funding availability, and large amounts of project-funds made available at a national level have already ensured that the United Kingdom maintains a leading position internationally in telematics. The push factors are supplied by methodology, according to Professor Morris who suggests that historians were asking questions and exploring methodologies which required the modern user–friendly, high-storage capacity, interactive machines long before they were available.

Methodology

Methodologies associated with computer-related or statistical work have been regarded as negative or lacking in 'Methodology'. It could be argued that IT is excellent at establishing the frequency of association between variables, but the nature of the relationship between the variables, unless indicated in the form taken by the information (as in poll books), is left to more traditional historical methods of interpretation and analysis. Professor Morris has made the point that historians tend to be extensive rather than intensive users of text and that Nominal Record Linkage, as a method, favours a synchronic rather than a diachronic or historical approach. However, methodology is subject to change as is technology. The proliferation of statistical societies in the United Kingdom (UK) in the nineteenth century comes to mind or the fact that, only fifteen years ago, a history seminar given at the Institute of Historical Research based upon a statistical approach was such a rarity that its very novelty was attractive. How the authority for different approaches changes over time is an interesting and complex question.

Authority

There is no doubt that telematics offers opportunities of distribution, participation and accessibility to a degree that was unknown before. Research and opinion may now be widespread at high speed, such as the electronic *Reviews in History*, which overcomes the delays in the distribution of scholarly reviews in more traditional journals and allows for an author's reply. Participation in the development of research is no longer geographically-limited and communication over any distance allows the immediate participation by any members of the national and international community of historians, as demonstrated by *Electronic Seminars in History*. Accessibility to information which promotes research and discussion of research is now easy in the UK and information on university teachers and their research, theses in progress and completed, the occurrence of seminars and conferences, is all searchable on the subject-based gateway and server on the internet for history, *IHR-Info/History UK*. All of the above examples have been created or developed as the result of national funding being available from the Joint Information Systems Committee in the last few years. The new technology offers two opposing developments: the very rapid extension of existing authority directly over a much wider population, and the promotion of a variety of new international rules of research.

The question of new sub-communities is demonstrated by the Association of History and Computing, which exists in very many countries. When a space for new development is created, it attracts pioneers, and there is a tendency to form a new community through common terms, skills, knowledge and method. When such sub-communities are based upon technology which becomes integrated into mainstream research, the excitement of the creative and multi-skilled frontiersperson in the covered-wagon subsides as the challenge is reduced and specific tasks assigned with perfunctory regularity to railway engineers and clerks with timetables. By far the greatest opportunity provided by telematics is the inspiration to reappraise historical methodology at an international level and to review the importance of the study of history in society.

Simulating the past: SOCSIM and CAMSIM and their applications in family and demography history

RICHARD SMITH

Cambridge Group for the History of Population and Social Structure
University of Cambridge

Abstract. This paper describes and reviews research in which computer-aided micro simulation techniques have been directed towards the understanding of demographic patterns, co-residential arrangements and kin sets in past societies. After a review of the techniques, two principal ventures by microsimulators of historical phenomena are considered. One area of emphasis appeared first in the late 1970s and early 1980s and was largely directed towards the use of simulation techniques as a means of improving scholars' comprehension of evidence, usually existing in the form of cross-sectional 'snap shots'. The other focus of research by microsimulators of past situations, currently under development, has been on the provision of information on features of the social structure that were and are largely unrecorded, but can be derived, within tolerable margins of error, provided sufficient information on the determining processes is available. Usually, however, there are no sources against which the simulated characteristics and patterns relating to the past can be compared. Examples of work directed to the understanding of family and kinship patterns in Ancient Roman society and the recent Chinese past are discussed.

Introduction

This paper, unlike that by Gilbert later in this volume, is somewhat narrowly focused in its attempt to describe and review a modest quantity of research in which computer-assisted microsimulation techniques have been directed towards the understanding of past societies. Two principal ventures by researchers who have utilized microsimulation will be considered. The earliest investigations of this kind dating from the late 1970s and early 1980s were largely directed towards the use of simulation techniques as a means of improving scholars' comprehension of evidence, usually existing in the form of cross-sectional 'snap-shots' of a society at a specific moment in time. Such cross-sectional evidence would usually exist in the absence of longitudinal information bearing upon processes through time that were responsible for the form assumed by the 'snap-shot'. More recently microsimulation has been increasingly used to provide information on features of the social structure that were (and are) largely unrecorded, but can be derived, within tolerable margins of error, provided sufficient information of the determining processes is available. Usually, however, there are no sources against which the simulated characteristics and patterns can be compared. Improvements in computer hardware in recent years have certainly facilitated work of this kind on modestly priced equipment within the grasp of most independent researchers.

Throughout the following discussion the focus will be on microsimulation and its application to historical problems. In microsimulation a series of hypothetical events is constructed by the computer, in a random fashion, but in accordance with specified probabilities, generally derived from empirical observations. As Gilbert has noted, this technique, often known as Monte Carlo, enables scholars to observe and chart the consequences for aggregate behaviour of assumptions about individual behaviour. The same instructions and probabilities can be given to the computer not just once but many times, holding everything the same except random numbers, the 'throws of the dice'. In principle, this allows outcomes to be observed in terms of random variation, without specifying any alteration to the structural characteristics of the situation or the model. This aim of repeating or replicating a process under constant or recurring conditions has suggested to some scholars the notion of 'experiment' for simulation exercises of this type. It has been suggested that computer microsimulation offers to historical social science many of the aids for conceptual clarity of laboratory science since 'history delivers us no retakes' (Wachter *et al.* 1978: 2). However, the computer can reveal what these retakes might have been if researchers are prepared to believe their own description of the processes in motion. One distinctive virtue of computer-aided microsimulation is that it obliges the researcher to make explicit his or her assumptions.

There is, at least superficially, the sense that by engaging in simulation researchers are venturing to capture something as it was, by constructing a copy as realistic as possible and more realistic than descriptive generalization will allow, of some process as it might have happened. But as Wachter (1988:215) pungently notes '...simulation connotes the making of a likeness. But the pursuit of realism through simulation is in fact a chimera. What is produced through simulation is not a likeness of the operation of the world, but a likeness of some set of our own ideas concerning the operation of the world'. Consequently, conclusions from a simulation are only as trustworthy as the rates and rules which the simulation takes as given.

Application of statistics to history is nothing new, and while there are some noteworthy exceptions (e.g., Wrigley and Schofield 1981), computers have had more variable success in furthering major paradigmatic shifts solely through their ability to process large bodies of data. However, what is commonly meant by the application of statistics to history is not what simulation is about. For certain purposes, the collection, processing and presentation of appropriate numbers suffice to shed light on historical problems. The numbers, once gathered, speak for themselves, or are assumed to speak for themselves. For other (indeed many) purposes, on the contrary, the numbers reveal little taken on their own. A great deal of effort expended in their interpretation is only justified when they are rare and precious. Microsimulation provides a framework within which much of the discussion concerned with uncertainty surrounding the meaning to be attached to these data can be undertaken.

Some subjects are undoubtedly more susceptible to careful consideration regarding the place of uncertainty in their interpretation than others. Microsimulation may well play a key role when that is the case. A pre-eminent area of this kind is demography which is a subject founded upon sets of statistical regularities of human births, marriages and deaths. The interactions of social structure with demography have proved to be a natural test site for statistical applications in history. It is perhaps no coincidence that applications of microsimulation have been especially effective in assessing patterns in data about pre-industrial European social structures that relate to small, but historically ubiquitous populations, such as parishes and townships. The problem of random variability is especially prominent in the analysis of such small populations. An additional difficulty or distinctive attribute associated with such contexts is that the inhabitants of such settlements cannot be regarded as statistically independent units for analysis in that they were often interrelated (e.g., parents, children, spouses, siblings) and, as a consequence, these kin links introduce statistical dependencies between age and other characteristics that they possess.

'Experimental history' (Hammel 1979), undertaken with the assistance of a computer programmed with a model that purports to simulate demographic and social processes, offers an opportunity for the practitioner to establish a set of controlled conditions. However, even a small pre-industrial village community provides conditions which are more complex than anything that can be modelled using a computer. But to reiterate, in microsimulation the aim is not to model the world in all its aspects with a computer. The intention is to model ideas about the world in that the aim is to test claims that certain patterns or conditions, other things being equal, should account for certain consequences. In the case of the issues with which this paper is concerned, the patterns are patterns of demography and social choice, and theories about these patterns can be reduced to computer programs in full detail. The effects of random variability can also be incorporated. Thus when the computer program is run, not only can the researcher test whether the assumptions do produce the consequences that they are supposed to produce, but the randomness to be expected in historical data can also measured.

The example of household kin composition in pre-industrial England

In the historical applications of microsimulation the most extensive applications have concerned issues to do with household and family demography. The problem under consideration has been posed in this fashion: could certain levels or differences in demographic rates account for certain levels or differences in the frequencies of occurrence of households of various types in a collection or sample of communities. There has been an articulate school of thought asserting that demography imposes quite severe constraints on the kinds of households in which people could live, by limiting the available relatives alive with whom to co-reside (Levy 1965). Whether such constraints have explanatory power in a particular setting depends on just how restrictive they are, relative to the range of demographic differences among communities being contrasted.

The hypothesis of this kind that has been most thoroughly evaluated is that which postulates that demographic constraints were sufficiently tight in pre-industrial England to account for the low observed levels of stem-family households there (a stem-family household is defined as one in which the domestic group consisted in an extended family of two married couples with their children, the head of the second being the child of the first), even if most opportunities to form stem-family households were being taken up when they appeared. The full account of this test or experiment is set out in exemplary detail in Wachter *et al.* (1978). The tests involved implementing three sets of detailed rules for decisions on household membership. Each set is a version of stem-family-forming behaviour. In one version (labelled primonuptial) the rules are designed more or less to maximize the time through the household cycle when the household would appear in cross-sectional data as a stem-family household, because the first-marrying child is the one chosen to bring the spouse into the household to co-reside. In the second version (labelled ultimonuptial), the rules are designed so as to minimize the time through the household cycle when the household appears of stem type, by forming stems through last-marrying heirs. Both versions are meant not to mimic reality, but to establish boundaries or maxima or minima for proportions of stem families. A third version of rules (primoreal) modifies the extreme character of the first version in line with certain features thought to be applicable to more realistic accounts of historical stem-family membership. There are other assumptions that are made, which are indeed problematic, including unchanging demographic rates and social homogeneity.

In combination with the residence rules, demographic mechanisms also have to be modelled and reduced to a representation in computer code. Rates for vital events have to be selected and the demographic regimes specified for the experiment. Attention there-fore has to be given to the relevance of the overall vital rates and of programming options to historical conditions. It was also necessary to ensure that there was consistency in the secondary statistics with the general knowledge of these past populations since rates under the direct control of the simulator, such as age-specific death and marriage rates, would have consequences for a gamut of secondary statistics such as age distributions of widows, durations of marriage and durations of widowhood, which are not based upon actual historical observations and are not explicitly determined. It is obvious how important actual documentation of both these primary and secondary statistics is for evaluation of the microsimulation's capacity to mimic conditions of the past.

The demographic assumptions of the experiment are fed into the computer in the form of tables of birth, death and marriage rates and a 'listing' of a starting population. The general demographic assumptions are built into the computer code itself for determining births, birth intervals, marriages, selection of spouses, fertility multipliers, remarriage, deaths and their probability distributions and interrelationships for the 'population' in the long run. By a 'population' in the computer, all that is implied is an artificial population whose existence is only as entries in a listing stored in the computer and refers to notional individuals, not to any real-world historical people. At any time in the simulation this listing can be printed and resembles in form the listing of a settlement that might be found in an actual parish except that it substitutes identification numbers for names and shows much more information about the life histories of the inhabitants and their relationship to each other, with greater detail and exactness, than any historical listing of inhabitants. The computer keeps track of time in notional 'months' and the population listing is updated each month to assimilate events generated for the individuals by the computer with its random number generator.

The range of random variation which occurs for a single set of rates is mapped out by repeating the simulation experiments using different random numbers each time. For each of 15 sets of tables, the experiment was repeated or replicated four times, tracing the evolution of the population over 150 years. The vital rates were controlled to be the same for each of these 64 times, and each of the 9 simulations (1 × 64) began with the same artificially-constructed population. The choice of starting population is not a matter of great concern since the evolution of these populations, whose vital rates were unchanging through time, becomes rapidly independent (within marginally more than a generation) of the composition of the initial population. While no simulation can do without a starting population, in history it is not possible (other than in an area of virgin land undergoing colonization by immigrants) to find the counterpart of a starting population.

There is another problem with which historians are obliged to grapple since they need to regard a settlement as an instance handed down to them at random out of some larger collection of possible settlements with the same structural characteristics. In principle they should be intent upon allowing, at least for the variance introduced into community statistics from year to year by the inherent variability of demographic processes, the source of randomness incorporated into the computer simulation. To allow for variance, as for other expressions of statistical dispersion, means to discover any contrasts in data which are too small to be statistically significant in the face of that much dispersion or variance. The amount of dispersion, measured by the variance, depends on the length of time the simulation runs. If this is zero, then variances are all zero. As the time over which the simulation runs is lengthened most variances increase.

Utilizing such procedures researchers can make allowances for the effect of demographic rates upon the choices of individuals and the occurrence of household types. They are also able to make allowances for random variation. They can begin to confront the following kinds of issues. Suppose 30 per cent of households in the listings of a place include three linearly-related generations. Is 30 per cent close to the maximum that could be expected, or is it so small in comparison with the maximum that it might occur reasonably often, as a random event, among communities with no special practices favouring multigenerational households? Until such questions can be answered as far as social practices are concerned, a figure like 30 per cent remains evidence for nothing. Similarly, if the community listing shows 30 per cent stem family households and another shows 20 per cent, is this 10 per cent difference a large one or a small one? Does it suggest a real cultural contrast? Could it be the by-product of demographic dissimilarities? Or is it likely to have occurred, without any systematic differences, by chance alone?

Wachter *et al.* (1978) were able to show that the differences between versions of stem-family formation behaviour were much greater than could be accounted for by differences in the demographic regimes tested. These regimes involved nine combinations, with expectations of life between 25.4 and 40.2 years, brides' mean ages of marriage between 19.1 and 28.9 years, average completed parities between 3.37 and 4.91 and growth rates between −0.006 and 0.035. Under none of the rules of household formation designed to favour the formation of stem-family households did simulation results create incidence levels as low as those observed in English evidence. Of the demographic influences, brides' mean age at first marriage exercises the most leverage; with the intermediate (primoreal) version of household formation rules, a contrast between 19 and 25 with heavy mortality corresponds to a contrast between 43 per cent and 30 per cent in the totals of multiple and extended family households.

The English pre-census setting thus provides an example where demographic constraints over household membership appear to be loose constraints and to have little explanatory power. Demography on its own explains little. Much more hinges on detailed features of household formation behaviour itself. One reason appears to be that even in the most straightforward and best thought-through example of a complex process of household formation, the stem-family process, large numbers of households do not follow the supposed 'typical' path through the successive stages of the household cycle. There are sufficient instances of deaths of heirs or their spouses, or failures to marry, or combinations of these eventualities that a model of household formation rules needs to treat the non-standard circumstances – the random occurrences– with some care. Microsimulation allows a more controlled consideration of the possible impact of such random events.

Micro-simulation, kin sets and kin counts in past demographic regimes

Micro simulation has also proved to be an invaluable tool in assessing the constraints and opportunities that kinship presents to individuals, groups and institutions. Studies of familial structure, support systems (particularly for the elderly), inheritances, family law and micro-economics have all benefited from its application. A particularly important subject concerns quantitative assessment of the various kin types or categories that might exist for an individual at the same time. In its simplest form a kin count is a single number, such as the number of that person's living brothers at his or her 65th birthday, or the number of children ever born to him or her during his or her lifetime. More complex kin counts may involve many numbers, such as a count of the number of various types of kin according to their age and sex, which an individual has at death.

In principle, kin counts can be obtained by empirical enumeration using genealogical, survey or census methods. But in practice it is often difficult or impossible to obtain kin counts by these methods. Genealogical research is labour-intensive and requires extensive (generally unattainable) archival data. Censuses seldom include any information about kin who live outside an ego's own household. (An ego is used as a marker individual.) Relevant surveys are hard to find, and to conduct special surveys is very expensive. All of these problems are compounded when kin counts are wanted for the past where genealogical and census data are even sparser and surveys are absent.

In this section of the paper the author reports on results from CAMSIM (Smith 1987, Smith and Oeppen 1993) – a Monte-Carlo simulation model that generates such marker individual or 'egos'. The egos are unrelated and represent a birth cohort – typically 10,000 egos are requested. Each ego is embedded in a kin-set of related individuals with life-histories dated to the nearest month. Events are drawn from mortality, fertility and nuptiality models controlled by a set of aggregate input parameters or schedules. The sex of the ego group, the number of ascendant and descendant generations and the width of the kin set are among the parameters set by the user. The set of all egos can be regarded as the result of a random sample drawn from the population defined by the interaction between the input parameters and the model, where all kinship relations are recorded. A feature of CAMSIM is its ability to allow the user to request that egos have special characteristics, without affecting the rest of the population. For example, one can require that all egos are eldest sons, or live to be over 90, while the rest of the kin-set reflects the normal population characteristics. This provides the 'heir's' or the 'old-old' view of the kin universe and is extremely efficient for the analysis of relatively rare characteristics.

If no special characteristics for ego are required, the set of all egos can be thought of as a sex-specific random sample from the population determined by the interaction of the model and the input parameters. If egos have been given special characteristics, they can be regarded as a random sample drawn from a sub-population. The kin-sets are aggregated across egos to produce standard tables of counts, proportions, age-distributions and shared life-times of kin as experienced by egos at each birthday.

The other leading micro-simulation model SOCSIM (Hammel *et al.* 1976), developed and used by Wachter and colleagues to undertake the research on the possible demographic constraints on the formation of stem-family households in preindustrial European households (discussed at length above), employs a different approach to CAMSIM. The simulation starts with a complete population cross section and projects it a month at a time, scheduling events to avoid conflicts. Unlike CAMSIM, which is an 'open' model where marriage partners are created as required, SOCSIM needs a marriage-preference function since partners must be selected from individuals who already exist within the simulation.

Both systems have many features in common, as well as advantages and disadvantages, so that they form a complementary pair. SOCSIM's closed marriage model is useful for anthropological and historical community-village-based studies and the projection approach is naturally suited to situations where demographic rates change, but the increased computer time works against the very large simulations needed for the generation of kin counts. In CAMSIM the kin-sets do not interact, so they can be generated sequentially, which allows larger simulations to be run.

As with other microsimulation models CAMSIM has the advantage over analytic and macrosimulation models that the variance of any measure, given the sample size, can be calculated and that behaviour need not be independent and homogeneous. It is also necessary to reiterate a point made above that aggregate measures can conceal heterogeneity.

Three classes of output are generated by CAMSIM. The first group gives the demographic characteristics of the population system defined by the microsimulation model and the user's parameters. The second group is based on a standard table where each row represents a type of kin and each column is a birthday of ego. Thus any cell in the table describes some characteristics of the living kin-set, defined by the kin type of the row, at a particular birthday of ego. The standard tabulations offer mean number and age of kin and proportion with at least one of that kin-type.

CAMSIM is written in C+ + and runs on personal and mainframe computers. The model is entirely self-contained, using its own tested portable random-number generator. The design is recursive, based on pointers to person and marriage records, and is highly modular to facilitate development and testing. Although dependent on the details of the input parameters, a typical run for 5000 egos and two ascendant and three descendant generations might take 30 minutes on an IBM-compatible 486DX personal computer.

Some historical case studies

Historical analyses utilizing simulated kin sets have assumed a diversity both in terms of time periods and geographical contexts. In the remainder of this paper certain examples of this category of research will be considered. One theme of growing interest, partly in response to contemporary concerns about community or kin-based care in relation to state or institutional support, concerns the viability of the family as a welfare-provider (Hammel *et al.* 1980, Wachter 1997). Kin availability and hence demography, is one important component in this area which interests a number of disciplines. Knowledge of the past is exceedingly sketchy and, as a consequence, reliable conclusions regarding change over time are few and far between.

The experience of China in the twentieth century provides a useful example of some of the central issues. There has been a widespread notion that, in the past, old people in China were always supported by their families, particularly by their sons. Partly because of such a belief, the rapid demographic change, especially the rapid change in the age structure of the Chinese population, has created some panic. Commentators and policy makers worry that because of the considerable reduction in the number of children and in the complexity of the Chinese family, which itself is partly a result of decreasing fertility, the long tradition of family support of the elderly is on the point of collapse or may collapse in the ageing society of the future. Before 1950 demographic conditions in China were characterized by high mortality, fairly high fertility, early age at marriage, universal marriage for women, and a high proportion of men marrying. Under such a demographic regime, was the reality of familial support such as that idealized in many folk accounts? Given the considerable demographic changes recorded during the last half century, how does the contemporary Chinese kinship network differ from those existing in the past? Finally, is the rapid decline in fertility observable in China since the early 1970s really going to cause great difficulties with family support for the elderly or even lead to the collapse of the traditional support system in the coming century?

Hardly any data exist from surveys or census-type materials to provide answers to such questions. Work at the Cambridge Group for the History of Population and Social Structure by Zhongwei Zhao (1993, 1998) utilizing CAMSIM has led to three simulations being carried out under different demographic conditions, thought to apply to Chinese society over the course of the present century. Each simulated population consists of 500 male egos and their kin. In the first simulation the input parameters were similar to the demographic rates recorded in China around 1930 and represent a high fertility and high mortality regime. In the second, the parameters are close to the demographic conditions of the mid-1960s, and represent a regime with high fertility, relatively low mortality, and very rapid population growth. In the third, the mortality rates and marriage patterns are close to those observed in the 1980s and early 1990s, and the fertility parameters are deliberately set at slightly below-replacement.

The results reveal that in the Chinese past (represented by demographic conditions measured in the 1930s) people might have preferred to form large multi-generational households and the younger generation was widely expected to take responsibility for supporting their old parents, but many people, perhaps even the majority, might not have been able to live in households of such a type because of the constraints imposed by mortality. Under these demographic conditions, even if each individual followed rules of family formation requiring all males to live with their parents when possible, nearly 60 per cent of those who reached age 70 would have spent more than 20 years in simple family households. A substantial part (40 per cent) of those aged 60 or 70 would have been found living in a household with a simple structure.

During the 1950s and 1960s, apart from the period between 1959 and 1962, the relatively low mortality and high fertility considerably increased the density of Chinese kinship networks. The traditional idea that many people survived to very old age and were supported by their sons, which had never been widely achieved previously, now became a reality. The simulations for the second period when compared with those for the first, show that the proportion of men with two or more married sons more than doubled. When egos reached ages of 60 or 70 close to 90 per cent would have at least one married son. Since the early 1970s China has been experiencing another dramatic change which is characterized by rapid decline in fertility. This change will have a significant effect on the availability of kin. If the current low fertility is maintained, simulation three reveals that the mean numbers of children and siblings for those over the age of 40 are likely to be maintained at very low levels and experience a further decrease. The lateral extension of Chinese kinship networks will be replaced by vertical extension. The probability of an elderly person living with more than one married son and the probability of forming a joint family will be markedly reduced. Furthermore, the proportion of those reaching their 60s or 70s with no married sons is substantially higher than the populations represented by the second simulation.

However, when these results are compared with those of simulation one, the following points are noteworthy. In spite of the fact that the total fertility rate in the third simulation is less than two-fifths of that in the first, the outcome of the third simulation shows that the proportion of those having at least one married son is even higher and the proportion having neither spouse nor children is considerably lower. These are primarily caused by the improvements in mortality. The surprising results indicate that under present conditions and those of the near future the feasibility of an elderly person's residing with one or two married sons might be even greater than that under the demographic regime which typified China half a century ago. The simulations also reveal that the situation after 2025 will be far less favourable for the elderly if support is sought within the family.

In a different geographical context and time period microsimulation has provided a powerful tool in deepening the Roman historian's understanding of family and kinship. This has intellectual implications that extend well beyond the field of classics. The Roman family and Roman Law as it relates to the family have had, for instance, a profound influence on social anthropology – the kinship terminology, for instance, that is used to describe a diverse array of societies has its roots in Rome (Morgan 1877). Like Lewis Morgan, Radcliffe Brown (1952: 14) looked to ancient Rome to define basic types of kinship system: 'In a system of father-right ... a man is largely dependant on his patrilineal lineage and therefore on his father's brothers, who exercise authority and control over him, while it is to them that he has to look for protection and for inheritance. Father-right is represented by the system of *patria potestas* of ancient Rome'. Furthermore, in a clear case of circularity of reasoning, the anthropological studies of kinship systems have now been cited by classical scholars for authoritative illumination of Roman social behaviour. This is a dubious enterprise because patria potestas and elaborate kinship classifications were legal constructs and their relationship to actual social practice is highly uncertain. In the absence of parish or census records outside the province of Egypt (a very special case), microsimulation offers the most effective tool for understanding the kin universe within which the legal rules and cultural paradigms could be brought into play.

While there is no space in this paper to discuss the basis of the demographic rates used in the simulation it should be noted that there are possible sizeable margins of error around the results based upon a regime that is summarized somewhat starkly as one in which high mortality prevailed, marriage was relatively late for males and relatively early for females and child-bearing was spread over a long period of the life course (Laslett 1988). Morgan, Radcliffe-Brown and many others identified the *paterfamilias* as the characteristic feature of Roman families. In law the *pater* retained his nearly absolute power (*patria potestas*) over the members and property of his *familia* for life. Because this paternal power normally ended only with the father's death, and not upon his children being married or reaching an age of majority, it is essential to know the probability of a Roman having a living father at certain points in his or her life. CAMSIM-derived kinship networks reveal that only half of the women marrying at twenty and only a quarter of the men marrying or women remarrying at age 30 would have had a living father (Saller 1986). To claim on the basis of the law that Romans submitted to marriages arranged by their fathers would be a partial truth with little bearing on the lives of most.

There is intriguing evidence from Egyptian communities under Roman rule that they were exceedingly endogamous, to a degree unparalleled in other historical societies. An analysis of census fragments suggest that 15 to 21 per cent of all identifiable marriages involved full brothers with full sisters (Hopkins 1980). Of course, by any yardstick 15 to 21 per cent is remarkable, but to know whether a sibling was the preferred marriage partner the 15–21 per cent should be placed in perspective by asking how likely an

Egyptian male of marriageable age was to have a younger sister (almost without exception the brother-husband in such marriages was older). A rough calculation based on the proportion of families in high mortality conditions having both a son and a daughter at the time of the father's death yielded an estimate that a suitable sibling would have been available to perhaps half of Egyptians, of whom a third married him or her. Microsimulation using CAMSIM permits refinement of that calculation by framing the question in terms of marriageable age rather than death of the father: what proportion of Egyptian men at age 25 would have had a younger full sister to marry? According to the simulation, no more than 34 per cent of men at age 25 would have had such a sister. In short the refinements of simulation lead to the conclusion that a majority of young Egyptian men with suitable sisters married them. The simulation also permits the researcher to discover just how impoverished were the kin networks of in-marrying Egyptians. For instance, fewer than half the children of brother-sister marriages would have had a living uncle, as opposed to two thirds of offspring in exogamous marriages.

Conclusion

Microsimulation studies, such as those discussed in this paper differ from traditional historical research which is primarily based on surviving documents and materials of other kinds. In contrast, simulation depends heavily upon computation. However, at the heart of every computer simulation lies an algorithm which itself depends heavily upon, or is the result of, historical research. SOCSIM and CAMSIM are alike in needing to establish a large number of relationships between variables. Such relationships, although they appear in a form of computer language or formulae, are all based on substantial empirical investigations. Data sets of this kind, when used within simulation studies, have enabled historians to enter and better understand worlds of the past that would never have been accessible through more conventional historical approaches and for which little written evidence exists. At the very least, using the tools of computer microsimulation, the historical demographer can paint the demographic background for broader discussions of the social, economic and political aspects of kinship in the past. Without such demographic background, there is a risk of mistaking what is extra-ordinary for the ordinary, and conversely, and researchers are left without the essential background necessary for contrast and comparison.

It is, however, necessary to emphasize that much of what has been discussed concerns simulated 'facts' which are stylized and subject to all the qualifications applicable to models of this kind. Ongoing efforts to widen the repertoire of processes replicated by CAMSIM and SOCSIM and more reliable specification of key parameters will undoubtedly lead to the generation of more and better results. The capacity to deal with changing rates, and the complex shifts in the age-patterns of mortality will need to be incorporated into these models as well as more empirical and cross-model comparison. The technical constraints of computing capacity no longer impose limits on an area of research in which historians and social policy makers, and analysts, indeed a broad array of scholars in quite diverse disciplines, are able to employ a common set of tools.

References

Hammel, E. A., Hutchinson, D., Wachter, K., Lundy, R. and Deuel, R. (1976), *The SOCSIM Demographic-Sociological Microsimulation Program*, Institute of International Studies, University of California, Berkeley, Research Series Number 27.

—— (1979), 'Experimental history', *Journal of Anthropological Research*, 35.

Hopkins, K. (1980), 'Brother-sister marriage in Roman Egypt', *Comparative Studies in Society and History* 22: 303–54.

Laslett, P. (1988), 'La Parente en Chiffres', *Annales (Economies, Sociétés, Civilisations)* 1: 5–24.

Levy, M. (1965), *Aspects of the Analysis of Family Structures* (Princeton) 1–63.

Morgan, L. H. (1877), *Ancient Society* (New York).

Radcliffe-Brown A. R. (1952), *Structure and Function in Primitive Society* (London).

Ruggles, S. (1987, *Prolonged Connections: The Rise of the Extended Family in Nineteenth-Century America* (Madison, Wisconsin).

—— (1990), 'Family demography and family history: problems and prospects', *Historical Methods* 23: 23–30.

Saller, R. (1986), '*Patria Potestas* and the stereotype of the Roman Family', *Continuity and Change* 1: 7–22.

Smith, J. (1987), 'The computer simulation of kin sets and kin counts'. In Bongaarts, J., Burch T. K and Wachter K. (eds.) *Family Demography: Methods and Their Application* (Oxford) 267–84.

—— and Oeepen J. (1993), 'Estimating numbers of kin in historical England using demographic microsimulation'. In Reher, D. and Schofield, R. (eds.) *Old and New Methods in Historical Demography* (Oxford) 280–317.

Wachter, K. (1988), 'Microsimulation of household cycles'. In Bongaarts, J., Burch, T. K. and. Wachter K. (eds.) *Family Demography: Methods and Their Application* (Oxford) 215–27.

—— (1997), 'Kinship resources for the elderly', *Philosophical Transactions of the Royal Society*, B 352: 1811–19.

—— Hammel, E. A., and Laslett, P. (1978), *Statistical Studies of Historical Social Structure* (New York and London).

Wrigley, E. A. and Schofield, R. S (1981), *The Population History of England 1541–1871: A Reconstruction* (London).

Zhao, Z. (1993) *Household and Kinship in Recent and Very Recent Chinese History*. Unpublished Ph.D. Thesis, University of Cambridge.

—— (1998), Demographic conditions and family support for the elderly in past, present and future China'. In Horden P., and Smith, R. M. (eds.) *The Locus of Care: Family, Neighbours and Institutions in Past Time* (London) 259–79.

Commentary

RICHARD BLUNDELL

Department of Economics
University College London

In my brief commentary I have decided to consider this area from my own perspective, i.e., that of an economist. In doing so I was impressed by the similarities with recent developments in Economics.

Information Technology has transformed the way we conduct research, increasing our ability to work with large complex models. It has removed the 'computational' justification for analysis based on the representative individual, thus allowing emphasis to fall on distribution effects, spillovers, social interactions and the formation of coalitions (see the selection of references below). The result has been not so much in the development of new theories but in the new understanding of empirical phenomena. In my view we are only just beginning to explore the possibilities for understanding and modelling interactions at the individual and household level. The research reported in this paper is an important step in enhancing our understanding.

But what kind of interactions should we look for or expect to uncover? In economics interactions are often simplified by the working of the 'market'. Thus, in a competitive market, there may be no direct interactions since the price system acts as a sufficient statistic for the way other agents' decisions affect the decisions of any particular individual under consideration. For example, the consumer of televisions does not have to interact directly with the producer; he or she can make a decision based entirely on the price and a list of attributes. This is less the case for a consumer of health services and consequently this simplifying result is rather exclusive to particular economic markets. In the case of interest here there is clearly no 'price' mechanism in the sense of 'formal' traded markets in demographic history! Given this lack of any market mechanism to simplify analysis, the question is whether observed behaviour can be represented through a set of simple deterministic rules.

There seem to be a number of important possible types of interactions. There are the individualist interactions, which are forward looking and incorporate learning from experience. These include models of the timing and spacing of births and decisions over employment. In terms of simulation modelling these can be solved as part of a stochastic dynamic program. Decisions are endogenous and there are no simplifying deterministic rules of behaviour. However, behaviour is completely determined by a set of parameters that define underlying preferences and constraints. Often one has to introduce concepts of bounded rationality to make the problem tractable. Next there are more passive interactions, for example, the impact of spillovers from society, companies or individuals investing in a 'stock of knowledge'. These are more likely to be taken as 'given' for individual decisions – much like prices in a competitive environment – and consequently are much simpler to simulate.

Finally there is the issue of how groups form or how matching takes place. The issue here is whether random matching processes of the type that lie behind many simulation models, including some parts of CAMSIM, really reflect the behaviour of individuals in terms of their choice of jobs, marriage and so on. Even if matches come about randomly, presumably this is not the case for dissolution. We are often interested in how equilibrium coalitions form and the stability of such groups in society, through trading relationships and marriage relationships, for example. Why do certain 'types' of coalitions disappear? In particular, how stable are coalitions and matches to external shocks?

Microsimulation methods are important in all of this. They have the advantage of allowing us to 'fit' simulated probabilities to observed frequencies. With sufficiently rich data this can allow us to test models against the data. If the data are not rich enough for this, at least we can calibrate the parameters of the simulation model to 'broad facts'.

Should we believe in the results of simulation models? What exactly is refutable? In economic research there has been a move away from complex models for the purposes of refutation and a move toward the use of 'natural experiments'. That is in the use of exogenous changes that affect one group but not another. This has clear similarities to treatment and control group analysis in more standard randomised trials. In micro-simulation models, refutation occurs when simulated probabilities do not match data for wide set of incidental parameters. However, this has proved very hard to operationalize in economics. Often, if the parameterization of the model is made general enough we need very precise data to refute. I would like to see a detailed assessment of the reliability of CAMSIM in terms of its underlying parametric assumptions and its ability to simulate existing historic scenarios. The interaction between simulation outcomes and observed frequencies in the data is now easily available with modern information technology and provides us with a more optimistic future for producing reliable microsimulation models.

Some References

Blundell, R. W. and Walker I. (1986), 'A labour supply model for the simulation of tax and benefit Reforms'. In Blundell, R. W. and Walker, I. (eds.), *Unemployment, Search and Labour Supply* (Cambridge).

—— Pashardes, P. and Weber, G., (1993), 'What do we learn about consumer demand patterns from micro data?' *American Economic Review*, 83(3): 570–97

Ellison, G. (1993), 'Learning, local interaction and co-ordination', *Econometrica*, 61: 1047–72.

Gorman, W. M. (1953), 'Community preference fields', *Econometrica*, 21: 63–80.

Grandmont, J. M. (1987), 'Distributions of preferences and the Law of Demand', *Econometrica*, 55(1): 155–62.

Hildenbrand, W. (1983), 'On the Law of Demand', *Econometrica*, 51(4): 997–1019.

Jorgenson, D. W., Lau L. and Stoker T., (1982), 'The transcendental logarithmic model of aggregate consumer behaviour'. In *Advances in Econometrics*, Bassman, R. and Rhodes G., (eds.), (Greenwich) I: 97–238.

Kirman, A. P. (1992), 'Whom or what does the representative individual represent?', *Journal of Economic Perspectives*, 6(2): 117–36.

—— Oddou C. and Weber S. (1986), 'Stochastic communication and coalition formation', *Econometrica*, 54: 129–38.

Stoker, T. M. (1986), 'Simple tests of distributional effects on macroeconomic equations', *Journal of Political Economy*, 94(4): 763–93.

How much has information technology contributed to linguistics?

KAREN SPÄRCK JONES

Computer Laboratory
University of Cambridge

Abstract. Information technology should have much to offer linguistics, not only through the opportunities offered by large-scale data analysis and the stimulus to develop formal computational models, but through the chance to use language in systems for automatic natural language processing. The paper discusses these possibilities in detail, and then examines the actual work that has been done. It is evident that this has so far been primarily research within a new field, computational linguistics, which is largely motivated by the demands of and interest in practical processing systems, and that information technology has had rather little influence on linguistics at large. There are different reasons for this, and not all good ones: information technology deserves more attention from linguists.

Introduction

There are two potential roles for information technology (IT) in linguistics, just as in other areas: as a means of developing and testing models and as a means of gathering and analysing data. For example, one may use a computer to help make some model of word formation properly specific, and also to gather and analyse some data on word forms. Linguistics thus has the same types of use and benefit for computing as other academic areas, such as archaeology or economics.

IT in linguistics can give both of these a sharper edge. Thus in the lesser case, data analysis, we can use the machine not merely to interpret data but to gather it. In the archaeological case, we can analyse supplied descriptions of pots to hypothesize a typological sequence, say, but the descriptions have to be supplied. Even with such aids as automated image analysis, the human input required is generally large. In the language case, in contrast, if we want to determine lexical fields, we can just pull text off the World Wide Web. We still need humans to supply the classification theory, but one cannot get everything from nothing, and the detailed human work is much less than in the archaeological case.

But much more importantly in relation to modelling, in the language case we can not only use computers to develop and test models in the normal way. We can apply computers operationally, and hence creatively, for the very same language-using tasks as humans do. For example, if we have a model of speech production, we can now build a speech synthesizer which can be attached to an advice system to generate new utterances in response to new inquiries. Again, with a translation system based on some model of translation, we can actually exercise this model, in an especially compelling way, by engaging in translation. But however good our archaeological models of the spread of neolithic agriculture are, they cannot go out and plough up untilled land at the rate of so and so many yards a day,

It is this productive new, i.e. *real*, application of computational models that makes interaction between IT and linguistics interesting, in the same way that the interaction embodied in biotechnology is. Model validation, with its supporting need for serious data, is a good reason for examining what may be called the IT push into linguistics. But the potentially productive use, in practical applications, *for* models, and the especially strong validation this implies, means that the IT pull from linguistics can also be assessed for what it has contributed to linguistics.

This is all an exciting idea; and it has stimulated a wholly new research field, computational linguistics. But IT has nevertheless had much less influence on linguistics in general than one would expect from the fact that words, the stuff of language, are now the pabulum of the networks and figure more largely in what computers push around than numbers do: computational linguistics remains a quite isolated area within linguistics. Linguistics has also had far less influence than might be expected on task systems that process natural language (in computing it is necessary to distinguish 'natural language' from 'programming language'). There are both good and bad reasons for this state of affairs, and these will be considered after an examination in more detail of specific forms of possible, and actual, interaction between linguistics and IT.

Exclusions

The range of specific areas to examine is large. Two will be excluded that, however intellectually important to their communities or practically valuable, are peripheral to the main topic of this paper.

One is the whole area labelled 'computers and the humanities', when this deals with language data for specific individuals or sources, considered in relation to author attribution or manuscript genealogies, say, or in content analysis, as in the study of the way political terms are used in newspapers. This is where all of the utilities exemplified by Standard Generalised Mark-up Language (SGML) have a valuable role in supporting scholarship see, e.g., Sperberg–McQueen (1994) on the Text Encoding Initiative (TEI); as illustrative titles for applications of this kind we can take such random examples from the ALLC-ACH 96 Bergen Conference as "The Thesaurus of Old English" database: a research tool for historians of language and culture'; ' "So violent a metaphor" Adam Smith's metaphorical language in the *Wealth of Nations*'; and 'Book, body and text: the Women Writers Project and problems of text encoding'. But this type of work is excluded as itself on the borderline of linguistics.

The other major area to be excluded is language teaching. Again, IT already has an established role in this, though far more as a dumb waiter than as an intelligent tutor that continuously adapts the content and presentation of lessons to the individual student. So far, there has been little progress in the development of teaching programs that would de facto constitute a serious test of alternative accounts of grammar or choose among performance models of language processing.

The author is no expert on speech research, so will only note some 'place-holding' points on spoken as opposed to written language.

For the moment, the scope and style of linguistics will be taken as properly large, and not restricted as an area of endeavour or discipline to a particular purpose or stance. The consequences of contemporary attitudes to these will be considered later.

Structure

The discussion begins by considering what IT can in principle (but also soberly) offer linguistics and then assesses how far linguists have exploited IT in practice. Finally, an attempt will be made to explain the present state of affairs. The focus is on the contribution of IT to linguistics, so the author will not attempt a systematic treatment of the work done, in natural language processing (NLP), by those who do not think of themselves as linguists, as opposed to engineers, or consider, in detail, the influence of linguistics on this work, although both will be referred to as necessary to round out the main argument.

Two main roles for IT in linguistics have been identified: data gathering and modelling. Of course these come together when corpus data are used to test some theory. However, there are in general marked differences between those who cut the corn and those who sharpen the sickles. Work with data will therefore be considered first and then the development of theory.

IT possibilities

Data work

Data, or corpus, work is a natural for IT. Computers can so rapidly and painlessly match, sort, count and so forth vast volumes of material, and as these are increasingly text that is already machine-readable, there is no data-entry effort for the linguist: IT would appear now to have much to offer. The points below refer primarily to natural independently-produced text rather than to elicited data, though they also apply to the latter; and automatic manipulation of data can also, of course, be useful for material marked up by the linguist.

Corpus work is of value at three levels: *observational, derivational,* and *validatory.* In the first, observational case, corpora – even processed as simply as by concordance routines – can usefully display language phenomena, both recording and drawing attention to them. This was one of the earliest uses of IT for linguistic study and remains important, although as corpora get larger it becomes harder to digest the concordance information.

Even at this level, however, there is the important issue of corpus coverage versus representativeness. While one obvious use of corpora is as a basis for grammars (Stubbs

1996), they have become increasingly important for lexicographers (see, e.g., Thomas and Short 1996). Here, while one function is to capture at least one example of every configuration, word or word sense (especially the latter), another has been to display the relative frequency of lexical usage (of value, for example, in building dictionaries for teaching). In both cases, however, the issue of corpus representativeness arises (Biber 1994, Summers 1996). What is the corpus supposed to represent? And how do we know it is so representative?

There is a presumption, for some, that a large enough mass of miscellaneous stuff taken from newspapers and so forth will be representative of common, regular, or mainstream phenomena. However, it is more usual, as with the British National Corpus (Burnard 1995), to develop some set of selection criteria that draw on conventional or intuitively acceptable notions of genre, and to gather samples of each. But this is a far from scientific or rigorous basis for claims of proper status for the resulting linguistic facts.

At the same time, while even a simple concordance can be useful, IT makes it possible to apply 'low-level' linguistic processing of an uncontroversial but helpful kind, for example lemmatization, tagging of syntactic categories, labelling of local syntactic constituents (e.g., noun or verb group) and even some marking of word senses (referring to some set of dictionary senses). Garside *et al.* (1987) illustrate both the possibilities and the important contribution Lancaster has made here. (It should be noted, however, that the opportunities for analogous automatic processing of speech data, presuming the ability to recognize and transcribe speech with reasonable accuracy, are currently much more limited.)

The second, derivative level of corpus use is potentially much more interesting, but is also more challenging. It is foreshadowed by the collection, even at the first level, of simple frequency statistics, but is aimed at a much more thorough analysis of data to derive patterns automatically: lexical collocations, subcategorization behaviour, terminological structure, even grammar induction (Charniak 1993). Such analysis presupposes first, some intuitive notion of the name of the game as the basis for choosing both the primitive attributes of the data and the specification for the formal model of what is to be automatically sought; and second, the actual algorithm for discovering model instances in the data, as indicated, for example, by Gale *et al.* (1994). The problems here are challenging and are well illustrated by the attempt to establish lexical fields objectively, by computation on data, rather than by introspection supported by data inspection. Thus what features of word behaviour in text are to be taken as the primitives for entity description? What measures adopted to establish similarity of behaviour, both between a pair of words and, more importantly, over a set of words to define a field, i.e., a semantic class? What operational procedure will be applied to deliver and assess candidate classes? Cashing in the notion of lexical field requires a whole formally and fully-defined discovery procedure, not to mention also some reasonable and possibly automatic way of evaluating the definitions applied as interpretations of the initial intuitive notion and, indeed, as justifications for the intuition itself.

The potential value of IT for extracting information from large-scale data bashing is obvious. But the difficulties involved, already indicated for the determination of lexical fields, are yet more evident in the idea of deriving the genres, even just for written discourse, of a language community by operations on a (very) large neutral corpus, say the entire annual intake of a major copyright repository. Genre is a function of many language factors – lexical, syntactic, semantic, pragmatic (communicative context and purpose) and, also, actual subject matter; so both specifying and applying the primitive attributes through which discourse sets will be differentiated, and hence genres defined, is clearly no simple matter. The example, however, also illustrates the range of useful outputs such a process can in principle deliver to the linguist: not merely indicative sets of actual discourses, but higher-order genre definitions based on class membership (by analogy with centroid vectors), as well as genre labelling for words in the lexicon.

The third level, theory validation, is where the two areas of the utility of IT for linguistics overlap. IT in principle offers great opportunities here, through making it possible to evaluate a theory of some linguistic phenomenon in a systematic, i.e., objective and comprehensive, way against some natural corpus. But what does it mean to test a theory against a corpus, informatively and unequivocally? If a researcher has some theory of the nature of syntactic or semantic representation, it can be checked for propriety and coverage using a corpus, by seeing whether representations can be provided for all the sentences in the corpus. However, such a test, as in other cases, is only a negative one. If processing succeeds, it shows that the theory holds for these data, but not that it is the only possible or the best theory. The obvious problems for theory evaluation are thus on the one hand the adequacy of the corpus, and on the other the explanatory adequacy of the theory. Taking these points further, natural corpora may be dilute, with a low incidence of test instances (e.g., occurrences of rare word senses for a model of sense selection); ambiguous, offering only very weak support for a theory because there are many alternative accounts of some phenomenon (e.g., sense selection either through lexical collocation or world knowledge) and opaque, too rich to allow sufficiently discriminating testing on some submodel through the interaction effects between phenomena (e.g., syntax and lexicon).

More importantly, using IT to validate a theory against a corpus requires an *automatic* procedure for theory application, the major issue for the model research considered in the next section.

The points just made have referred to the analysis of running text data. But there is also one important, special kind of corpus to which increasing attention is being paid, namely that represented by a lexicon. A lexicon may be viewed as providing second-order data about language use, rather than the first-order data given by ordinary discourse. While the information supplied by a dictionary has the disadvantage that it embodies the lexicographer's biases, it has the advantage of providing highly concentrated information, often in a relatively systematic way that reflects the application of a special-purpose sublanguage. Exploiting this information may involve hairy conversions from typesetting tapes, as well as the further regularization required to develop a so-called lexical database. But it is then in principle possible to derive a higher-level classificatory structure over words from the bottom-level entries. Early ideas here are illustrated by Spärck Jones (1964/1986), more recent ones by Boguraev and Briscoe

(1989). Of course, corpus analysis for text and lexicon can be brought together, for example to select a domain sub-lexicon, which may be linked with the syntactic and semantic preferences of a domain grammar that is grounded in the text corpus.

Model research

The importance of IT for linguistic theory goes far beyond the stimulus to model formation that browsing over volumes of data may provide and even (though this is not to imply that such evaluation is not of critical importance) beyond the testing of a theory against a corpus. This is because, as mentioned earlier, computing offers not only a natural context for the development and expression of *formal* linguistic theories; it also places the most demanding, because of necessity principled, requirements on theory, through theory application in systems for implementing language-using tasks. This is not to imply that useful systems cannot be built without theory, or at any rate without careful and rigorous theory as opposed to some ad hoc application of some plausible general idea. But the fact that Natural Language Programming (NLP) systems, for language *interpretation* or *generation* for some purpose, can be built is both a challenge for, and a constraint on, those concerned with linguistic theory.

There are indeed several specific benefits for linguistics from IT here. In relation to IT as a stimulus to formal model development, the most extreme position is that the style of formal language theory that computer science has also stimulated and enriched is the right kind of apparatus for the formal characterization of natural languages (see, for example, Gamut 1991). This is a complicated matter because programming languages gain their special power from eschewing the ambiguity that characterizes natural language. However, as computing systems have become more complex, computer science theory has been obliged to seek a subtler and richer expressivity (for example, in capturing temporal phenomena), and thus might possibly provide the means for characterizing our language without damaging over-simplification. The crux here is thus whether computer science offers well-founded ways of cashing in the computational metaphor now common, in both vulgar and philosophical parlance, for human activities, including the use of language.

This still leaves open, however, both competence and performance-oriented approaches. Thus taking language production as an example, we can have both a formal, computational, *competence* theory characterizing a syntactic model that would hopefully generate all and only the syntactically legitimate sentences of a language. Or we can have a formal, computational *performance* theory intended to model the way humans actually go about producing syntactically acceptable strings. Such a theory could indeed in principle encompass performance in the behavioural limit by including, for example, mechanisms for restarting sentences under certain production conditions. Thus because computation is essentially about actually, as oppposed to possibly, doing things, it invites an attack on flowing rather than frozen language. Dowty *et al.* (1985) and Sowa (1984) illustrate the wide range of possibilities for such performance modelling.

The business of processing naturally leads to the second level of IT relevance for linguistics, that associated with building IT systems for *tasks*. The point here is that such systems are not just ones capable of exercising language-using *functions*, like interpreting and answering a question, responding to a command, endorsing a statement, i.e., systems with the necessary bottom-level capabilities for language *use*. Even here such systems have taken a critical step beyond the treatment of language as a matter of words and sentences, and an ability to handle forms like interrogatives or imperatives as defining sentence types. The absolutely minimal level of functionality is represented by what may be called 'checking' responses, for example to some question by noting that it is a question asking whether X or not, or to a statement by offering a paraphrase. It is possible to view such a form of model evaluation as purely linguistic and without any real invocation of communicative purpose or utterance context, but with the advantage that the model evaluation involved does not depend on inspecting model-internal representational structures such as (parse trees and logical forms) for plausibility, a very dubious way of validating representations of language form or meaning.

But since language is used for communication, IT would seem to have a more substantive role in model testing even at the level of individual functions, e.g., by answering a question rather than by merely reformulating it in some operation defined by purely linguistic relationships. Answering a question appears to imply that a fully adequate interpretation of the question has been attained. Thus we may imagine, for example, some 'database' of information to which questions may be applied. But such strategies for model evaluation are of surprisingly limited value both because of the constraints imposed by whatever the example data are, and because of the essentially artificial restrictions imposed by the treatment of sentence (utterance) function independent of larger communicative purpose and context. Even the idea of answering questions implies relations between different sentence functions, and models that attempt to account for anaphor, for example, invoke above-sentence discourse. This is evident in both Gazdar and Mellish (1989)'s and Allen (1995)'s treatments of computational processing, for example.

NLP systems are built for tasks like translation, inquiry, or summarizing that go beyond sentence function by requiring accounts of communication and discourse (and therefore typically also have not only to address a range of sentence functions but also themselves to subsume different tasks). In general, properly done and not in such limited application domains as to justify wholesale simplification, task systems exercise the ability to determine meaning from text, or to deliver text for meaning. They thus constitute the best form of evaluation for linguistic models. They can do this for the competence-oriented linguist if required. But their real value is in performance modelling: what are the *processes* of sentence and discourse interpretation or generation? More specifically, if language has 'components' – morphology, syntax, semantics, pragmatics, the lexicon (and these also above the sentence, in discourse grammars) – how do these *interact* in processing, i.e., what is the processor's architecture in terms of control flow? How do components impose *constraints* on one another? Winograd (1972) amd Moore (1986) equally show, in different situations and applying rather different ideas, how significant the issue of processor architecture is.

It is possible to address process for single components, for example, in whether syntactic parsing is deterministic (Marcus 1980). But if IT offers, in principle, the 'best' form of testing for language models because it avoids the danger of pretending that humans can assess objects that are really inaccessible, namely 'internal' meaning representations, this is also the toughest form of testing, for two reasons. First, how to evaluate task performance, given that this is the means of model assessment: for example, how to rate a summarizing system when in general there is no one correct summary of a text? While linguistics makes use of judgement by informants, e.g., (and notoriously) about grammaticality, informant judgements about system performance for complex tasks are much harder to make and much less reliable; but in a disagreeable paradox, human participation with the system in some task, for example in reading a summary in order to determine whether to proceed to the full underlying text, is either too informal at the individual level or too rough when based on many user decisions, to be an informative method of model evaluation. This exacerbates the problem, for task systems that are inevitably multi-component ones that depend both on individual language facts in the lexicon and on general rules, of assessing the validity of model detail. It should also be recognized that task systems normally require knowledge of the non-linguistic world to operate, so attributing performance behaviour to the properties of the linguistic, as opposed to non-linguistic, elements of the system as a whole can be hard. These challenges and complexities of evaluation are further explored in Spärck Jones and Galliers (1996).

But it is further the case that while task systems can in principle offer a base for the evaluation of linguistic theory, in practice they may be of much more limited value, for two reasons. One is the 'sublanguage' problem, where tasks are undertaken in particular application domains: this makes them suspect as vehicles for assessing the putatively general models that linguists seek. The other is that practically useful systems, e.g., for translation, can be primarily triumphs of hackery, with little or only the most undemanding underpinning from models, which makes their contribution to model evaluation suspect unless, as discussed further later, this is taken as a comment on the whole business of language modelling. Nevertheless, the key role that computation offers research on models is in forcing enough *specificity* on a theory for it to be programmed and operationally applied in autonomous action: humans can rely on hand waving, but machines cannot.

IT actualities

Having rehearsed the potential utilities of IT generally (and hence also of computer science) for linguistics, we can now ask: how far has IT actually had any impact on linguistics? Further, has any impact been direct, through computationally-derived data, or through model validation? Or has it been indirect, through the recognition of computational paradigms? In relation to data this influence would be most clearly shown by a respect for statistics, and in allowing that language-using behaviour may be influenced by frequency. This last may seem an obvious property of language, but acknowledging the computational paradigm brings it into the open. At the theory level, the computational paradigm focuses not so much on rules – a familiar linguistic desideratum – as on rule application. Even when computational work adopts a declarative rather than procedural approach, concern is always with what happens when declarations are executed and so, for example, with compositional effects in sentence interpretation.

Overall, although this is an informal judgement (and also an amateur one by a nonlinguist), the impact of IT on linguistics as a whole has been light, and more peripheral than substantive, certainly if the evidence of the linguistics shelves in a major Cambridge bookstore is anything to go by. An attempt will be made to summarize the relevant work, and identify its salient features, and then to seek reasons for the lack of impact and interaction.

Data exploitation

It is clear that natural corpora can supply test data bearing on all of morphology, syntax, semantics, pragmatics and the lexicon, although the processing for this (and indeed the linguistic knowledge presupposed in this processing) can vary. For example, while it is relatively easy in English simply to pick up all the word tokens (though, of course, also names, misspellings etc.) in a corpus, this may be rather less useful in, e.g., German, where freely-formed compounds may have to be deconstructed. Similarly, for those interested in syntax, offloading some of the data assembly work to the machine depends on bootstrapping via a surface parser, say. But setting this aside, what work under the heading of computational data exploitation has actually been done?

Corpus use at the lowest, observational level appears to be spreading – indeed has been referred to as one of the fastest growing areas of linguistics (cf. Stubbs 1996), even if it is not yet widespread: it is illustrated, for example, by past uses of the Brown or Lancaster/Oslo-Bergen Corpora, and the use that is beginning, especially by lexicographers, of the British National Corpus (Burnard 1995). It is hard to measure in any precise way how valuable such browsing and observational use of simple word concordance and frequency data is, but the fact that serious publishers are willing to put money behind corpus construction suggests that, at least by such 'applied' linguists, corpora are seen as useful, even essential. The range of possible corpus uses for descriptive purposes by linguists in general rather than by lexicographers is well-illustrated by, for example, such ALLC-ACH '96 Conference titles as 'Collocation and the rhetoric of scientific ideas: corpus linguistics as a methodology of genre analysis'; (see also Stubbs 1996, Thomas and Short 1996). Corpora of a relatively considered, rather than casually assembled, kind are also becoming increasingly common through the efforts of organizations such as the Linguistic Data Consortium and several European groups. These descriptive uses of corpora have also been taken further, via the application of taggers and parsers (e.g., Garside *et al.* 1987, Brill 1995), to gather information about syntactic constructions or about words that is dependent on syntactic contexts.

Processing in this way leads naturally to the derivational use of corpora. It may, for instance, be exploited to establish preferences between parsing paths for NLP. This is one example of the increasing interest in exploiting corpora at the derivational level, which also includes analysis for such purposes as establishing selection criteria for word senses and identifying synonym sets. The range, both of techniques and data types, to explore is well shown in *Computational Linguistics* (1993) and Boguraev and Puste-jovsky (1996). Much of this work is restricted to finding pairwise associations between 'objects' and has not progressed to full-scale classification, but is already showing its value. It should also be noted that at both this level and the next, corpus analysis can provide useful information about the lexical and structural properties of particular language worlds, e.g., of financial news stories. Equally, derivational work on lexical as well as text corpora is in progress, including work on multilingual databases (Copestake *et al.* 1995).

Finally, corpora have not only been used observationally or derivationally: they have to some extent been used to validate theory. This is often indirect, in the sense that, for example, corpora have been used to test syntax analysers where evaluation is of the parser used, or of the specific grammar, rather than of the grammar type; but it still constitutes model evaluation. While simply running a parser with grammar against a corpus can be very instructive, performance evaluation may also be by comparing output with the reference analyses of a 'treebank' (Marcus *et al.* 1993, Black *et al.* 1996).

Theory development

In respect of language modelling, and starting with IT as a stimulus to the development of formal theories, there has been work on all aspects of language.

There have been accounts of morphology, as by Kaplan and Kay (1994) and Koskenniemi (1983); views of grammar, with Lexical Functional Grammar (Kaplan and Bresnan 1982), Generalized Phrase Structure Grammar (Gazdar *et al.* 1985), Head Phrase Structure Grammar (HPSG) (Pollard and Sag 1994) and Tree Adjoining Grammar (Joshi 1987), where the influence of the computational paradigm is not only in formal definition but in a concern with computability in a real and not merely notional sense; work on semantics covers both lexical aspects – see for example Saint-Dizier and Viegas (1995), and the representation and derivation of semantic structure, say compositionally (e.g., Alshawi 1992). In pragmatics there has also been work on computational implicature (see Cohen *et al.* 1990), and computational, because essentially algorithmic, accounts of discourse phenomena like the use of anaphoric expressions and focusing (e.g., Grosz *et al.* 1995): the emphasis on mechanisms underlying anaphors and focus, for instance, has helped to throw light on their roles. Computational modelling of the structure of the lexicon is an area of growing interest, extending from the form of individual entries to the (inference-supporting) organization of a lexicon as a whole (Briscoe *et al.* 1993, Pustejovsky 1995).

In general, IT's distinctive orientation towards process, discussed earlier, has stimulated both process-oriented views of grammar, as in Shieber (1987), and an enormous amount of work on generic parsing technologies, which can be seen as abstract performance modelling (cf. for example, Gazdar and Mellish 1989 and Allen 1995). One feature of this research has been attempts to capture bidirectionality as an operational rather than a purely formal property of grammars. Alongside all of this, and again motivated by computational principles, there has also been effort on generic formalisms for the specification of grammars, e.g., PATR (Shieber 1992), and for the definition of lexical information, as in DATR (Evans and Gazdar 1996).

Some of this work has been done in what may be called an academic spirit and informally evaluated, in the style of mainstream linguistics, by examples. However, the implementational philosophy of IT in general has also stimulated an interest in descriptive coverage for the relevant language component, for instance of syntax, and in the objective assessment of an abstract language model by automatic processing with some instantiation of the model, as in sentence parsing with some particular grammar. In this context it is worth noting that the notion of test data can be extended to cover not only natural corpora but also so-called test suites, specifically-constructed data sets designed to optimize on discriminative power and focus in testing. At the same time, grammar construction and testing tools have been developed, as by Carpenter and Penn (1993) and Kaplan and Maxwell (1993).

However, the really important point about this work as a whole is that it has been closely tied to work on building systems for NLP tasks, such as translation or data extraction from text, as illustrated in Grosz *et al.* (1986) and Pereira and Grosz (1993). The stress to which computational models have been subjected by being adopted for real systems has been of benefit to theory development; and the business of building task systems, especially for dealing with the interpretation or generation of dialogue or extended text, has led directly to attempts to provide rigorous and detailed accounts of language 'objects' and language-using operations in two important areas. These are of dialogue and discourse structure, as in the computational refinement and application of Rhetorical Structure Theory (compare Mann and Thompson 1988 and Moore 1995), and the organization of *world knowledge* for application in conjunction with purely linguistic information. Building and using discourse models, where text and world interact and where discourse referents including events are characterized, has stimulated significant, concrete work in the computational community on the treatment of important language constructs, namely anaphoric and temporal expressions. The issues that arise here, of how to represent and reason with world knowledge as required for language interpretation or generation have, as Sowa (1984) or Allen (1995) illustrate, to be tackled by any system builder, and thus pervade the NLP literature. But while this area is particularly important because it addresses what is properly a determinant of adequate linguistic theory, it is one in which linguists have generally not been explicitly or specifically interested.

General observations

When we look carefully at all this actual IT-related work, which is indubitably respectable and informative in itself, there are two significant points about it. The first is that, at the intellectually challenging derivational and model validation levels of work with data, and even more in all the research aimed at theory development, this is primarily done by those who label themselves at least as Computational Linguists, and perhaps as Language Engineers, that is, by those whose who are either committed even as descriptive or theoretical linguists to a computational perspective or by those engaged in practical NLP. Thus innovative statistical corpus and lexicon work has been stimulated by operational needs, including those for sublanguage grammars for particular applications. The second is that this work appears to have had little impact on the linguistic community at large, even with the computer only in the role of humble handmaiden. Those giving realistic, or real, computation a role in work on language appear to be a distinct community, neither influencing not interacting with the larger world of linguistics.

The separation is of course not absolute. Thus Cole, Green and Morgan (1995) show there is some contact between the two sides, some work on morphology, for instance, draws on computational sources (cf. e.g., Fraser and Corbett 1995), and HPSG is a fruitful area of mutual influence. However in general, even where there appears to be connectivity, this is either a consequence of the ineluctabilities of language facts or, as in the area of formal semantics, less attributable to the influence of IT than to pressure from a common higher cultural authority, namely logic. Thus even if Kamp's Discourse Representation Theory (Kamp 1981, Kamp and Reyle 1989) is of increasing interest to computational linguists and even to those building NLP systems, insofar as linguists also engage with it this because it is part of a tradition, exemplified in the work of Montague and Partee (Partee, ter Meulen and Wall 1990), that has been one common element of linguistics at large. This is indirectly illustrated by the *Handbook of Contemporary Semantic Theory* (Lappin 1996), which has one computational chapter out of twenty two. At the same time, computational metaphors, like online processing in psycholinguistics, all too often lack substance of the kind needed to write a parsing program or to define an architecture so as to deliver phone-by-phone flow of control in speech understanding.

Why, therefore, since IT in principle offers linguistics so much, has it in practice contributed so little?

Analysis

Linguistics' influence on IT

So far, the discussion has focused on the contribution by IT to linguistics. As an additional input, in trying to explain why IT appears to have had so little influence on linguistics in general, it is useful to ask whether linguistics has figured with those engaged in computational work in the language area, and in particular has affected those building NLP task systems, for translation, database access and so forth. Of course, anyone building operational systems is bound to use language objects like actual grammars and dictionaries. The question is rather whether practitioners respond to the general style of linguistic research (whatever that is) or adopt specific linguistic theories, for example Chomsky's, which have dominated linguistics for the last decades. It might be expected that if linguistic research were to play a significant part in NLP, this would help to promote feedback from NLP into linguistics generally.

On the whole, the influence of linguistics, and especially linguistic theory, on NLP has been slight, other than in the shared area of formal semantics and in some rather particular and local respects where individual pieces of work have been exploited (for example, discussions of prepositions). Moreover, even if it takes time for linguists' work to have an impact, as is interestingly shown by the slow spread of longstanding contributions from the Prague School (Hajicova *et al.* 1995), the way Halliday's Systemic Grammar (Kress 1976) has been applied in sentence and text generation is the exception rather than the rule; and indeed it is arguable that philosophy, in the shape of Grice's maxims, has had more influence on NLP than linguistics proper. Some of this disconti-nuity is, regrettably, attributable to ignorance and laziness on the part of those who build systems, fuelled by an assumption that linguists do things so differently there is no point in checking what they say. There is a good deal of what may be labelled 'wheel rediscovery' where, after computational practitioners have become alerted to some topic, e.g., pragmatics and discourse, have worked on it for a while and had, maybe, some ideas, they have found that the linguists have been there before them and have already made some descriptive or analytic progress which could with advantage be exploited.

However, there are also more respectable reasons why those who might be interested in applying the ideas and findings of linguistics have not done so. One is that these are in fact inapplicable because of fundamental differences of paradigm. This is well illustrated by work done in the past on applying Chomsky's theories, where attempts to build transformational parsers were misguided and unsuccessful, even if Government and Binding has fared a little better (Stabler 1992). The second, which is more likely to affect system developers, is linguists' 'selectivity': it is perfectly legitimate for the linguist to concentrate on some particular feature of language, e.g., tense and aspect, or nominaliza-tion and compound nominals, and to offer a potentially valuable account of it, in isolation. But the system builder *cannot* leave things in such isolation: he must, for instance, treat the parsing of compounds as only one aspect of sentence processing. Yet he often finds that he cannot just plug a linguist's account of a phenomenon, such as compound interpretation, into some slot in his system: it rests either on incompatible presuppositions about the rest of language, or is essentially lonely as a cloud. The third reason is simply that the linguists' work is not carried through to the level of specificity where it can be taken to provide even the beginnings of a grounding for programs. This is illustrated by Kintsch and van Dijk's approach to discourse representation (e.g., in van Dijk and Kintsch 1983) where, for all the attraction of their ideas on the formation of 'summarising' structures and interest of their experiments with human subjects, there is a huge gaping hole for anyone seeking to cash in, at the level of specificity required for programs, on the notions of propositional inference involved. The same holds for any attempt to exploit Sperber and Wilson (1986)'s Theory of Relevance – compare Ballim *et al.* (1991), for instance. But these problems also arise in much less obviously challenging areas such as syntax and the lexicon. Even where an explicitly formal viewpoint has been adopted, the outcome may be more descriptive than analytic, or a mere sketch with voids of raw canvas.

The pragmatics case that Sperber and Wilson represent nevertheless also draws attention to the limits on the *potential* benefits to be gained from linguistics. Though definitions of the scope of linguistics vary, linguists generally agree in eschewing the nonlinguistic world. Now while practically useful linguistic systems can be built with very little reference to any kind of world, or *domain*, model of what is out there to be or being talked about, many tasks, of which information inquiry is one, do require such domain models; and providing these is often the hardest part of building useful systems. These domain models require generalizations about the kinds of things there are in this world, particularities about individual entities, and inference capabilities subsuming both the types of reasoning allowed and search procedures for executing these on the knowledge base. The need to engage in reasoning on world knowledge in order to support the interpretation of input discourse, to carry out some consequent task activity, and to provide for the generation of output discourse places particular emphasis on the properties required of *meaning representations* so that this *operational* interaction between language and thought can be effected. Those linguists, generally cognitive linguists, willing to push far into this area, of whom Lakoff and Jackendoff may be taken as instances (e.g., in Jackendoff 1994), neverthless fail to tackle the issue in a manner, and at a level of detail, appropriate for system builders (even those willing to undertake a lot of hard graft themselves).

This point suggests some of the reasons why, in turn, IT has had so little impact on linguistics.

IT's influence on linguistics

Some of these reasons are good, others are bad. They apply primarily to the more important area of model formation and evaluation. There are good reasons to do with principle, and also ones to do with practice.

First, at the level of principle, there are genuine (even if ultimately metaphysical) differences of view about the scope of theories about language and, on a narrower view, of the scope of linguistics as oppposed to, say, philosophy. Thus some linguists may argue that IT's concerns with the connection between language processing and reasoning in NLP systems should have no bearing on linguistics, though this is not a reason for rejecting computational linguistics altogether. Second, there may be different views of what may be called the style of linguistics, according to the relative emphasis placed on formal theories of language or on descriptive coverage of languages, even where everyone would like to think that their work has *some* theoretical underpinning. Certainly there are fashions, with theoretical linguistics currently so dominant that comprehensive description has little status. On this view, while it is the business of theorists to account for linguistic phenomena, this can perfectly well be done by means of critical cases and illustrative examples, supported by sensitive sampling: it is no concern of linguistic theorists to engage in comprehensive grammar or lexicon writing. Again, this differentiates linguistics more from those working on NLP than from all of computational linguistics.

As practical reasons, it is first the case that much of what computational linguistics, or NLP, has been able to do so far is rather, even very, crude in relation to the linguistic data. IT has not been able to capture many of the phenomena, and refined distinctions (lexical, syntactic or semantic), that descriptive linguists have noted and for which theoretical linguists seek (though not necessarily with complete success so far) to account, for example,the subtleties of adverbials, or of register. It is also the case that IT has been primarily devoted to English, and otherwise concerned only with major languages including the main European ones, Russian, Japanese and Chinese and, increasingly, Arabic, but has paid no attention to the many languages, ranging from Djerbal to Huichol, that figure in linguistics. Moreover, as at least some NLP systems are rather more hackwork than could be wished, there are cases where linguists genuinely have nothing to learn from the IT side.

It has also to be recognized that the arrogance so characteristic of those connected with IT – the self-defined rulers of the modern world – is not merely irritating in itself, it is thoroughly offensive when joined to ignorance not only of language, but of relevant linguists' work.

So while IT claims to offer linguistics an intellectual resource, especially through its methodology, it does not appear to demonstrate its value convincingly to the linguistics community.

But the potentialities in IT for linguistics that were presented earlier, and the actualities that have been illustrated, are both important enough to suggest that the main reasons for the lack of interest in linguistics in IT, and the lack of computational linguists' influence on their mainstream colleagues, are due primarily to bad rather than good reasons. Again, these are at both principled and practical levels.

In the author's view, *coverage* (as for a complete syntactic grammar), *interaction* (as between syntax and semantics), *process* (as in identifying the sense of a word in a sentence), and *integration* (as in combining morphological, syntactic and lexical evidence in processing operations) are all proper concerns for linguistics, and there is no proper justification for neglecting or excluding them. Not being willing to learn from IT's fundamental grounding in process, in particular, is placing crippling limits on the power and interest of linguistic theories. Thus the crux in computational language processing is in dealing with the *ambiguity* – lexical, structural and referential – that is a fundamental feature of language: to interpret linguistic utterances the system must resolve ambiguity, and to generate effective utterances the system must minimise ambiguity. Doing this requires precisely that a system has coverage, manages interaction, and executes process to combine different sorts of information. It is not possible, as is so often the case in the linguistics literature, to focus only on one aspect of language and ignore the others, except as a temporary strategy; nor is it legitimate, as is also so often the case in the linguistics literature, to take for granted that understanding of a sentence or text it is the whole object of the enterprise to achieve and explain. Again, not taking computational output, delivered by an independent black box, as a superior way of testing a theory seems deliberately unscientific: what better way of evaluating an account of the distinctions between word senses than to see what happens when a translation program uses it? (Indeed, testing by system performance is exciting as well as principled.) But even the specificity required for computation, in itself, is an object lesson for formal theoretical linguists. Those linguists who reject the lessons of computational linguistics and NLP are thus also mistakenly, or wrongly, subverting their own cause.

On the practical side, it is impossible not to conclude that many linguists are techno- and logico-phobes. It is true that understanding logic, formalisms and computational concepts requires training to which some may be unwilling to dedicate themselves. But, less defensibly, the business of working out, in the necessary grinding detail, what a program should or does do is so exhausting that it is easier to say that doing it is irrelevant.

Conclusion

It may be that, although it is hard to discern significant impact by IT on linguistics outside the area labelled 'computational linguistics', IT is now so generally pervasive that it has begun to invade linguistic thinking. But it is doubtful, for example, whether Chomsky's minimalist programme (Chomsky 1995), which appears to invoke some notions also encountered in computational linguistics, in fact demonstrates there is any material influence from IT.

However, as NLP is forced, by tackling some tasks like interactive inquiry, to address topics such as dialogue structure, and automatic speech and language processing continue to make progress, often with surprising success by alien means, as in the use of Hidden Markov Models for speech 'recognition', there is much for linguistics to gain from looking both at how computation does things and at what it finds.

It is something of a caricature to see those engaged with computation as crass technocrats for whom the expression 'non-computational theory' is an oxymoron, and linguists as toffee-nosed snobs unwilling to inspect the rude mechanicals' cranks and levers, and a huge chasm between the two. But there is a gap that deserves to be bridged because for linguists, and especially theorists other than those whose metaphysic is resolutely anti-computational in any sense whatever, there is everything to be learnt from appreciating the distinctions between assumed, ideal, and real computation.

Acknowledgement

I am most grateful to Professor Gerald Gazdar FBA for comments on my draft.

References

Allen, J. (1995), *Natural Language Understanding*, Second Edition (Palo Alto, CA).
Alshawi, H. (1992) (ed.), *The Core Language Engine* (Cambridge, Mass).

Ballim, A., Wilks, Y. and Barnden, J. (1991), 'Belief ascription, metaphor, and intensional identification', *Cognitive Science*, 15(1): 133–71.

Biber, D. (1994), 'Representativeness in corpus design'. In Zampolli, Calzolari and Palmer (1994) 377–407.

Black, E., Eubank, S., Kashioka, K., Magerman, D., Garside and Leech (1996), 'Beyond skeleton parsing: producing a comprehensive large-scale general-english Treebank with full grammatical analysis', *COLING-96, Proceedings of the 16th International Conference on Computational Linguistics*, Copenhagen, 107–12.

Boguraev, B. K. and Briscoe, E. J. (1989) (eds.), *Computational Lexicography for Natural Language Processing*, (London).

—— and Pustejovsky, J. (1996) (eds.), *Corpus Processing for Lexical Acquisition* (Cambridge, Mass).

Booij, G., and Marle, J. van (1995) (eds.), *Yearbook of Morphology* 1994, (Dordrecht).

Bresnan, J. (1982) (ed.), *The Mental Representation of Grammatical Relations* (Cambridge, Mass).

Brill, E. (1995), 'Transformation-based error-driven learning and natural language processing: a case study in part-of-speech tagging', *Computational Linguistics*, 21(4): 543–65.

Briscoe, E. J., Copestake, A. and de Paiva, V. (1993) (eds.), *Inheritance, Defaults and the Lexicon*, (Cambridge).

Burnard, L. (1995), *Users Reference Guide for the British National Corpus*, Oxford University Computing Services, (Oxford).

Carpenter, R. and Penn, G. (1993), *ALE: The Attribute Logic Engine*, Version 2.0 User's Guide and Software, Laboratory for Computational Linguistics, Department of Philosophy, Carnegie-Mellon University.

Charniak, E. (1993), *Statistical Language Learning* (Cambridge, Mass).

Chomsky, N. (1995), *The Minimalist Programme* (Cambridge, Mass).

Cohen, P. R., Morgan, J. and Pollack, M. E. (1990) (eds.), *Intentions in Communication* (Cambridge, Mass).

Cole, J., Green, G. M. and Morgan, J. (1995) (eds.), *Linguistics and Computation* CSLI Lecture Notes 52, (Stanford: Centre for the Study of Language and Information).

Computational Linguistics (1993), Special Issues on Using Large Corpora, I and II, 19 (1) and 19 (2), 1–177 and 219–382.

Copestake, A., Briscoe, T., Vossen, P., Ageno, A., Castellion, I., Ribas, G., Rigau, G., Rodriquez, H. and Samiotov, A. (1995), 'Acquisition of lexical translation relations from MRDS', *Machine Translation*, 9: 183–219.

Dijk, T. A. van and Kintsch, W. (1983), *Strategies of Discourse Comprehension*, (New York).

Dowty, D. R., Karttunen, L. and Zwicky, A. M. (1985) (eds.), *Natural Language Parsing* (Cambridge).

Evans, R. and Gazdar, G. (1996), 'DATR: A language for lexical knowledge representation', *Computational Linguistics*, 22(2): 167–216,

Fraser, N. and Corbett, G. (1995), 'Gender, animacy, and declensional class assignment: a unified account for Russian'. In Booij and van Marle (1995), 123–50.

Gale, W. A., Church, K. W. and Yarowsky, D. (1994), 'Discrimination decisions for 100,000-dimensional spaces' . In Zampolli, Calzolari and Palmer (1994) 429–550.

Gamut, L. T. F. (1991) *Logic, Language and Meaning*, 2 vols. (Chicago).

Garside, R., Leech, G. and Sampson, G. (1987) (eds.), *The Computational Analysis of English* (London).

Gazdar, G., Klein, E., Pullum, G. K. and Sag, I. A. (1985), *Generalized Phrase Structure Grammar* (Oxford).

—— and Mellish, C. (1989), *Natural Language Processing in Prolog* (Reading, Mass).

Groenendijk, J., Janssen, T. and Stokhof, M. (1981) (eds.), *Formal Methods in the Study of Language*, Mathematical Centre Amsterdam.

Grosz, B. J., Joshi, A. K. and Weinstein, S. (1995), 'Centering: a framework for modelling the local structure of discourse', *Computational Linguistics*, 21(2): 203–25.

—— Spärck Jones, K. and Webber, B. L. (1986) (eds.), *Readings in Natural Language Processing* (Los Altos, CA).

Hajicova, E., Skoumalova, H. and Sgall, P. (1995), 'An automatic procedure for topic-focus identification', *Computational Linguistics*, 21(1): 81–94.

Jackendoff, R. (1994), *Patterns in the Mind: Language and Human Nature* (New York).

Joshi, A. K. (1987), 'Introduction to tree-adjoining grammars'. In Manaster-Ramer (1987) 87–114.

Kamp, H. (1981), '*A Theory of Truth and Semantic Representation*'. In Groenendijk, Janssen and Stokhof (1981) 277–322.

—— and Reyle, U. (1989), *From Discourse to Logic*, 2 vols. (Dordrecht).

Kaplan, R. M. and Bresnan, J. (1982), 'Lexical-functional grammar'. In Bresnan (1982) 173–281.

Kaplan, R. M. and Kay, M. (1994), 'Regular models of phonological rule systems', with comments by M. Liberman and G. Ritchie, *Computational Linguistics*, 20(3): 331–80.

—— and Maxwell, J. (1993), '*Grammar Writer's Workbench*', ms, Xerox Palo Alto Research Centre, Palo Alto.

Koskenniemi, K. (1983), *Two-Level Morphology: A General Computational Model for Word-Form Recognition and Production*, Publication 11, Department of General Linguistics, University of Helsinki.

Kress, G. (1976) (ed.), *Halliday: System and Function in Language* (London).

Lappin, S. (1996) (ed.), *The Handbook of Contemporary Semantic Theory* (Oxford).

Manaster-Ramer, A. (1987) (ed.), *The Mathematics of Language* (Amsterdam).

Mann, W. C. and Thompson, S. A. (1988), 'Rhetorical structure theory: towards a functional theory of text organization', *Text: an Interdiciplinary Journal for the Study of Text*, 8(2): 243–81.

Marcus, M. P. (1980), *A Theory of Syntactic Recognition for Natural Language* (Cambridge, Mass).

—— Santorini, B. and Marcinkiewicz, M. (1993), 'Building a large annotated corpus of English: the Penn Treebank', *Computational Linguistics*, 19(2): 313–30.

Moore, J. D. (1995), *Participating in Explanatory Dialogues* (Cambridge, Mass).

Partee, B. H., ter Meulen, A. and Wall, R. E. (1990), *Mathematical Methods in Linguistics* (Dordrecht).

Pereira, F. C. N. and Grosz, B. J. (1993) (eds.), Special Volume: Natural Language Processing, *Artificial Intelligence* 63(12): 1–492.

Pollard, C. and Sag, I. A. (1994), *Head-driven Phrase Structure Grammar* (Chicago).

Pustejovsky, J. (1995), *The Generative Lexicon* (Cambridge, Mass).

Saint-Dizier, P. and Viegas, E. (1995), *Computational Lexical Semantics* (Cambridge).

Shieber, S. M. (1987), *An Introduction to Unification-Based Approaches to Grammar* (Chicago).

—— (1992), *Constraint-Based Grammar Formalisms* (Cambridge, Mass).

Sowa, J. F. (1984), *Conceptual Structures* (Reading, Mass).

Spärck Jones, K. (1986), *Synonymy and Semantic Classification*, Published Thesis, 1964 (Edinburgh).

—— and Galliers, J. R. (1996), *Evaluating Natural Language Processing Systems*, Lecture Notes in Artificial Intelligence 1083, (Berlin).

Sperber, D. and Wilson, D. (1986), *Relevance* (Oxford).

Sperberg-McQueen, C. M. (1994), 'The Text Encoding Initiative'. In Zampolli, Calzolari and Palmer (1994) 409–28.

Stabler, E. P. Jr (1992), *The Logical Approach to Syntax* (Cambridge, Mass).

Stubbs, M. (1996), *Text and Corpus Analysis* (Oxford).

Summers, D. (1996), 'Computational lexicography: the importance of representativeness in relation to frequency'. In Thomas and Short (1996) 260–6.

Thomas, J. and Short, M. (1996) (eds.), *Using Corpora for Language Research* (London).

Winograd, T. (1972), *Understanding Natural Language* (Edinburgh).

Zampolli, A., Calzolari, N. and Palmer, M. (1994) (eds.), *Current Issues in Computational Linguistics: In Honour of Don Walker* (Dordrecht).

Commentary

HENRY S. THOMPSON

Human Communication Research Centre
University of Edinburgh

Introduction

In her paper, Karen Spärck Jones offers a useful taxonomy of possible interactions between Information Technology and Linguistics, and on investigating each of them finds little evidence of a significant impact. In this brief follow-up I will disagree mildly with her taxonomy, emphasise two potentially important dichotomies, and then focus on a few areas which she perhaps slightly neglected, where I think the evidence for influence is stronger.

Beyond data and models

Nearly 15 years ago I presented a paper (Thompson 1983) at a workshop co-hosted by Karen Spärck Jones. That paper included Figure 1.

Interestingly enough, I think Spärck Jones's two main 'potential roles for information technology (IT) in linguistics' are *both* subsumed under what I label here *Computation in service to linguistics*. What I think Spärck Jones underestimates is the extent to which the area I call *Computational Linguistics proper*, that is, the conduct of the project of Linguistics in an inherently computational way, is a significant factor in the current intellectual landscape. It will not do to re-label practitioners in this area as *computational* linguists and thus irrelevant to the question of impact on Linguistics itself – the fact of the matter is that in many areas (and this is a change from 1982 and my conclusions in the earlier paper), the nature of linguistic theorizing, by card-carrying linguists, is essentially computational. Examples include most of non-Charles-River syntactic theories (e.g., Lexical Functional Grammar and most sign-based grammatical theories such as Head-Phrase Structure Grammar and its many variants), many semantic theories oriented to structure beyond the sentence level (e.g., Discourse Representation Theory), lexical and morphological theories in which both object-oriented inheritance and finite-state technologies play a crucial role (e.g., DATR, Finite State Morphology) and

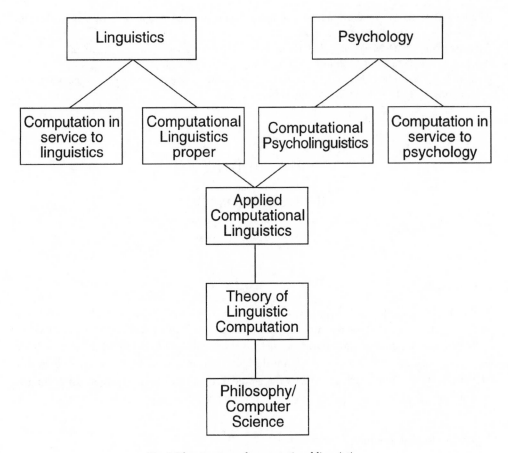

Fig. 1. The structure of computational linguistics

finally process-oriented approaches to phonetics and phonology, which I will take up at more length below. In the first and the last of these areas, I believe, there is almost no *non*-computational linguistic theorising of any significance underway. I recognize that in sheer numeric terms, the dominance of contemporary syntactic theory by the Charles River school is nearly overwhelming, but the fact that virtually all the competition is computational in inspiration surely counts for something.

Qualitative versus quantitative

Let me turn next to the matter of information technology as a means for 'gathering and interpreting data.' Although at first this would seem by its very nature to be a kind of impact which could not be qualitative, and which can therefore be dismissed from consideration (after all, more and faster does not change *what* I do, just my rate of progress), in fact I think in several areas this is a mistake. Sufficient quantitative change can result in qualitative change. In several areas (see below) the nature and scale of the data which information technology makes available for linguistic investigation has substantially transformed the very nature of that investigation.

Rationalist verus empiricist

The philosophy of linguistics is a minefield where I am ill-qualified to tread, but it is I think worth noting the extent to which the rationalist/empiricist dichotomy has been appealed to from within computational linguistics over the last five years in order to explain the impact of the availability of large volumes of speech and language in computationally accessible form. On the one hand 'the new empiricism' is an accurate label for the dominance of statistical modelling in the construction of useable language and speech technology for practical application. Fifteen years ago the expectation was that such artefacts would be constructed on the basis of computational realisations of linguistic theory. In fact few if any such systems were successful, and the most significant practical impact (in the areas of speech recognition and synthesis, information retrieval and message processing) has come from systems which eschew theory-based rules in favour of data-intensive statistical models.

But this triumph of empiricism in the practical domain has not so far extended to linguistic theory. As suggested in the previous section, the *nature* of theories is evolving under the influence of computational ideas, but the *goal* of theorizing, the project of linguistics, is still explanatory accounts of language at many levels. Or rather, there has been a change, but in methodology, not in aims. Theory *validation* is more and more seen in terms of ability to account for the wealth of empirical data now available, but the usefulness of theorising itself is not in doubt.

Phonetics and Phonology

The study of the sounds of language, both at the level of production, transmission and perception, and at the level of formal system, shows perhaps the greatest change as a result of the advent of information technology. In a very clear case of quantitative change (the amount of data a single phonetician could be expected to explore grew by at least a factor of 100 between 1970 and 1985) giving rise to qualitative change, the theory and practice of phonetics has changed substantially. Both the nature of experimentation and the kinds of theories have changed. The change in theory is even more vivid at the level of phonology, where finite-state and constraint-based computational substrates play an increasingly central role in mainstream phonological theories.

Dialogue

At the other end of the speech chain lies another example of how information technology, specifically the advent of high-quality digital recording of natural dialogue, is beginning to make a qualitative change in how science is done. If our interest is the question of how participants in a conversation time their contributions thereto, this shift in technology, from audio tape to digitised speech file, quite simply changes what the facts of the matter are. The limitations of the old technology meant theory in this area was perforce founded on subjective impressions of the timing of contributions, impressions which are known to be at risk when the conversation includes stretches where more than one party is talking at the same time.

It is my own view that existing theory, based on a claim that people do their best to 'take turns', is actually false to fact. But I can only say this because I have access to the facts in a new way, I can actually determine objectively when overlapping speech starts and stops, in absolute terms of milliseconds, not in relative terms of perceived co-occurrence. Of course the point here is not whether I'm right or not, but simply that information technology has irrevocably changed the nature of the scientific debate in this area of linguistics.

Conclusion

As a linguist and a computer scientist, I would say this, but none-the-less I think information technology has in fact had a major impact on linguistics, for the better. On the one hand, the nature of the data we consider and which our theories are measured against has changed enormously, and in many areas this change has had to be matched by quite fundamental changes in methodology. On the other hand, concepts and approaches from computer science have contributed to theory development in many areas of linguistics, usually for the better. I expect both these trends to continue, and I welcome them.

References

Thompson, H. S. (1983), 'Natural language processing: a critical analysis of the structure of the field, with some implications for parsing'. In Spärck Jones and Wilkes, (eds.) *Automatic Natural Language Processing* (Chichester).

'Eke out our performance with your mind': reconstructing the theatrical past with the aid of computer simulation

RICHARD BEACHAM

School of Theatre Studies
University of Warwick

Abstract This paper focuses on the role of computer-based simulation of three-dimensional models of theatrical space, based on specific examples, ranging from temporary Roman stages, through permanent Roman theatres, to 18th century London theatres, culminating in the work in progress to restore the Hellerau Festspielhaus near Dresden as a venue for advanced experimental performance. The raw materials for the three-dimensional models range from two-dimensional paintings, site plans and fragmentary elements to the surviving buildings themselves. Particular attention is given to Rome's first permanent theatre, the largest the Romans ever built and now largely hidden by later building in the centre of Rome, making excavation impossible and three-dimensional simulation the only feasible approach.

Introduction

The subjects addressed at this symposium and the variety of methodologies and disciplines encompassed by them indicate the diverse and complex manner in which Information Technology (IT) has already insinuated itself into how we view and pursue our scholarship. The subject area to be considered in this paper, although sometimes struggling for a name – whether 'Performance Studies', 'Dramatic Arts' or '*Theaterwissenschaft*' and a relative new-comer to the formal 'Academy', has long been a lively, many faceted, and familiar element in the cultural life of western civilization, and in recent years, Information Technology has been enlisted in its service. One could note, for example, such things as computer-controlled lighting plots, which have been in use for many years, or soon no doubt the virtual box-office where one will place one's finger upon a seating chart of the theatre, and immediately see on a screen the view attainable there of both the stage and one's neighbours in the audience.

In addition theatre, both as a subject for scholarly enquiry as well as a cultural or professional activity, is well-represented in a quickly growing range of web sites devoted to the various ways it may be evaluated, studied, described and recorded. A good selection of such sites (including academic courses, training programmes, libraries, museums and theatre history resources) is listed on *Theatre Central Resources* (http://www.theatrecentral.com/). The Société Internationale des Bibliothèques et Musées des Arts du Spectacle (*SIBMAS*) is currently constructing a site based at the University of

Amsterdam which aims both to be a forum for researchers and to provide guidance and data (http://www.let.uva.nl/vg/sibmas.html). In the United States, an ambitious project in association with the American Society for Theatre Research, 'Performance in History', is currently being set up, which intends ultimately to make available a very wide-ranging selection of theatre historical materials on the web. In the United Kingdom (UK), as one of five providers forming the syndicate of the Arts and Humanities Data Service, a Performing Arts Data Service (*PADS*) has been established at the University of Glasgow (http://pads.ahds.ac.uk/). Both this and *PATRON*, the Performing Arts Teaching Resources Online Service (http://www.surrey.ac.uk/Library/research/PATRON.html) at the University of Surrey (part of the Electronic Libraries Programme), are funded by the Joint Information Systems Committee of the UK's Higher Education Funding Councils.

The intention here, however, is not to survey the wide-ranging implications of IT for the study and practice of theatre through such broad initiatives but rather to focus on one particular but important corner of the discipline: the organization, analysis, and use of theatrical space. The crucial and definitive thing about theatre after all – its almost unique claim amongst the arts – is that it takes up both time and space: quite literally it 'takes place'. The understanding of any work of drama is vitally informed by an assessment of and due regard for the original spatial conditions, which, in a most literal sense, shaped and conditioned it. Theatre is also of course quintessentially a visual medium. The Greeks had a word for it, *Theatron*: literally, the 'seeing place'. And this quality has always been absolutely central to the nature of theatre and our under-standing of it, whether like the Romans we call it *spectaculum*, with Inigo Jones characterize it as 'nothing else but pictures with light and motion' (*Tempe Restored*: 49–50), or simply advertise it as 'a Show'.

Where therefore do computers come into this most lively art? In one quite real sense, of course, the art of the theatre is itself the earliest known form of 'virtual reality' – indeed, quite a sophisticated form of it, both for the performers as they impersonate people, places, emotions and the like which are not in fact real, as well as for the spectators as they 'willingly suspend disbelief'. And hence, of course my Shakespear-ean title (*Henry V*, 3. Chorus 35), from one whose art constantly and triumphally draws into a virtual reality the complicit recipient of his work; whether as spectator of the enacted outer events and inner mindscapes of his characters; or as reader, fashioning with one's mind's eye a veritable universe. The purpose of this symposium is to explore some of the ways in which the application of IT in the humanities and social sciences has affected our own research and that of our colleagues. This paper will to do so focusing closely upon several examples of the manner in which computer simulation of historical theatre architectural and scenic elements may facilitate, contribute to, and enlarge this particular area of scholarly enquiry. Most of the examples cited below represent aspects of work being conducted by *THEATRON* (Theatre History in Europe: Architectural and Textual Resources Online), a Consortium associated with the School of Theatre Studies at the University of Warwick (http://www.theatron.co.uk). However, related work in computer aided reconstruction of historic theatres and stage settings, as well as the use of computer technology in contemporary theatre design, is beginning to appear from both individual researchers and academic departments, worldwide. One particularly promising example of such initiatives is that of the Theatre Computer Vizualization Center at the University of Indiana (URL http://appia.tcvc.indiana.edu/~tcvc/pr.html).

The Theatre of Dionysus at Athens

There is, of course, a lively argument (illustrated in the content of this symposium) concerning the extent to which much of the assistance offered by computers to our investigations is essentially that of effective tools which do not, however, fundamentally alter the nature of research or its outcome. This is something of a moot point – obviously tools do not 'think', and neither (yet!) do computers in the normal sense of the word. But they most certainly can both free scholars from mind-numbing drudgery and greatly facilitate new ways of looking at the evidence, thus more readily collected, for analysis. Much of what will be discussed – still photos of computer-animated interactive architectural models – could, painstakingly, have been created by traditional means. What is particularly novel and requires one therefore to 'eke out with your mind' is that crucial quality of time and motion, providing in synthesis with the visual element, the very essence of theatre, and which has been extremely difficult for previous generations of theatre historical scholars – and their students – to conjure up.

It is important to keep students in mind in this discussion, because much of the value to be perceived in the type of work outlined here is that it greatly improves the communication – and hence the understanding – of the insights achieved by scholarly research. It is difficult therefore to make much meaningful distinction between employing this type of tool for research on the one hand, or for effective teaching on the other. Both undertakings surely (and particularly in a discipline based on the type of formal elements outlined above) are aimed at clear perception, valid interpretation and cogent understanding.

The first example is a basic one. Wilhelm Dörpfeld's site-plan (1896) of the Theatre of Dionysus at Athens (well-known to generations of theatre students) showing his interpretations of the remaining physical evidence to suggest the stages of architectural evolution on the site It is not particularly difficult to 'read', but on the other hand it (and the information it seeks to convey) are not notably clear or easy to envisage (see, e.g., Bieber 1961: 55, 64). By converting its information into a relatively simple three-dimensional architectural model, the data are both more readily communicated, and easier to extend into plausible architectural options (Figures 1,2). Both the relationship between the surviving physical remains, and the transformation of the site over many centuries – including, crucially, the modifications in the use of theatrical space and architecture – become easier to perceive and communicate, or conversely, to question. So too, by placing the 'viewer' at different points in the model the immensely important qualities of space and distance, and consequently what members of the audience actually saw in their *Theatron*, become evident: elements which in turn are vital to any understanding or analysis of acting style, type of language, use of costumes, masks and props

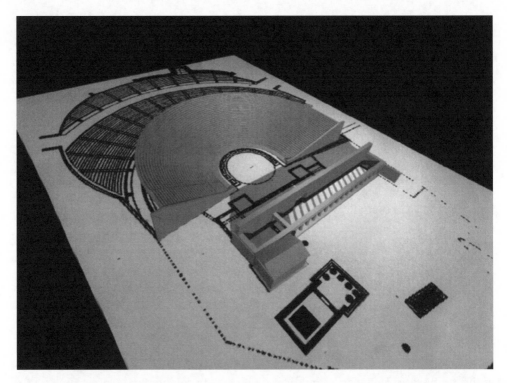

Fig. 1. A computer 3D depiction of the evolution of the Theatre of Dionysius at Athens

Fig. 2. A computer depiction of the site plan of the Theatre of Dionysius

and the like. The study of theatre is composed of elements which are difficult to manipulate both physically and intellectually. Short of 'being there' IT offers the readiest and most satisfactory access to these materials.

Roman wall painting and temporary stages

For the first several centuries of its existence – including crucially the period during which most of its surviving plays were written – the Roman theatre was performed on temporary stages put up for a particular festive occasion and then dismantled. For those wishing to understand the nature of that theatre, including the performance of its drama, some attempt at 'reconstructing' those temporary stages is invaluable. A long-term project undertaken at the University of Warwick has used as evidence an analysis of ancient Roman wall paintings that survive, primarily at Pompeii and Herculaneum. Such paintings were unusual in that they used sophisticated perspective technique on flat walls to create the subtle illusion of complex three-dimensional structures. This technique of perspective painting was called *skenographia*. It had originally evolved, as the word suggests, in the Greek theatre of the fifth century BC where it was used to embellish the flat facade of the stage building, the *skene* (Aristotle. *Poet*. 4. 17, Vitruvius. 7. *Praef*. 11, cf. Richter 1970). Later, the Romans used the same method to decorate the walls of their homes and, by a strange cross-fertilization, to then introduce theatrical motifs which had developed in the theatre into domestic settings. The Roman architect Vitruvius tells us they even went so far as to depict actual theatre scenery and stage sets (7. 5. 2; cf. Cerutti and Richardson 1989, Moorman 1983).

Most of the wall paintings thought to contain theatrical elements are difficult to interpret, since such elements are usually embedded in more extensive and elaborate decorative schemes. Moreover, Roman perspective technique – sometimes employing multiple vanishing points – can result in problematic images. It is often impossible to discern the stage image within the imaginary and fantastic architecture surrounding it (cf. Little 1971, Ling 1991:75–8). A few paintings recently discovered, however, are easier to interpret, and in turn may be used as models to help 'unravel' those that are more complex and ambiguous. For example, a painting from the 'Room of the Masks' in the House of Augustus at Rome (Carettoni 1961) was employed as a sort of 'Rosetta stone' to analyse a great many other paintings. In addition, after first constructing a small wooden model of the architecture depicted in the painting to determine that the theory was plausible, a full-scale version was built at Warwick, upon which a series of Roman comedies was then staged. The insights which this project provided into the nature of the style, language, and staging of Roman comedy – is another story (Beacham 1987 video, 1992: chaps. 3–4).

In respect of the painting, with the aid of computer modelling it was possible to pursue this entire process 'virtually' – to in effect 'draw out' the 'real' architecture from the painting and then to test the nature of the performance space which, hypothetically, it represented. Moreover, this same computer model could then in turn be applied to the analysis of a substantial body of other, less straightforward paintings to identify

Fig. 3. A painting from the Villa of Oplontis near Pompeii

Fig. 4. A computer-generated 3D depiction of the architectural elements on that painting. (A colour version of this figure is at http://www.britac.ac.uk/pubs/it-schol)

common architectural, decorative and spatial elements and to analyse the manner in which these have been modified in each case. Essentially the value of the model is that it facilitates three-dimensional perception and greatly helps to distinguish between plausibly 'real' and 'fantasy' architecture in such paintings, and the manner in which the one may have stylistically evolved into the other.

A second example is from the Villa of Oplontis near Pompeii (de Franciscis 1975; Malandrino 1977). Taking the model from the 'Room of the Masks', it was easy to identify common architectural properties in the work, and similarly to create a three-dimensional model based upon it (Figures 3,4). From this, it was a short step (assisted to be sure by the generous application of much money) to fashion a full-scale version of this, and stage the author's translation of Plautus' comedy *Casina* upon it at the Getty Museum – itself a replica of a Roman villa – at Malibu in 1994 (Shirley 1994, Hornby 1995, Hamma 1995, Gamel 1995). Many of the paintings on the walls of the Getty museum-villa are themselves of the *skenographic* variety, and therefore easily, as it were, 'cross-referenced' to the temporary stage erected there which was itself based on such paintings: thus aesthetically 'closing the circle'. (Figure 5).

The depiction and analysis of Roman permanent theatres

The theatre historian examining the remains of Roman permanent theatres is, in a literal sense, on firmer ground. But again, much can be learned through the judicious

Fig. 5. A temporary replica stage built at the J. Paul Getty Museum. (A colour version of this figure is at http://www.britac.ac.uk/pubs/it-schol)

application of computer simulation. Pompeii contains the architectural skeleton of its large theatre – where, according to Dio Cassius (66. 23. 3), the population was assembled at the actual moment of Vesuvius' eruption – the ultimate in scenic pyrotechnics and surprise endings. Before its demise and preservation that theatre had gone through successive architectural incarnations from the second century BC to AD 79, and again, as in the case of the Theatre of Dionysus, these can readily be depicted and analysed as the site evolved from a Hellenistic format into the earliest surviving example of the Roman 'type'. (Figure 6).

But it is also possible to, in a phrase, 'let the mute stones speak' by carefully reincarnating them into a computer-generated three-dimensional model. SIMLAB, a research initiative in networked virtual reality affiliated with the Department of Art and the School of Computer Science at Carnegie Mellon University, has recently prepared as part of a "virtual Pompeii" project such a model of the large theatre at Pompeii (Holden 1996). This very effectively demonstrates (taking just two areas of investigation) both the decorative embellishment and the careful organization of scenic and social space which were so crucially a part of the aesthetic and ideological nature of the Roman theatre (Figure 7). It also helps us once again subsequently to apply and test an architectural 'template' against the remains of other Roman theatres both to assist in identifying their structural elements and to determine the manner in which these have been modified, and why.

A particularly intriguing example is at Rome itself, where in 55 BC the triumphal general Pompey the Great persuaded the authorities to allow him to construct the City of Rome's first permanent theatre – the largest the Romans ever built, anywhere – and to name it (with characteristic modesty) after himself (Beacham 1992: 157–63; Beacham 1999: chap. 2). This was no ordinary theatre, and it has exercised a fascination upon generations of scholars. It was the site of some of the most momentous events in the political and cultural life at Rome – Caesar was assassinated in part of it – and remained in constant use for over five centuries, to the end of antiquity. It was throughout its history one of the great showplaces of the City; last restored and refurbished under the Ostrogoths in the sixth century AD; and remained a major 'tourist' site during the Middle Ages (Cassiodorus *Chron*, for AD519). Today, however, there is little to see of it – above ground. Just a remarkable ghostly image in the urban landscape (Capoferro Cencetti 1979, Richardson 1987).

Imaginative recreations have been proposed with greater or lesser attention to the evidence. Some beautiful (if rather fanciful) ones were done in the last century (e.g., Beltard). Scholars are fortunate in that the so-called 'marble plan', a map of Rome created early in third century AD, preserves a depiction of a portion of the site, allowing us to locate and identify many of its elements (Almeida 1980: tab. 32, 39; Coarelli 1972; Sear 1993; Figure 8). This can then be augmented by, literally, piecemeal evidence found in unlikely places such as the basements of restaurants (preserving the substructural vaulting of the theatre), and the occasional column brought to light behind the walls of later buildings. The problem, of course, is to assemble this jigsaw into a coherent whole. Comprehensive excavation of the site, although briefly contemplated in a fit of *Caesar-*

Fig. 6. A view of the remains of the large theatre at Pompeii

Fig. 7. A computer model reconstruction of the large theatre at Pompeii

omania by the fascists in the thirties, is quite impractical, since it would involve wholesale destruction of a major, architecturally irreplaceable, section from the heart of Rome (Galassi Paluzzi *et al.* 1937).

Computer modelling now offers a uniquely effective and appropriate means for overcoming these local difficulties. Currently initial work is being carried out as part of an intriguing and promising application of what might be termed 'computer archae-ology', in the 'Pompey Project'. This involves initially, the creation of a computer model of the site based on existing information and leavened by plausible hypotheses. This model will then be systematically tested and continuously refined, in the light of emerging new evidence or analysis, which can be incorporated incrementally into it. It enables the viewer to explore the site in some detail, and eventually will incorporate links to primary and secondary written accounts, allowing the many decisions and choices made in creating elements of its design to be evaluated and alternative possibilities scrutinized. With the support and assistance of the office of the Soprintendenza Archeologica di Roma, 'key-hole' excavations will be focused at particular tightly targeted sites where information crucial to verifying or modifying the model is likely to be found. The attraction of such an electronic model is its malleability, the capacity quickly to incorporate and react to new data. If for example, the initial model assumes that the height of the columns in the great *porticus Pompeii* (which was part of the complex) was twelve feet, but subsequently this is revised to fifteen feet, these data can be 'fed into' the model and can then be used in turn to generate necessary or appropriate modifications elsewhere (Figure 9).

One of the enigmas posed by the surviving evidence, for example, is the nature of the architecture schematically depicted by the marble plan at the end of the portico immediately adjacent to the back wall of the *scaena*. Professor James Packer, who has for two decades worked to produce the definitive study of the Forum of Trajan, has observed that this depiction (about which little else is known) is nearly identical with that depicting an equivalent position in Trajan's Forum, about which a good deal more is known (Packer 1997: vol. 1, 265 n. 23). In the light of the fact that this Forum frequently 'quoted' other notable earlier monuments at Rome, and applying the theorem that 'things equal to the same thing are equal to each other', we can tentatively modify the Pompey model to reflect this hypothesis.

In addition to the theatre itself, the architectural complex – which was designed as a single integrated unit (Velleius Paterculus 2. 48. 2) – included an assembly room or *curia*; a new meeting place for the Senate, dominated by a statue of Pompey himself, provided by the Roman people to demonstrate its gratitude (Plutarch, *Brut.* 14). It was here that 'even at the base of Pompey's statue which all the while ran blood, great Caesar fell' (*Jul. Caes.* 3. 2. 189–90; Sapelli 1990). Both this, and a nearby sumptuous house which Pompey provided for himself, were located within a spacious park extending some six hundred feet behind the theatre. It quickly become one of the most popular places in Rome to stroll, escape from the summer heat, or arrange amorous assignations (Cicero *De Fat.* 8; Catullus 55. 6; Ovid *Ars Amat.* 1. 67; Propertius. 2. 32; 4. 8). Within were rows of trees, shaded streams, and fountains. Along the north side was the *Hecatostylon*, 'the portico of

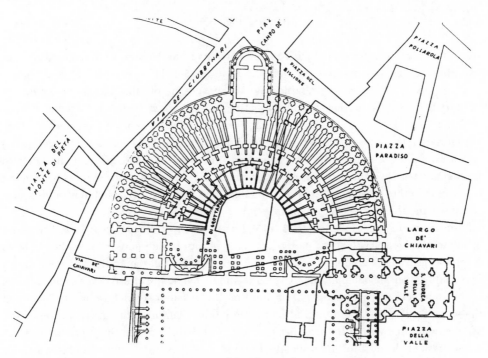

Fig. 8. Plan of a portion of the Theatre of pompey complex

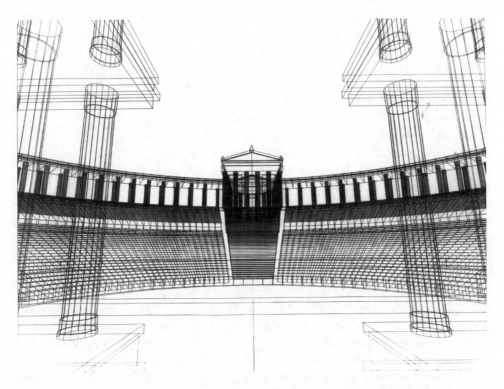

Fig. 9. A prelininary 3D computer model of the interior of the Theatre of Pompey

the hundred pillars', festooned with golden curtains from Pergamum, and a collection of valuable statues and paintings (Pliny *Nat. Hist.* 35. 59). The large central court had a double grove of trees, and probably rows of statues or plinths displaying Pompey's military trophies. At its western end, along the back facade of the theatre's *scaenae frons* which faced out over the park, it seems likely that Pompey placed fourteen statues personifying the nations he had conquered (Pliny *Nat.* Hist. 36.41; Packer 1997: vol. 1, 273 n. 27) This park was used on the days of performance as a place for the audience to promenade between the entertainments without leaving the theatre complex or causing disruption in the streets. As Vitruvius noted (5. 9), it could also be used to provide space for preparing the stage sets and machinery.

According to Pliny (*Nat. Hist.* 36. 115), Pompey's theatre could seat forty thousand spectators, a figure which has long been doubted, but which may turn out not to have been too greatly exaggerated (Goldberg 1996: 265–6). The computer model enables reasonably accurate calculations to be made and tested, using alternative configurations of the architecture. The diameter of the auditorium was almost five hundred feet (120 m); the stage itself was three hundred feet wide (90 m). Behind it the great facade of the *scaena*, which may initially have been of wood, probably rose to the full height of the upper tiers of the auditorium opposite: three stories. The outer semi-circular wall was composed of three tiers of engaged columns carved from red granite (Pliny *Nat. Hist.* 36. 41) This massive facade was adorned with stone and stucco and embellished with numerous statues of stone and bronze (Pliny *Nat. Hist.* 7.34). It formed a series of forty-four huge vaulted arches at street level, from which a system of passages and staircases efficiently conducted spectators to their seats above. Computer aided design techniques, when applied to the various hypotheses which have been proposed for the precise structural organization of the building, will allow these to be systematically tested and evaluated for the first time, taking into account all the available surviving evidence, and with due regard to Roman building technology.

The most striking element of the theatre was the provision of a temple to Venus *Victrix* (Pompey's patron goddess) crowning the top and rear of the auditorium. It was the largest of several shrines along the colonnade at the upper rim in honour of *Honos, Virtus, Felicitas* and *Victoria* (Pliny *Nat. Hist.* 8. 20) (see Hanson 1959:44–55). Apparently this temple was constructed so that the monumental ramp of steps leading up to it formed the central bank of seats in the auditorium. It was said that when Pompey's political rivals objected to a permanent theatre, he claimed that in fact he was building a lofty temple beneath which steps would be provided for watching games honouring the goddess (Tertullian *De Spect.* 10.5; Tacitus *Ann.* 14.20; Gleason 1994: 21; see Gruen 1992: 205–10). Both the foundations of this temple and substantial portions of its walls survive, having been incorporated into a complex of subsequent building on the site, which still towers over the surrounding urban landscape just at it did in antiquity; these architectural elements and the evidence they may provide for the nature of the ancient structure have never before been scientifically analysed (Coarelli 1977).

At regular intervals around the external perimeter of the upper colonnade were attached the vertical masts from which projecting horizontal booms suspended a huge brightly coloured linen awning, the *vela*, that shaded the audience. The building also used water flowing down the aisles to cool it, as well as a device for spraying a fine saffron-scented mist (Val. Max. 2.4.6). Recently developed software for environmental design when applied to the model allows detailed calculations of acoustics, lighting and 'climatic' conditions within the theatre to be made, and can even take into account its orientation to the sun at different times of the day and year.

Pompey's complex was an amenity with a message. To walk through the central court of the park (easily simulated using the computer model) was to be impressed both with the munificence and military accomplishments of its patron (cf. Gleason 1994). Moreover, the site and its architecture communicated an ideological concept. Because the complex was located in the Campus Martius which – in addition to its venerable military connection – had long been a place where voters were impressed by monumental architecture (and from time to time bribed with largess or handouts); in effect it extended and refined associations which this area already had (Frezouls 1983). The layout of the buildings – very clearly illustrated by the model – and in particular the placing of the theatre and the *curia* at opposite ends of the central axis, tended to raise the status of the former (crowned by its temple) to that of a formal political space when faced from the front porch of the *curia* which was also itself a sacred precinct (Aulus Gellius 14. 7. 7 Marchetti-Longi 1960). The entrance to the latter was dominated by a huge painting of a warrior by the fifth century painter Polygnotus, which may have served to remind visitors of the military prowess of its builder (Pliny *Nat. Hist.* 35. 59). The political/ religious nature of the building dominating each pole of the axis was therefore visually emphasized by being mirrored in its opposite; the effect of which can be graphically demonstrated by the model (Figure 10).

Fig. 10. General view of a preliminary 3D computer model of the Theatre of Pompey complex

The Pompey model represents an early example of the use of computer technology and virtual imaging which is currently being encouraged by the Council of Europe sponsored MINOTEC initiative. This project (under the auspices of the European Network of Ancient Places of Performance) seeks to explore the manner in which new technology can be used simultaneously to protect, enhance and educationally exploit ancient places of performance. Among other undertakings, MINOTEC hopes to produce a range of electronic publications and research which have careful regard for the fact that 'with the current vogue for synthesised images, there is a great risk that beautiful images will be given preference over archaeological and historical knowledge' (FEMP 1996: 4). By demonstrating the manner in which computer modelling may function not just as a medium to illustrate or publish the results of research, but as a uniquely valuable new research tool in its own right, the Pompey project is an important and promising initiative.

The Restoration and Early Eighteen Century Stage

At Warwick University, David Thomas has recently used computer modelling to assist his analysis of early English playhouses, including the first Theatre Royal Drury Lane of Sir Christopher Wren, and Sir John Vanbrugh's Queen's Theatre in the Haymarket (Thomas 1996 video).

A drawing in Wren's papers called simply 'Playhouse' is thought to be a section of his design for Drury Lane which was constructed in 1674. However, the drawing is deliberately torn through in two places, indicating perhaps some element of doubt or dissatisfaction by Wren (see Thomas 1989:70–1). Functionally, this design seems unsatisfactory by virtue of a row of massive pilasters along the sides of the auditorium. Computer simulation quickly demonstrates that anyone seated behind these in the boxes would have seen little of the action on the apron stage, and nothing at all of the scenic settings located on flats further upstage (Figure 11). The pilasters would also have hidden from the view of the rest of the audience, a sizeable proportion of those most high-ranking members seated in the boxes; which would have been quite unacceptable.

By closely examining both written and visual evidence for the layout of Drury Lane in the early eighteenth century, it becomes clear that the only major discrepancies with the plan suggested by Wren's damaged drawing do indeed relate to the use of the pilasters; in other respects the major details in the earlier drawing are confirmed by the later evidence (Thomas 1989:268–70). Using a second computer model it is possible to suggest how Wren modified his initial plan (presumably before the original version was actually built) in order to improve the functional effectiveness of the auditorium and its physical relationship to the stage area (see Thomas 1996 video).

In 1705 Sir John Vanbrugh (playwright and architect) built the Haymarket Theatre to his own design, boasting that it was unlike any other existing theatre (Thomas 1989: 73–7). No undisputed visual illustration of its interior exists. What is known is that it suffered from a number of design flaws that needed to be rectified within three years of the building's completion. However, from Colley Cibber's detailed written critique a number of vital clues emerge (see Thomas 1989: 75). These suggest that in his attempt to

Fig. 11. A 3D computer model of Wren's original design for the Drury Lane Theatre

fashion a classically 'pure' design, Vanbrugh created a semi-circular auditorium which curved well beyond the width of the proscenium opening. This, together with other recorded flaws, when simulated in a three-dimensional computer model, readily indicates why the initial layout was unsatisfactory (Figure 12). A significant proportion of the audience could neither see nor hear what was presented to them on stage.

In 1708 Vanbrugh was forced for financial reasons to relinquish control of the theatre. Under new management a number of substantial alterations were made to the building to remedy its defects. Again, relying upon contemporary descriptions and some later visual evidence, it is possible to create a model of what the altered theatre was like. This reveals that the changes completely wreck the visual purity of Vanbrugh's original design, but what has been lost in terms of purity of form has been gained in terms of functional effectiveness.

The Hellerau *Festspielhaus* and Appia's 'Rhythmic Spaces'

The modern theatre has also produced some notable and suggestive works of architecture, and the final example presented here is based on one of these, the *Festspielhaus* at the Garden City of Hellerau, near Dresden. Conceived by the theatre designer, theore-

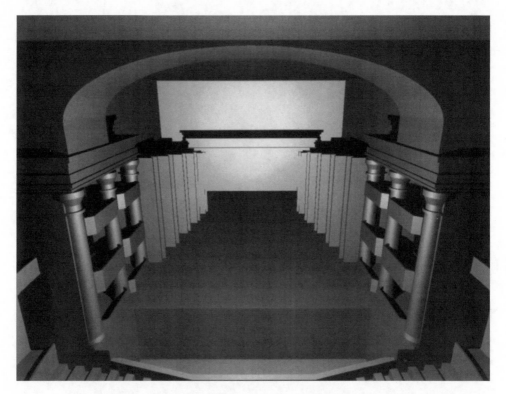

Fig. 12. A 3D computer model showing the stage and pit of Van Brugh's Haymarket Theatre

tician and aesthetic visionary Adolphe Appia, and built by the proto-Bauhaus architect Heinrich Tessenow, it was constructed in 1910 to house a school for 'Rhythmic Gymnastics', or *Eurhythmics*. Here the Hellerau *Bildungsanstalt* was engaged until the outbreak of the First World War in extraordinary and immensely influential experiments in the use of light, movement and space; those fundamental elements of theatrical art cited at the beginning of this paper (Giertz 1975). The innovative work at Hellerau has become almost legendary; some have seen it as marking the birth of the modern theatre, as well as contributing substantially to the early development of modern dance (e.g., Feudal 1960). The list of those who worked, studied or simply came to view exhibitions of its work reads like a 'who's who' of the most influential shapers of modern performance (see Beacham 1994: 79–137).

The centrepiece of the site was a large open hall which abolished the proscenium arch and raised stage. It was lit by thousands of lights installed behind translucent linen, operated centrally to radiate light which was orchestrated to express in space the emotional nuance of the music, and complement its physical embodiment as expressed both through the revolutionary abstract settings and the gestures and movements of the performers. In a word, '*Total Theatre*' (See Beacham 1992 video).

After the First World War the building was used as a recreational facility by the SS,

Fig. 13. Current state of the Hellerau Festspielhaus

and then after the Second, as a Soviet garrison until just 3 years ago. Symbolic of its extraordinary history, the *yin yang* symbol, international sign of Eurhythmics, was until recently displaced by the Red Star (Figure 13).

Recently after a long campaign an international organization, the Förderverein für die Europäische Werkstatt für Kunst und Kultur Hellerau, has been given responsibility both for the conservation and restoration of this building and its rededication as a site for advanced experimental performance (Festspielhaus Helleran, Karl Leibknechtstrasse 56 01109 Dresden). To assist its work a detailed three-dimensional electronic model of the site has been created. This was used to help win a highly competitive conservation grant for $250,000 from the J. Paul Getty Trust, and to secure the building's formal listing amongst the one hundred most important threatened architectural sites under the 'World Monument Watch' Programme (Burnham 1996: 26). The model is useful on several levels. It allows the viewer to 'de-construct' the building to show how, conceptually it was put

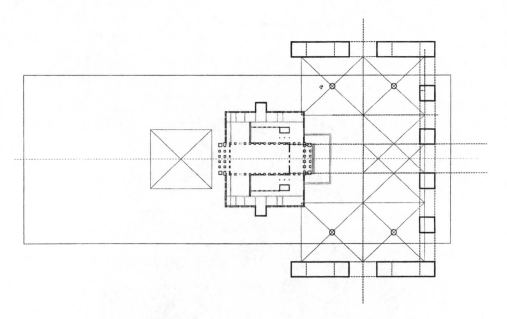

Fig. 14. Site plan showing the arrangement of buildings in the hellerau complex

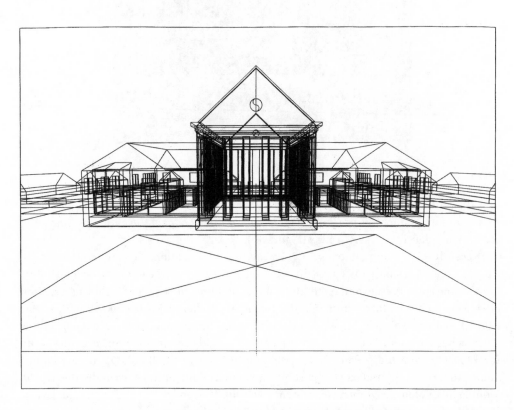

Fig. 15. A preliminary 3D model of the Hellerau Festspielhaus

together carefully drawing upon classical architectural precepts, as well as the particular scenic concepts of Adolphe Appia, which it everywhere embodies. The Institute at Hellerau was strongly influence by concepts which today would be termed 'holistic', and which sought to condition and modify at conscious and unconscious levels both the aesthetic perception and experience of well-being of those taking part in its activities. Indeed, a central tenet of its work was that visitors should no longer remain what Appia termed 'eternal spectators', but should themselves become actively engaged as the traditional barriers between performer and audience were progressively removed (Beacham 1994: 218–9). In using computer reconstruction to examine closely the layout of the *Festspielhaus* and its site, and to simulate movement within it, it emerges that well before visitors took their seat in its great hall, they had already in effect undergone a carefully structured, modulated (and quite deliberate) 'rhythmic' exercise as they approached the building, entered through its front portals, walked through its foyer and climbed the stairway to reach their destination (Figure 14).

Quite apart from revealing these intriguing insights into the aesthetic concepts 'embedded' in the building and conditioning the original visitor's experience of it, the model also assists those now undertaking its conservation. It invaluably enables them to examine the site in great detail in order to identify both the alterations which the original structure as first conceived has undergone in the course of its subsequent uses (the earliest drawings no longer exist), and to determine how the building in its current state may best be restored to its pristine condition, and conserved (Figure 15).

The model also extends into another related aspect of theatre historical research, by enabling the designs of Appia to be projected into a virtual reconstruction of an architectural space originally intended for them, and there to be examined and analysed while simulating the conditions under which they were first presented. In creating these settings Appia conceived of them not as autonomous pretty pictures, and still less as fictive backdrops or illustrations for the staging of conventional dramas. Rather as 'living space', they were intended to clarify the relationship between music, time, space and movement. Appia perceived that the way to bring these settings to life was by contrasting them with the human body. Their rigidity, sharp lines and angles, and immobility, when confronted by the softness, subtlety and movement of the body, would by opposition take on a kind of borrowed life (Giertz 1992). Moreover, by applying music and – crucially – carefully 'orchestrated' lighting to them, they could themselves convey psychological or emotional meaning to become not just static settings, but rather directly 'expressive elements' of theatrical art. This concept (embodying one of the fundamental principles of contemporary stage production) is one of several which has justified Appia's position as a 'prophet of the modern theatre' (Volbach 1968).

Computer simulation allows one both to illustrate this approach and to examine effects under different conditions. As part of unpublished research, Kent Goetz at Cornell University has recently taken examples of a series of designs which Appia termed 'rhythmic spaces', and demonstrated how, by modifying them with the application of various lighting conditions and textures, they become a virtual commentary on and extension of Appia's own theoretical analysis. Appia had pointed out in regard to these

Fig. 16. Rhythmic Space design of Adolphe Appia 1909

Fig. 17. Computer 3D model of a Rhythmic Space. (A colour version of this figure is at http://www.britac.ac.uk/pubs/it-schol)

designs that

> the active role of light developed naturally from a spatial arrangements which demanded it, and everything thereby took on the *appearance of expectancy*: the nature of the space made the presence of the body indispensable. By means of these designs I gradually achieved a purity of style which was composed for the most parts of lines and solid forms. The resistance they provide to the movement of the body complements its expressive quality and creates a three-dimensional effect. (Translated and quoted by Beacham 1994: 119).

The computer models are ideally suited not just to demonstrate different lighting conditions, but of course to present Appia's models not as flat designs, but as what he emphasized above all and which gave them their particular value: their intended solidity and three-dimensional quality (Figures 16–17).

Conclusion

They also provide an appropriate conclusion to this paper, which began by pointing out something that Appia was himself always at great pains to articulate: that the unchanging essence of an ancient or modern theatrical art (which he more than any other reformer wished to renew and return to its roots) consists of such primary expressive elements as space, light, form, movement and the human body. All but the last have now been opened up to intriguing and promising research through computer simulation, the furthest realms of which are not yet in sight. As for the simulation of that most fundamental and primal element of all – the living performer, that remains for us 'to eke out with our minds, or even – dare one suggest it in so cerebral a context? – articulate with our bodies.

References

Books and Articles

Almeida, E. (1980), *Forma Urbis Marmorea, Aggiornamento generale* (Rome).
Baltard, V. (1837), *Mémoire explicatif de la Restauration du Théâtre de Pomee* (Paris).
Beacham, R. (1992), *The Roman Theatre and its Audience* (Cambridge Mass.).
—— (1994), *Adolphe Appia: Artist and Visionary of the Modern Theatre* (Chur).
—— (1999), *Spectacle Entertainments of Early Imperial Rome* (New Haven, Conn.).
Bieber, M. (1961), *The History of the Greek and Roman Theater* (Princeton).
Burnham, B. (1996) (ed.), *World Monuments Watch* (New York).
Carettoni, G. (1961), 'Due nuovi ambienti dipinti sul Palatino', *Bolletino d'Arte*, 46: 189–99.
Capoferro Cencetti, A. (1979), 'Variazioni nel Tempo dell'identita funzionale di un monumento: Il Theatro di Pompeo', *Revista di Archeologia*, 3: 72–85.
Cerutti, S. and Richardson, L. (1989), 'Vitruvius on stage architecture and some recently discovered *Scaenae Frons* decorations', *Journal of the Society of Architectural Historians*, 48(2): 172–9.
Coarelli, F. (1972), 'Il complesso Pompeiano del Campo Marzio e la sua decorazione scultorea', *Rendiconti della Pontificia Accademia Romana di Archeologia*, 44: 99–122.
—— (1977), 'Ill Campo Marzio occidentale. Storia e topografia', *Mélanges de l'Ecole Française de Rome*, 89: 807–46.

De Franciscis, A. (1973), 'La villa romana di Oplontis', La Parola del Passato, 28: 453–66.

—— (1975), Pompeian Wall paintings in the Roman Villa of Oplontis (Recklinghausen).

De Michelis, M. (1991), Heinrich Tessenow (Stuttgart).

Dörpfeld, W. (1896), Das Griechische Theater (Athens).

FEMP: Fondation Européenne pour les Métiers du Patrimoine (1996), 'MINOTEC. New Technologies and Enhancement of Ancient Places of Performance' (Strasbourg).

Feudel, E. (ed.) (1960), In memoriam Hellerau (Freiburg im Breisgau).

Frezouls, E. (1983), 'La construction de Theatrum Lapideum et son contexte politique', Théâtre et Spectacles dans L'antiquité (Leiden).

Galassi Paluzzi, C., Giglioni, G. Q., Bartoli, A., Lugli, G., Marchetti-Longhi, G. and Collini, A. M. (1937), 'Il problema archeologico del Teatro di Pompeo', Capitolium, 12: 99–122.

Gamel, M. (1995), 'Review of Menander's The Woman from Samos, and Plautus' Casina', Didaskalia, 2.1 [URL: http://www.warwick.ac.uk/didaskalia/didaskalia.html].

Giertz, G. (1975), Kutus Ohne Gotter (Munich).

—— (1992), 'La Gymnastique rythmique au service du théâtre', Adolphe Appia ou le Renouveau de l'esthetique Théâtre (Lausanne).

Goldberg, S. (1996), 'The fall and rise of Roman tragedy', Transactions of the American Philogogical Society, 126: 265–86.

Gleason, K. (1994), 'Porticus Pompeiana: a new perspective on the first public park of Ancient Rome', Journal of Garden History, 14(1): 13–27.

Gruen, E. (1992), Culture and National Identity in Republican Rome (Ithaca).

Hamma, K. (1995), 'A Production of Plautus' Casina and Menander's Samia', Didaskalia, 2.3 [URL:http://www.warwick.ac.uk/didaskalia/didaskalia.html]

Hanson, J. (1959), Roman Theatre-temples (Princeton).

Holden, L. (1996), 'Virtual Pompeii', V.R. News, 5(1): 33.

Hornby, R. (1995), 'Review of Ancient Theatre at the Getty Museum', Hudson Review, 48(1): 113–14.

Ling, R. (1991), Roman Painting (Cambridge).

Little, A. (1971), Roman Perspective Painting and the Ancient Stage (Kennebunk, Maine).

Malandrino, C. (1977), Oplontis (Naples).

Marchetti-Longhi, G. (1960) 'Curia Pompeja', Studi Romani, 5: 642–59

Moormann, E. (1983), 'Rappresentazioni teatrali su scaenae frontes di quarto stile a Pompei', Pompeii Herculaneum Stabiae, 73–117.

Packer, J. (1997), The Forum of Trajan. A Study of The Monuments, 3 vols. (Berkeley Calif.).

Richardson, L (1987), 'A note on the architecture of the Theatrum Pompei', American Journal of Archeology, 91: 1236.

Richter, G. (1970), Perspective in Greek and Roman Art (London).

Sapelli, M. (1990), 'Restauro della statua di "Pompeo"', Bollettino di Archeologia, 56: 180–5.

Sear, F. (1993), 'The Scaenae Frons of the Theater of Pompey', American Journal of Archaeology, 97: 687–701.

Shirley, D. (1994), '"Samos", "Casina": Ancient Comedies With a Lot of Life', The Los Angeles Times, 20 Oct., 1994: F2.

Thomas, D. (1989) (ed.), Theatre in Europe: A Documentary History. Restoration and Georgian England 1660–1788 (Cambridge).

Volbach, W. (1968), Adolphe Appia, Prophet of the Modern Theatre (Middletown Conn.).

Videos

Beacham, R. (1987), *Ancient Theatre and its Legacy. Staging Roman Comedy: Pompeian Painting and Plautus* (Warwick).

—— (1992), *Ancient Theatre and its Legacy. Revolution and Rebirth: The Theatrical Reforms of Adolphe Appia* (Warwick)

Thomas, D. (1996), *Ancient Theatre and its Legacy. The Restoration Stage: From Tennis Court to Playhouse* (Warwick).

Commentary

MEG TWYCROSS

Department of English
University of Lancaster

As in a medieval scholastic debate, I am restricted as respondent to the topics introduced by the first speaker. So I cannot talk about three of the four areas of computing which seem particularly germane to theatre research, and which our York *Doomsday* Project is exploring. I cannot mention the uses of multimedia; nor may I talk about hypertext; I shall not even enter into the heady realms of interactive performance. (The reader will recognize the rhetorical device of *occupatio*, invented by late Roman orators for precisely such a situation as this.)

I must concentrate on the fourth, in which we share an interest: theatrical archaeology, the speculative restoration of vanished playing spaces. Both Professor Beacham and I have spent some time physically recreating these structures – though mine have been mostly on wheels – because theatrical space determines the nature of performance and vice versa. As a result we have both moved into computers.

As a tool, Virtual Reality (VR) has its attractions and its shortcomings. Our Theatre Studio Manager at Lancaster trains students on AutoCad, a standard set-design package. He confirms that drawing in 3D improves their clarity of vision and avoids some of the worst lunacies of unskilled 2D design. They can also judge perspective and scale, which is difficult with maquettes, where you always play Gulliver; and they can print off measured drawings.

For the researcher, it has the same advantages, with the addition that we have a mass of disparate data to feed in. Most is secondary evidence, visual and verbal: occasionally we have primary evidence, as with the 16th-century Valencia Corpus Christi pageant-waggons.

As Professor Beacham says, Information Technology provides us with the best tool we have had so far for testing our theories economically. Reification provides a 'proof by construction' – *proof* in both senses: 'confirmation', but also 'trial'. Once your theory is externalized in Virtual Reality (VR), it is there to be critiqued, first by yourself, then by others. You cannot, as in a verbal debate, defend your position by sneakily redefining your terms halfway: you have to alter your model. In theatre, in any case, our theories have to stand up to demonstration in a very material way: if my pageant waggon falls over, it will damage more than my professional pride. Which is why some of my best friends are engineers – and another reason why VR is useful: it provides a safe, immaterial, laboratory.

But Virtual Reality is not real, in some very significant ways. VR objects are built up of polygons. The processing of data therefore has to obey the laws of geometry: but it does not have to obey the laws of physics – such as gravity, or the impermeability of brick walls. This is apparently because the processing power needed to apply all the constraints of real life is so huge that no ordinary computer can currently cope with it: hence, by default, the popularity of Superman effects in video games. But it also means that in the virtual environment, the resurrected Christ could pass effortlessly through the wall of the pageant waggon; or that you could design a Roman theatre supported by a giant banana, and then tip it on its apex: and most programmes would let you.

And it looks very plausible. An elegant VR design can convince students, funding bodies, ourselves. This is dangerous in many ways. Especially with early theatre, we will never have all the necessary information. To be honest to ourselves and to others, we need to find some way of indicating where the gaps are in our data. There needs to be a decorum of signalling fakes. (Arthur Evans' Knossos springs to mind.)

Finally: how far are our results conditioned by our software, how far by our data, and how far by our own research backgrounds?

The assumption behind the handsome reconstructions we have been shown seems to be that all Roman theatres have a basic blueprint in common: an 'architectural template' which can be applied for verification. This may well have been true of the Roman stage. So here the computer is being used to determine a norm or, if you like, to apply Ockham's Razor.

My approach and that of my colleagues is that the computer allows us to produce a whole range of possible solutions, and then weigh – and, by using manipulable objects, allow students to weigh – which one is the most *likely* in those particular circumstances, while still being aware that there are other options. VR, and re-creation in general, does provide a test-bed, but it cannot prove that your theory is right: it can only show that it is not impossible. This undermines the whole wishful assumption of research so far, that you can come up with a 'correct' solution. But then I know that the York *Doomsday* play (of which we have no pictures) could not have been produced on the Antwerp *Doomsday* waggon (of which we do). Moreover, the production details of the York Plays changed over the years, just as, on the micro level, no one theatrical performance is identical with any other. So my research background suggests multiplicity of solutions rather than uniformity, and Ockham's Razor is irrelevant. Is this because our source material differs? or because we have been working in hypertext and Professor Beacham has been working with construction packages?

So I would like to start the discussion by asking him what software he uses, and how he uses it to establish his 'real' from his 'fantasy' architecture.

Art History and the Digital Image

WILLIAM VAUGHAN

Department of History of Art
Birkbeck College

Abstract. After a review of the resistance of art historians to computerisation, the necessity of such a move is recognized. Art history is unique in terms of imagery, in that the image is its text. This poses two problems – the importance of the quality of the image and the method of codification, since there appears no discrete equivalent to the letter, number or musical note. However, the process of ditigization does produce such an equivalent, the individual picture element (pixel). This process provides stability, and the product is readily transferable and manipulable, permitting the analyses of image. One problem for the scholar is access to digital sources because of copyright and the relative lack of resources of good quality. Attempts are being made to develop expert systems, but one system described, though successful, is very specific in its application. A possible complementary 'bottom up' approach is represented by the author's Morelli system, which provides a simple unique identifier for each image, thus facilitating searches of catalogues of digital imagery. The paper also explores the role of multi-media and the Internet, the latter particularly for access to digital sources and for communication between scholars. Digital sources have the potential for formal and structural analysis and hence the consideration of form, a return to the original emphasis in art history, replacing the modern tendency to see images purely iconically.

Historical background

Like every other group of scholars, art historians have found themselves making increasing use of computers in recent years. The use has grown exponentially, particularly since the arrival of the latest generation of Internet facilities provided via the World Wide Web. But it remains highly questionable what the implications of this situation are. Is it simply the application of a new tool, a useful aid for gathering and processing information which enhances existing potential, but does not basically change the nature of the subject or the conceptual patterns of its practitioners? Or is it a fundamental reordering of a discipline, in which interests and modes of interpretation will become irrevocably changed?

Perhaps one of the most potent forces at work at present is the fear of what might happen. It is no exaggeration to say that, by and large, the response to computerization in the history of art – as in other humanities subjects – has been defensive. At its crudest level, it is seen as the invasion of raw technology into the refined sanctum of the arts – yet another stage in the ongoing struggle between the opposing practices of the sciences and the arts. Ever since computers first began to emerge outside the confines of pure scientific research in the 1950s, there have been stories told of their destructive effects – sometimes comic, sometimes horrific. Yet despite this, more and more humanities scholars use computers. Their application is as inevitable as that of any other modern technological advance. Like these other advances, too, the pressure for their use has been primarily economic. The academic community does not like to be reminded how dependent it is upon the broader demands of the economies in which it is situated. But the bare truth of the matter is that the new technology is part of the contemporary world and the academic scholar has to adapt his practices to accommodate it. The question is not 'should this happen?', but 'in what ways will it happen?'.

It is here that the debate is at its most extreme. Those who have been involved most closely in the application of the new technology in the humanities have pointed out frequently how much is to be lost by a failure to engage in the issue in a positive manner. At the economic level this comes down to the lack of adequate resources being made available and a failure to develop appropriate techniques. There are many computer scientists who stress how much innovative work there is to be done in devising new processes to aid research in the humanities. There are places indeed where such work does occur in an exemplary manner – as for example in the new methods for text analysis and image research that have been pioneered by the Humanities Computing Centre at the University of Oxford (BLRD 1993:4). But important though these are, they touch only a small part of the problem. In an age of increasing networking of systems and enhancement of multimedia potential, there needs to be a more global response to ensure that humanities research in general gains access to appropriate resources and uses these fruitfully.

These are pragmatic reasons for the engagement – and probably the ones that will be most powerful agents for change. But it should also be remembered that there is an intellectual basis as well. The view of computers as a philistine intrusion into the sanctum of the humanities is somewhat misleading from this point of view. For while a confrontation between arts and sciences practices might always be present, this is in fact more of a dialogue than a disagreement. For more than a generation now, it has been understood that modes of scientific enquiry are as engaged with the conditions of a given society as are those of 'artistic' culture. These areas are never totally divorced from each other. Indeed they share fundamental perceptions far more often than is commonly imagined. This is certainly true in the case of the computer, which is very much a product of the prevailing intellectual practices of western societies.

It is, of course, perfectly possible to make use of computers without engaging with these issues. It is not necessary to know how they work, or what they are doing with a scholar's material, to profit from their services. This is, in effect, how most scholars use them, but they should also recognize that when they do so they are working at second hand. They are making use of processes devised by others, usually for other purposes. All too often in the humanities, scholars accept what is on offer without thinking about whether they could not in fact be doing something quite different with the machine, something that might in fact be much more relevant to their inherent modes of enquiry.

Computers and the image

Imaging techniques; storage and analysis

Many of the problems that are raised by computers for art historians are the same as those for other scholars in the humanities. Those relating to text analysis, databases, provision of information via the Internet are no different from those encountered in other scholarly disciplines. However, the situation is different in the case of imagery.

At first sight this might not seem to be such a difference, since visual information is used in a wide number of other disciplines. In the sciences, of course, highly sophisticated image recognition and management techniques have been developed in areas such as geography and medicine. In the arts the image is used as a matter of fact in archaeology and increasingly by the historian. But while admitting all this, the art historian has had two particular problems with the image up to now.

The first is the question of quality. This is a difficult one to put across, as it smacks of connoisseurship; but the central point is that the image is the *text* for the art historian. Other scholars use images by way of illustration or documentation – to reveal evidence about a specific point. But the art historian explores the image as a phenomenon. There is, ultimately, no substitute for exploring the image directly. This has led to art historians treating the reproduction in a certain way. They see its function as being analogical, and require it to simulate as closely as possible the experience of confronting the work of art directly. Early computer imagery came a poor second to conventional photography from this point of view, a circumstance that has led to a prejudice against the medium that is only now beginning to dissolve.

The second problem is more conceptual. One of the most stimulating aspects of computer technology is the way in which it employs a process of codification that, while being mechanical and therefore in some sense limited, is nevertheless capable of translating the codes of traditional forms of communication. In the first instance the computer was used to simulate the codes of mathematics – to such an extent that some people still believe that computers work fundamentally by calculation (which they do not). Then it became adapted to handle the conventions of the alphabet as a means of accessing the structures of writing. Since music – like writing – used a codified form of notation, it was not long before this, too, became a field for computerized analysis. But what of the image? While theorists might interpret images as forms of codified communication, they manifestly do not depend upon a discrete set of conventions for their transcription. In the jargon of the age, the traditional image, however made, is 'analogue'. It is constructed by a process of simulation without the use of invariant coded sub-units. There is no equivalent of the letter, the number or the note in the traditional image. This situation has seemed to make the possibility of 'automated' pictorial analysis comparable to that used in linguistic, literary and musical studies unattainable. There would always have to be a phase of human intervention, of interpretative codification, before the analysis could proceed.

The digital image

Although this seems to be the case, the computer does in fact offer a fascinating possibility which has only recently begun to be explored. This is the fact that the very process whereby the computer stores and produces images does provide a type of codification. Computers can only work by means of the manipulation of symbols, coded assemblages of digits; to manipulate an image the computer has to transform the image into such a set of codes. This is done through the process of digitization. Essentially what digitization does is to break down any pictorial phenomenon into a set of discreet units. Each of these units will have a coded value (typically relating to hue and/or luminosity in the case of a picture) and an 'address' – that is a set of co-ordinates that give the precise location of the unit, or 'pixel' (picture element) as it is called. By subdividing an image into a series of 'pixels' each with an address and value (or set of values), the digitization process does, in effect, create a 'text' out of an image.

This might seem to be a purely formal point, but in fact it is much more. There are three fundamental effects that emerge as a result of this process that have implications for the subsequent usage of the image.

i) The first is **stability** of record. Once the visual impression has been codified, it is unchanging in the way that letters and numbers are unchanging. No longer is the record of an image dependent upon its actual effect – as it is, say, in a conventional photograph of an image; as long as the code is expressed in symbols (for example, those of letter or number), then the physical changes to those symbols have no effect on their meaning. Once captured digitally the image can be relayed to another medium – it could even be printed out as a text – without the information deteriorating in any way. This stability does, of course, present one practical problem, namely, that to be made visible the code has to be 're-interpreted' by another machine. But this is a practical problem that does not affect the integrity of the record. This stability has been one of the reasons why so much interest has been expressed in the digital image by restorers and conservationists, but it has implications beyond. All art history departments, for example, have the constant problem of obsolescence in their slides. The digital image is one that does not deteriorate

ii) The second important feature of the digital image is its **transferability**. It can be disseminated in a way that no conventional photographic image can.

iii) The third important feature is its **manipulability**. In other words, that it is possible to perform analysis on digital images. This is interesting for both identity and analysis.

The ability to perform specific calculations on a digital image makes it a powerful tool in reconstruction, for example, in the reconstruction of partially preserved three-dimensional objects. One recent example of this is the use of computer modelling to reconstruct the original appearance of Inigo Jones' facade of the Whitehall Palace (Hart *et al.* 1993). There have also been extremely impressive uses of the computer image to aid the infilling of lost parts of paintings – such as that used to help reconstruct the Cambia Madonna damaged in the Florence flood of 1967, and to penetrate beneath the surface of pictures in a far more accurate way than is provided by the conventional use of x-rays or infra-red photography (SBSV 1984).

Yet the problem remains: how much such work can be made available to scholars outside the specialized laboratory. Here the problem seems to hang on the accessibility of the digital image itself. Very gradually museums and other custodians of pictures are beginning to address this problem, with a view to making such imagery available either on-line, or on computer disk form. There are, as well, 'Rolls Royce' solutions – notably that of the pioneering Vasari project, which is in the process of digitizing works in the Louvre, the Neue Pinakothek in Munich and the National Gallery in London to the level of 30 lines per millimetre – a standard that would meet the most exacting professional requirements (Figure 1) (Hamber 1991). At the same time many commercial companies are offering to produce digitized images of works in museum collections of a lower quality that would still be useful for general purposes.

As yet the pool of good quality digital images limited. It is likely to remain so until a larger demand is evident and problems of copyright have been resolved.

Copyright is a great and as yet intractable problem. The possibility of more rapid and universal provision of visual imagery via the Internet has exacerbated an already tense situation. It is not surprising that those who have a vested interest in a picture or its reproduction should seek to gain some revenue when it is being used, but charges

Fig. 1. Detail of a Vasari high resolution digital reproduction of the Arnolfini Portrait. (A colour version of this figure is at http://www.britac.ac.uk/pubs/it-schol)

suggested at the moment are of a kind that would make normal scholarly activities virtually impossible. On the other hand, the temptations for piracy have never been greater. Even when a user is not deliberately setting out to break copyright, this may well happen through the simple inability to find out the identity of all who might have a copyright. Typically this can involve the owner of the picture, the artist or artist's family, the photographer and (in the case of a reproduced work) the publisher. The way forward here is to establish some kind of clearing agency but no-one has come forward here who is prepared to operate at a level that would make scholarly research viable. Those involved in managing copyright are on the whole too accustomed to the huge sums that can be commanded from commercial users, such as television and film studios, to be prepared to contemplate the kind of modest operation that would be appropriate for scholarly usage.

Digitzed reproductions and pictorial analysis

Digitized reproductions and pictorial analysis are an area that has immense potential. As noted , the digital image offers the possibility of picture recognition and picture analysis by automated means. It will be necessary to develop some form of picture recognition by motif and visual form (as opposed to by textual description) if the true potential of visual databases is to be exploited.

There are many schemes being planned. To a large extent they are dependent upon experiments conducted by psychologists into pictorial recognition (Anderson 1964: Kohonen 1988: Simson 1990). But there are also more pragmatic approaches available which might in the end be of more practical use.

Attempts have been made to use this potential to create 'expert systems' that will simulate the formal elements used by certain connoisseurs to identify various artistic schools and individuals. In the University of Bergen Kroepelien (1995) has developed the means for making an 'expert system' out of the criteria used by Garrison for the identification of Medieval Italian wall paintings (Figure 2). Such systems are important, not just for testing the ability of the machine to simulate the expertise of a connoisseur, but also for testing the degree of consistency that might exist within a particular method. This is not just to test the reliability of a particular scholar. It is also a test of the assumption that formal features are sufficient to characterize a style. Either style is a formal quality, which possesses certain constant objectively observable features, or it is not. In the case of Garrison, Kroepelien had to construct a set of principles from the scattered observations made over a wide range of articles. In fact, the attempt proved remarkably successful. Not only did she succeed in finding a series of clearly designated determinators of style which seemed to support the notion that style could (at least in the case of early Italian murals) be described in terms of formal constants – such as the line shapes used to describe drapery, hair and other such features. She was also able to develop the means by which these could be read unequivocally by the machine. The problem behind her experiment was that the process proved enormously time-consum-

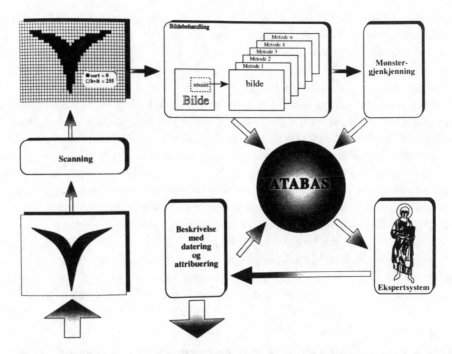

Fig. 2. Illustration from B. Kropelien's Fra Stil til Agoritme

ing. If her expert system could be adapted easily to fit other situations, then it might be practical to adopt it – much in the way that expert systems have been adopted to help doctors in the diagnoses of certain diseases (in fact it was a medical expert system that formed the model for her own). But the criteria that Garrison used for his analysis of style were peculiar to the particular type of painting that he was investigating. In themselves these would not be appropriate for art forms dependent upon different formal and thematic criteria.

Kroepelien's study is important for opening up a set of problems and suggesting solutions for them. One can only hope that more investigations of this kind will take place. If they are successful, they could revolutionize current thinking about the notion of style, and return one once again to the 'scientific' connoisseurship that was proposed at the end of the last century. But while this process is taking place, there is still the possibility of using simpler means to achieve some less ambitious forms of picture recognition. Whereas Kroepelien's approach is 'top-down', working from a developed concept towards implementation, such an approach would be 'bottom up', working from the simple practical tools available towards increasingly more complex achievements.

This is essentially the principle behind Morelli, the picture recognizing system that has been developed by the author. It works on the principle of deriving a unique identifier of the smallest and simplest possible kind for each picture. This identifier is linked to a more sophisticated digitized version, which allows the possibility of searching for further characteristics. Whereas Kroepelien's system is built upon a highly-specialized knowledge of the works of art being investigated, Morelli works in a totally arbitrary way, deriving similar sets of data from any image presented to it by entirely automated means.

Morelli has proved effective in being able to get a machine to recognize other reproductions of the same work of art by a simple matching process. It has further been able to range these with close variants of the pictures being explored (Figure 3). While this might seem to be of limited use in the area of style analysis, it has proved to be of practical use as a visual tool for exploring picture archives that have been digitized. Since the unique identifiers created for each image are remarkably small – using no more than 67 bytes per image – it is practical to have the identifiers stored in fields in parallel with textual information in the database managing a visual archive. This also raises the fruitful possibility of making combined text and image searches.

Essentially Morelli functions in a manner similar to the program that manages a text database. In a text database management program, a key word is entered as the basis for a search of the database. In Morelli an image is used to search through a visual archive. The image can be a reproduction scanned in from 'outside' the system, a sketch image

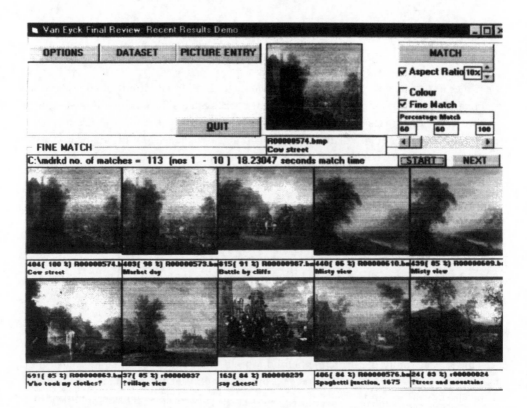

Fig. 3. Example of a Morelli Search

drawn by the user, or an image that has been drawn out of the database itself. If, for example, a researcher had come across an unidentified picture and wanted to see if anything similar was already recorded in a picture archive, the image and use could be scanned in and used to search the visual archives for the nearest related works stored in them. Alternatively the researcher could 'block out' a design and see whether the database had anything of a similar kind. Or it would be possible to select an image already in the database and see if there was anything similar that had been done by some other artist.

The Morelli system has been tested on a group of 2,000 images, and results have been encouraging (Vaughan 1992). However, its full value would be realized only if it were applied to a large archive of digitized images and this has not yet happened. At the moment, Morelli is being integrated into the Van Eyck system devised under the sponsorship of the European Commission to provide a standard for constructing on-line database for visual archives. This system is being developed in collaboration with the Witt Library, the Courtauld Institute, University of London, and partners in the Netherlands and the Irish Republic (Hourihane 1995).

The Morelli system differs from other picture-matching systems currently available commercially in a number of ways (Grout forthcoming). First, it works with the overall configuration of a picture, rather than by searching for motifs within it. This is useful when one is looking at works of art, which have a fixed appearance and (usually) a determined edge. It is not so useful when images are being used principally as a description of objects rather than as important in their own right. A journalist wishing to survey a collection of photographs for an image of the Pope would not find this system useful; an art historian searching an archive to spot a particular religious painting would. It is because Morelli measures at its basic level only the characteristics of the total picture that it is able to make accurate matches with so little information. This makes it practical for it to scan very large archives of several million images in a way that other searching techniques, dependent as they are on large bodies of data and highly complex algorithms, cannot. The second major difference is that it focuses exclusively on shape and tone, and ignores colour. The reasons for this are purely pragmatic. First, most existing photo-graphic archives of works of art are predominantly of images in black and white. It would therefore be useless to use colour matching to scan them. Second, colour reproduction is so notoriously varied, that it would be impractical to use colour matching as a way of linking different reproductions of the same objects. Most commercially-available systems use colour as matching criteria, but they are dealing typically with colour photographs of a particular type, where colour matching may be effective. User trials have, however, suggested that even in these cases, colour matching appears to be limited in its effectiveness.

It may be that the two different approaches represented by Kroepelien's research and the Morelli system could be brought together. The low level data of Morelli can be linked to higher level digital reproductions in which more sophisticated formal features could be explored, but such an experiment is in the future. As yet developments in this area are restricted, but the potential is immense.

Hypertext and multimedia

The procedures discussed above are all individual techniques, to be used for specific purposes. But the arrival of multimedia systems – in which text, image, film and sound can all be brought together and managed on a personal computer – has stimulated the interest in providing systems in which all these operations can be managed as a single process.

This concept is epitomized in the notion of 'hypertext', a term that has become highly suggestive since it was coined by Theodore H Nelson in the 1960s. Hypertext is a text that is read in a non-linear manner, and which can be accessed by many different routes. This possibility has entranced a number of people working in the art historical field, such as Landow at Brown University and Veltman at the Marshall McCluhan Institute, Toronto. Landow (1991a) has published a series of studies on the relevance of hypertext for critical studies. He has also addressed the issue more specifically in relationship to the potential of uniting the new hypertext with the new generation of digital imagery and with networking. 'Computer hypermedia, which produces texts in ways that differ fundamentally from those created by printing, therefore offers the promise of threat of thus changing the conception and practice of art history.' (Landow 1991b:77)

One implication of the new flexibility that such methods provides in the employment of images has been noted by Benedictis (1994), who has used multimedia in under-graduate teaching. It removes the pressure to teach the subject using the dialectical process established by Wölfflin and others in the late nineteenth century, namely the comparative method of lecturing using two-screen projection. In multimedia applications a user can move from one to any number of images simultaneously, thus allowing for a far richer range of types of analysis and association.

In his publications Landow has given convincing and impressive accounts of how hypermedia can be used to gather and collate a plethora of data. This facility certainly turns the computer into a powerful tool for the exploration of data and for making new types of connections.

Landow's work is based on practical example at Brown University, where he uses a hypertext system developed on an Apple Macintosh personal computer. In an article 'Connected images: hypermedia and the future of art historical studies' (1991b) he gives an account of how his system will enable a scholar to bring to bear a seemingly endless body of information about his investigations. For example, he mentions a case where an art historian might wish to link a motif in one picture with that of another. The picture in question here is Holman Hunt's Lady of Shallott.

> Looking at William Holan Hunt's large version of the subject, which is now in Hartford, Connecticut, our art historian wishes to determine how closely the lady's discarded clogs resemble those in paintings by Van Eyck and Memlinc, so she searches through folders until she finds reproductions of the relevant works. Then, using Intermedia's recently developed capacity to permit full-text searches, she uses the computer mouse to begin one. When a dialogue box appears, she types 'Hunt Van Eyck Memlinc Composition' and after waiting twenty to thirty-seconds, she receives a hierarchically arranged list of all documents on intermedia ... in which these terms appear. (Landow, 1991b:89).

All of this is very impressive, and lends substance to Landow's conclusion that,

> clearly, working in a hypertext environment permits the scholar to obtain information far more rapidly than has been otherwise possible (assuming, of course, that the textual or visual information appears on the system), and it also permits the scholar to make annotations, comments, and working notes. Most important, a hypermedia environment allows art historians far more easily to do what a recent study (AHIP 1988) suggests is their primary scholarly act – perceiving, recording and analysing relations among large amounts of data.

All this may be very true, but there are also problems. No-one would deny the uses to which hypermedia can be put. Landow's global approach is one that has been adopted by others. Veltman has similar ambition for this SUMS system (System for Universal Media Searching) at Toronto. In other fields, classical studies have greatly benefited from Harvard University's Project Perseus, which includes an impressive textual and visual database for Classical Greek art, as well as for other aspects of Ancient Greek civilization. Historians are developing similar types of hypermedia workbenches, such as the Hides project at the University of Southampton, or the Cleio database devised by Thaller (1992) at Gottingen. Nevertheless, some problems remain.

First is that phrase of Landow's '(assuming, of course, that the textual or visual information appears on the system)'. This is an obvious limitation, but it begs the question – who is going to input such information? The problem might not be so acute in teaching – where it can be seen as an extension of the concept of preparing material. But in the context of research there is an obvious limitation. Most researchers are involved in one way or another in 'primary' material which, by definition, lives somewhere outside the system. It may be a document in an undeciphered hand in some distant archive. It may be some previously unobserved part of an ancient building in an out of the way place. However good the system is at offering an unheard of number of new possibilities and connections with the data already available, it cannot provide what no-one has gathered.

Networking and the World Wide Web

It may well be that this situation will change through the possibilities offered by networking. As has already been discussed, impressive numbers of collections and archives are now entering material about their holdings onto computer systems of one sort or another. Through the process of networking, it is possible for one individual user in theory to gain access to any of these from his personal machine. Even now, it is possible to see breathtaking examples of the transfer of such information, such as the delivery of a high definition reproduction of an image stored in New York in a matter of seconds in London. There is, it is true, a host of logistical problems that still have to be resolved, for example the sheer cost of the venture. At present huge sums of money are being poured in by governments and other agencies keen for these processes to be developed. But this cannot go on for ever, and someday individual users will have to start paying the cost. Then there are problems to do with the compatibility of the different systems in which data are stored. There is no standard at the moment – although standards are being hotly debated (Roberts 1988). It may be that standards will be firmly established in the end, but it will be a difficult business. There will always be the nagging feeling that, whatever standard has been adopted, some kind of data will have had to be distorted to accommodate it. Finally, for objects, at least, there are horrendous problems of copyright. It may be that in the end principal holders of images and reproductions will be persuaded that it is in their interests to allow images to move through the ether with the speed and mutliplicity that will make true networked investigation a possibility. But most at present are unwilling to sign away rights to what seems to them to be a potential gold mine. Without such agreements the cost of any but the simplest searching will be prohibitive for the average academic user.

Undoubtedly the development of the World Wide Web over the past few years has had a great effect both on freeing up information in general and of making images more generally available for usage. With the emergence of the Web, it is possible for every user to set up a graphics environment on a 'page. Anyone who can use a scanner can thereby communicate images throughout the world. Already vast banks of images have been made available in this form, for example, by Michael Greenhalgh at the National University of Australia. While problems of copyright still exist, the technical difficulties involved in monitoring them have become so large as to be virtually uncontrollable. For the private user, at least, it has never been so easy to become a pirate. Quality is equally hard to monitor, in all sense of the word, but several helpful indexing systems have been set up to guide users towards useful resources, such as those at the Art History Research Centre. Such resources can easily be found by browsing through the World Wide Web. It remains to be seen whether this monitoring process will eventually be brought together into a centralized system.

Even if all these problems are resolved, it will remain the case that multimedia and the Internet will have little to offer in the acquisition of primary archival research material, however helpful it is for subsequent investigation.

This does not mean that scholars should not make use of such resources. Apart from anything else, the World Wide Web offers unrivalled new powers for sharing information and for the development world wide of special interest groups, which can hold online conferences and seminars, and can comment on each others research prior to its appearance in more conventional published form. All this is admirable, and will undoubtedly help to facilitate both teaching and research.

But none of this obviates the continued need to conduct primary research at the traditional archival level. Multimedia and Internet facilities should be used like other computer applications, as a tool, and not as a total environment that subsumes a scholar's whole working practice. The sheer ability of multimedia to present multiple choices should not conceal from scholars the analytical processes of which the computer is capable of, some of which were outlined above in the discussion on the image.

It is one of the ironies of the subject that digitization does bring within the art historian's grasp the possibility of formal and structural analyses that have been carried out by literary scholars and musicologists. But to do so, it would be necessary for art historians to return to the consideration of the significance of form. In modern studies – under the heavy influence of linguistics, the tendency has been to see images purely iconically – as though the formal basic unit of a picture was the interpretable sign, rather than existing at a more primitive level of signification, that driven by the interpretation of form. This is ironic since the whole structure of history of art as an independent discipline with its own particular contribution to knowledge was based initially on the scientific analysis of form of the generation of Morelli and Wolfflin. It remains to be seen whether the art historian will now be tempted to return to this more primal area of pictorial analysis with the aid of the new process of picture analysis that the computer is offering.

References

Anderson, A. R. (1964) (ed.), *The Mechanical Concept of Mind* (London).

AHIP (1988), *Object Image Inquiry: The Art Historian at Work*. Getty Art Historical Information Program, (Santa Monica, CA).

Benedictis, E. de (1995), 'Teaching with multimedia in the art history undergraduate classroom', *Computers and the History of Art*, 5(1):, 53–64.

BLRD (1993), British Library Research and Development Report 6097, *Information Technology in Humanities Scholarship* (London) p.4 ff.

EVA (forthcoming), *Electronic Imaging and the Visual Arts* Conference Papers, National Gallery, 24–6 July 1996 (London).

Grout, C. (forthcoming) 'From "Virtual Librarian" to "Virtual Curator', in EVA (forthcoming).

Hamber, A. (1991), 'The Vasari Project', *Computers and the History of Art*, 1(2): 3–19.

Hart, V., Day, A. and Cook, D. (1993), 'Conservation and computers: a reconstruction of Inigo Jones's Original Whitehall Banqueting House, London c. 1620', *Computers and the History of Art*, 4(1): 65–9.

Hourihane, C. (1995), 'The Van Eyck Project. Information exchange in art libraries', *Computers and the History of Art*, 5(1): 25–41

Katzen, M. (1991) (ed.), *Scholarship and Technology in the Humanities*, (British Library, London).

Kohonen, T. (1988), 'An introduction to neural computing', *Neural Network Magazine*, 5(1): 10–17.

Kroepelien, B. (1995), *Fra Stil til Algoritme* (Bergen).

Landow, G. (1991a), *Hypertext; The Convergence of Contemporary Critical Theory and Technology*, (Baltimore, Md). 1991.

—— (1991b), 'Connected images: hypermedia and the future of art historical studies'. In Katzen (ed.). 77–94.

Lyotard, J. F. (1987) *The Post-Modern Condition* (London).

Roberts, D. A. (1988), *Collections Management for Museums*. Museum Documentation Association. (Cambridge).

SBSV (1984) Soprintendenza ai Beni e Storici de Venezia, 'Riflettoscopia All'Infrarosso Computerizzato', *Quaderni della Soprintendenza ai Beni e Storici de Venezia*, 48–53.

Simpson, P. K. (1990), *Artificial Neural Systems* (New York).

Thaller, M. (1992), (ed.), *Images and Manuscripts in Historical Computering* (St Katharinen).

Vaughan, W. (1992), 'Automated picture referencing: a further look at Morelli', *Computers and the History of Art*, 2(2): 7–18.

Commentary

ERIC FERNIE

Cortauld Institute of Art
University of London

My comments on Professor Vaughan's paper fall under the two heads of Opportunities and Problems, each subdivided into Quality, Access and Analysis.

Opportunities

Quality. This is perhaps the most important desideratum for art historians given that the image is our primary source. With the right hardware for recording and retrieving (from the Leaf lamina camera to the high-resolution Visual Display Unit (VDU) digitized images can be of the very highest quality. Combined with the stability of its stored image this technique should therefore be superior to all others for recalling images, whether in the form of slides for lectures or prints for sale.

Access. The market offers an increasing number of ways of gaining access to information concerning the visual arts. Databases range from collections of paintings or manuscripts to compilations of moulding profiles, presented either as raw data or accompanied by extensive catalogues in hypertext, while interactive programs in multi-media reconstruct how objects might have been experienced by those who made and used them. All of these are increasingly available both on-line and on CD-ROM, though more are relevant to teaching than to research.

Analysis. The transmutation of the image into digital form carries revolutionary implications for the history of art since, as Professor Vaughan says, the work of art thereby changes from something which is experienced into something which can be manipulated, like a text. This raises the possibility that it might be possible to quantify styles by breaking them down into their component parts, as in Dr Brit Kroepelien's programme based on the Garrison Collection of Italian images or in the development of a search tool like Birkbeck's Morelli program.

Problems

Quality. Opinions differ over the extent to which we can achieve high quality storing and copying of images, and film still holds the edge for certain kinds of specialized publication.

Access. The hardware available may not be good enough to enable the data to be used to best advantage; conversely, if the technology with which the information was stored has become obsolete, it may no longer be possible to retrieve it. In the case of multimedia, the reconstruction can seriously mislead (though this may be no more than a sophisti-cated version of the poor or deteriorated colour slide).

Analysis. Programs for reading or recognizing shapes have not progressed as far as had been hoped. Subject recognition still depends on descriptions in the form of words or codes being supplied by the laborious inputting of data, as with the Iconclass system.

Experience also suggests that style is very difficult to establish on a quantifiable basis. The sorts of criteria which work (such as amount of yellow paint, distribution of shaded areas) can produce results, but it is difficult to assess their reliability and they run the risk of including irrelevant material in the calculations. Where more sophisticated criteria have been tried, the art-historical model on which they are based may not convince the researcher. The task should be easier with architecture, where component parts of buildings are identifiable by definition, but here again we should note the problems encountered by scholars such as Frankl and Harvey who have attempted to define the Gothic style in terms one major architectural feature. This may, however, be an overly pessimistic assessment, especially given the success which has been achieved in speech technology research.

Practicalities. At present the costs of services such as the Internet and Superjanet are reasonable; there is no reason to suppose that they will remain so. Those who own copyright over visual material should be wary of relinquishing it in exchange for, for example, digitization of the collection and distribution of the resulting CD. Digitized systems suffer from the disadvantage of always being able to provide an answer, which, given the garbage in, garbage out principle, may be no answer at all.

Training is essential if we are not to spend swathes of time unprofitably 'exploring' the possibilities of the digitized world. We shall get full value from our computers only if our software is tailored, which demands a high level of expertise and the diverting of time, energy and talent into learning the relevant computing skills. Equally, ergonomic problems such as repetitive strain injury and posture should form part of any competent training regime.

Conclusion

The effect of the digital revolution on the humanities will no doubt be extensive, but computer programs may remain tools aiding a pre-existing process, rather than goads to the formulation of a new kind of discipline.

The impact of information technology on legal scholarship

RICHARD SUSSKIND

Centre for Law,
University of Strathclyde

Abstract. The paper summarizes and explains the impact that information technology (IT) has had so far on the conduct of two traditional branches of legal scholarship: legal exposition and legal studies. Although it is suggested that the impact to date has been slight, it is claimed that affordable emerging technologies and shifting attitudes will result, in years to come, in far greater usage in both these branches of legal scholarship. It is also argued that IT will itself bring about a fundamental shift in paradigm in the provision of legal services, a shift which will radically transform the emphasis and scope of legal exposition and will raise fundamental issues for legal studies about the nature of law. This shift in paradigm is clarified in two ways: first, by reference to the changes in the information substructure in society, as progress is made from a print-based industrial society to an IT-based information society; and, second, in the context of movement along a legal information continuum on which information technologies are positioned between written legal sources and human legal experts. The paper concludes by demonstrating the limitations inherent in any legal information system.

The impact of IT on legal exposition and legal studies

Most legal scholarship belongs to one of two broad, overlapping categories. One category can be termed legal exposition (or legal science) and this is devoted to providing statements of what the law is at particular moments in time. A legal textbook which seeks to describe the current rules and principles of the English law of contract is one example of legal exposition. The second category of legal scholarship, which might be called legal studies, seeks to assess and clarify the role of law in society. Illustrations of this second category are legal philosophy, the sociology of law, legal history and legal anthropology.

It has been argued for over twenty five years by leading commentators in the field of computers and law that information technology (IT) could have a profound impact on legal exposition (Tapper 1973, Bing and Harvold 1977). Early research and development focused largely on the use of full text legal information techniques for the retrieval of potentially relevant primary source material (legislation and case law). It transpired, however, that these early legal information systems were to exert very little influence on those who were the authors of secondary sources in the Scottish and English legal systems. While legislation and case law have, in principle, been more widely available to legal scholars through a variety of legal information retrieval systems, the best known of which is Lexis, the reality was that few have chosen to use the facilities. Through the 1980s, this was frequently noted by the commercial distributors of these systems.

This lack of uptake by legal scholars was generally attributed to two factors (Susskind 1987). First, these systems required dedicated hardware which was not, in the event, widely available and easily accessible to the academic legal community, and the technology was costly, difficult to use and physically located beyond scholars' usual working environments. More fundamentally, full text retrieval systems provided an inappropriate model for legal research, resulting in crucial sources not being retrieved or an excess of irrelevant materials being identified. The occurrence of keywords within documents was recognized to be an insufficient criterion of relevance in the search for relevant legal sources (Tapper 1982).

More recently, especially since 1994, the increasing and widespread interest in the Internet and the World Wide Web in the academic legal community provides some corroboration for this view of the shortcomings of legal information retrieval systems. The availability, on a global basis, of vast quantities of legal materials, coupled with ease of accessibility through low-cost personal computer technology, have been welcomed by academic lawyers involved with research. Moreover, the shift from text retrieval technology to hypertext browsing, occasioned by the move away from systems such as Lexis to the more intuitive legal web sites, has been similarly well received (Paliwala 1996).

Gradually, in the United Kingdom (UK), there is also growing acceptance of the publication of learned articles on the web sites of law faculties so that the Internet is quite rapidly providing valuable sources of legal information as well as a medium through which scholarship can be placed in the public domain (Paliwala 1996). Furthermore, Internet electronic mail is encouraging and enabling legal scholars across the world to communicate with one another, not just by transmitting documents but by less formal groups, scattered internationally, who are now able to exchange ideas and experiences where this would not have been practicable or possible in the past.

In summary, IT had little impact on legal scholars until the early 1990s, since when the World Wide Web and global electronic mail seem to have been embraced with some considerable enthusiasm. In due course, it is realistic to assume, these changes in working practice and in attitude will affect both the research which underlies legal exposition as well as the medium through which legal exposition is published.

As for legal studies, the second category of legal scholarship identified earlier, perhaps the most striking impact of IT has been on one branch of jurisprudence (legal theory or legal philosophy) in relation to the development of expert systems in law. Serious and sustained work in this field began around 1970 (Buchanan and Headrick 1970), with the aim of developing computer programs that contain human legal expertise which can be applied in simulating legal reasoning and legal problem solving.

Although the value and point of jurisprudence have frequently been doubted by legal practitioners, students and academics alike, one aspect of the discipline – analytical jurisprudence – is of central importance to expert systems in law. For that part of legal theory strives to promote a systematic, theoretical and general understanding of issues such as the structure of legal rules and legal systems, the nature of legal reasoning, the role of logic in the law, and the interpretation of legislation and case law. It transpires that each of these issues is crucial for building expert systems that reason in law (McCarty 1977, Susskind 1987, Gardner 1987, Zeleznikow and Hunter 1994, Popple 1996).

As a matter of necessity, all expert systems in law make assumptions about the nature of law and the nature of legal reasoning. It is apparent, then, that the enterprise of constructing these systems is laden with jurisprudential (particularly analytical) implications. It can be argued, therefore, that jurisprudence is pertinent for legal knowledge engineering in two significant ways. First, jurisprudence can be deployed as a source of practical, sound guidance for those developing expert systems in law. Secondly, through jurisprudential discussion and argumentation, the latent theoretical implications, pre-suppositions and assumptions of existing systems can be articulated and thereby the potential, as well as the practical and jurisprudential limitations, of these systems can be pinpointed.

These uses of jurisprudence have now become quite widely accepted and so the application of legal studies (as a branch of legal scholarship) has itself been extended by IT – to inform the development of expert systems (and advanced legal information systems more generally). Furthermore, exploration of the use of the technology of expert systems in law has offered scholars new ways of looking at traditional questions of legal theory. The challenge of actually representing legal knowledge within the knowledge base of an expert system, for example, has provided jurisprudents with a new context within which to debate the nature of law and of legal sources, while the design of inference engines for expert systems in law has, similarly, given rise to a novel backdrop for discussion of the topic of legal reasoning (Susskind 1987, Gardner 1987, Ashley 1990).

In years to come, as IT comes to be more widely used for the purposes of legal exposition, then it can reasonably be expected that legal scholars will more naturally and frequently refer to computational models and IT metaphors in pursuing even the most traditional areas of legal philosophy.

The legal information substructure

The argument of this paper so far is that the effects of IT on legal scholarship have been modest to date, although far greater impact is expected in the coming years, both in legal exposition and legal studies. The remainder of the paper advances a related but more fundamental and radical claim – that, with the advent of IT and progress towards the information society, legal scholarship and legal practice are on the brink of a shift in legal paradigm as profound in its impact as the previous shifts brought about by the transition from the age of orality to the era of script; and from the era of script to print-based society.

The starting point in substantiating this claim is consideration of the significance for the law of what can be called the 'information substructure', a term that used here to refer to the dominant mechanism by which information is transmitted and conveyed in society. One model which is useful for this analysis proposes four phases of information substructure, where societies are dependent, respectively, on orality, script, print and then IT (Ong 1988, Katsh 1989, Katsh 1995). The subject which deserves great scrutiny is how the substance of the law and the way it is administered differ across these four phases.

It is intuitively obvious that the nature of law and the way it is administered are conditioned by the information systems which are available for its storage and its dissemination. Thus, the information substructure, no doubt in complex and subtle ways, to some extent determines and constrains the quantity of law, the complexity of law, the regularity with which the law changes and the people who are able to advise on the law. It is clear from research and writings on the history and development of communication as well as from legal anthropology, the sociology of law and jurisprudence more generally, that the information substructure of society impacts considerably on each of these factors (Ong 1988, Hoebel 1961, Hart 1994). And, it is submitted, when this impact across the four fundamental stages of development and communications is examined – through these stages which are dominated in turn by orality, script, print and then IT – then it becomes possible to project with some greater confidence about future developments in the administration of justice and the practice of law.

The transition into the age of IT has brought the capability for everyone to engage in printing and publishing from their own desktop computers. With powerful word processors available, legislators and draftsmen are not contained in their capacity to generate the printed word. The reproduction of printed material has also entered a new era: first with photocopying technology; later with transferable word processing files and high capacity laser printers; and, more recently, with telecommunications technology, text can be transmitted and disseminated electronically and at minimal cost.

IT cannot be blamed entirely for the huge quantity of legislation and case law which is now available (both in print and in electronic form in massive databases), but it has certainly not helped to check the verbosity of legislators around the world. In part, IT has a case to answer in helping to engender the proliferation of legal material which gives rise to what can be called 'hyperregulation'. Being hyperregulated means there is too much law to be managed (Susskind 1996).

Similarly, in the age of IT legal provisions are of unparalleled complexity. The specificity and detail of so much legal material today often renders the law impenetrable and too complex. Moreover, IT facilitates change in the law. In contrast with the eras of orality and script when change was a rarity, with IT available, the prevailing attitude towards documentation is that it is dynamic *by nature*, and subject to regular alteration, rather than static. At all stages in the life cycle in the generation and application of the law, IT supports rather than inhibits change.

With more legal source material than ever before and with the added challenge of some of it being available in legal databases that are themselves impenetrable, are specialist lawyers more or less in demand in the era of IT? In fact, this situation appears to have led to an increasingly lawyered society, with vast and growing quantities of legal material of unparalleled complexity, which are subject to unprecedented frequency of change.

On this view, should it not be concluded that IT is having a tragic effect on the law?

This inference need not be drawn, for to do so would be to make the mistaken assumption that the move from industrial print-based society into what can be called the IT-based information society has been completed. There are strong grounds for believing instead that lawyers are still in a transitional phase between these two eras and what have just been identified are some of the rather unfortunate consequences or features of being in this transition.

Once fully ensconced in the IT-based information society, many of the current shortcomings in the law may be seen, in retrospect, as transient features of the transitional period. At the heart of this prediction is what can be termed *The Technology Lag*, whose explanation demands a brief digression (Susskind 1996).

The capacity of today's computer technology to capture, store, retrieve and reproduce data greatly surpasses its ability to use technology to help analyse, refine and render more manageable the mass of data which data processing has spawned. Feeding information into systems poses few problems, but IT is less impressive at enabling users to extract the information that they want. This disparity can be characterized as *The Technology Lag* – the vital lag between data processing and knowledge processing.

The key point about *The Technology Lag* is not just that computer scientists have been more successful in programming computers to process data than knowledge. Rather, there is a far more significant phenomenon here, namely, that data processing, through technologies such as photocopiers and scanning machines, has actually created problems which knowledge-based systems are not yet sophisticated enough to overcome.

In law, for example, senior barristers and judges regularly reminisce about trials in the past when complete document sets could be held under the arm or in a briefcase. They curse the photocopier and attribute today's escalating costs and delays in the courtroom to the document analysis and management tasks which that technology seems to require. Current litigation support systems, based on data processing, go only some small way to conquering the document mountains and it will be some years yet before advanced enabling techniques, such as conceptual retrieval, expert systems and hypertext, are refined and applied successfully to help manage the difficulties which earlier technology has left as its legacy. So, too, with massive legal information retrieval systems such as Lexis, which may indeed hold vast quantities of data (Nichols 1991) – the problem is that the searching techniques are not yet sufficiently knowledge-based to help users secure *all but only* the relevant documents for their particular purposes.

The Technology Lag is not exclusive to legal information processing. It is said that during the Gulf War, satellite technology, which enabled the capture of millions of digitised images of enemy camps and movements in troops and armoury, was not matched by computer-based tools for analysing such images, so that much potentially vital data went unanalysed. Generally, across industry, commerce and government, managers and workers bemoan the quantities of information they are expected to digest. So far, IT is said to have given rise to less rather than more control over information – a product of *The Technology Lag*, in that users suffer from the technologies which allow more documentation to be produced and disseminated with relative ease but with no commensurate facilities to help sift through and identify relevant information.

In the discussion above of the four phases of information substructure, the perceived shortcomings of the transitional phase are compelling illustrations of *The Technology Lag*, of the way in which data processing capabilities have, so far, surpassed knowledge processing capacity. Word-processing, database and electronic transmission technologies are all classic applications of the world of data processing, in which the creation, reproduction and dissemination of printed text have become an art form. Data processing supports quantity, complexity and change in the law. But techniques in the field of knowledge processing are being refined and gradually systems are being developed which will help analyse and manage vast bodies of information. And these systems will themselves help lawyers pinpoint *all but only* the relevant material relevant to the particular purposes of users.

Once these technologies are in place, quantity ceases to be a problem because users will be assisted with accuracy in the retrieval of manageable quantities of legal materials; complexity will largely be hidden from them, as systems will effortlessly guide hitherto perplexed users through the labyrinths of the law; and change will either be hidden from the user with updating a continuous phenomenon or, more proactively, be brought to the attention of users by systems which themselves have the ability to monitor all relevant developments for individuals.

Perhaps even more radically, knowledge processing may well spawn a multitude of legal information products and services for direct consultation by non-lawyers and so, in the information society, it is suggested there will be less rather than more reliance on specialist legal advice.

It must be stressed that this vision of a transformed legal service on the strength of knowledge processing is not one which is likely to be realized in the next few years. Researchers have battled for a quarter of a century in trying to develop knowledge-based systems for lawyers and the results so far have been modest. It may well be twenty five further years before the transitional period is complete and progress is made into the fully fledged, IT-based information society.

The legal information continuum

The shift in paradigm anticipated here, for the law and lawyers, can be analysed from another perspective which is quite different from that of the information substructure. Consider instead a spectrum of legal information, with the written, formal sources of the law (legislation and case law) at one extremity (the left-hand side) and human legal experts dispensing legal advice at the other (the right-hand side). At each end, there are the two extreme categories of sources from which legal guidance can be drawn. The formal legal sources are the raw data of all legal processes; whereas the expertise brought to bear by lawyers in specific cases is the product of extensive analysis, manipulation and application of those data.

This spectrum can be called *The Legal Information Continuum* (Susskind 1996). On it, as shown in Figure 1, can also be placed a variety of enabling techniques which can serve as vehicles for the delivery of legal guidance – leaving the technical details aside,

The Legal Information Continuum

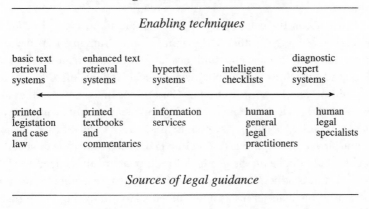

Enabling techniques

basic text retrieval systems	enhanced text retrieval systems	hypertext systems	intelligent checklists	diagnostic expert systems
printed legistation and case law	printed textbooks and commentaries	information services	human general legal practitioners	human legal specialists

Sources of legal guidance

Fig. 1. The legal information continuum

these are software techniques which allow legal information to be packaged and presented in a variety of ways.

The techniques have been placed along the continuum, in positions which indicate their proximity either to the conventional publication of information on the one hand or to human legal advisory service on the other. Generally, the nearer a technology is to the right-hand side, the more sophisticated and useful its guidance will be. An expert system, as a legal problem solving system, will hover quite close to the human end of the continuum. Where, in contrast, a technology is closer to the left-hand side it is therefore thought to have greater affinity with the presentation of legal information in its conventional published form. Basic text retrieval systems, which store searchable text in a form much like that found in books, are at home nearer the formal sources.

Also on the continuum are general legal practitioners, who are, of course, providers of legal information, but not advice as focused or polished as that provided by the specialists. Not very far from the other end sit published secondary sources, such as textbooks or articles, which are not the embodiment of the law but are descriptions of the law, often prepared by legal scholars. *The Legal Information Continuum* serves as a useful model for analysis of a wide range of phenomena.

With movement along the continuum, from left to right, the blurred and much debated boundaries between legal data, legal information, legal knowledge and legal expertise are no doubt passed across. Consistent with this, it follows that the reliable disposal of a legal problem can be achieved either by a human being in isolation or through the application of various techniques of IT where the guidance of systems is often supplemented by human advice. And as the continuum is traversed from left to right, these techniques that are deployed will need to be accompanied by progressively less human involvement, intervention and supplementary advice. For example, legal textbooks on their own will rarely yield a legal solution for a non-lawyer, but will require substantial additional analysis by a human legal adviser. A hypertext system further along the contimuum may offer a non-lawyer some considerable guidance and provide a useful frame of reference which will often (but not always) require supplementary human legal input.

Much will depend on the complexity of the legal matter at issue, but for any given single issue, it is clear that the further to the right one moves amongst the technologies on the continuum, the more focused the guidance should be and, in turn, there should be relatively less need for additional human assistance. It follows also that as one moves towards the right of *The Legal Information Continuum* the guidance offered becomes more directly usable. This does not mean that legal experts should be more user-friendly than, say, legal hypertext systems (although this may be so). Rather, given that the guidance as one moves in a rightward direction is of a higher degree of specificity, then the more focused it should be on the particular requirements of the user (or client, as the case may be). The end product, in other words, becomes more usable for most purposes.

The legal continuum also serves as a useful model for analysing the implications for legal liability implications of computer systems which offer legal guidance. At one end, as any practising solicitor will be quick to agree, most legal advisers can most certainly be held liable for losses resulting from advice which was negligently provided. At the other end of the continuum, however, the English courts have always been reluctant to attach liability to authors whose negligent misstatements have allegedly caused loss to readers who relied upon them. Scholars and students of computer law have for long agonized over the place along the continuum where the courts might chose to draw a line between systems which give rise to actionable loss and those that do not (Capper and Susskind 1988).

It is unlikely that the courts would simply draw a line in some one-dimensional fashion. Rather, they will more probably look also to the broader circumstances of any case and the extent to which it was reasonable for a given user to rely on the guidance offered; to the relationship, if any, between the system provider and the user; to the commercial context of the operation of the system; the level of expertise (legal and technical) of the user; and to the nature of any supplementary human guidance which might have been sought. *The Legal Information Continuum*, therefore, brings the issue sharply into focus but does not provide any shortcuts to the likely judicial view on the matter.

The Legal Information Continuum also highlights the likelihood of legal publishers competing directly with lawyers in the provision of legal information. Both traditional legal publishers around the world and smaller, entrepreneurial firms are now investing heavily in IT and firmly recognize that it is important for the delivery of their conventional products. As publishers produce text retrieval systems on CD-Rom and using hypertext, for example, *The Legal Information Continuum* is regarded as representing a marketplace, the legal publishing world is seen to be striding forcefully from left to right.

Certainly, they have made greater progress than practising lawyers moving in the other direction. It is true that some more innovative legal practices are charging clients for remote access to their in-house know-how systems; or delivering large contracts in hypertext form, together with additional commentary on the impact of clauses; or developing electronic checklists and prompts to help clients manage their legal risks. But these initiatives remain exceptional amongst legal practices.

It also seems to be a good time for new entrants to the market: electronic publishers (not specifically legal) are information service providers who will find in law a fruitful area for diversification. And so too might other professional services organizations such as the international accounting and consulting practices.

As a simplified model of the legal marketplace, therefore, *The Legal Information Continuum* can show quite starkly why fierce competition for lawyers might be imminent. The packaging and delivery of legal information services using IT may become attractive to other information service providers. So far, in moving from right to left along the continuum, in using IT in the provision of legal service, the legal profession's response has been appreciable if not dramatic. This move combines with progress through the transitional phase between print-based and IT-based societies to suggest that the delivery of legal service in society is set to change radically in coming years.

A shift in legal paradigm

The fundamental claim of this paper is that IT will enable and help bring about a shift in paradigm of legal service, a fundamental change from a service that is substantially advisory in nature today to one which will become one of many information services in the IT-based information society of the future. In turn, basic aspects of the legal process and the administration of justice will also alter radically.

Despite the burgeoning performance of IT, the shift in paradigm cannot be complete until *The Technology Lag* is eliminated. Much of what is said here, therefore, as has been stressed, is premised on great advances in knowledge processing as a counterbalance to the great strides already made in data processing. Once developed and refined, it is suggested that the principal role of knowledge processing will be in innovating and re-engineering legal service and legal processes rather than automating and streamlining legal practice of today. In this way, the delivery of legal service and the administration of justice will move gradually from right to left along *The Legal Information Continuum*, away in most cases from the legal advisory services of experts towards the IT-based packaging of legal guidance. Even in the current legal paradigm, there are indications of the emergence of the legal information services market. Imaginatively produced legal information packs are now being sold in book shops, offering guidance, for example, on landlord and tenant agreements, debt recovery, the pursuit of small claims, as well as taxation, conveyancing and the drafting of wills. Standard form documentation is provided alongside step-by-step help, which takes the user patiently through each phase of the process in question. These would sit on the right-most edge of the parts of *The Legal Information Continuum* which are allocated to conventional publications, because they go well beyond the declaration or recasting of the law and distil the sources into directly usable form.

IT has already taken these packs a further step, mainly for lawyers at this stage, but paving the way for legal products for the consumer. Illustrative applications are the computer-based debt collection systems, computer-assisted conveyancing and tax calculation systems that are now readily available. These operate on processes which, in the past, required the one-to-one attention of lawyers' advisory skills, each time afresh. They have now been routinized and systematized.

With the great leaps in IT which it is reasonable to expect, such systems and many others will be upgraded and become available for direct use by non-lawyers. In turn, IT will help realize what can be called the *latent legal market* – the myriad of circumstances, in domestic and business life, in which non-lawyers today are generally unable to benefit from the legal input they require because conventional legal service is too expensive or impractical in the circumstances. It is submitted that IT will help bring the legal guidance to this *latent legal market*, giving everyone – and not just lawyers – ready and inexpensive access to legal guidance obtained through a variety of legal products and information services. The focus of these services will be on helping individuals and businesses with their legal affairs where direct consultation with lawyers would, in the past, have been too costly or simply not practicable. Thus, legal guidance will become one of countless sorts of information available on the global information highway. The law will no longer be the exclusive preserve of lawyers.

That said, in the enthusiasm of anticipating a shift from advisory to information service, it is vital not to overlook these areas of legal life which will remain the province of lawyers – for these, it transpires, will often be of great social significance and commercial value. This province itself can be divided into two: the specialist function and the judicial function.

Both for commercial reasons and because of the nature of law, there will still be a need for specialist lawyers in the information society. The strongest candidates for assuming this role in England are barristers and specialist solicitors. From the commercial point of view, there will still be many situations where the value of a transaction, dispute, project or activity will be so high that the stakeholders will inevitably be prepared to invest in a second opinion. This will be so even if the scenario at issue is one which seems to be routine and well proceduralized and systematized in readily-available legal information services. Where the guidance offered by legal information systems supports the position of the stakeholder involved, then consultation with a specialist may either be a matter of prudence and caution or another layer of legal risk management. When, however, the legal input offered by information systems inclines the other way and is potentially or actually contrary to the stakeholder's substantial financial interest, then direct consultation with human specialists will be with a view to investing in expert legal advice which either challenges the guidance of the information system or argues that the stakeholder's particular circumstances are not so straightforward as to be covered completely by the routinized rendition of the law.

It is realistic and not cynical to anticipate this latter deployment of lawyers, because this is precisely what happens today. When there is enough at stake, the services of the very best lawyers are invoked either to challenge and destroy the arguments of others, or to suggest that there has been a category error and that the client's circumstances are actually governed by other rules and principles (inevitably in their favour).

Beyond the commercial imperatives which might drive users of legal information services to call upon specialists, there is a further set of compelling reasons why the services of conventional legal specialists will still be in demand in the future. These have their roots in the very nature of law. To address this issue, it is necessary to take a minor philosophical tour and delve briefly into issues which properly belong to the discipline of jurisprudence (the branch of legal studies discussed earlier).

For present purposes, it is important to clarify one particular topic, that of the impossibility of creating a legal information system which can cover all eventualities and so have no gaps. It can be argued that this is impossible for four reasons, no matter what enabling techniques or applications are used to package the law (Susskind 1987).

The first is to do with language. Because the law and legal information are expressed in natural language, there can always be doubts or arguments over whether the particular circumstances of one's case falls within a category presented by some information system. For example, if a system makes it clear that a user is not permitted to drive a vehicle in the public park, does this rule extend to skateboards? In this, and many other instances, because language is indeterminate, parties to a dispute are not given water-tight help. Sometimes there may seem to be little doubt – it seems to be clear that one should not take a 10-ton truck through a recreational area.

A second kind of gap is where there does not seem to be any law or legal information governing particular circumstances. This is to be expected because legislators, judges and developers of legal information system have limited foresight and cannot anticipate all situations which may arise. Thirdly, on some occasions legal information systems (like lawyers) might seem to provide a series of suggestions, some of which contradict one another, and this uncertainty with which the system speaks can be regarded as another sort of gap.

Finally, there will be gaps in any legal information system that are due to the possibility of any guidance being subject to implied exceptions. No representation of the law can be regarded as fixed and static, but can always be refined or disregarded in the context of a particular case because of some overriding purpose of the law or because of some legal principle. For example, the 10-ton truck in the earlier illustration may transpire to be acceptable for the park in the light of the future information that the purpose of its entry is by way of some war memorial gesture. In these circumstances it might be said that the *purpose* of the regulation was to promote a harmonious community facility and the memorial gesture may be construed as supporting rather than defeating that purpose. An instance of the application of legal principle is the legendary jurisprudential example of the man who murdered his grandfather to inherit under the latter's will. Although the rule of testate succession seemed to point to the murderer as the rightful inheritor, the courts found this rule subject to the implied exception that 'no man may profit from his own wrong', a legal principle inherent in the legal system in question. Similarly, when enough is at stake, clever lawyers always seem to able to contrive to find similar such countervailing principles and bring these to bear in opposition to any unacceptable guidance offered by legal information systems.

This dip into legal theory (which itself supports an earlier claim of this paper that jurisprudence can help identify the limitations of advanced information systems) suggests that on those occasions where the language of a system is indeterminate, or there is an absence of relevant information, or a conflict in the information or there is a realistic prospect of some exception being implied, then the legal information system may not be sufficiently powerful to help the user, and recourse to the specialist adviser would still be necessary.

In respect of the judicial function, speculation about the future of computers and the law often leads to debate on the impact of IT on judges. There are three distinct questions here. First, will the more widespread use of legal information services reduce the number of cases which come before the courts? Second, will IT help judges in the conduct of their work? And, third, can computers replace judges? The second question is dealt with in detail elsewhere, for example by Lord Woolf, in his reports, entitled *Access to Justice* (Woolf 1995, 1996). Here, the first and third questions are addressed.

As legal guidance becomes readily available and increasingly usable and useful, it may well be, in the future, that recourse both to lawyers and to the courts will be made less frequently. On this view, legal information systems will of themselves reduce the number of formal disputes before judges. If there is a shift in society away from legal problem solving towards legal risk management, then this may lead, more generally, to a culture where dispute pre-emption is pervasive rather than dispute resolution.

It may be that only a subset of those cases which, for the commercial or jurispru-dential reasons just discussed, would be handled by specialists, may thereafter require the attention of the courts. Yet this has extremely profound implications for the law. It is possible, for example, that the information which will be accessible on the global highway will guide our social, domestic and working lives more directly than the primary sources (legislation and case law) themselves. In a sense, this legal guidance itself may come to be regarded as the law itself and not just a representation of it. This may indeed become the prime illustration of what legal sociologists have come to call the 'living law' – the law which actually reflects and conditions behaviour in society (Ehrlich 1975).

That such a representation could ever assume this status (as a quasi legislative source) may challenge the constitutional purist who will say that valid law can only emanate from a properly-elected legislature or a duly-appointed judiciary. Yet there is some precedent, in Scotland at least, for commentators' writings becoming the law itself: the so-called Institutional Writers were scholars whose analysis and synthesis of the law came to be treated later as authoritative and binding sources.

Certainly if legal information systems were regarded by non-lawyers as constituting the law itself, then this should encourage legal institutions to seek to set standards for legal guidance being widely available in this form and perhaps also to establish some central body or to appoint individuals (perhaps judges) with responsibility for reviewing and even endorsing materials of sufficient quality.

But what of those cases which do seem to call for resolution by some impartial authority? Might computers ever assume the judicial function? Can judging, in large or small part, be mediated by machine? Is this just fertile ground for science fiction writers or can automated dispensers of justice be expected? (Detmold 1984, Susskind 1986).

First, it is clear that the jurisprudential limitations of legal information systems as discussed in relation to specialists apply equally to the concept of judicial systems. In fact, it is precisely when there are gaps in the law (in the senses identified) that judges are most urgently required today and no doubt tomorrow. The technical limitations of IT are also relevant here because the technical problems associated with natural language processing and common sense reasoning, for example, are at the heart of the current inability to program computers to display the creativity, individuality, intuition and common sense that is expected of judges acting in their official role.

Moral issues come into play here too. The considerable disquiet that has been expressed in relation to the notion of the computer judges (Weizenbaum 1984) is, at root, a moral claim which might be extrapolated to run as follows: so long as we accept the primacy of human beings as the basic moral unit in society (mainly Western democracies) then we would have difficulty in justifying certain sorts of conflicts between human agents being resolved by non-human forces. Even if it were possible, therefore, to program computers to exhibit, for example, moral, religious, social, sexual and political preferences akin to those actually held by judges and applied in their dispensing of justice, we may reject it as morally undesirable. We might do so because this may require the design of systems which would generalize in these various dimensions where the judicial system has always presupposed uniquely human, empathetic focus on the part of judges in dealing with very specific details of particular cases.

Yet the jurisprudential, technical and moral arguments cannot be stretched too far, because there are no doubt all kinds of legal dispute to which they do not apply; there are many cases with no significant moral dimension which may, in principle, be disposed of more effectively by some form of system, even if the techniques and technology to enable this are not yet sufficiently refined.

Existing research in artificial intelligence and law does hold some promise of systems which will help choose between diverging accounts of the facts of cases – by applying probability theory together with the rules of evidence, for example. And, using diagnostic expert systems techniques, systems are also able to apply complex bodies of rules to the facts presented to them. Systems which can solve legal problems and choose between competing arguments under some sets of circumstances are entirely conceivable, although the process of handling these situations through IT might come to be no longer regarded as judicial but may be looked upon as a matter of public administration instead.

In the future, the judicial function may then be confined largely either to what computers cannot do, or (on one view) ought not to be doing. Today these two categories seem to coincide in the functions of making moral and ethical judgements about the circumstances of individuals or the interests of society more generally. Such decision-making will no doubt continue to involve human beings of integrity, knowledge and experience acting as impartial arbiters in relation to related disputes over fact or law. Additionally, it may be that judges will also come to have a vital role to play in reviewing the new 'living law', the content of the legal information systems used in society; and in hearing appeals resulting from the operation of these systems.

The limits of legal information systems

A distinction can be drawn, therefore, between legal questions and circumstances which can be disposed of or handled through the use of legal information systems and other situations when, for commercial reasons or because of the nature of law, specialist human legal input is required.

The distinction is, of course, an over-simplification because there will be some borderline situations so that allowance should be made for a grey area between these two categories. The far more fundamental problem, however, is that everyday circumstances do not come neatly packaged or labelled as capable of disposal by a legal information system or requiring the attention of a human specialist or belonging to the grey area. A citizen or business person (as distinct from a lawyer) who uses a legal information system as his or her first port of call may not receive guidance on this initial question of classification. Can the system offer sufficient guidance or is specialist human help needed?

On some occasions, for example, on the strength of the extensive financial implications of the user's position, it may be fairly obvious that a specialist is needed. In other situations, profound financial implications or the considerable legal complexity may not be apparent to the non-specialist. Consequently, legal information systems may surely be used on occasions which are contrary to the interests of the user.

This is an extremely vexing issue – if users themselves cannot be relied upon to recognize the limitations of the systems, is the whole enterprise then not fatally flawed? Certainly, there is a challenge here to the social utility and reliability of legal information systems, but it is not a devastating one. For the argument presented here rests on a conviction about what is the most socially significant impact of IT on law in the information society – the realization and emergence of *the latent legal market*. With numerous legal information products and systems widely available, it is suggested that it will be possible, in respect of both social and working affairs, readily and easily to obtain legal guidance in circumstances -and this is vital – where in the absence of IT it would be impractical or too costly to seek traditional legal advice.

The dilemma can, therefore, be summarized as follows. Should IT be embraced so that, in the information society, legal information products and systems are developed which will guide non-lawyers far more extensively than would otherwise be possible on the understanding that these same products and systems may fail, on occasions, both to notify users that more complex issues may be at play and that human specialist advice is needed? Or should the new technology be rejected on the grounds that even although the law will be invoked far less frequently, on those fewer occasions there can nevertheless be complete confidence in the reliable, expert disposal of the problems in question?

More crudely, and no doubt tendentiously, should we prefer a society in which the law is fully integrated with society but not applied correctly on all occasions to one in which it remains alienated from our social and working lives but gets it right on the rare occasions it is invoked? The issue clearly requires further debate but, the utilitarians would no doubt favour the adoption of IT.

The dilemma points to other fruitful areas for further research and practical development, for it is surely crucial to pursue the development and implementation of techniques to enhance the ability of systems to help users classify their problems as appropriate for disposal by the system or not.

It is a striking thought, in any event, for those readers of jurisprudence who are used to dwelling on debates over 'hard cases' (Hart 1994, Dworkin 1986), that the widest use of legal information systems, even on occasions which are more properly the province of lawyers, could itself create a culture in which the application of the law is assumed to be straightforward rather than subject on all occasions to endless debate of legal minutiae.

Of itself, this could engender a culture which is driven less by literal interpretation of highly-detailed rules and adversarial attitudes than by legal guidelines pitched at a higher level of generality where confrontation is exceptional. In the end, the availability of legal information systems for *the latent legal market* could begin to align the legal method of common law systems with that of civil jurisdictions where today they are already more liberal and broad-brush in their approach to interpretation and less inclined to launch into combative legal dispute.

Thus the shift in legal paradigm anticipated in this paper not only sets new challenges for the branch of legal scholarship devoted to legal exposition, in that the new discipline of legal information engineering may soon underlie the statements of the law which are most widely consulted; it also raises fundamental issues for the jurisprudential branch of legal studies, given that so many crucial questions about the nature of law in society are raised by the projected availability of legal information systems.

Acknowledgement

Many of the arguments and concepts of this paper are taken from the author's book, *The Future of Law*, with the permission of the publishers, Oxford University Press, to whom the author is most grateful.

References

Ashley, K. (1990), *Modelling Legal Argument* (London).

Bing, J. and Harvold, T. (1977), *Legal Decisions an Information Systems* (Oslo).

Buchanan, B. and Headrick, G. (1970), 'Some speculation about artificial intelligence and legal reasoning' *Stanford Law Review*, 23: 40–62.

Capper, P. and Susskind, R. (1988), *Latent Damage Law – The Expert System* (London).

Detmold, M. (1984), *The Unity of Law and Morality: A Refutation of Legal Positivism* (London).

Dworkin, R. (1986), *Law's Empire* (London).

Ehrlich, E. (1975), *Fundamental Principles of the Sociology of Law* (New York).

Gardner, A. (1987), *An Artificial Intelligence Approach to Legal Reasoning* (London).

Hart, H. (1994), *The Concept of Law* 2nd edition (Oxford).

Hoebel, E. (1961), *The Law of Primitive Man* (Cambridge, Mass.).

Katsh, M. (1989), *The Electronic Media and the Transformation of Law* (Oxford).

—— (1995), *Law in a Digital World* (New York).

McCarty, L. T. (1977), 'Reflections on TAXMAN: an experiment in artificial intelligence and legal reasoning' *Harvard Law Review*, 90: 837–93

Nichols, S. J. (1991), *Law Databases* (London)

Ong, W. (1988), *Orality and Literacy* (London).

Paliwala, A. (1996), 'From academic tombstones to living bazaars – the changing shape of law reviews', *The Journal of Information, Law and Technology* < http://elj.warwick.ac.uk/elj/jilt/issue1/1abdul/ > .

Popple, J. (1996), *A Pragmatic Legal Expert System* (Aldershot).

Susskind, R. (1986), 'Detmold's refutation of positivism and the computer judge', *Modern Law Review*, 49: 125–38.

—— (1987), *Expert Systems in Law* (Oxford).

—— (1996), *The Future of Law* (Oxford).

Tapper, C. (1973), *Computers and the Law* (London).

—— (1982), *An Experiment in the Use of Citation Vectors in the Area of Legal Data* (Oslo).

Woolf, Lord, (1995), *Access to Justice*, Interim Report (London).

—— (1996), *Access to Justice*, Final Report (London).

Weizenbaum, J. (1984), *Computer Power and Human Reason* (Harmondworth).

Zeleznikow, J. and Hunter, D. (1994), *Building Intelligent Legal Information Systems* (Deventer).

Commentary

NEIL MACCORMICK

Faculty of Law
University of Edinburgh

A by-law prohibits sleeping in the railway station. Late one evening, the trains being delayed, a commuting business man was found to have nodded off on a bench on the platform. Meantime, on an adjacent bench, a tramp had settled down for the night with newspapers and blankets to try to keep warm. But he was afflicted with insomnia and unable to get to sleep.

This problem case, like that of the vehicles in the park cited by Richard Susskind in his excellent paper, comes from the fertile pen and imagination of the late Lon Fuller (Fuller 1958: p.664). It invites us, of course, to reflect on the question whether either the businessman or the tramp has broken the by-law. On a literal reading, it seems that the former, by being actually asleep, has done so; the latter, by being however regretfully awake, not. Judging by the presumed spirit of the regulation rather than its letter, the reverse is the case.

As this reminds us, problems involving the manipulation of legal texts are primarily practical. The search is not for detached understanding of a text, but for a way to make practical sense of it in applying it to concrete problem instances. Legal information has the particular character of belonging to what my colleague and co-author Ota Weinberger has called 'practical information' (MacCormick/Weinberger 1986, Chs 1 & 3). It is information which guides, regulates, or motivates conduct, and which is most appropriately read for the sake of the guidance it gives. Even a detached and scholarly or academic interpretation aimed at a pure understanding has to give primacy to its action-guiding character. To fail to understand that it has this character is to fail to understand it at all.

In his discussion of the continuum of legal information, Susskind makes a certain allowance for this, for he does acknowledge the omnipresence of interpretational problems, and the value-laden character of practical-interpretational reasoning. But I think I wish to lay upon it yet greater emphasis than he does, and to advert yet more pointedly to the problem this poses for some of the developments of legal informatics envisaged in Susskind's paper.

Faced with texts that are bearers of practical information in the context of institutional normative order as exemplified in state legal systems, or transnational legal systems such as that of the European Community, we frequently find disputes arising about their proper meaning in connection with their relevance for application to specific situations. The public prosecutor decides to prosecute the business man or the tramp or both; they or their representatives dispute the relevancy of the charge given the situation in which they found themselves. Such an eventuality is by no means unusual. The practical character of legal information entails that competing interests may be satisfied by competing interpretations, and so competing interpretations are worked out and put forward, and disputes abound.

There are three broad areas of interpretative argument; the first is, of course, the linguistic – in the context of this sentence in English in a by-law, what does 'sleep' mean, does either person count as having 'slept' in a relevant sense? The second is the systemic. Real statutes, by-laws, precedents and the like are part of the fabric of large and ever-more-complex bodies of similar information constituting what most lawyers conceptualize as 'legal systems', and the meaning of a legislative provision must be gathered in the context both of the whole relevant enactment and of related elements of the same general branch of the law, as well as perhaps overriding pervasive norms of constitutional law, including fundamental rights. (Compare MacCormick/Summers 1991, Ch 2).

Even in the trivial example of the sleepers in the station, we can imagine the defence posing the question whether any form of criminal intent is required – the businessman, we may suppose, fell asleep involuntarily, and is not to be blamed for that. (This sounds rather convincing, yet in a different department of criminal law, we may find that someone who falls asleep when driving a car is guilty of carelessness for failing to take adequate precautions to avoid drowsiness. We had better be ready to show that the cases are distinguishable.)

A further element is teleological and evaluative. What purposes do we find in or ascribe to laws of the kind in view; with what general conceptions of rights, rightness and justice do we expect them to be compatible? That no valuable purpose could possibly be served by harassing weary travellers is one way or the other a strong reason for not prosecuting the businessman, or for rejecting any proposed prosecution, regardless of the literal purport of the words.

The systemic and the evaluative elements of interpretation are the ones that it is hardest to envisage being embraced by legal IT in the foreseeable future, and it is open to doubt whether IT is in principle capable of doing this kind of work. It does not follow that IT has no valuable contribution to make. Much of the complexity of law, especially in the context of what Susskind neatly dubs 'hyperregulation', consists in the working together of almost impenetrable concatenations of rules. Here, problems are syntactic as much as, or more than, they are semantic. Susskind and Capper have shown with great skill how expert systems can give substantial help here. I salute the work Richard Susskind has done in bringing IT closer to law and law closer to IT. I find his vision of the future of law challenging. (See References in Susskind's paper.) But I see many problems involved in adapting machines such as we presently have to the intelligent processing of practical information given its practical character.

References

Fuller, L. L. (1958), 'Positivism and fidelity to law: a reply to Professor Hart' *Harvard Law Review* 71: 630–72

MacCormick, D. N. and Summers, R. S. S (1991), *Interpreting Statutes: A Comparative Study* (Aldershot).

MacCormick, N. and Weinberger, O. (1986), *An Institutional Theorv of Law* (Dordrecht).

Information technology in the social sciences

ALAN WILSON

Vice Chancellor
University of Leeds

Abstract. To assess the impact of information technology (IT) in the social sciences, it is argued that generic soft technologies and generic theories should be sought and identified. This argument is illustrated by four examples: accounts in demography and economics, health service delivery, urban development and site identification in archaeology. It is argued that the potential of these developments has not been fully realized because social science research has been under-funded rather than properly treated as 'big' science.

Introduction

The impact of *IT* in the social sciences is obviously driven by the hard technologies which have delivered computing power. It is more interesting, however, to focus on the impacts of what might be called *soft* technologies which are facilitated by computers and which change the ways in which research is undertaken in the social science disciplines: ideas which become in some sense practicable for the first time; new ideas whose development is somehow encouraged by the technology; new theories. The aim will be to go beyond the obvious impacts using the software of word processing through to relational databases and number-crunching to focus on new kinds of conceptual development. It is recognized, in stating this, that the potential in areas like relational databases should not be under-estimated: the tools can generate new and more systematic ways of thinking (see Lee 1995). In this introductory paper to the social science contributions to this symposium, the aim is to try to articulate *generic soft technologies*, perhaps even *generic theories* – with the implication of the 'generic' being that they are applicable across a range of social science disciplines. These topics are introduced in turn. Even general arguments of this type are often best presented through example, and this method is adopted here. Four examples are offered: accounts in demography and economics; performance indicators in health services delivery; urban development modelling; and site prediction in archaeology.

Generic soft technologies

System representation

A subject within a particular discipline can be thought of as a 'system of interest', and then it is usually taken for granted how that system is represented. This means that the representation of the system as it has evolved within the discipline historically tends to be the accepted one. One of the impacts of *IT* is to make it worthwhile to open up this question. First, relational databases provide effective means of storing large amounts of information, and this already poses questions of categorization. It also raises interesting research questions, for instance, when different elements of a population database do not 'match'. For example, there may be two characteristics of a population, from different sources, each broken down by age; but the age categories are different. How can the database be built in a consistent way? This question can be answered and *IT* provides the framework for providing the answers – though the critical element will turn on having a good *theory* of the system of interest.

A second example is provided from within geography. Geographers are obviously interested in space and this must be reflected in the characterization of the system of interest. Space can be treated continuously or discretely. Historically, the great theorists of geography have tended to treat space continuously (Wilson 1989, 1995). However, it is only when there is a shift to a discrete representation that the full powers of *IT* can be brought to bear.

There are many issues of these types within the social science disciplines and it is worth making them explicit. This will generate new perspectives and therefore new routes for ongoing research – and it will generate new research questions. When these issues are resolved (albeit temporarily) in a particular case, the resulting database provides the foundations for the applications of the formal methods of classification and statistical analysis and for calibrating and testing system models. Large databases also generate their own distinct research questions. For example: how can they be intelligently *navigated*?

Accounts

An intermediate step between building a database and a good theory (perhaps as a model) is often the articulation of *accounts*. These provide the framework in which all the elements of the system, and what happens to them over time, can be accounted for. Units of money in financial accounts provide an obvious example; economic accounts and population accounts others. The frameworks of accounts in the social sciences are long established, e.g., Leontief (1967), Stone (1967; 1970) or Rees and Wilson (1976). What *IT* offers, is the potential for implementing these accounts (and then furthering the related development of theory) either in their original (usually matrix) form or through some new representation such as micro-simulation (a topic which will be taken up again below).

Modelling

IT obviously has a particularly sharp impact in those parts of the social sciences which lend themselves to quantification. In these areas, the move beyond system representation and accounts towards theory can be characterized in terms of model building. A good theory is represented as a model – of an economy, a population, a city or whatever. (A by-product of model development and testing is the estimation of 'missing' data – or making incompatible data sets consistent.)

There are two broad approaches: the statistical (such as the econometric) and the mathematical. In a particular field, the statistical usually precedes the mathematical, the latter becoming more feasible as theory develops. Models are usually represented as sets of equations and one of the obvious areas of impact of *IT* has been its number-crunching potential: 'solving' larger and larger sets of equations, usually through some sort of simulation method. Indeed, there is a half-way house between statistical and mathematical modelling – and that is simulation modelling, presented, for example, as 'system dynamics' whose original exponent was Forrester (1968, 1969) and now incorporated in computer packages such as ITHINK. There are of course many other forms of simulation.

The power of IT opens up new methods: the exploitation of parallel processors for number crunching in modelling is one example. In spatial interaction modelling, for instance, Alvenides *et al.* (1996) are modelling migration flows for wards in England on the basis of a 9930 × 9930 matrix. This power can be enhanced through new methodologies from other fields: the exploitation of neural network ideas to underpin simulation is one (Openshaw 1996); the notion of genetic programming, borrowed from evolution theorists (see Kauffman 1993 for an overview) and applied by Openshaw (1988), is another. A simulation methodology devised by Langton *et al.* (1995) from the *artificial life* research group has been applied in geographic modelling (Openshaw 1992, Dibble 1996) and theoretically this opens up new perspectives on the agency-structure problem because it directly simulates the behaviour of agents.

Visualization

Much of what has been described so far would have been feasible on 1960s, 1970s or early 1980s mainframe computers. There are beginning to be major new opportunities which arise, as already noted, from the sheer size and power of super-computing facilities. But it is necessary also to take into account another dimension of the impact of powerful personal computers (PCs) and UNIX workstations. What has already been argued about databases overlaps here: although there were the beginnings of powerful relational databases on mainframes, they have developed significantly since the advent of PCs. This illustrates the key to what PCs have to offer: they are much more user friendly and have better presentation facilities. This objective of the manufacturers and software developers has had more far-reaching consequences than they can have envisaged. The ease of use – and power – of even word processing, but then of relational databases and, more generally, visualization, has had a significant impact in its own right.

Of course, the argument about PCs and mainframes can now be combined: most research PCs are linked to networks, and through these networks to the most powerful servers and mainframes. This will be particularly significant for data access in social science research: it will be possible to develop the idea of social science *data warehouses* – cf. Kelly (1996) – with wide access through networks. This connects to the issues raised earlier of navigation and search. Cockcroft (1996) uses the concept of metadata – which divides into *dictionaries* (what are the data?) and *directories* (where are they?). These search issues are also pursued by Stewart (1996) from a particular visualization perspective: virtual reality.

There is an obviously striking geographical example (with implications for related map-needing disciplines): *geographical information systems* – or *GIS*. Geographers, along with historians and social scientists need maps to illustrate arguments and computers can now deliver these with great accuracy. The fundamental change is that there is less need for the kinds of choices that authors of atlases had to make because, for a country or a region or a topic, it is now possible – through GIS – to generate self-designed maps for the immediate scholarly purpose in question. In effect, millions of maps are available to the researcher and this provides a powerful new tool – see Coppock and Rhind (1991) for an historical account. If there is a problem with this development, it is if the GIS business becomes an industry in its own right, divorced from an analytical drive and substantive research purposes (Birkin *et al.* 1996).

However, maps are but one form of visualization. More generally, the outcomes of model calculations can be displayed visually and this is a significant advance. It becomes possible to display, for example, solutions spaces of systems of complicated non-linear equations in such a way that further research development is facilitated. This will be pursued below in the context of the study of urban development: it may be possible to recognize 'types' of development from this kind of visualization which would not be possible by any other means. This kind of work depends critically on combining human intelligence with the computational power of the machine – and the power of personal computers in this context is critically important.

Integration

A critical task in any research project will always be to achieve the effective integration of all the conceptual and technological power which can be brought to bear on the problem at hand. If theory building – and its application – is of the essence, the impact of *IT* should be viewed in the light of what it can offer when combined with other approaches – and the extent to which it can be the foundation for inventing new approaches to either old or new problems. This latter distinction is worth making, because in a number of instances – the analysis of dynamical systems is one – a particular mixture of new theory or technique and computing power enables the formulation of problems which could not be considered earlier.

Generic theories

System types

The ways of classifying systems of interest can point to methods for modelling or theory building in particular contexts; knowledge can be shared across disciplines; new generic research problems can be exposed. In urban geography, a valuable categorization has been adapted from that of Weaver (1948): systems can be simple, of disorganized complexity, or of organized complexity. The first type can be tackled with the tools of straightforward mathematics; the second by the tricks of statistical averaging; and the third, which contained the issues which seemed particularly difficult – and therefore interesting – to Weaver at the time he was writing, requires the tools of nonlinear dynamical analysis. What is particularly interesting in the present context is the potential of the class of methods which become available through the contemporary power of *IT*. An interesting research question is then: are there new model types which can be conceived because this power exists?

Model types

It is now possible to combine the argument of the section on Generic Soft Techniques with that of the above introductory paragraph. An example of a 'simple' model is an account-based model: articulate an appropriate way of counting, and identifying changes of state through time, and use this as a framework for calculating rates – such as birth and death rates – and there is the basis of a model. *IT* makes such modelling feasible because it can handle the sizes of the matrices which are necessary to characterize systems of interest to social scientists.

A statistical averaging model (Wilson 1970) is at the core of much geographical analysis through the concept of *spatial interaction*. An individual travels from home to work (or to shop or to hospital or whatever). The decision structure which underpins this outcome may be complicated and idiosyncratic, and certainly not modellable or predictable. However, it is possible to average over the behaviour of (say) a city's population and to produce rather good models and predictions. Again, the relevance of *IT* is that it has become feasible to handle large systems. At a more general level, this kind of thinking potentially has something to say about the agency-structure problem: what is predictable and what is essentially unpredictable?

The concept of optimization is the basis of many economic models: through, for example, individuals maximizing utilities or firms maximizing profits. The interaction of these agents is difficult to model, but again an averaging process offers solutions in appropriate cases.

Statistical averaging does not work when there are non-linearities and strong interactions in the system. These kinds of systems have become known as dynamical systems and the appropriate mathematics began to be available for modelling from about the mid-1970s, initially through the work of Thom (1975) in *catastrophe theory*. This would have been an interesting curiosity, offering insight, but no possibility of calculation, but for the power of *IT*. What is revealed for this kind of system is that there are many possible 'solutions' to the model equations. Computing power, combined with human intelligence through its facilities for visualization, permits a systematic and intelligent search of such solution spaces.

Examples

The argument now proceeds by example. Three examples are considered in turn: of a simple system – account-based population and economic models; a system of disorganized complexity – the geography of health service delivery; and a system of organized complexity – the city. As a fourth example, an archaeological application of these ideas is examined. In each case, the achievement which has arisen from *IT* developments and, where appropriate, the new research challenges which have been opened up, are emphasized. The examples have a geographical bias, but each illustrates more general issues – and the systems are each of interest to the practitioners of a wider range of disciplines.

There is perhaps another general theme to be developed on the basis of this argument: if it were possible to *teach* this kind of generic thinking, then the next generation of researchers would be better equipped to undertake multidisciplinary research and to tackle the 'big' social science research issues to be discussed briefly in the final section.

Example 1: demography and economics

Rate-based population models have a long history, dating back to Malthus. Three points are worth emphasising in relation to *IT* developments and ongoing research. The first point arises because , since it becomes feasible in *IT* terms to handle large systems, it is possible to add a fine-scale geographical dimension to the models (see Rees and Wilson 1976; and for more recent applications, Rees 1996, and Rees and Phillips 1996). The second point then shows how concepts have to evolve as models are refined. The geographical dimension complicates the apparently simple concept of a demographic rate – because both numerator and denominator have to be corrected for cross-boundary flows.

The third point turns on the issue of system representation and illustrates why the question is worth asking explicitly. Populations are likely to be characterized by, say, age (a), gender (s), social class (m), place of residence (i) and so on. Hence $P(a,s,m,i,t)$ might be the population in categories (a,s,m,i) at time t. In accounting, the population by category can be traced through time, to time $t+1$ say, and the relevant array is then, using an obvious notation, $P(a,s,m,i,t,a',s',m',i',t+1)$. All this is simply to make the point that very quickly, very high-dimensional arrays are generated, and many of the cells in these arrays will be empty, making this form of storage very inefficient. An alternative is to simulate a hypothetical population directly as a long list – so constructed that this population has the required characteristics. This technique has now been exploited by a number of research groups: for example, in Leeds by geographers (Wilson and Pownall 1976, Duley and Rees 1991), in Cambridge, by historical demographers (Smith in this volume), in Surrey by sociologists (Gilbert, 1995) and at the LSE by economists (Harding 1990, Hancock and Sutherland 1992) showing not only the developing record of the power of the technique, but also that it can be applied in a range of disciplines.

A similar argument applies to account-based economic models. These models originated in the work of Leontief (as reviewed in his 1967 book); in the 1970s, again on the back of greater computing power, these models were given a geographical dimension – either as single regional input-output models or, more interestingly, as multi-regional input-output models. In this case, the theory is relatively well worked out; the research challenge remains that of building these models on a systematic basis – a topic that will be returned to in the final section in discussing *IT*- based social science as, potentially, 'big science'.

Example 2: health service delivery

A key concept in geographical analysis, with a long history, is that of *spatial interaction*. The interactions might be travel to work, travel to shop or travel to hospital. The delivery of health care will be used here to illustrate how the development of large systems can facilitate the construction of performance indicators which are of the greatest importance in policy analysis.

How can (a) the efficiency of a hospital and (b) the effectiveness of delivery of health care to the residents of an area be measured ? These questions are much more interesting when tackled at a small area scale. Conventionally, a hospital will be considered to have a catchment population which will be taken as the whole population of, say, the city in which it is located, and this provides the denominator for the calculation of various performance indicators, e.g., operations per head of population. A little thought, however, shows that except in the simplest of circumstances, there will be several hospitals in the region and these will share that simply-defined catchment population. So the concept needs to be refined. Conversely, the population of a zone will be served by several hospitals, and this fact needs to be taken into account in constructing indicators of effective service delivery. If crude indicators are used, then it will be perfectly possible to have hospitals which are deemed to be 'efficient' with pockets of population in their areas which are badly served; or, it is possible to have a situation where all zones are well-served but the system is inefficient.

The spatial interaction concept provides a solution. Suppose that the city or region is divided into N zones – 1, 2, 3, ..., N. Let S_{ij} be the flow of patients from residential zone i to a hospital in zone j. Then $\Sigma_j S_{ij}$ is the total flow of patients from i and $\Sigma_i S_{ij}$ is the total flow of patients into j. If P_i is the population of zone i and W_j is a measure of the total size or activity level of a hospital in j, then a sensible definition of catchment population is

$$C_j = \Sigma_i [S_{ij} P_i / \Sigma_j S_{ij}] \tag{1}$$

and a measure of what is delivered to the residents of i is

$$D_i = \Sigma_j [S_{ij} W_j / \Sigma_i S_{ij}] \tag{2}$$

Then, performance indicators such as W_j/C_j and D_i/P_i are sensible measures of efficiency and effectiveness respectively. For a fuller discussion, see Clarke and Wilson (1985a) or Chapter 6 in Birkin, Clarke, Clarke and Wilson (1996).

Clearly this argument needs to be refined, but it presents the basis of an important idea. Birkin *et al.* (1994:121) show that when considered for small areas, an indicator like rates of hospitalization varies tremendously. Deeper analysis is likely to show that a component of this is explicable in terms of geographical access to hospitals – but there is also a possibility that some of the variation is explained by some treatment procedures not being available in particular hospitals.

This example illustrates the application of *IT* in the social sciences in a particularly clear way. The analytical work is only possible because of the number-crunching capabilities available. These facilitate conceptual developments. Visualization is important because it enables the rapid scanning of large numbers of mapped indicators. There is then tremendous potential for the deployment of the results of this kind of analysis in policy making and planning although there has been a marked reluctance to realize this potential.

Example 3: urban development

A model of a city has many interacting components. The discussion in each of the two preceding sections is relevant: population and economic account-based models are important elements to provide macro frameworks. Typically, the city should then be considered to be a system of zones and spatial interaction models of which those representing population-work and population-service and business-business interactions are critical components. (cf. Bertuglia *et al.* 1987: 339 for an example.) These models are all well understood. The emphasis in this section is on the harder problem of urban development dynamics because this illustrates a new facet of *IT* in the social sciences and reaches to the front line of research. Account-based models can be handled by modelling the steady state; spatial interaction models are essentially equilibrium models – the 'fast dynamics'; the more difficult topic is the slow dynamic – the evolution of urban spatial structure. To illustrate the argument, a measure of spatial structure is needed. A simple but well-developed and rich example is provided by retail structure. Let P_i be the population of zone i and W_j be a measure of the size of the retail centre in zone j (and it can of course be zero if there is no such activity). The vector $\{W_j\}$ is then a simple representation of urban retail structure. A very dispersed city would have many small values in the vector; one with a strong centre would have a large W-value for that centre, with the rest of the W_js small or zero. A variety of possible patterns can be generated in simulations and interpreted in terms of the parameter values in the models (for example, see Clarke and Wilson 1985*b*).

Interesting research questions are: can the evolution of such structures be modelled? When (and under what conditions) can one type of structure be expected to transform into another? In one obvious sense, and this is true of many social science research questions, it would be absurd to pretend that detailed predictions could be made. The form of structure will be influenced by the idiosyncratic behaviour of individual agents – and in this case, 'averaging' will not provide a solution because the numbers involved are likely to be too small. However, it can be hypothesized that the rate of growth of a particular centre is proportional to its profitability. Its profitability will, of course, also be a function of what is happening in other centres so that the mathematical representation of this hypothesis is a set of nonlinear simultaneous differential equations in many variables. It then turns out that these equations have *types* of solution; and that there are interesting transitions from one type to another under conditions which can be identified.

How does the history of this example illustrate the present argument? The answers have something in common with the health delivery services: computational capacity is needed to make any progress at all. New concepts evolve to meet the need – almost certainly in parallel with the increase in that capacity. These concepts are those of nonlinear mathematics which have become fashionable as *chaos theory*, though it should be emphasized that it is the sub-chaotic behaviour which is interesting in this context – and that also may be part of a more general argument (Cohen and Stewart 1995). (The same equations occur in other disciplines – ecology and physical chemistry for example – see Wilson (1981) – indeed whenever there are competing 'elements' in a dynamical system, and this shows the continuing importance of cross-disciplinary fertilization.) It is also again true that visualization plays an important role in this kind of research: computer simulation *and display* of the range of possible solutions facilitate understanding. This example, however, also illustrates another feature of the current situation. Although these equations have a long history (see Harris and Wilson 1978, again, for example, for the urban development application), the full fruits of their potential have yet to be realized.

Example 4: archaeology

This last example is added to show some of the unexpected benefits of cross-disciplinary linkages but also to show another kind of benefit of the ideas presented in this paper. That is, these kinds of models can often help in situations where the data are very poor: add a good theory (or model), and it may be possible to estimate some of what is missing. In a typical situation in archeology, what is known is the set of point locations of archaeological sites at which there is evidence of settlement; needless to say, relatively little is known about the relative size of settlement at each site. In this example, the case study is Greece in the late Geometric period (around 700–600 BC). It is thought that the basis of the spatial organization in that time was the *polis* – which typically involved some kind of central settlement and some smaller dependent ones. We can therefore take a vector such as $\{W_j\}$ from in the urban development (see above) retail example as a representation of this structure. It is then possible to run a model, on a variety of possible assumptions, to see if a plausible structure can be identified. Rihll and Wilson (1987a, 1987b, 1991) carried out many simulations using only point location information and, of course, some trial model parameters. The important interactions (and hence the centres) could then be presented as a network structure. Perhaps not surprisingly, but still pleasingly, those centres known to be particularly significant were reproduced in the model runs, at least for certain parameter values: Athens, Corinth, Argos, Thebes and Khalkis for instance. What proved particularly interesting was the prediction of a large site at Akraiphnion which has been recognized as an important site only in recent times. Would this model run have been sufficient evidence to make the investment in a major dig worthwhile if it was the only pointer available!?

Concluding comments: social science as 'big' science?

Inevitably in an introductory paper only glimpses can be offered of the potential of *IT* for social sciences research, and then, in this case, glimpses with a disciplinary bias. However, the potential is clear and conclusions can be drawn by building on the examples and looking forward.

Note that, while the research areas used as examples and many more, are of significant scholarly interest, many of them have obvious policy implications; and the benefits of effective application would be considerable. It should be noted in passing, because the emphasis of this paper has been on the science and not on planning and policy, that another set of massive and fascinating research problems opens up with this extension – all associated with the *combinatorial* problem of design. Searching for good solutions means, technically, searching high-dimensional spaces in which there are almost always multiple solutions – and this is the design equivalent of number-crunching. Designers, architects or planners, for example, are more likely to proceed incrementally, both in practice and conceptually, rather than face this problem! (cf. Alexander 1964, whose arguments still hold weight.)

It is becoming frustrating, given the obvious potential, that more progress has not been made in the last twenty five years (cf. Wilson 1985). The first three examples are each areas which illustrate this. Demographic modelling is generally good – but it could be further developed at a small area scale – and with finer social categories, and then deployed in areas such as housing research. There have been important developments in microsimulation of populations. There must be a case, however, for having a national model. This would facilitate policy applications in many fields and it would, in effect, become a learning system as data were added to it. In the economic case, the investment has never been put into regional or urban input-output modelling (see Jin and Wilson 1993, for a multi-regional formulation). In a situation where cities and regions routinely compete with one another for inward investment, either individual areas could benefit from the knowledge of using a model to indicate what would most strengthen their economy for the long run; or a multi-regional model could be used at the national scale to help determine regional policy. There is also the tantalizing but unfulfilled prospect of building multi-regional input-output models on a really small zone basis – say for local authority wards.

It has already been noted that in the health policy field, there has been no significant enthusiasm for the development of a good analytical capability. Indeed, it is notoriously an area where very large sums of money – tens of millions of pounds – have been squandered on the development of ineffective databases. When the sums of money involved in such exercises are compared to the funds available to support academic social science research, there must be a strong *a priori* case for devising a system with stronger intellectual foundations. Preliminary analyses of the work presented here indicate huge inequities in health service delivery and treatment outcomes and relatively cheap responses would be possible – for example through spatial reorganization.

The understanding of the urban development process is one of the great challenges of this century. Tremendous progress has been made, but again, the investment is too low to carry the programme through as effectively as it might have been. The potential benefits of such a programme – in tackling the problems of inner cities for example – would be considerable.

In conclusion, therefore, it is appropriate to compare the examples of social science research presented in this paper with 'big science'. The problems which can be articulated by the social science community are as large and complex as those in the physical or biological sciences or engineering – and the potential cost savings or quality benefits to society are almost certainly just as great – though this is a calculation which has not been done – another research challenge! Because the funding has not been available for major team projects, researchers in the social sciences have become accustomed to working as individuals or in small groups. The pool of researchers with experience of conducting such large-scale research is therefore under-developed. There is a strong argument for a government with the necessary imagination to fund some 'big' social science. And, of course, there are postgraduate training implications of this argument.

Acknowledgements

I am grateful to Professors Coppock, Haggett and Openshaw for comments on an earlier draft. This author remains responsible for any remaining weaknesses.

References

Alexander, C. (1964), Notes on the Synthesis of Form, (Cambridge Mass.)

Alvanides, S., Boyle, P., Duke-Williams, O., Openshaw, S. and Turton, I. (1996), Modelling migration in England and Wales at the ward level and the problem of estimating inter-ward distance. Mimeo, Proceedings, First International Conference on GeoComputation, School of Geography, University of Leeds, 4–5.

Bertuglia, C. S., Leonardi, G., Occelli, S., Rabino, G. A., Tadei, R., and Wilson, A. G. (1987) (eds.), Urban Systems: Contemporary Approaches to Modelling, (London).

Birkin, M., Clarke, G. P., Clarke, M. and Wilson, A. G. (1996), Intelligent GIS: Location Decisions and Strategic Planning (Cambridge).

Clarke, M. and Wilson, A. G. (1985a), 'A model-based approach to planning in the National Health Service', Environment and Planning, B, 12: 287–302.

—— and Wilson, A. G. (1985b), 'The dynamics of urban spatial structure: the progress of a research programmes', Transactions, Institute of British Geographers, NS 10: 427–51.

Cliff, A. D., Gould, P. R., Hoare, A. G. and Thrift, N. J. (1995) (eds), Diffusing Geography: Essays for Peter Haggett 342–52 (Oxford).

Cockcroft, S. (1996), 'First experiences in implementing a spatial metadata repository', Mimeo,

Proceedings, First International Conference on GeoComputation, School of Geography, University of Leeds, 111–20.

Cohen, J., and Stewart, I. (1994), *The Collapse of Chaos: Discovering Simplicity in a Complex World*, (London).

Coppock, J. T. and Rhind, D. W. (1991), 'The history of GIS'. In Maguire, Goodchild and Rhind, D.W. (eds.) (1991) 21–43.

Denley, P. and Hopkin, D. (1987) (eds.), *History and Computing*, (Manchester).

Dibble, C. (1996), 'Theory in a complex world: agent-based simulations of geographic systems', Mimeo, Proceedings, First International Conference on GeoComputation, School of Geography, University of Leeds, 210–2.

Duley, C. and Rees, P. H. (1991), Incorporating migration into simulation models, in Stillwell, J. C. H. and Congdon, P. (eds.)

Fischer, M. M. and Nijkamp, P. (eds.), (1993) *Geographic Information Systems, Spatial Modelling and Policy Evaluation (Berlin).*

Forrester, J. W. (1968), *Principles of Systems* (Boston).

—— (1969), *Urban Dynamics* (Cambridge, Mass).

Gilbert, N. (1995), 'Using computer simulation to study social phenomena'. In Lee (ed.), 208–20.

Hancock, R. and Sutherland, H. (1992) (eds.), *Microsimulation Models for Public Policy Analysis: New Frontiers* (London).

Harding, A. (1990), 'Dynamic micro-simulation models: problems and prospects', Working Paper 48, London School of Economics Welfare State Programme (London).

Harris, B. and Wilson, A. G. (1978), 'Equilibrium values and dynamics of attractiveness terms in production-constrained spatial-interaction models', *Environment and Planning, A*, 10: 371–88.

Jin, Y-X. and Wilson, A. G. (1993), 'Generation of integrated multispatial input-output models of cities', *Papers in Regional Science*, 72: 351–67.

Kauffman, S. A. (1993), *The Origins of Order: Self-organisation and Selection in Evolution* (Oxford).

Kelly, S. (1996), *Data Warehousing* (Chichester).

Langton, C., Minar, N. and Burkhart, R. (1995), 'The Swarm simulation system: a tool for studying complex systems' , Santa Fe Institute, www.santafe.edu/projects/swarm.

Lee, R. M. (1995) (ed.), *Information Technology for the Social Scientist* (London).

Leontief, W. (1967), *Input-Output Analysis*, (Oxford).

MacMillan, B. (1989) (ed.), *Remodelling Geography* (Oxford).

Maguire, D. J., Goodchild, M. F. and Rhind, D. W. (1991) (eds.) *Geographical Information Systems: Principles and Applications, Volume 1* (London).

Openshaw, S. (1988), 'Building an automated modelling system to explore a universe of spatial interaction models', *Geographical Analysis*, 20: 31–6.

—— (1992), Some suggestions concerning the development of artificial intelligence tools for spatial modelling and analysis in GIS', *Annals of Regional Science, 26*, 35–51.

—— (1993), 'Modelling spatial interaction using a neural net'. In Fischer, M. M. and Nijkamp, P. (eds.) 147–66.

Ratcliffe, P. (1996) (ed.), *Ethnicity in the 1991 Census* (London).

Rees, P.H. (1996), 'Projecting the national and regional populations of the European Union using migration information'. In Rees, P. H., Stillwell, J. C. H., Convey, A. and Hupiszewski, M. (eds.)

—— and Phillips, D. (1996), 'Geographical spread: the national picture'. In Ratcliffe, P. (ed.) 23–109.

—— Stillwell, J. C. H., Convey, A. and Hupiszewski, M. (1996) (eds.), *Population Migration in the Soviet Union* (Chichester).

—— and Wilson, A. G. (1976), *Spatial Population Analysis* (London).

Rich, J. and Wallace-Hadrill, A. (1991) (eds) *City and Country in the Ancient World* (London).

Rihll, T. E. and Wilson, A. G. (1987*a*) 'Spatial interaction and structural models in historical analysis: some possibilities and an example', *Histoire et Mesure* 2(1): 5–32.

—— and Wilson A. G. (1987*b*) 'Model-based approaches to the analysis of regional settlement structures: the case of ancient Greece'. In Denley, P. and Hopkin, D. (eds.), 10–20.

—— and Wilson, A. G. (1991), 'Settlement structures in Ancient Greece: new approaches to the polis'. In Rich, J. and Wallace-Hadrill, A. (eds.) 58–95.

Stewart, V. (1996), 'Interacting with the data warehouse: applying virtual reality technology for exploratory data analysis', Mimeo, Proceedings, First International Conference on GeoComputation, School of Geography, University of Leeds, 766–76.

Stillwell, J. C. H. and Congdon, P. (1991) (eds.), *Modelling Internal Migration* (London).

Stone , R. (1967), *Mathematics in the Social Sciences* (London).

—— (1970), *Mathematical Models of the Economy* (London).

Thom, R. (1975), *Structural Stability and Morphogenesis* (Reading, Mass.).

Weaver, W. (1948), 'Science and complexity', *American Scientist*, 36: 536 – 44.

Wilson, A. G. (1970), *Entropy in Urban and Regional Modelling* (London).

—— (1981), *Catastrophe Theory and Bifurcation: Applications to Urban and Regional Systems* (London).

—— (1985), 'Raising the levels of ambition in research: some lessons from the journal', *Environment and Planning, A*, 17: 465–70.

—— (1989), 'Classics, modelling and critical theory: human geography as structured pluralism'. In Macmillan (ed.) (1989) 61–9.

—— (1995), 'Simplicity, complexity and generality: dreams of a final theory in locational analysis'. In Cliff, Gould, Hoare and Thrift (eds.) 342–52.

—— and Pownall, C. M. (1976), 'A new representation of the urban system for modelling and for the study of micro-level interdependence', *Area*, 8: 256–64.

The simulation of social processes

NIGEL GILBERT

Department of Sociology
University of Surrey

Abstract. Computer simulation is not just a new method to add to the social researcher's armoury, but a new way of thinking about society, and especially social processes. Conventional methods have some difficulty in investigating social dynamics and in testing theories of social processes. Recent advances in computer technology have for the first time made it possible to carry out complex simulations and this has given rise to a burgeoning interest in the opportunities for theoretical and methodological developments in simulation within the social sciences. This paper reviews a variety of examples of present day simulation studies taken from anthropology, social psychology and economics as well as sociology. It identifies some theoretical ideas that have been inspired by simulations and considers some methodological issues applicable not only to simulation but to the social sciences in general.

Introduction

To see why simulation has the potential to be of great significance in the social sciences, consider the following propositions:

1   Simple patterns of repeated individual action can lead to extremely complex social institutions.
2   It is impossible, in principle, to predict the outcome of some social changes.
3   Even when there are powerful processes tending to convert a population to a consensus view, minorities may persist.
4   Members' mis-perception and mis-belief can be functional for groups and societies.

These propositions are all to some degree counter-intuitive. They are concerned with processes, although little present-day sociology is about understanding the general processes of social dynamics. They use words like 'functional', although functionalist explanations are now extremely unfashionable in British sociology. Yet as this paper aims to demonstrate, they are all conclusions which can be derived from a significant new trend in contemporary social science: the use of computers to simulate social processes and social phenomena.

Computer simulation is a child of the extraordinary advances in information technology (IT) of the last fifteen years. Some of the ideas now being developed by those involved with simulation were proposed long before computers became readily available, but they were neglected or regarded as curiosities because there was no means of studying their implications. Since experiments on society itself are obviously fraught with practical and moral difficulties, simulation is providing the first chance that most sociologists have had to adopt an experimental paradigm. However, the simulation of social processes is almost always difficult, involving substantial computer resources and some complex algorithms and techniques. Only within the last few years have adequate computer hardware and software become available at reasonable cost to support social simulation. Now, however, the opportunities afforded by advances in information technology are allowing social scientists to engage in new and fascinating explorations using computer simulation.

The growth of simulation research has coincided with an increasing impatience in sociology with approaches which are not explicitly process-oriented. For example, much functionalist sociology of the 1940s and 1950s concerned itself only with *synchronic* analysis, that is, as though from a single snapshot at a moment in time. This was partly in reaction to previous highly speculative 'evolutionary' theories. For example, early twentieth century anthropologists had proposed that some of the customs of patrilineal societies were leftovers from previous times when those societies were matrilineal. Unfortunately, these pre-literate societies had left no records about their earlier organization with the result, as functionalists were keen to point out, that this kind of evolutionary explanation was untestable (Cohen 1968).

Synchronic analysis

Synchronic analysis rules out an important class of explanations, those based on process. To understand action, it is certainly possible to look around in the immediate environment for an explanation. But often one needs to look also, or perhaps primarily, at events that occurred in the past and at how the present situation developed from previous circumstances. This was an approach to explanation in which functionalists were not much interested and their reluctance to explain in terms of processes through time is one that has left its mark even on present-day sociology.

Consider, for instance, the two main methods of empirical analysis sociologists use today: statistical tools such as regression and its more complex variants, and the whole gamut of qualitative analysis of interviews and observational data which can be loosely characterized as 'ethnography'. In the case of ethnography, it is rare for the analyst to have access to data about processes, that is, data about how things came to be as they are. Interviewing people will provide an insight into their present ideas. Asking them to recount their biographies or explain their careers is possible, but the picture obtained will inevitably be influenced by their current circumstances and their current percep-tions. For example, if women doctors are interviewed about their careers and their decisions about whether to have children, the sample will not include those women who decided not to qualify as doctors because they realized that it would be difficult to combine a medical career with bringing up a family. Moreover, the accounts that they provide of their decisions will undoubtedly be coloured by their subsequent experiences. This is not a criticism of ethnography as a method; just that it is an almost inevitable consequence of this type of data collection that the analyst's attention will be shifted away from processes towards synchronic explanations.

As far as statistical analysis is concerned, until quite recently the only data which have been available have been from cross-sectional surveys, that is, from surveys of people at one moment in time. Gradually over the last ten years the inadequacies of these data have been realized and increasing attention is being given to mounting panel studies. These are surveys in which the same people are asked the same or similar questions regularly over a period of years, so that it is possible to determine how the attitudes and circumstances of individuals have changed. In the United Kingdom (UK), the best examples are the pioneering National Child Development Study (Ferri 1993), which is collecting data about all the people in the UK born during one week in 1953, and the British Household Panel Study (Buck *et al.* 1994), which is interviewing a random sample of households annually.

Together with the increasing availability of such longitudinal data has come the development of new statistical methods of analysis. For example, event history analysis aims to show how the characteristics of an individual can be used to explain the timing of that person's life events. Given some data at the individual level from a panel study on when people enter and leave unemployment, one might use event history analysis to explain the duration of a period of unemployment in terms of a person's education, previous spans of unemployment, age and similar variables.

Individualistic explanation

Even these new methods of statistical analysis, however, leave something to be desired. If we use event history analysis to explain length of unemployment, we do so in terms of each individual's own characteristics: their own education, their age, their past history of employment and so on. The only way in which the society enters into the explanation is as a substrate in which there is a rate of unemployment and an education system, but these characteristics are taken as givens and are not themselves explained.

Explanations provided by techniques such as event history analysis also fail to suggest the processes which generate the observed relationships. An analysis of unemployment might show that the expected length of a span of unemployment is related to the unemployed person's previous employment history. It could provide a beta coefficient to measure the strength of this relationship, but what it could not do is provide an explanation of why the relationship holds: just what is it about previous unemployment that tends to lengthen the duration of current unemployment? Not only does it not offer an answer to this question, but it also fails to offer any clues about where we should look to discover more.

An approach which might help to overcome these problems is the construction of *models of social processes*. Model-building has a long history in sociology, but nowadays it tends to be assumed that a model necessarily takes the form of a statistical equation. This is because statistics offers a highly refined technology for model-building which has come to dominate social science.

Within the last few years, however, new opportunities for building computational models have arisen, inspired partly by the extraordinary advances in computing hardware and software and partly by influences from other disciplines, particularly physics, artificial intelligence and theoretical biology. Since the mid-1980s there has been rapidly increasing interest world-wide in the possibility of using simulation in sociology and the other social sciences (Chattoe and Conte 1995, Gilbert and Conte 1995, Gilbert and Doran 1994) as sociologists have realised that it offers the possibility of building models which are process-oriented and in which the mechanisms of social life can be explicitly represented. The following sections will explore the potential of computer simulation in the social sciences by describing some recent examples. The examples have been chosen to give a flavour of the range of simulation methods and the variety of research areas which are now using simulation as a research tool. It should be emphasized that these examples have been chosen for illustration and what follows is not intended as a comprehensive survey.

Computational models of social life

Micro-simulation

One of the earliest and probably the best known type of social science simulation is 'micro-simulation' (Harding 1990), developed primarily for investigating the consequences of changes in social policy on populations. It has been used to predict the financial effects of pension changes on future generations and for investigating the implications of welfare benefit and tax changes on households (Hancock and Sutherland 1992, Harding 1996). Previously most fiscal projections were made by rather simple extrapolations of past trends into the future. Micro-simulation aims to provide much better grounded estimates (see the paper by Sutherland in this volume).

The basic idea is simple: collect data about a random sample of a few thousand households at one moment in time from a national survey such as the Family Expenditure Survey, then simulate the effect of the passage of a year on each of the households in turn. For example, all the members of the household will get one year older. This means that some of the children will leave school and join the labour market; some of the older members will leave the labour market and retire. Some women will give birth to children and some people will die during the year. Each of these life course events is simulated with a specified probability, the probability varying according to the situation of each person. Thus a woman aged between 16 and 25 will have a certain probability of becoming pregnant, while a man will have a zero probability of doing so. After simulating demographic changes during the year, consequential changes to income and expenditure are made (for instance, people who retire lose their salary but gain a pension). More complex models may also simulate the break-up and formation of households. Once the effects of one year have been calculated, the simulation advances to the next year, building on the previous results.

At the end of each simulated year, aggregate statistics about the sample such as the proportions in and out of the labour force or the total expenditure on benefits can be calculated and grossed up to predict what would be the case for the whole population. In this way, forecasts about changes years ahead at the level of a whole society can be made which are based on simulations of the behaviour of individual households.

Micro-simulation is usually aimed at providing answers to matters of social policy. As such it is at the applied end of the spectrum of social research. It suffers from some of the same points of criticism as have been levelled at more conventional methods. For example, it treats each household as an isolated entity. In practice, proponents concentrate almost exclusively on prediction, what the situation will be like in, say, twenty years time, rather than on explanation, why it should be like that. Nevertheless, micro-simulation is interesting because it shows how behaviour at one level – national taxation and benefit expenditure – can be modelled by a simulation of households at a lower level of analysis. As will be seen in subsequent sections, the relationships between levels of analysis, individual, organizational and societal, are matters of central concern in social simulation. Some more advanced micro-simulation programs are now modelling not only households but also the business sector. They are also beginning to use simulated changes at the aggregate national level to influence behaviour modelled at the individual level, for example, the effect of national unemployment rates on the probability of individuals securing employment.

Cellular automata

The micro-simulation approach treats the units of analysis, households, as isolated agents. Work based on a different approach suggests one way of going beyond this to model interactions between people. Cellular automata are arrays of simple processes arranged so that each process can be affected by the state of its neighbours. One of the first and simplest cellular automata models was the so-called Game of Life (Berlekamp *et al.* 1982). Imagine a rectangular grid of cells. Time proceeds in discrete steps. At any time step, a cell can either be 'alive' or 'dead'. Two rules determine the state of a cell. A living cell remains alive only if it has two or three living neighbouring cells. Otherwise it will die, either of 'loneliness' or of 'overcrowding'. A dead cell starts to live if there are exactly three living cells around it. Although these two rules are very simple, the effect at the macro level, that is at the level of the grid as a whole, can be very complex, with different starting configurations of live and dead cells giving sequences of patterns arising and evolving, sometimes remaining stable and sometimes dying away. The form of these dynamic patterns is normally impossible to predict analytically; the only way of discovering the patterns is to simulate. The patterns can be said to 'emerge' from the life and death of the individual cells.

Cellular automata (CA) have been used to investigate the properties of physical materials (e.g., magnets), and engineering problems (e.g., fluids in pipes) and have been of great interest to mathematicians (Toffoli and Margolus 1987, Wolfram 1986). Now they are beginning to be used for investigating social phenomena (Hegselmann 1996). Of course, a cell in a grid is not intended to be a fully-fledged simulation of a person. Rather, CA models are used to investigate the abstract properties of interacting agents. In some of these models, as in the Game of Life, the cells remain fixed on the grid. In others, the cells are allowed to move over the grid like pieces on a draughts board, again dependent on the results of applying simple rules about the state of neighbouring cells.

An example is the study by Schelling (197, 1978) of ethnic segregation. Segregation into distinct geographical neighbourhoods was and still is often considered to be a product of direct discrimination (e.g., estate agents dissuading black people from moving into white areas) or the indirect effects of economic constraints (e.g., poor black families being able to afford housing only in deprived areas). But by investigating the properties of a CA model, Schelling pointed out that if families, both black and white, prefer to live in neighbourhoods in which there are at least some of their own ethnic group, and they are able to move to the nearest location which satisfies this desire, segregation will inevitably emerge. This is the case even if none of the families actually wants to be segregated, or even desires a location in which their group is in the majority. An unintended outcome emerges from the effect of many individual decisions.

Schelling's experiments were mainly carried out with paper and pencil, a very laborious procedure prone to error, because adequate computer support was not available in the early 1970s. The conclusions which took him so much effort to arrive at can now be obtained in a few seconds because the simulation can be programmed on a computer and can be run with a graphical interface which demonstrates immediately and clearly the segregation which results (e.g., Epstein and Axtell 1996).

Modelling dynamic social impact

Latané has put the cellular automata model to good effect in exploring the implications of the theory of dynamic social impact. Social impact is defined quite generally as a change in a person's subjective feelings, motives, emotions or beliefs as a result of the actions of other individuals. In an early paper, Latané (1981) proposed that social impact is proportional to the product of the number of people influencing an individual, their strength (e.g., the amount of status, persuasiveness and attractiveness) and their immediacy (e.g., their closeness in space or time to the person being influenced). During the following ten years, the relationship was shown to hold in a wide variety of situations. However, as formulated, social impact is a static and individualized theory. What happens if we have a population of people, all influencing each other? Until the advent of computer hardware capable of supporting simulation experiments, it was hard to answer this question.

Latané (1996) used computer simulation to explore the reciprocal effects of social impact within interacting populations. Imagine a population of some hundreds or thousands of people whose attitudes to three different and independent issues are known. Suppose also that to begin with, 60 per cent of the population follow the majority view on each issue and the remaining 40 per cent have the contrary view, but these attitudes are distributed among the individuals entirely at random, with no correlation between individuals' attitudes on the three issues. Furthermore, suppose that the people vary in how influential they are, again at random. A cellular automata model can be set up with each cell representing a person and with state change rules that implement the principle of dynamic social impact, so that if the sum of the influences on a particular person in one direction exceeds the sum of the influences in the other direction, that person flips their attitude correspondingly. We can then watch what happens as people influence their neighbours and their neighbours in turn influence them.

First, rather than being overwhelmed by the combined influence of the majority view, the minority survives although with a reduced percentage of adherents. While individuals continually change their affiliation as a result of social impact, overall there remains a minority of more or less constant size. Secondly, the distribution of attitudes changes from the initial random distribution to being spatially clustered. That is, people with similar attitudes are grouped together, influencing each other to stay in line. It is the clustering that protects the minorities from extinction, because it is only the cells on the edges of clusters which are exposed strongly to the other attitude. Thirdly, although changes of attitude on the three attributes are modelled as being entirely independent at the individual level, the three attributes become correlated at the level of the population. This is because as the simulation proceeds, clusters of like-minded people develop. These clusters are different for each of the three attributes, but because a person in one cluster is somewhat more likely than random chance to be in another cluster (or vice versa), at the population level there will apparently be a correlation between the attitudes.

This result has some sociological implications. A set of correlated attitudes or beliefs can be described as an ideology and it is assumed that ideologies arise as coherent groups of beliefs from social movements. But here we have modelled the emergence of a prototype ideology literally from nothing. The model suggests, for example, that the cluster of attitudes called a class ideology could arise not only from people's relationship to the mode of production but also from their spatial clustering and their interaction, and it proposes a mechanism for this.

Latane's results are robust. It does not matter what the initial random starting configuration of attitudes is, nor the distribution of strengths, nor the number of people in the simulation, nor the number of attitudes modelled; the clustering and the survival of minorities occur every time. Those features of the simulation which *are* essential and without which interesting behaviour does not occur are: people must be located in social space so that they have more influence on near neighbours than on distant strangers; attitudes must be on a discrete rather than a continuous scale (this introduces non-linearity into the system); and the distribution of strengths in the population must not be uniform (the strong individuals protect the borders of minority clusters).

Models based on Artificial Intelligence

The result of this kind of simulation can be fascinating to watch, and the advent of powerful personal computers has meant that graphical displays are relatively easy to create, but it nevertheless requires much theoretical imagination to move from patterns of cells on a grid to conclusions about societies. This is partly because the individuals are modelled as such very simple units. Another strand of recent simulation research has favoured using rather more complex models in which individuals are simulated using 'agents' based on techniques derived from Artificial Intelligence (AI).

A model of budgeting

Chattoe and Gilbert (1995) have been building a simulation of how people divide their income between major categories of expenditure such as rent, food and leisure, based on data obtained from interviews with consumers. Existing economic theories about consumption behaviour are based on rational choice but tend to be poor at predicting actual expenditure, partly because they have difficulty in incorporating factors such as social influences, personal rules of thumb and the fact that consumption decisions are made over time. Because most people most of the time make budgetary decisions from habit, Chattoe and Gilbert interviewed people who would be most likely to be budgeting explicitly: the recently retired, many of whom will have had a major change in their economic circumstances and who will therefore have had to adjust their purchasing, and postgraduate students who often have some difficulty in making ends meet.

The respondents were asked to give details of their major sources of income and expenditure using their own categories. They explained how they dealt with regular outgoings such as rent, how they would deal with unexpected expenses and which categories they regarded as fixed or negotiable. Their replies were formalized as a set of rules which drove a simulation. One conclusion was the importance of planning for consumption. The respondents were able to forecast their likely future expenditure and appeared to use this to decide whether they had to economize. The effect of such projections could be examined by running the simulation both with and without modelling the ability to project. Without projection, the simulation would rapidly get into dire trouble. With projection and the same stream of income and bills, the simulated agents were able to survive for months on end.

Thus the simulation serves as a way of capturing and experimenting with the rules that people say they use in budgeting. The model provides a formal notation for expressing respondents' budgeting rules and it allows the rules to be checked for consistency and completeness, pointing out areas and issues that neither the researchers nor the respondents had realised needed to be considered. The research, however, aims to move beyond this descriptive mode to explore the consequences of different budgeting behaviours.

Deciding what to spend one's money on is not a purely individual matter of strict economics. Very few people are so poor that they do not have some choice about what they buy and the great majority probably have much more potential choice than they can possibly cope with rationally. It may be for this reason that rational choice theories of consumption work so badly. Instead, one might assume that people make decisions on consumption on the basis of social learning and social imitation. That is, people adopt bunches of consumption decisions or 'lifestyles' from a selection available to them from their friends and family and these are then adjusted in the light of circumstances through a process of trial and error or evolution. Chattoe and Gilbert (1996) experimented with this notion by building a simulation in which the agents evolve their own budgeting rules under the constraint that they have to live on their income, just as people do. The simulation uses a technique called genetic programming which is loosely based on biological evolution.

Living things evolve through a process of repeated reproduction in which the genes, a way of coding information about the characteristics of an individual, are transmitted from parent to offspring. Genes are combined from both parents in sexual reproduction and occasionally mutate. The chances of an individual reproducing and passing on their genes depends on the 'fitness' of that individual in its environment. These basic ideas of evolution have been simulated in computer programs using sequences of bits as a model for a gene, and implementing sexual reproduction and mutation by combining and randomly changing those bit sequences. Such 'genetic algorithms' now have a respectable history and have been applied in many domains: not just for biological research, but also in engineering and financial applications where the algorithm is used to evolve designs which fit their environments well (Goldberg 1989, Koza 1992). In Chattoe and Gilbert's simulation, budgeting rules are evolved and can then be compared with the ones described by the respondents.

Collective mis-belief

Another, rather different example of the use of artificial intelligence techniques started as a study of the emergence of social complexity among pre-historic hunter-gatherers in south-west France about 20,000 years ago. Archaeologists believe that around this time there was a change from societies with a rather simple organization of small groups of close relatives to much larger bands with a clearly identifiable leader or 'big man', the development of status differences and the evolution of ritual and decoration, including cave art. Two slightly different theories have been proposed (Gamble 1991; Mellars 1985) to account for the emergence of social complexity, both of them suggesting that population concentration resulting from glaciation during the ice age was an important factor. Distinguishing between the theories on the basis of the very limited archaeological evidence is difficult and so Doran proposed to compare the theories by examining their implications through a simulation (Doran and Palmer 1995, Doran *et al.* 1993).

To do so, he created a simulated landscape, a large virtual space over which his agents could move. Agents could harvest food resources which were distributed randomly in this space. One could imagine them to be herds of reindeer or salmon rivers. Agents were also randomly distributed over the landscape. Each agent has a working memory, in which facts are stored (or strictly speaking beliefs, since its knowledge may not be true). For example, the working memory could hold the location of the last food resource encountered. In addition the working memory stores 'perceptions' recorded by simple simulated sensory organs. Agents also have a set of rules of the form 'if this is the situation, then carry out this action'. For example, one rule might be, 'if next to a food resource, eat it'. In order to determine whether the condition part of the rule is true, the agent looks in its own working memory. The action part of the rule may either instruct the agent to carry out some kind of action (e.g., move or eat) or may change the state of the working memory (e.g., 'remember that there is a food supply here'). Finally, there is a part of the agent which repeatedly scans the rules to find one whose condition part is true and then carries out the action specified in that rule. All the agents share the same set of rules (but not the same memory) and interact within the same environment. They can send each other messages. As time goes on, they use up energy which has to be replenished by eating food and they come to learn about each other's existence and positions. If they fail to find and eat enough, they starve to death. The agents are set up with rules to: consume food that is immediately adjacent; move towards food to which they believe they are the nearest agent; or move randomly a small distance.

With this system, various experiments can be performed to find factors which increase or decrease the overall likelihood that the population of agents will survive (that is, not die of starvation). Doran (1985) has carried out experiments in which the agents form themselves into groups of 'friends' which collectively carry out plans to obtain resources. He has also experimented with the consequences of mis-beliefs. In the latter experiments, agents can attack other agents and take over their food. But agents will not attack agents whom they believe are their friends, nor agents who have a friend in common with them. The agents are programmed in such a way that they can make mistakes that lead them to believe in the existence of 'pseudo-agents', agents which do not in fact exist. Because agents exchange beliefs with their friends, such mis-beliefs may spread, leading to the formation of what Doran calls a 'cult', a group of agents all of whom believe they have a pseudo-agent as their friend. The consequence is that cult members will not attack each other and this leads to an overall higher rate of survival. Because pseudo-agents, being only beliefs in the 'minds' of the agents, never die nor move out of range, cults survive much longer than groups focused around 'real' agents.

The hypothesis that the existence of mis-belief in a society may be functional can lead to a number of philosophical and methodological problems if it is considered simply in functionalist terms. However, recast into the framework of computational modelling, it is much more precise and, in particular, testable. We can specify what we mean by 'a society', we can define 'functional for' in terms of the average survival time (or any other indicator we choose) and we can then, crucially, carry out experiments to see whether the hypothesis is true under controlled conditions. Of course, these experiments are performed not on a society itself, but on a model of a society. Nevertheless, there is nothing unusual or unsafe about this provided that one is aware of the limits of the conclusions that can be drawn.

An approach to social processes

Non-linear dynamics

These examples can be used to draw out some general principles about social phenomena which seem to be suggested by current work in the field. One of the themes of social simulation research is that agents can be programmed with very simple rules (consider, for example, the simulation of social impact) but the behaviour of the system as a whole can turn out to be extremely complex because of non-linearities in the models. Conventional statistical methods are almost all based on the assumption of a linear relationship between variables, that is, the effect on the dependent variable is proportional to a sum of a set of independent variables. But this is a very restrictive assumption. A new interdisciplinary field called Complexity Theory (Waldrop 1992) is trying to develop general results about non-linear systems. As an example, consider pouring a steady stream of sand out of a pipe so that it mounts up into a pyramid. As more sand is added, there will be little landslides down the side of the pile. While the pyramidal shape of the pile and, in particular, the angle of the side is predictable, depending on the properties of the average sand grain, the timing, location and scale of the landslides are unpredictable because the slippage is non-linear: once a grain of sand starts sliding, it pulls others along with it and there is positive feedback leading to a mass of sand slipping. Similar non-linearities are thought to cause stock market crashes.

From the point of view of the scientist or mathematician, non-linear systems are difficult to study because most cannot be understood analytically. There is often no set of equations which can be solved to relate the characteristics of the system. The only generally effective way of exploring non-linear behaviour is to simulate it by building a model and then running the simulation. Even when one can get some understanding of how non-linear systems work, they remain unpredictable. However much one studies stock markets or the properties of sand, it will still be impossible (in principle) to predict the timing of a crash or a landslide.

Explanation and prediction

This experience does have some lessons for sociological explanation. For instance, the philosophy of social science has often made too ready a connection between explanation and prediction. It tends to assume that the test of a theory is that it will predict successfully. This is not a criterion which is appropriate for non-linear theories, at least at the micro scale. There is an interesting consequence for debates over free will and determinism, but sociologists hardly seem to worry about this issue any more. This is as it should be, because the classic debate assumed incorrectly that if we were ever in a position to understand human action completely, we would then be able to predict it, leaving no room for free will. Complexity theory shows that even if we were to have a complete understanding of the factors affecting individual action, that would still not be sufficient to predict behaviour. The message is even stronger if we make the plausible assumption that it is not only social action that is complex in this sense, but also individual cognition.

Emergence

A formal notion of emergence is one of the most important ideas to come from this approach. Emergence occurs when interactions among objects at one level give rise to different types of objects at another level. More precisely, a phenomenon is emergent if it requires new categories to describe it which are not required to describe the behaviour of the underlying components. For example, temperature is an emergent property of the motion of atoms. An individual atom has no temperature, but a collection of them does.

That the idea of emergence is not obvious is attested by the considerable debate that sociologists, starting with Durkheim (1895), have had about the relationship between individual characteristics and social phenomena. Durkheim in his less cautious moments alleged that social phenomena are external to individuals while methodological individualists argued that there is no such thing as society (e.g., Watkins 1995). Both sides of this debate were confused because they did not fully understand the idea of emergence. Recent social theorists (Archer 1995, Kontopoulos 1993) are now beginning to refine the idea and work through the implications. Simulations could provide a powerful metaphor for such theoretical investigations.

We can see social institutions as emergent from individual action, just as clusters emerged from the interacting influences of Latané's cells. There is, however, a difficulty with this view. It appears to leave human organizations and institutions as little different in principle from animal societies such as nesting wasps. They can all be said to emerge from the actions of individuals. The difference is that while we assume that, for instance, wasps have no ability to reason, but just follow instinct and in doing so construct a nest, people do have the ability to recognize, reason about and react to human institutions, that is, to emergent features. The institutions which result from behaviour which takes into account such emergent features might be called 'second order emergence'. The fact that humans engage in such behaviour might be one of the defining characteristics of human societies, distinguishing them from animal societies (Gilbert 1995). It is what makes sociology different from ethology. Not only can we as scientific observers distinguish patterns of collective action, but the agents themselves can also do so and therefore their actions can be affected by the existence of these patterns.

This point can be illustrated by returning to the example of the simulation of budgeting decisions described earlier. It may be that one of the influences on people's patterns of budgeting decisions is their adoption of a 'lifestyle', that is, a collection of predigested consumption decisions. There are two ways in which this could happen. On the one hand, people might adopt a lifestyle without any recognition that they are so doing, and this is probably the way it works for most people most of the time. It is only when the sociologist or economist studies their consumption patterns that it becomes clear that those patterns fit into a widely shared template. On the other hand, there are some people who quite consciously adopt lifestyles and others who discover after the fact that they have adopted a lifestyle. These people are quite likely to categorize themselves as 'the sort of people who follow this lifestyle', to band together as a group (e.g., 'punks', 'students', 'old age pensioners') and to contribute explicitly to the evolution of the lifestyle.

A simulation of such a process would therefore have to model:

1   the emergence of patterns of consumption in the society as a result of the social imitation of individual agents' decisions on consumption;

2   the perception by agents that these patterns exist;
3   the categorization ('social construction') by agents of these patterns into some small number of 'lifestyles';
4   the influence of agents' adoption of these lifestyles on their consumption decisions, leading to the evolution of adapted or new patterns of consumption.

The simulation would thus have to model both the emergence of societal level properties *from* individual actions and the effect of societal level properties *on* individual actions. The latter in turn may affect the societal level properties and so on. One of the present-day challenges for computational simulation in the social sciences is to develop convincing examples of such models. It would be fair to say that at the moment we do not know how to do so.

Conclusion

This paper began by presenting four propositions which might be considered to be rather unusual. In the course of this review of recent computer simulation in the social sciences, each of them has been mentioned and shown to be worth consideration. They thus illustrate the particular value and fascination of simulation: it is both a practical enterprise, requiring the full resources of contemporary information technology and sometimes resulting in conclusions which can be applied directly to questions of social and economic policy, and an exercise which can illuminate fundamental issues of social theory. It is this duality, together with the new opportunities available from more powerful hardware and the influence of ideas brought in from other disciplines, which is now making computer simulation one of the fastest growing and most exciting areas of social research.

Acknowledgements

This paper has benefited from comments from Edmund Chattoe and Anthony Heath. Previous versions have been presented at the conference on New Technologies in the Social Sciences, 27–29 October, 1995, Bournemouth, UK, at a seminar at LAFORIA, Paris, 22 January 1996 and at a meeting of the British Academy on Information Technology and Scholarly Disciplines, London, 18–19 October 1996.

References

Archer, M. (1995), *Realist Social Theory: the Morphogenetic Approach* (Cambridge).
Berlekamp, E., Conway, J. and Guy, R. (1982), *Winning Ways for Your Mathematical Plays* Volume 2: Games in particular (London).
Buck, N. Gershuny, J., Rose, D. and Scott, J. (1994) (eds.) *Changing Households: the British Household Panel Survey, 1990–1992* (Colchester).
Chattoe, E. and Conte, R. (1995), (eds.) *Third Symposium on Simulating Societies* (Boca Raton, Fla).
—— and Gilbert, N. (1995), 'A simulation of budgetary decision-making based on interview data'.

In Discussion paper 3, ESRC Economic Beliefs and Behaviour Programme, electronic document: http://snipe.ukc.ac.uk/ESRC/papers/chatto/chatto1.html

—— and Gilbert, N. (1996), *The Simulation of Budgetary Decision-making and Mechanisms of Evolution* (Guildford).

Cohen, P. (1968), *Modern Social Theory* (London).

Doran, J. and Palmer, M. (1995), 'The EOS project: integrating two models of Palaeolithic social change'. In Gilbert, N. and Conte, R. (eds.) *Artificial Societies* (London) 103–25.

—— Palmer, M., Gilbert, N. and Mellars, P. (1993), 'The EOS Project: modelling Upper Palaeolithic change' In Gilbert, G.N. and Doran, J. (eds.) *Simulating Societies* (London) 195–222.

Durkheim, E. (1895), *The Rules of Sociological Method* (Chichester).

Epstein, J. M. and Axtell, R. (1996), *Growing Artificial Societies: Social Science from the Bottom Up* (Cambridge, Mass).

Ferri, E. (1993) (ed.), *Life at 33: the Fifth Follow-up of the National Child Development Study* (London).

Gamble, C. (1991), 'The social context for European Palaeolithic art'. *Proceedings of the Prehistoric Society* 57: 3–15.

Gilbert, G. N. (1995), 'Emergence in social simulation'. In Gilbert, N. and Conte, R. (eds.) *Artificial Societies: the Computer Simulation of Social Life* (London) 144–56.

—— and Conte, R. (1995) (eds.), *Artificial Societies: the Computer Simulation of Social Life* (London).

—— and Doran, J. (1994), *Simulating Societies: the Computer Simulation of Social Phenomena* (London).

Goldberg, D. E. (1989), *Genetic Algorithms in Search, Optimization and Machine Learning* (Reading, Mass.).

Hancock, R. and Sutherland, H. (1992), *Microsimulation Models for Public Policy Analysis: New Frontiers* (London).

Harding, A. (1990), 'Dynamic microsimulation models: problems and prospects', Discussion Paper WSP/48, London School of Economics, Welfare State Programme.

—— (1996), *Microsimulation and Public Policy* (Amsterdam).

Hegselmann, R. (1996), 'Cellular Automata in the social sciences: perspectives, restrictions and artefacts'. In Hegselmann, R., Mueller, U. and Troitzsch, K. G. (eds.) *Modelling and Simulation in the Social Sciences from the Philosophy of Science Point of View* (Berlin) 209–34.

Kontopoulos, K. M. (1993), *The Logics of Social Structure* (Cambridge).

Koza, J. R. (1992), *Genetic Programming* (Cambridge, Mass).

Latané, B. (1981), 'The psychology of social impact'. *American Psychologist* 36: 343–56.

—— (1996), 'Dynamic social impact' in Hegselmann, R., Mueller, U. and Troitzsch, K. G. (eds.) *Modelling and Simulation in the Social Sciences from the Philosophy of Science Point of View* (Berlin) 287–310.

Mellars, P. (1985), 'The ecological basis of social complexity in the Upper Palaeolithic of South-western France'. In Douglas-Price, T. and Brown, J. A. (eds.) *Prehistoric Hunter-gatherers: the Emergence of Cultural Complexity* (New York) 271–97.

Schelling, T. C. (1971), 'Dynamic models of segregation'. *Journal of Mathematical Sociology* 1: 143–86.

—— (1978), *Micromotives and Macrobehavior* (New York).

Toffoli, T. and Margolus, N. (1987), *Cellular Automata Machines* (Cambridge, Mass.).

Waldrop, M. M. (1992), *Complexity: the Emerging Science at the Edge of Chaos* (New York).

Watkins, W. J. N. (1955), 'Methodological individualism: a reply'. *Philosophy of Science*, 22: 58–62.

Wolfram, S. (1986), *Theory and Applications of Cellular Automata* (Singapore).

Commentary

ANTHONY HEATH
Nuffield College
Oxford

Professor Gilbert is right to identify computer simulation as a new way of thinking about social processes. It offers the possibility of understanding in a formal and rigorous way the underlying processes, particularly those involving social interaction, that generate the observed regularities in social behaviour. He is also right to distinguish between the enterprises of statistical analysis and of computer simulation. While they often use the same terminology and talk of models and explanations, I agree with him that there is a major difference between their uses in sociology. The most successful examples in sociology of statistical analysis have tended to be descriptive of regularities or associations between observed measures of behaviour. Computer simulations, on the other hand, are essentially hypothetical models which postulate mechanisms and processes that generate the observed regularities.

Perhaps the most attractive feature of computer simulation is its ability to model social interaction (that is, the reciprocal influences of individuals on each other) and to explore the emergent, unintended consequences of social interaction. It thus can move beyond the typically individualistic approach of conventional statistical analysis and can move towards a model that captures the distinctively social aspects of human behaviour. Moreover, these processes of interaction also generate nonlinearities which, as Professor Gilbert rightly observes, are particularly difficult to handle with conventional statistical methods.

Having said this, I was unconvinced that Professor Gilbert's first example of computer simulation really did mark much of a break with conventional statistical analysis. Micro-simulation of changes in household composition, income and expenditure is certainly useful for planning purposes, but it seems to be largely an extension of standard statistical analyses of survey data: in the example that Professor Gilbert gives, micro-simulation starts with the observed relationships between social positions and, say, expenditure patterns and with the observed probabilities of people changing their social positions over the course of the year. On the assumption that the observed conditional probabilities in the past will hold true in the future, it is possible to combine these two sets of observed conditional probabilities in order to predict aggregate expenditure in future years. This kind of model does not move away from the conventional individualistic assumptions of statistical analysis nor does it take any account of processes of social interaction (which might in principle lead the future conditional probabilities to be unlike the past ones).

Other examples given by Professor Gilbert, such as Latane's use of cellular automata to model the persistence of deviant minorities, represent a more radical break with conventional statistical modelling. These models of cellular automata move away from the individualist assumptions of micro-simulation and explore the dynamic processes of mutual influence between individuals.

Interesting though they are, these examples seem to be rather remote from the real-world problems that exercise contemporary sociologists. While they may shed useful light on the properties of fundamental social processes, they may have more interest to the social psychologist than to the sociologist. Latané's models, for example, fall within the scope of social psychological research on intergroup relations and they lack the substantive content that sociologists tend to prefer. The artificiality of Latané's assumptions makes for elegant modelling but perhaps for limited applicability.

The challenge for computer simulation, therefore, is to show that it can help us understand real-world problems. One example which does begin to do this is Gudgin and Breen's dynamic model of unemployment in Northern Ireland (Gudgin and Breen 1996). Catholics have typically experienced much higher unemployment rates than Protestants (the Catholic rate being around 2.5 times as high as the Protestant one), and this has come to occupy a central place in discussions of fair employment in Northern Ireland. Gudgin and Breen use a computer simulation in order to try to understand the evolution of Catholic:Protestant differentials in unemployment. Their model takes account of differences in the rate of natural increase of Catholics and Protestants, in their rates of migration and labour market participation, and on the overall rate of growth of employment in Northern Ireland. They conclude from the results of their simulation that it is possible to generate a Catholic:Protestant; unemployment ratio in excess of 2.0 without any assumption about discrimination (Gudgin and Breen 1996, p.40).

Gudgin and Breen's conclusion has proved somewhat controversial (see Murphy 1996 and Rowthorn 1996), but it does demonstrate the value of computer simulation for understanding real-world problems. Their model has perhaps more in common with microsimulation than with the abstract automata of Latané's model. Like the micro-simulations, it uses survey-based evidence to provide the key empirical inputs into the model (on the rate of natural increase and so on), and unlike the cellular automata it does not attempt to model complex processes of social interaction. Like the micro-simulations, therefore, it builds on conventional statistical modelling rather than providing a radical challenge to it, and it may well be that this is the course that computer simulation will tend to take in sociology, leaving the artificial world of the cellular automata to the social psychologists.

Reference

Gudgin, G. and Breen, R. (1996), 'Evaluation of the ratio of unemployment rates as an indicator of fair employment'. Central Community Relations Unit, Studies in Employment Equality, Research Report no 4, Part 1, (Belfast) 1–68.

Murphy, A. (1996), 'Comment'. Central Community Relations Unit, Studies in Employment Equality, Research Report no 4, Part 2, (Belfast) 69–77.

Rowthorn, R. (1996), 'Comment'. Central Community Relations Unit, Studies in Employment Equality, Research Report no 4, Part 2, (Belfast) 78–81.

Information technology and psychology: from cognitive psychology to cognitive engineering

ANNE H. ANDERSON

Department of Psychology
University of Glasgow

Abstract. Cognitive psychology is a large sub-domain of psychology concerned with identifying and understanding the processes which underlie human cognition. It developed following a paradigm shift in the 1950s when psychologists abandoned 'Behaviourism' with its stimulus-response models of behaviour and became interested in the internal processes and representations involved in human information processing. The introduction of computers provided a powerful analogy for these mental operations. Thus the introduction of information technology (IT) had a profound impact on the way psychologists modelled behaviour. In the 1980s there were challenges to the computational metaphor. Psychologists who adopt a 'Connectionist approach' claimed that cognition should be explained in terms of interactions between connected neural-like elements. Models should correspond to the neural processes of the human brain. Connectionists use powerful computer simulation techniques to model human information processes and regard this as a second paradigm shift based upon the appropriate use of IT. This paper will concentrate on a third aspect of the relationship between IT and psychology: the desire to understand the way in which human users interact with the technology, its impact upon human activities such as communication and decision making, and how the technology should be designed to facilitate these processes. The goals of this 'Cognitive Engineering' approach will be illustrated in terms of developing design guidelines for technologies and understanding human behaviour in new technologically-mediated milieus.

Introduction: information technology as a metaphor for the mind

Cognitive psychology is concerned with understanding the structure and functions of the human mind and assumes that mental processes are linked with observable behaviour. The cognitive mental processes which have been the main focus of study have been those involved in memory, attention, communication, perception and problem solving.

Cognitive psychology came into being as a result of what is generally regarded as a 'paradigm shift' (Kuhn 1962) in the 1950s when psychologists largely abandoned 'Behaviourism' (Watson 1914, Skinner 1938) with its stimulus-response models of human behaviour. In its place psychologists became interested in the internal processes and representations which are involved in human information processing, and the

development of serial computers provided a powerful analogy for these mental operations. Thus the introduction of information technology (IT) had a major impact on the
way in which psychologists modelled behaviour.

The impact of IT on cognitive psychology has been profound and pervasive. From its
impact as a metaphor for the workings of human information processing systems, to a
method of simulating human cognitive processes, IT has had significant effects at every
level of the discipline. Almost all cognitive psychologists would agree on its historical
significance (see, for example, Sanford 1985, Solso 1995, Haberlandt 1994). This paper
includes a sketch of recent historical changes which have occurred as a result of the
development of computing and a personal view of the present position and future
directions in the relationship between IT and cognitive psychology. It will focus on the
need to understand the way in which human users interact with IT, its impact upon
human activities such as communication and decision making, and how the technology
should be designed to facilitate these processes.

This approach has a distinguished academic pedigree beginning with the wartime
studies at the Applied Psychology Unit in Cambridge on aircraft displays. Researchers
tried to understand the problems of human interactions with technology, and so to assist
in designing systems which would maximize human performance. Broadbent noted that
people were guided by the information provided for them by machines. Airline pilots had
many displays which they could view but not all the information on display was being
used as the pilot flew the aircraft; instead, certain dials were monitored more frequently
than others. It appeared that too much information was on display, and pilots could not
attend to it all at once; they had to monitor dials in turn and this was a laborious process.
The pilots were seen to be actively planning and anticipating future actions and as a
result seeking particular kinds of information from their environment. This field research
was later replicated in laboratory studies on attention and information processing, and
published in a number of papers and reports (Broadbent 1950, 1953, 1955; Broadbent and
Ford 1995).

This example of human information processing in a highly technical applied setting
had considerable implications for psychological models. The prevalent Behaviourist
models of human behaviour, such as those proposed by Skinner (1938), did not provide a
good account of such purposeful information seeking. The pilots were not passively
waiting for stimuli to impinge upon them as in stimulus-response accounts of behaviour.

Applied research encouraged psychologists to consider human behaviour in terms of
information processing and this approach was given a huge impetus by the development
of computers in the 1950s. The publication of Broadbent's classic text *Perception and
Communication* in 1958 drew on such observations and their implications for a wide
range of human cognitive processes. In this text an information processing account was
developed from the applied and laboratory studies. This work is widely credited as one of
the major foundations of cognitive psychology (see, for example, Eysenck 1984, Best
1995). This kind of research combined with developments in Information Theory
(Shannon and Weaver 1948, Weiner 1948), and the invention of the digital computer
led to great changes in the way psychologists thought and the kinds of research they

conducted. Studying the interaction of men and complex technology had revealed the shortcomings of existing psychological accounts, and the advent of the new computer technology provided powerful analogies which would assist psychologists such as Broadbent as they tried to develop better psychological models. As Broadbent (1958:205) states in his concluding chapter:

> Computing machines operate on a binary basis; they have long term and short term stores; servo systems seek goals by negative feedback. But it is often argued that these analogies are of no worth unless there is evidence that organisms operate in the same way: and it is sometimes assumed as a further step that no such evidence exists. This book is intended to show that ... a general layout of this type is entailed by the detailed evidence about behaviour

The computational metaphor provided the new cognitive psychologists with a precise and objective means of describing possible internal information processing and structures. It allowed them to hypothesize about the internal states involved in human activities such as memory and attention, without recourse to the introspectionist and 'unscientific' methods used by nineteenth century psychologists such as Wundt, as described by Boring (1950) in his history of psychology. The precision of the new computing technology, with its binary codes and storage devices, provided analogies with all the scientific rigour which had been the main benefits of Behaviourist accounts such as those of Watson (1914) and Skinner (1938) but which could now be applied to quintessentially human mental activities as well as to observable behaviour.

The advent of the digital computer showed how a suitably programmed electronic device could perform tasks which previously were thought to be extremely complex and achievable only as a result of intelligent human action. Even by the 1950s there were computers which could play a reasonable game of chess and solve geometry problems (for an account of such early research in Artificial Intelligence, see Newell and Simon 1965, Feigenbaum and Feldman 1963). The power of conceptualizing mental operations as a series of procedures for operating on abstract symbols became very attractive to psychologists. The stores and processing components of digital computers were translated, consciously or unconsciously, into the stores and processing components of cognitive models. The power of the computational metaphor led to a true paradigm shift in psychology. This was reflected in the influential text *Cognitive Psychology* (Neisser 1967), in which the author defined the remit of cognitive psychology to include exploring the mental processes involved in storing, elaborating, retrieving and using information derived from sensory inputs.

An example of a classic information processing model which is clearly heavily influenced by the computer analogy is Atkinson and Shiffrin's (1967) model of memory. In this account (in which all terms in bold reflect the analogy with IT) memory is viewed as consisting of two types of stores, a **short-term memory store** (STS) and a **long-term memory store** (LTS). They describe how information flows through the memory system, beginning with stimuli from the environment being **registered** by the appropriate sensory register and then **entering** the short-term memory store. While in the STS the information may be **copied** into the long-term store. Relevant information in the LTS may become activated and may enter the STS. This transfer of information between STS and LTS is determined by the individual's use of **control processes** such as rehearsal of information, retrieval strategies and coding decisions.

Such information-processing approaches are often described as a form of abstract analysis. The biological and neural processes which underpin cognitive processes are not explicitly described in these models. The models make no claims about the neurological basis for any of the stores or processes in the model. There is no simple or necessary correspondence between the links in such models and neural connections or the existence of particular stores such as short term memory and discrete locations in the brain. The usefulness of such models depends, not on a biological level of analysis, but rather on what the models illuminate about the abstract cognitive processes involved.

IT as a support for scientific methods

The impact of IT upon psychology is not just as a metaphor for models of the mind. As in many scholarly disciplines, psychologists' research methods and techniques have been revolutionized by the advent of IT. Almost every aspect of the day-to-day work of researchers has been profoundly influenced by the use of computers. This has changed the way stimulus material is presented in experiments to explore cognitive processes, the way that data are captured during the course of such experiments, the analytical methods applied to the data, and the way in which the results of such research are disseminated. The impact of IT in research and teaching in psychology seems likely to grow with increased access to high-speed and high-powered computers and to net-worked resources such as the World Wide Web, as well as high bandwidth connectivity between universities and research laboratories.

As in many other disciplines the use of IT in psychology has made some kinds of scientific investigations vastly more efficient. Research techniques which required extreme ingenuity and extensive preparation and effort are now relatively trivial tasks owing to the computer and specially-designed software. As Mollon (1997) points out, psychologists who were researching visual processing in the 1950s, such as those described in Gibson (1950), could spend many weeks carefully preparing by hand random arrays or patterns of blocks or dots or other kinds of stimuli, to investigate the visual cues used in the perception of depth or movement. Statistical techniques used to explore the data gathered from experiments, for example on reaction times to different kinds of stimuli presented in different experimental conditions, are often complex in the computation they require. Before the advent of accessible IT, such data analysis techniques could require weeks or months of the researcher's effort, whilst now every undergraduate can conduct several such analyses on a data set by pressing a few key strokes on a desktop personal computer (PC).

IT has not only made psychological research easier, it has also changed the nature of the scientific investigations which can be conducted. There is a wide range of such new research techniques which has been made available by developments in IT, of which the following are two contrasting examples.

If psychologists wish to explore human perception and in particular to investigate the visual cues which are used when a human face is processed to decide if it is happy or sad or male or female, the computer can now take existing images of faces and alter them in specifiable ways. For example, by taking two images, one of a happy face and one of a sad face, combination faces can be produced by the computer with known proportions of components. So images can be presented to participants in experiments with a range of specific combinations of features ranging from say 100% of the features of a happy face, 80% of the features from a happy face seamlessly merged with 20% of the features from a sad face, down to 10% of the features of the happy face combined with 90% of those of the sad face. By presenting such computer-interpolated or 'morphed' faces very precise information can be obtained about the exact combination of features which are used in human perceptual judgements or the particular difficulties experienced by patients with certain kinds of brain injury or disease (see, for example, Campbell *et al.* 1996, Sprengelmeyer *et al.*, 1996).

In a different context computer imaging techniques such as PET scans (Positron Emission Tomography) or MRI (Magnetic Resonance Imaging) or ERP (Event Related Potential) can be used to observe various aspects of brain activity during cognitive activities such as remembering or reading or listening to words or texts, among healthy or brain-injured individuals. By measuring changes in blood flow or the extent of electrical activity, psychologists can begin to map the architecture of cognitive processing within the brain (see, for example, Posner *et al.*, 1988, Friedman and Simpson 1994).

AI and computer simulations

In addition to the kinds of research techniques described above, there are computational techniques which provide alternative methods of scientific exploration. One important example of such an alternative approach is the process of computer simulation. From the very earliest days of computer science there has been a strong interest in using computers to simulate human cognitive processes. This interest has led to the development in the 1950s of the discipline of Artificial Intelligence (AI), which is concerned with developing computer systems which can perform complex tasks 'intelligently' (see Feigenbaum and Feldman (1963) for an account of many of the earliest AI simulations).

Artificial Intelligence, like traditional information processing models in psychology, separates software and hardware; in other words it treats cognitive processes as 'the mind' as distinct from the 'brain'. AI simulations are generally conceived as symbol-processing systems which can be implemented without detailed concern about the underlying computer hardware.

In some areas of AI, researchers tried to model intelligent human processing, (e.g., Newell and Simon (1972) on problem solving), whereas other researchers were only concerned with an intelligent outcome irrespective of whether the internal processes of the system resembled human cognitive processing. So most computer chess programs play an intelligent and skilful game of chess, but achieve this using computer capabilities such as large and reliable memories which allow the system to look ahead at very large sets of possible moves, which is different from the way that skilled human chess players operate (see Newell and Simon 1965, DeGroot 1965, and Chase and Simon 1973, for accounts of research on chess playing by humans and machines).

Many other AI programs have been developed in vision, language processing and problem solving which attempt to operate according to what is known about human cognitive processing. Some such as Schank and Abelson's (1977) account of scripts for language processing or Anderson's (1983) ACT general model of cognition, are explicitly attempting to simulate human cognitive processing.

The benefits which the AI approach have brought to cognitive psychology are in part due to the discipline of having to formulate the processing stages and representational systems of mind or machine in an explicit and well-defined manner. This leads to testable models of mental processes. For example, Schank and Abelson (1977) developed the notion of the 'script', a package of stored general world knowledge about the sequence of events and activities which surround stereotypical events such as visiting a restaurant. This was derived from earlier notions such as the 'schema' suggested by the psychologist Bartlett (1932). The discipline of producing a working computer program which could read stories and answer questions about them because of its stored 'scripts' required the concept to be specified and formalized to a far greater extent than those found in earlier purely psychological accounts. The development of the Script Applier Mechanism simulation (SAM, Shank and Abelson 1977), which used scripts, in turn stimulated psychological studies on how stories were read and remembered, motivated by the desire to see if the detailed specifications of how the general knowledge was stored and activated during story processing by SAM corresponded to human processing (see for example, Bower *et al.*, 1979, Anderson *et al.*, 1983; Yekovitch and Walker 1986).

AI also provided psychologists with a greatly increased range of concepts for considering cognitive processing. Just as the advent of the first serial computers provided very general metaphors for processing abstract symbols and storing information, the much richer array of current AI tools and techniques has provided a whole range of terminology and concepts such as indexing, addressing, storage buffer, modularity, subroutine and parsing.

In the 1980s a particular form of computer simulation was developed which was concerned with modelling, not just abstract cognitive processes but also the underlying computational or neural processes. This new approach challenged the traditional metaphor of computational information processing. Psychologists who adopted a 'Connectionist approach' claimed that cognition should be explained in terms of interactions between connected neural-like elements. Models of cognition should correspond to the neural processes of the human brain. Ironically Connectionists use powerful computer-based simulation techniques, based upon parallel distributed processing, to model human information processes such as reading, recall and learning. Advocates of Connectionism would regard this as a second paradigm shift in cognitive psychology based upon a more appropriate use of IT.

IT and connectionism

Researchers who adopt a Connectionist Approach emphasize the biological and mathematical bases of their models, claiming that their theories are modelled on the process of the brain (Rumelhart and McLelland 1986). Neuroscience research on the cerebral cortex of the brain (e.g., Mountcastle 1979), had shown that there are very many more connections between the cortical cells than had been thought. The system of neural connections in the cortex was also found to be distributed in a parallel array in addition to serial pathways. It seems that the brain functions by having parallel processing networks which are distributed throughout the cortex. This helps solve one of the fundamental problems in cognition, that cognitive processes can be so rapid but must depend on neural transmissions which are relatively slow. The answer appears to be that a great many of such neural activities are happening simultaneously in parallel.

Such advances in neuroscience inspired connectionist or parallel distributed processing (PDP) models in cognitive psychology. Connectionists claim that their theories are modelled on the processes of the brain. Rumelhart and McLelland (1986), who adopt this approach, assume that information is processed through the interactions between a very large number of simple processing units which each send excitatory and inhibitory signals to other units. The human information processing system is thus a massively distributed mutually-interactive parallel system. The appeal of such models is in part their clear analogy with the neural anatomy of the brain. The other attractions of such accounts lie in their ability to use computer simulation techniques to test the details of their models and the way the resulting PDP simulations can mimic human performance, including errors, on a growing array of cognitive tasks such as letter and word recognition, learning the past tense of English verbs and remembering the properties of individuals. The classic text on Parallel Distributed Processing, edited by Rumelhart and McLelland (1986), describes a wealth of PDP simulations of such human processes.

Connectionist models involve a set of interconnected simple processing units. There are three types of units, viz., input units, output units and hidden units. Input units take in information, directly from the senses, or indirectly from other parts of the network of connected units. Output units put out information and control responses directly or send information to other parts of the network. Hidden units communicate with both input and output units but not directly with the environment. In distributed models the units do not represent whole meaningful entities such as words or concepts but stand for constituent features. The complete entity emerges in distributed systems when units interact. The units and their connections are the most important aspects of a connectionist model, the processing and the representation of information are distributed across the network. There are various kinds of connections between units, excitatory and inhibitory, and different connection weights on the links between units which modify the way that activation spreads through the network. Mathematical equations about the nature of these various levels of activation have been calculated and have allowed learning rules to be developed in connectionist simulations.

These learning rules enable the network to modify its behaviour and are one of the most attractive features of connectionist simulations. Dynamic processes such as how children gradually learn the rules about the way to form past tenses for regular and irregular English verbs can be modelled (Rumelhart and McLelland 1986). As this simulation progresses through many cycles, it models the three stages in children's spoken production: Stage 1, where children use a small set of verbs, including irregular forms such as 'went' correctly; Stage 2, where they begin to make mistakes and use forms such as 'goed' where the regular past form + ED has been used incorrectly; and Stage 3, where both regular and irregular forms are produced correctly.

Other impressive features of connectionist models are they way they continue to operate when some of their connections are damaged. This feature, known as 'graceful degradation', means that performance deteriorates when connections are damaged but the network still functions, and seems analogous to the human response to various kinds of brain injury. Again there have been very impressive connectionist simulations of specific problems following brain damage such as the condition known as 'surface dyslexia' (Marshall and Newcomb 1973, Patterson *et al.*, (1985). These patients have particular difficulty in reading words with irregular pronunciations, so that words such as 'pint' and 'yacht' are read as if they rhymed with 'mint' and 'hatched'.

Patterson *et al.*(1989) produced a connectionist model of surface dyslexia, by setting the sum of the connection weights and activation levels to zero, in an attempt to mimic the effects of brain damage. The simulation produced outputs very similar to the performance of surface dyslexic patients, with more errors for irregular words.

Connectionism is a very impressive addition to the scientific techniques available to cognitive psychologists, although critics such as Besner *et al.* (1990) and Pinker and Prince (1988), among others, have questioned the range of psychological phenomena which can be modelled in this way. Some critics doubt whether such techniques will be as useful for modelling 'higher level' processes such as problem solving, planning or reading complete texts. Connectionists are trying to make progress on simulations of such complex processes and their success can only be judged over time. A more salient criticism might be that the level of explanation offered by connectionist models is not particularly helpful for **understanding** cognitive processes. Do psychologists really know any more about memory or reading by having a mathematical account of connection weights between layers of processing units? Such reservations might lead those in the future to develop hybrid models of the mind that incorporate more general abstract information processing levels of explanation with very precise connectionist type models as precise alternatives of the underlying processes.

Cognitive engineering: understanding interactions with IT

IT has provided psychologists with tools and techniques of increasing power and sophistication to explore cognitive processes but is this battery being directed at the right targets? One of the most influential figures in cognitive psychology, Neisser (1978) issued a challenge to the discipline. He wished psychologists to come out of the laboratory and into the world as they conducted investigations of cognitive processes such as memory. These views were controversial but some psychologists responded to the challenge and began to study cognitive processes in real settings.

This challenge to study cognition in the world was couched in general terms, but people's interactions with IT, which have become so pervasive, provide particularly fascinating examples of real world domains where cognitive processes can be studied. Psychologists have begun to try to answer questions about the psychological processes involved in interactions with and through IT.

In addition to attempting to answer psychological questions posed by IT, researchers have also been involved in studying human-computer interactions to provide information for the designers of computer systems. The goal is to provide guidelines about the design of IT which will enable systems to be produced which are truly 'user friendly', that is, which support easy and effective interaction between user and machine. Studying human-computer interaction (HCI) in this way has become known as **cognitive engineering** (Norman 1987). This approach usually involves studying the performance of people in real work settings, or realistic simulations of such settings, where information, often in very large quantities, has to be processed and where tasks to be completed are often complex, ill-defined, and interrupted by other activities which are competing for attention, and depend upon co-operation from other people.

One of the goals is to design the demands of the job and the associated technology so that they best match the capacities and skills of the users of IT. In addition, researchers also hope that this work will illuminate models of cognitive processing, which are often based on the performance of individuals in rather artificial laboratory conditions, with insights from real life performances. As Norman (1987) suggests, studying the interactions between people and computer systems reveals the gaps in scientific understanding of what is involved in accomplishing real world tasks.

Norman (1987) has described how he discovered in his own research that he had to develop a new theory of action, in response to the perceived gap between existing psychological theories and the observed interactions between people and computers (Norman 1986). This modern example of the feedback loop from studying applications to altering or redefining existing theoretical models has close parallels with the classic wartime studies of human factors which had a major impact on psychological models in addition to their practical applications.

The new discipline or sub-discipline of cognitive engineering, however, faces some stiff challenges and Landauer (1987) has described some of the problems that limit its application. One is that psychologists have usually focused on phenomena which illuminate abstract theories of information processing rather than on concrete real-world applications. A related problem is that many principles of cognitive psychology which are thoroughly researched in the laboratory have had little impact on the design of technology. One reason may be poor communication between psychologists and IT designers, but another contributory factor is the relatively small absolute size of the effects that laboratory studies have demonstrated. Very small but consistent differences in the speed with which people perform certain cognitive tasks may be very important in understanding mental processes but completely unimportant for decisions about the optimum design of information technologies. Landauer, however, is equally concerned with the potential contribution studies of human computer interactions could make to psychology, or the science of mind. Landauer (1987: 112) writes:

> The science of the mind is ... not the science of what the mind can do in a laboratory situation artificially rigged to make it relevant to one of our theories ... the abstracted laboratory experiment is an essential tool, but it must answer questions raised by nature, and its answers must be tested against nature.
>
> ... we need to study it (the mind) in the habitats in which it frequently finds or wishes to find itself. At the moment it seems to wish to find itself in constant interaction with computer systems so this is where we must track it down.

He is optimistic about the future and hopes that a new cognitive psychology can be developed which draws on what is known about cognitive processes in the laboratory and in realistic contexts. The hope is that cognitive psychology will make an important contribution to the design of new and better technologies and that studies of HCI can also make a significant contribution to psychology in general.

Cognitive psychology has largely been concerned with modelling cognitive processes from the viewpoint of the internal representations and processes of the individual. Similarly human-computer interactions were traditionally viewed as those between a single user interfacing with the a single computer system, usually through some form of text-based commands. These kinds of human-computer interactions seemed to offer analogies to the existing individualistic models of cognitive psychology, although Landauer and others have pointed out the limitations of this apparently simple translation from theories to applications. Recent technological developments in network-ing computers and applications plus the advent of multimedia information technologies, underline the need to extend psychological models to accommodate cognitive processes which depend upon multiple users and multiple modalities.

An example of research on people's interaction with multimedia IT is described in a paper by Sproull *et al.* (1996). They compared the effects on users of two different kinds of computer interfaces, one where the user received messages on the computer screen as text and one where a realistic but computer generated face appeared and spoke the same messages. The users' task was to participate in a prototype career counselling service. All the users knew that the face was a computer artefact but this still influenced how they responded to standard questions about their interests and personal attributes. Users who interacted with computer-generated faces, presented themselves in a more positive light, reporting themselves to be significantly more socially desirable and altruistic than those users presented with the questionnaire as text on the screen.

This study highlights the impact on users of visual as well as verbal messages. It emphasizes that, as computer applications are developed which involve more complex psychological processes than those involved in relatively straightforward tasks such as word processing or database searching, important social dimensions emerge. These are not necessarily covered by traditional HCI concerns of computer interfaces as a means of delivering fast and efficient task performance.

Following on from the views of psychologists such as Neisser, Norman and Landauer, and given the rapid pace of technological developments in IT, cognitive psychologists are studying the way people interact with these new technologies and exploring what these new forms of interaction reveal about cognitive processing.

The ESRC Cognitive Engineering Programme

To encourage just such research endeavours, the Economic and Social Research Council (ESRC) launched a research programme in Cognitive Engineering in 1995. Fifteen research teams throughout the United Kingdom are investigating different aspects of the way people interact with IT. The goal is to understand more about the nature of such interactions so that design guidelines for improved IT systems can be produced and to appreciate what the details of such interactions reveal about cognitive processes such as communication, decision making and problem-solving. As well as producing guidelines for future design technologies based on a greater understanding of these human processes, the research explores whether the cognitive processes themselves are altered by the interaction with the technologies, e.g., are communication, problem-solving or decision making different when supported by IT and what are the nature and consequences of such differences?

Cognitive Engineering projects are tackling a wide range of topics. One project is investigating the way children learn from interacting with multimedia CD-ROMs, and the role in problem solving of the various kinds of external representations provided by such IT including diagrams, graphics and animations (Scaife and Rogers 1996). The research tackles a number of important questions, such as how multimedia IT can be exploited to support effective learning and what contribution the unique features of interactive multimedia can make to learning and problem-solving.

A second project is exploring the nature of medical decision making in neonatal intensive care units, and examining the role of medical data presented by computerized monitoring in the clinical decisions made by nursing and medical staff (Logie *et al.* 1997). By exploring how senior and junior staff use the available data the researchers hope to learn about the nature of expertise in medical decision making and how this interacts with the use of IT. A third project is investigating the way in which users retrieve information from complex on-line information resources and how this process is influenced by factors such as knowledge of the domain and of the problem space and the nature of the computer interface (Sutcliffe and Ennis 1998).

As research in all the cognitive engineering projects is at an early stage, this paper will use examples from studies the author has conducted with colleagues, exploring human communication which illustrate how studies of people's interactions with IT challenge psychologists to develop richer models. Earlier in this paper, attention was drawn to the very fast pace of technological developments in IT. One aspect of the developments in linking computers over local-area and wide-area networks is that the distinction between communications technology and information technology has become blurred. For the user the so-called 'information age' results from the seamless merging of these technologies. Human-computer interaction is no longer characterized by an individual using a stand-alone computer and its software. Instead, people can use their desk-top computers to access information resources across the world through the World Wide Web, they can use facilities such as desktop video conferencing to communicate and collaborate with colleagues in the next building or in the next continent, they can jointly access a wide variety of software and information resources which can in theory revolutionize how they work and learn. These fascinating technological developments pose huge challenges to psychologists trying to understand the nature of these new forms of human-computer interaction. Most of the HCI research to date might be characterized as focused on individual users and their interactions **with** IT; the research to be described in the following sections begins to study the way computer users interact **through** IT. In the initial attempts reported here to grapple with these new forms of interaction, the researchers focus on pairs of users and their collaboration and communication. Studying pairs of users is, however, only the first step in understanding the full impact of new multi-user information and communications technologies, and the research will expand to include groups of users in both laboratories and in real work settings.

Cognitive engineering: understanding interactions through IT

Over the last few years, with collaborators at the Universities of Edinburgh (Bard and colleagues), Stirling (Doherty-Sneddon and Bruce) and Nottingham (O'Malley and Langton) the research team has been investigating the way people communicate and solve problems in different communicative contexts. One important context for communication which has emerged in recent years is where the interaction is supported by various forms of IT. Communication and problem solving have been compared where two people co-operate face-to-face, when they are screened from one another and cannot share visual information, and where they interact with IT providing the communication channels. The work has both theoretical and applied aspects. The researchers are interested in issues concerned with the use of visual and verbal signals in communication and how these are combined. By understanding more about such issues they hope in time to develop a better account of multimodal communication, i.e., that which depends upon and deploys a range of sensory modalities.

As Landauer suggested about IT in general, the emergence of new technologies of multimedia communication presents an opportunity to explore such issues in realistic settings. It also provides a milieu where the outcomes of the research might have salient implications for the future design of such technological systems. In a series of studies the researchers have examined how the processes of communication and problem solving are influenced by the presence or absence of visual as well as verbal signals, and whether the impact of visual signals is similar or dissimilar to those exchanged in face-to-face conversation when provided by IT.

Study 1: The role of visual signals in face-to-face interaction

In work on collaborative problem-solving the researchers have found that, in face-to-face interaction, participants needed to say significantly less to achieve the same level of performance than in conditions where visual signals are not shared (Boyle *et al.* 1994). This study shows subtle but significant benefits of the availability of visual signals for collaborative problem-solving.

The task used in the study by Boyle *et al.*, and in subsequent explorations of video-mediated communication, is a form of collaborative problem solving known as the Map Task (Brown *et al.* 1984). This is a laboratory task, but it elicits a range of communicative behaviours which are typical of many real world tasks. In Landauer's terms, the researchers believe that it 'answers questions raised by nature.' The task sets pairs of participants a goal, to reproduce a route on a map and to overcome a set of constant problems, but the way the task is accomplished is determined entirely by the participants. The dialogues which result are lengthy, spontaneous and individualistic in character. They represent a far richer and less restricted sample of communicative behaviour than is usually gathered in laboratory studies.

In face-to-face dialogues speakers used 28 per cent fewer turns and 20 per cent fewer words than in the audio-only condition. Yet face-to-face participants achieved equally good levels of task performance with this reduced verbal input. These face-to-face advantages suggest that speakers can use visual signals to supplement the information presented verbally.

Dialogue analysis

What kinds of communicative functions are visual signals being used to convey? To answer this question the researchers made detailed comparisons of all 128 dialogues in their corpus of problem-solving interactions. What kinds of communicative functions caused the greater length of audio only dialogues, and thus what kinds of functions may be substituted by the visual signals in face-to-face communication?

Detailed analysis of the dialogues was carried out using a system of coding called Conversational Games Analysis (Kowtko *et al.* 1991), which charts the kinds of communicative behaviours in which speakers are engaging as they attempt to achieve their communicative goals. Analyses of face-to-face dialogues showed that speakers less often check that their listener understands them, or that they have understood their partner, than in audio-only interactions. There were significant increases of 50 and 28 per cent respectively in the frequency of these communicative behaviours where speakers were not communicating face-to-face. Where visual signals are not available speakers do more verbal checking, whilst in face-to-face conversations non-verbal signals may be substituted (for a full account of these data see Doherty-Sneddon *et al.* 1997). The research team is pursuing the investigation of the role of visual and verbal signals in communication by exploring interactions between people supported by multimedia IT systems.

Study 2: The role of visual signals in video-mediated communication (VMC)

IT systems now support the exchange not just of text or numerical data but also of video and audio data. These multimedia systems potentially offer considerable benefits to users but can they provide the benefits of face-to-face communication? What impact do such IT systems have on cognitive processes such as communication and problem-solving? The answer to these questions depends at least in part upon the nature of the IT, so in different studies a range of different multimedia communication systems has been explored. From earlier research such as O'Connail *et al.* (1993) and Barber and Laws (1994), it is known that the technical properties of systems such as the rate at which the video images are refreshed and the presence or absence of a delay between audio and video signal transmission have impacts upon users and their cognitive processes.

The study described here explored the impact of technologically-mediated visual signals which were as similar as possible to the visual signals transmitted in face-to-face interaction. It investigated whether high-quality high-bandwidth VMC, namely 'video-tunnels' (see Smith *et al.* 1991), could replicate the advantages of face-to-face interaction. These are laboratory-based simulations of high-quality multimedia communication systems which are being developed and tested by many IT producers. A high-resolution video link was provided as a substitute for face-to-face communication and the system could be set to allow direct eye-contact between speakers. It also provided almost life-size images of the conversational partner's face as well as high quality sound. The impact of three conditions was compared: VMC where participants could make eye contact with their partner, VMC where eye contact was not possible, and an audio-only condition.

If VMC is to confer the benefits observed for face-to-face interactions, then the high-quality VMC condition where users can engage in eye contact should elicit similar benefits in communication over audio-only conditions as shown in the study by Boyle *et al.* (1994). The researchers predicted that task performance would be comparable across conditions but that task dialogues would be expected to be significantly shorter in the VMC plus eye contact condition, as this condition most closely resembles face-to-face interaction. These efficiency gains should be derived from similar changes in dialogue structure described earlier.

As predicted, no differences in levels of task performance were obtained across conditions. But dialogues from the condition of VMC with eye-contact were significantly LONGER than dialogues under the other two conditions, containing 11 per cent more turns and 10 per cent more words than with the other two conditions, which did not differ. A full account of the results of performance and conversational analyses from this study is described in Doherty-Sneddon *et al.* (1997). As the level of task performance was the same, not only did VMC with eye-contact not replicate the length advantage of face-to-face communication, but it was significantly LESS efficient. More speech was used to achieve the same level of performance as in audio only communication.

What was happening to cause these longer VMC interactions? Was there something about large, high-quality video images with eye contact which encouraged greater interaction and hence more dialogue? When the amount of gazing in VMC conditions was compared, there was significantly and substantially more gazing in the condition where speakers and listeners could have eye-contact. As the rate of gazing was more than double that recorded in face-to-face interactions it seems that VMC with eye-contact may encourage participants to 'over-use' the visual channel.

This level of gaze behaviour is unusual for a collaborative task and may be counter-productive. In several previous studies, for example Goldman-Eisler (1967) and Beattie (1981), it has been suggested that gaze may interfere with cognitive processing and speech planning. With the high levels of gaze which were observed in VMC + eye contact dialogues, the benefits of having access to visual signals may be counterbalanced by users becoming distracted by their partner's face and so using significantly more speech to achieve a comparable level of task success.

In this study the impacts of technologically-mediated visual signals were rather different from those observed in face-to-face conversations. The 'added value' of visual signals in VMC was not the gains in efficiency observed in face-to-face interactions where fewer words were needed to achieve a given level of task performance. The impact of technologically-mediated visual signals seemed instead to be primarily social. Speakers felt able to engage in interaction more freely than in audio-only conditions. The appeal, perhaps even the novelty of having high quality video images of the conversational partner, encouraged participants to look at one another much more frequently than they would in face-to-face interactions. These social benefits of the availability of visual signals had, however, unexpected consequences. The high levels of gazing observed in this study may have led to longer dialogues as gazing has been found to interfere with speech planning.

Several recent papers support the idea that IT systems which relay images of faces may be distracting but socially rewarding for users. When the computer interface includes a realistic computer-generated face with which the user interacts, Koda and Maes (1996), Takeuchi (1995) and Walker (1994) all report that users find such interactions require more effort and attention but are more engaging and satisfying than alternative interfaces.

If a purely cognitive view of communications is adopted, that communication is concerned solely with the way information flows between speakers and listeners, then the efficiency of a given dialogue would be assessed by comparing the verbal effort and resulting task performance. From this stand-point IT-mediated visual signals seem to lead to less efficient communication. An alternative and perhaps more attractive conclusion is that this research demonstrates that technologically-mediated visual signals demonstrate a combination of social and cognitive effects. This emphasizes the importance of the social as well as the cognitive dimension of communication even in a carefully-designed laboratory study. As Norman (1987) suggested, studying the interactions of people and technology highlighted the omissions in current psychological thinking. From this research it appears that IT offers considerable benefits to users but can have unexpected impacts on cognitive processes.

Communication has been a central concern from the earliest days of cognitive psychology, as indicated by the title of Broadbent's classic text *Perception and Commu-*

nication (1958). However psychological research and theorizing about communication, or language processing as it has come to be known, has focused very heavily on characterizing the way in which speakers and listeners produce and interpret verbal utterances in social isolation.

Since the 1980s there has been increasing interest among psychologists in what has come to be called the 'interactionist' or 'collaborative' approach to language processing (Clark 1985, Schober and Clark 1989). The interactionists are concerned with those aspects of language processing which depend upon the interplay between participants in a linguistic exchange and with how speakers and listeners collaborate with each other moment by moment to try to ensure mutual understanding.

The results of recent studies of interactions with and through IT suggest that such a view must be augmented with an understanding of the impact of social aspects of communication. Psychologists need to describe how the social features of an interaction shape the structure and content of face-to-face and IT-mediated dialogues and the role that visual as well as verbal signals play in this process. To develop models which will deal with rich and complex communicative environments is an exciting challenge and one which will need to draw on insights from those who have studied interactions with IT from sociological and anthropological as well as psychological perspectives.

Conclusions

Information and communications technologies are revolutionizing many aspects of work, education and leisure. For psychologists the challenge has always been to to understand human behaviour and mental processes. As developments in IT change the way in which people behave by providing them with new resources and allowing them to conduct intellectual activities such as communicating, collaborating, problem-solving in new ways, then these become fascinating areas of psychological research in their own right.

Studying human behaviour in these new IT-supported settings also offers methodological challenges to psychologists. Psychology in general and cognitive psychology in particular have adopted a scientific approach to studying human behaviour which has involved simplifying and abstracting away from the complexities of everyday life and studying the behaviour in the controlled conditions of the laboratory. It has attempted to identify the critical dimensions of any human behaviour which can then be studied in controlled laboratory experiments. Whilst this has led to considerable advances in understanding of many cognitive processes, studying the way people interact with and through IT in real or realistic settings highlights salient aspects of human behaviour which current psychological models tend to ignore. This need to consider the ecological validity of psychologists' work accords with the suggestion that psychology has been influenced too heavily by the methodologies of the physical sciences, and that biological sciences such as ethology, which have studied behaviour in rich and complex natural environments, might offer an alternative more fruitful research methodology.

From the advent of the first computers, IT has provided psychologists with powerful metaphors for its theoretical models, and a powerful set of computational techniques with which to investigate and simulate mental processes. It has also provided a fascinating field of study in its own right. By studying a wide range of human-computer interactions, psychologists may be able to make significant contributions to broaden the scope of future models of cognitive processes, although whether this represents a 'paradigm shift' or merely improved 'normal science' remains an open question.

Acknowledgements

Some of the research described in this paper was supported by an Economic and Social Research Council grant to the Human Communication Research Centre at the Universities of Glasgow and Edinburgh, and an Economic and Social Research Council Award no. R000233560 to C. O'Malley, V Bruce, and A H Anderson.

References

Anderson, A. H., Garrod, S. and Sanford, A. (1983), 'The accessibility of pronominal antecedents as a function of episode shift in narrative text' *Quarterly Journal of Experimental Psychology*, 35: 427–40.

Anderson, J. R. (1983), *The Architecture of Cognition* (Cambridge, Mass.).

Atkinson, R. C. and Shriffrin, R. M. (1967), 'Human memory: a proposed system and its control processes. In Spence, K. W. and Spence, J. T. (eds). *The Psychology of Learning and Motivation* (New York) 163–178.89.95.

Barber, P.and Laws, J. (1994), 'Image quality and video communication'. In Damper, R., Hall, W. and Richards, J. (eds.) *Proceedings of IEEE International Symposium on Multimedia Technologies and Their Future Applications* (London) 163–78.

Bartlett, F. (1932), *Remembering.* (Cambridge).

Beattie, G. (1981), 'The regulation of speaker turns in face-to-face conversations: some implications for conversation' *Semiotica*, 34: 55–70.

Besner, D., Twilley, L., McCann, R. and Seergobin, K. (1990), 'On the association between connectionism and data: are a few words necessary?' *Psychological Review*, 97: 432–46.

Best, J. (1995), *Cognitive Psychology* (St. Paul, Minn.).

Boring, E. (1950), *A History of Experimental Psychology* (Englewood Cliffs, N.J.).

Bower, G., Black, J. and Turner, T. (1979), 'Scripts in memory for text', *Cognitive Psychology*, 11: 177–220.

Boyle, E. A., Anderson, A.H. and Newlands, A. (1994), 'The effects of eye contact on dialogue and performance in a cooperative problem-solving task'. *Language and Speech*, 37: 1–20.

Broadbent, D. E. (1950), 'The twenty dials test under quiet conditions'. *Applied Psychology Unit Report No. 130.* (cited in Broadbent, D. E. (1958) *Perception and Communication*).

—— (1953), 'Economising VHF channels: synthetic trials of a technique.' *Flying Personnel Research Committee Report No. 831.* (cited in Broadbent, D. E. 1958).

—— (1954), 'The role of auditory localisation in attention and memory span'. *Journal of Experimental Psychology*, 47: 191–6.

—— and Ford, H. K. (1955), 'Two channel listening in the Aircraft Situation.' *Flying Personnel Research Committee Report No. 945.* (cited in Broadbent, D. E., 1958).

—— (1958), *Perception and Communication* (London).

Brown, G., Anderson, A. H. Shillcock, R., and Yule, G. (1983) *Teaching Talk* (Cambridge).

Campbell, R., Woll, B., Benson, P., and Wallace, S. (1996), 'Categoricity in communicative face actions: surprised, puzzled and question faces in and out of sign', unpublished paper delivered to the Experimental Psychology Society 50th Anniversary Meeting, Cambridge, 1996.

Chase, W. and Simon, H. (1973), 'The mind's eye in chess'. In Chase, W. (ed.) *Visual Information Processing* (New York) 215–81.

Clark, H. H. (1985), 'Language use and language users'. In Lindsey, G. and Aronson, E. (eds.) *The Handbook of Social Psychology* (New York) 179–231.

DeGroot, A. (1965), *Thought and Choice in Chess* (The Hague).

Doherty-Sneddon, G., Anderson, A. H., O'Malley, C., Langton, S., Garrod, S. and Bruce, V. (1997), 'Face-to-face and video mediated communication: a comparison of dialogue structure and task performance', *Journal of Experimental Psychology Applied*, 3: 105–25.

Eysenck, M. (1984), *A Handbook of Cognitive Psychology* (London).

Feigenbaum, E. and Feldman, J. (1963) (eds.), *Computers and Thought* (New York).

Friedman, D. and Simpson, G. (1994), 'ERP and scalp distribution to target and novel events: effects of temporal order in young, middle-aged and older adults' *Cognitive Brain Research*, 2: 49–63.

Gibson, J. J. (1950), *The Perception of the Visual World* (Boston).

Goldman-Eisler, F. (1967), 'Sequential temporal patterns and cognitive processes in speech'. *Language and Speech*, 10: 122–32.

Haberlandt, K. (1994), *Cognitive Psychology* (New York).

Koda, T. and Maes, P. (1996), 'Agents with faces: the effects of personification of agents'. In Blandford, A. and Thimbleby, H. (eds.) *Adjunct Proceedings of HCI96*, 98–103 London, 20–23 August, 1996.

Kowtko, J. C., Isard, S., and Doherty-Sneddon, G. (1991), 'Conversational games in dialogue'. Human Communication Research Centre Technical Report No HCRC-RP 24, Lascarides, A. (ed.) (Edinburgh).

Kuhn, T. S. (1962), *The Structure of Scientific Revolutions* (Chicago).

Landauer, T. K. (1987), 'Cognitive psychology and computer system design'. In Carroll J. M. (ed.) *Interfacing Thought* (Cambridge, Mass.) 1–25.

Logie, R., Hunter, J., McIntosh, N., Gilhooly, K., Alberdi, A., & Reiss, J. (1997), 'Medical cognition and computer support in the intensive care unit: A cognitive engineering approach. In Harris, D. (ed.) *Engineering Psychology and Cognitive Ergonomics: Integration of Theory and Application* 167–74 (Aldershot).

Marshall, J. and Newcomb, F. (1973), 'Patterns of paralexia: a psycholinguistic approach', *Journal of Psycholinguistic Research*, 2: 175–99.

Mollon, J. D. (1997), '...on velocity cues alone: a review of perception 1946–1996', *Quarterly Journal of Experimental Psychology*, 50A (4): 859–78.

Mountcastle, V. B. (1979), 'An organising principle for cerebral function: the unit module and distributed system.', In Schmitt, F. O. (ed.) *The Neurosciences: Fourth Study Program* (Cambridge, Mass.).

Neisser, U. (1967), *Cognitive Psychology* (New York).

—— (1978), 'Memory: what are the important questions?' In Gruneberg, M., Morris, P. M. and Sykes, R. (eds.) *Practical Aspects of Memory* (London) 3–24.

Newell, A. and Simon, H. (1965), ' An example of human chess playing in the light of chess playing programs'. In Weiner, N. and Schade, J. (eds.) *Progress in Biocybernetics*, Amsterdam 2: 19–75.

Norman, D. A. (1986), 'Cognitive engineering'. In Norman, D. A. and Draper, S. W. (eds.) *User Centred System Design:New Perspectives on Human Computer Interaction* (New Jersey).

—— (1987), 'Cognitive engineering – cognitive science'. In Carroll, J. M. (ed.) *Interfacing Thought* (Cambridge, Mass.) 325–36.

O-Connaill, B., Whittaker, S., and Wilbur, S. (1993), 'Conversations over video conferences: an evaluation of videomediated interaction', *Human- Computer Interaction*, 8: 389–428.

Patterson, K., Marshall, J., and Coltheart, M. (1985), (eds), *Surface Dyslexia: Neuropsychological and Cognitive Studies of Phonological Reading* (Hove, Sussex).

—— Seidenberg, M., and McLelland, J.L. (1989), 'Connections and disconnections: acquired dyslexia in a computational model of reading processes'. In Morris, R. G. (ed.) *Parallel Distributed Processing* (Oxford).

Pinker, S. and Prince, A. (1988), 'On language and connectionism: analysis of a parallel distributed processing model of language acquisition', *Cognition*, 28: 73–193.

Posner, M., Peterson, S., Fox, P. and Raichle, M. (1988), 'Localisations of cognitive operations in the human brain' *Science*, 240: 1627–31.

Rumelhart, D. E. and McLelland, J. L. (1986), *Parallel Distributed Processing: Explorations in the Microstructure of Cognition (Vol 1)* (Cambridge, Mass.).

Sanford, A. J. (1985), *Cognition and Cognitive Psychology* (New York).

Scaife, M. and Rogers, Y. (1996), 'External cognition: how do graphical representations work?' *International Journal of Human Computer Studies*, 45: 185–213.

Schank, R. and Abelson, R. (1977), *Scripts, Plans, Goals and Understanding* (Hillsdale, NJ.).

Schober, M. J. and Clark, H. H. (1989), 'Understanding by addressees and overhearers'. *Cognitive Psychology*, 21: 211 – 32.

Shannon, C. E. and Weaver, W. (1949), *The Mathematical Theory of Communication* (Urbana, Ill.).

Skinner, B. F. (1938), *The Behaviour of Organisms* (New York).

Smith, R., O'Shea, T., O'Malley, C., Scanlon, E., and Taylor, J. (1991), 'Preliminary experiments with a distributed, multi-media, problem-solving environment'. In Bowers, J. and Benford, S. (eds.) *Studies in Computer-Supported Co-operative Work: Theory, Practice and Design 31–48* (Amsterdam).

Solso, R. L. (1995), *Cognitive Psychology* (Boston).

Sprengelmeyer., R., Young, A. W., Calder, A., Karnak, A., Lange, H., Homberg, V., Perrett, D. and Rowland, D. (1996), 'Face perception and emotion recognition in Huntingdon's Disease: loss of disgust', unpublished paper delivered to the Experimental Psychology Society 50th Anniversary Meeting, Cambridge, 1996.

Sproull, L., Subramani, M., Kiesler, S., Walker, J. and Waters, K. (1996), 'When the interface is a face'. *Human Computer Interaction*, 11: 97–124.

Sutcliffe, A. G. and Ennis, M. (1998), 'Towards a cognitive theory of information retrieval. Interacting with Computers, 10(3): 321–51.

Takeuci. A. (1995), 'Situated facial displays: towards social interaction'. In *Proceedings of CHI95 Human Factors in Computing Systems* (New York) 450–54.

Walker, J. (1994), 'Using a human face as an interface'. In *Proceedings of CHI94, Human Factors in Computing Systems* (New York) 85–91.

Watson, J. B. (1914), *Behaviour: An Introduction to Comparative Psychology* (New York).

Weiner, N. (1948), *Cybernetics* (Cambridge, Mass.).

Yekovich, F. and Walker, C. (1986), 'Retrieval of scripted concepts', *Journal of Memory and Language*, 25: 627–44.

Commentary

CHARLES CROOK

Department of Human Resources
Loughborough University

This paper conveyed a good sense of what preoccupies academic psychologists. It reminded us how our dominant theoretical traditions have been guided by both information theory and information technology. Dr. Anderson addressed three themes: method, theory and practice. So we encountered the computer as laboratory tool, the computer as cognitive metaphor, and the computer as a machine that people interact with (and whose working practices are therefore researchable).

In relation to method, research technique certainly has been transformed by information technology. But it should not be thought that psychologists are concerned only with designing visual stimuli or with recording reaction times. Much of what constitutes data in contemporary psychology is talk – reports, accounts, conversations. Software for qualitative analysis plays an increasingly central role in systematizing such talk. Thus the influence of new technology on method is even more far reaching than was implied.

The second theme was theory. Dr. Anderson gave an honest history of a changing conceptual landscape. Behaviourism did indeed dominate early theorizing – promoting that comical analogy between the human condition and rats negotiating a maze. It is also fair to claim that behaviourism was overturned by a cognitive revolution. Cognitive psychologists recovered the discarded world of private events that occur between stimuli and responses. Our new task was to model cognition by reference to concepts from the emerging technology: information processing systems. Cognitive science dominated psychology and the computational metaphor dominated cognitive science.

But notice: academic psychology is about as old as the century. So cognitivists have been mobilising the rhetoric of revolution for half the lifetime of the discipline – continuously since the 1950s. Yet has a real revolutionary liberation taken place? Has this computational metaphor been influential outside of the academic forums of psychology? For example, has it led to psychology having a greater impact upon practitioners or upon persons in the street? I am struck by how infrequently the mass media bother to report our research. Television documentaries rarely recruit academic psychologists. There are no widely recognised popularisers – no Blakemores, Attenboroughs, Dawkins, Patrick Moores. There is Cracker of course. But the cognitive revolution does not surface there (although the computer-based 'profiling' of forensic psychologists offers interesting parallels to certain analytic uses of information technologies in the humanities). This may seem harsh, but Dr. Anderson shares some of my scepticism. Moreover, I think we both believe there are ways forward for psychology – ways that implicate information technology.

Such promise arises from the third theme above (practice). Here we are reminded that psychologists do apply their theories to real world problems – such as interacting with computers. This particular concern defines 'cognitive engineering'. Yet I do not share an excitement about this applied work in quite the same way. Dr. Anderson applauds the fact that theory gets exercised by the demands of addressing practical problems. But we need theory to be transformed by this contact.

My own view is that psychological analysis has become trapped by a suffocating individualism. Even in cognitive engineering, the focus remains a 'model of the mind'; and the'mind' remains something located firmly between our ears. Yet how could it be otherwise? And why should it be otherwise? Consider the urging to 'study cognitive processes such as memory in real world settings'. To be radical, this must mean more than taking models of mind away from the laboratory and applying them to people 'outdoors'. Being radical here means incorporating the real world into models of mentality. So to theorize memory, for example, we must confront it as 'remembering'- acting in a world of artefacts, institutions, rituals, and social interaction. Consider this claim : a child with pencil and paper has a better memory than an adult without. Cognition is mediated. The very vivid illustration of using writing to record experience reminds us of this. Thus, growing up involves appropriating the various technologies and interpersonal practices provided by our social niche. Cognitive development is a process of enculturation: its analysis must address individuals acting with mediational means. In this way, culture becomes integral to accounts of cognition, not some benign backdrop to human action.

So I welcome the ingenious reference to cognitive engineering when seeking to define new energies for psychology. But for me, reflecting on people's use of new technology provides a different and more radical inspiration. Peoples' use of computers is not simply some novel form of real world activity against which to test our models of mind – like observing people playing chess or riding bicycles. People using computers force us to notice the dramatic reorganization of human cognition that is possible through mediated action. The sheer drama of this has prompted many theorists to incorporate the context of action (mediational means) into the vocabulary of theories. Information technology forces us to notice the mediation of intelligent activity and. thereby, helps us foster more cultural theories of cognition.

Information technology and the development of economic policy: the use of microdata and microsimulation models

HOLLY SUTHERLAND

Department of Applied Economics
University of Cambridge

Abstract. After some general reflections on the differences that information technology (IT) has made to the practice of applied research in economics, the main focus of this paper is on the use of microdata in policy simulation models. These models are in principle accessible to a wide range of users and it is important that their advantages and limitations are fully understood. Some of the issues are illustrated by an application of the Microsimulation Unit's model, POLIMOD. The widespread use of such models is potentially threatened unless a new framework for the regulation of the use of microdata can be developed. Advances in IT have meant that the distinctions between data and other model components are increasingly blurred. A new approach to data access needs to take account of the increased integration of the processes involved in data analysis and policy evaluation.

Some general issues

The use of Information Technology (IT), particularly personal computers, networks and the Internet, has become integrated into the work of applied economists to the extent that it is difficult to isolate the aspects of these developments that simply allow work to proceed more quickly or efficiently from those that carry research into new and innovative areas. Most economists active in research are not old enough to remember what pre-digital computing was like, and take for granted such features as the speed of analysis, lack of direct dependency on the work of others and rate of development of IT generally that exist today.

The main focus of this paper is on the impact of IT on the construction and use of policy simulation models based on microdata. But this discussion is preceded by some general remarks about other kinds of economic models. There is a growing literature on the history of econometrics, which is now one of the most computer-intensive parts of economics (although not the only one). Analogue methods of computation preceded the widespread use of digital computers, and these machines are now literally museum pieces. Examples include the Phillips machine, which was a model of the economy using hydraulics to imitate economic flows. Restored versions are on display in the Science Museum and at a number of universities in the United Kingdom (UK) and overseas. Another example was Orcutt's electronic analogue machine, known as a regression analyser, which made possible tests of significance of apparent relationships between autocorrelated time series, using Monte Carlo simulation methods (Berndt 1991). Both machines involved some type of highly visual display, an aspect which is returned to below.

One aspect of quantitative economics as it existed before electronic computers was the constraints that were imposed by the need to do calculations by mechanical methods. Durbin's comments to Phillips (1988: 131) showed that there were a number of concerns in the Cambridge of the 1950s that do not typically trouble researchers there today:

> We thought at the time that they were horrendously difficult calculations, but one of the assets of the DAE [Department of Applied Economics] was that we had a room there with perhaps eight or ten young ladies operating desk calculators, supervised by an older lady of forbidding demeanour. They did the computing.... We were very concerned about the accuracy of these tables, as everybody was, doing computing in those days. What we tried to insist on was for the girls to do all the calculations twice. But of course this was rather boring from their point of view. To some extent you had to play a game when you were organising this type of computing, in getting the right amount of checking and getting it done properl.... There was always a doubt in our mind whether the tables really were accurate to the order that we claimed they were.

In fact, later electronic calculations showed the mechanical calculations to be accurate. However, this vivid picture suggests a number of ways in which the practice of applied economic research changed with the development of IT. First, the personnel management role has virtually disappeared: there is increasingly less division of labour (or other divisions) between the different functions that make up a research project. Typically these are far more integrated, with all the necessary tools provided by a desktop personal computer. Even where hierarchies remain within larger research teams, forbidding older ladies tend not to have a role and most members of the team are expected to develop and maintain a wide range of skills. A second difference is the importance of getting the design of an application right first time. Today, there are few constraints on the number of times that applications can be revised and re-run. Projects are often designed in this way, suggesting that perhaps there may be less *thought* and more volume of research output than previously. This comment amounts to a criticism only if truly original thought is crowded out along with the need for crystal clear thinking at the design stage.

There are also aspects of the conduct of research that have not changed in the last forty or fifty years; for example, concern with accuracy and replicability is still an issue today.

Computer-intensive economics

With the exception of mathematical software, used to solve equations that are difficult or impossible for a human, most uses of IT are in applied research rather than in theory. Computable General Equilibrium (CGE) models characterize the behaviour of representative agents and take account of the sorts of economic interactions that are predicted in theory between the sectors of the economy. Clearly the complexity of such a model depends on computer power. Macroeconomic forecasting models are also obviously computer intensive: they estimate many equations describing aspects of the economy, either simultaneously or, more usually, by linking the equations through a system of calibrations that maintain consistency. It is less obvious that the basic questions that they address or the general type of technique that they use are substantially different from those used before the development of modern IT. Allowing for rational expectations – the notion that if models predict a certain outcome, economic agents will adapt their behaviour to take advantage, thus ensuring that the predicted outcome will not take place – is feasible only with considerable computer power. However, without complex models of the economy and the signals they provide, such feedback effects may be less likely to occur, and in turn would be less of a focus for modellers' concerns.

In similar vein, the widespread use of IT has changed the economy itself and the way it operates. These changes need to be appreciated by any study of the economy and hence need to be captured in models. Examples include changes in the labour market illustrated by the quotation above describing manual computation: for the nature and importance of clerical work has changed entirely. Account also needs to be taken of financial liberalization which in part can be explained by IT. The increased importance of information as a commodity and the difficulty of accounting for this and other intangibles present problems for national accounts and for taxation, as well as their more general treatment in economics. Put baldly, accounting for *stocks* becomes less relevant and less straightforward, and *flows* become more important. The advent of modern IT may represent a change in our notions of time and space on the same scale as that brought about by the railways or electricity (Neuburger 1996). Traditional economic concepts – such as inputs and outputs – need to accommodate to this change.

Use of large and complex sets of microdata sets in a range of types of application is also clearly computer intensive. Not only does processing a large number of records take time and is therefore most conveniently done as fast as possible, but data storage is also an important requirement, as is the software necessary to handle complex data structures and for data management generally.

Typically, the microdata available for academic social science research are survey data, either collected as part of a project and integral with it, or collected by government or other statistical agencies and made available for research. Administrative data and census data are also used. The use by economists of such data is similar in its relationship with IT to that in many other social science and related disciplines, such as social policy, geography, epidemiology and demography.

Of course, social surveys were undertaken and analysed before computers were available to help. Seebohm Rowntree's surveys of York in 1899, 1936 and 1950 are good examples Although for their respective times they were each extremely innovative, sophisticated and influential, by current standards they were primitive. Their samples were drawn using eccentric methods; the samples were relatively small; a limited amount of information was collected from each respondent; and standards of checking and verifying data were poor. Prospects for handling each of these limitations can be seen to have been immeasurably improved by the use of IT. Large-scale survey sampling is typically carried out using computerized registers of various kinds (such as postcodes). Expansion of sample sizes and numbers of questions asked, while certainly influenced by other factors, was also affected by the ability to analyse quantities of large records, once the data were collected. Checking, and validating are much simplified by the use of automated checks, including the recently-introduced use of computer-assisted interviewing which allows checks to be made and information verified as the interview proceeds.

Perhaps the most significant change brought about by the advent of computers is the ability to store and archive the data effectively. The history of the data from Rowntree's 1950 survey is a case in point (Rowntree and Lavers 1951). Interview schedules were completed for each household in the form of a single sheet of paper and tabulations were computed by hand of such variables as income, household size, occupation and Rowntree's own measure of poverty. In the late 1970s the 1950 schedules plus the published report, together with Rowntree's notes and correspondence on the 1950 project, provided the basis for a study on intergenerational mobility: the children of the 1950 respondents were traced and their economic and social position compared with that of their parents (Atkinson *et al.* 1983). When the number of interview schedules was compared with the implied number of observations in the published report, it was discovered that about a third of the records of the interviews from 1950 were missing. No explanation for this gap was found and the follow-up project proceeded with a reduced sample. Atkinson *et al.* (1981) provide a comparison of the characteristics of the reduced sample with that reported in Rowntree and Lavers (1951). With the advent of computers, the loss of this irreplaceable information would probably not have happened: it would have been archived by the Data Archive at the University of Essex.

Microdata on households such as those collected by Rowntree and now collected regularly in several surveys by the government can be used for a range of types of research. Descriptive statistics measuring poverty and inequality have been moved beyond those available to Rowntree by the use of software developed for the purpose (see, for example, Cowell 1992). Ease of calculating measures of inequality and related phenomena using powerful computers has encouraged the development of new measures and the proliferation of approaches and interpretations. In a similar manner, the development of econometric techniques for the analysis of both cross-sectional and time series issues has been facilitated considerably. In particular, econometric studies that depend on non-parametric methods – those which do not from the outset impose functional forms on the relationships under consideration – may be very dependent on computer power and have developed as a practical option only as developments in IT permitted.

The Rowntree follow-up study was one of the first studies in the UK to produce longitudinal data on incomes, i.e., data collected at different points in time for the same (or related) individuals. Although an interest in the dynamic aspects of income, living standards and welfare, as well as related work on social mobility, pre-dates the development of the computer hardware and software that facilitates such analysis, these developments have clearly allowed an expansion of such activity. Household panel data such as those collected for the British Household Panel Study (Buck *et al.* 1994) would have been extremely difficult to manage, store, link and analyse effectively twenty years ago. Plentiful data storage and powerful computers permit new techniques for managing and linking multiple sets of microdata to be explored. The use of these data to explore questions of mobility and the dynamics of personal economic change is facilitated by developing new analytical methods and the software tools to implement them. Each of these is IT-dependent.

A further application of microdata has been in the development of microsimulation models, which are the subject of the next section.

Microsimulation models

Microsimulation means the use of *micro*-data on individuals to *simulate* the effect of changes in policy or the economic environment. It is the dependence on a wide range of individual characteristics in the microdata and at every stage of the analysis that distinguishes microsimulation models from other sorts of economic, mathematical, statistical or descriptive models. The use of microdata, representative of the population in question, allows the distributional effects of a policy change to be modelled and can also give greater precision in the estimates of aggregate change. Reliance on a large quantity of data in itself means that microsimulation models are highly dependent on IT.

Such models are usually divided into two sorts: dynamic and static. Three kinds of dynamic model can be identified. The first sort incorporates the effects of changes in individual behaviour by modelling, usually econometrically, any change in economic-related activity such as working or saving, fertility or retirement, that results from a change in policy. This is seen as necessary when a significant change in behaviour is expected, since it will need to be captured if the revenue effects of the policy change are to be estimated accurately. Furthermore, if the *purpose* of the policy is to change behaviour – to make work or saving more attractive, for example – then a full evaluation of the change will need to estimate how many people do change what they do and the extent to which these changes are in the direction intended by the policy initiative.

The second kind of dynamic model attempts to capture macro (second order) effects. These may occur as a result of changes in behaviour by persons, firms or other institutions in response to changes in policy. For example, following a reform to indirect taxes, changes in levels or patterns of personal spending will eventually have an impact on macroeconomic activity, which will affect government finances. The particular demand that such models make of IT arises from the need to carry out econometric estimation, which may be repeated many times.

The problem with these approaches arises because modelling human behaviour is extraordinarily difficult. People do not necessarily act in the ways supposed by economists. There are too many dimensions in which rationality may exist, too many interrelated factors involved for the task to be straightforward. Information Technology gives economists tools with which to explore these questions: but it cannot answer them.

Thirdly, some dynamic models operate by ageing a sample of units (such as individual people) so that projections or lifetime profiles are obtained. These can be generated under a range of scenarios, thereby aiding the evaluation of the long-term effects of changes in policy or testing the sensitivity of the outcomes to changes in assumptions, or indeed in any underlying theory on which the simulations are based. These dynamic microsimulation models are huge enterprises which are enormously resource-intensive. Problems arise because of lack of information about certain key transitions between states conditional on other key variables – such as family formation being dependent on participation in the labour force (and vice versa). The problems inherent in predicting changes in individual behaviour may apply in two ways. First, in the dynamic ageing process and secondly, in the *different* behaviour that results from different policy scenarios. Dynamic microsimulation models are naturally highly computer-intensive, particularly of storage space for actual and synthetic data, but also of computer power when stochastic simulation is involved.

In contrast with dynamic models, tax-benefit models, or static microsimulation models, are used for the analysis of policy that has its impact in the short term. They simulate tax liabilities and benefit entitlements of individual households in a sample which are then grossed-up to be representative of the total population. These calculations are performed for the current system and for a policy change which has been specified by the model user. The difference between the weighted sum of net incomes before and after the policy change is equal to the revenue gain to the government. The information on individual household is stored and re-assembled to give tables showing gains and losses for households at different points in the income distribution, or of different characteristics. The model makes the calculations of each element of the tax-benefit system so that interactions between different elements of the system – for example, some social security benefits that are taxable and others that depend on after-tax incomes – are fully taken into account.

Simulations using POLIMOD, the Cambridge Microsimulation Unit's model (Redmond *et al.* 1996) illustrate the approach below. Several other tax-benefit models exist for the UK, including that of the Institute for Fiscal Studies, TAXBEN2 (Giles and McCrae 1995) and IGOTM, the model maintained by the Office for National Statistics on behalf of government departments. Similar models exist for most European and other OECD countries (see Sutherland 1995 for a survey of models in some European countries). The prospects for a Europe-wide model, EUROMOD, are currently being researched (Sutherland 1996*b*).

POLIMOD is essentially arithmetic and addresses some of the same issues as manual calculations for individual hypothetical or 'model families' did before electronic data processing was commonplace. At the same time, the use of a computer-based model with a nationally representative database extends what was possible using manual calculations in two ways. First, as shown by Atkinson and Sutherland (1983), example family calculations can represent only a small proportion of actual families in the UK. Use of microdata allows the full range of living circumstances to be taken into account. Secondly, microdata made representative of the population permit estimates of the revenue effect of a change to be made. Not only is this essential for costing a particular policy, it also enables the distributional effect of the change to be established, conditional on a particular revenue constraint. This has the effect of prompting the designer of policy to consider how expenditure is to be paid for, or alternatively, of suggesting that revenue-raising schemes might incorporate compensation for unintentioned losers. While the advent of computer-dependent tax-benefit microsimulation models has not changed the fundamental approach to inquiry into the effects of changes in public policy, it has changed its focus, heightened awareness of distributional issues and had a major impact on the way that the research interacts with the processes of policy-making and policy evaluation.

The focus in designing POLIMOD has been to make it as user-friendly, flexible and durable as possible. User-friendliness has a number of dimensions, an attractive user-interface being one, but not necessarily the most important. For POLIMOD to be a genuinely useful as a tool for policy analysis it is vital that it is also transparent and that its limitations are understood. One of the other important aspects of a model that is designed to be widely used and understood is that its output should be as visually compelling and informative as possible. This is an aspect that today's models have in common with the two analogue models mentioned above. Portability is another consideration, as is illustrated by Orcutt describing the demonstration of his prototype analogue machine during the last months of World War II:

> I took my regression analyser with me to Cleveland and demonstrated it at the annual Christmas meetings. Since I was grossly overloaded, I was unable to take along the cathode ray tube which served as a graphical display device for showing time series and scatter diagrams derived from the three time series segments being read into the regression analyser. But I was able to borrow one from Case University in Cleveland. (Quoted in Berndt, 1991, 3).

Portability is an aspect of model accessibility which the development of personal computers and particularly laptops has greatly aided. Bringing interactive and sophisticated analysis into the lecture theatre, into committee meetings and onto the kitchen table has the potential to change completely the process of policy formation and to extend the ability to make informed comment and criticism to a wide range of interested groups, individuals and institutions. A brief example follows.

An example: taxing child benefit

The following example serves to illustrate the advantages and limitations of access to computer-based models such as POLIMOD and is designed to explore the implications of the speed, flexibility and user-friendliness that the use of IT brings to such an exercise. Suppose an analyst had been asked to consider the revenue and distributional implications of taxing child benefit. Currently this benefit is payable to the parent – usually the mother in the first instance – of all children under 16 or under 19 and in full-time non-advanced education. It was paid at a rate of £8.80 per child per week in 1996–7, with an additional £2 for the first or only child in the family. It is not means-tested or otherwise conditional and is tax-free. Indeed, it should be remembered that child benefit was introduced in the late 1970s in part to replace child tax allowances, so the logic has always been that it was not itself taxed. However, this does not rule out the possibility that it *could* be included in the tax base. One of the advantages of a computer model is that it requires its instructions in a precise form: the user is forced to focus on the detail that is required. Using POLIMOD to evaluate the general proposal raises a number of detailed but important questions about this apparently simple reform. First, is the benefit to be taxed as the income of the mother or of the father? Since 1990 the British tax system has treated the individual as the tax unit so that a person's liability for income tax is independent of the income of the spouse. An alternative would be to tax the child benefit as the mother's income, transferable to the father in cases where her income is not high enough to attract tax. Given that mothers have substantially lower incomes on average than fathers this choice has major implications for the revenue that is raised.

Secondly, at which rate would the benefit be taxed? Would it attract tax at the individual person's marginal rate and hence raise more tax from people with higher incomes? Or would it be taxed at a flat rate, and if so, what would this be? Thirdly would all of the payment be taxed, including the addition for the first child. Would one-parent benefit also be taxed? Fourthly, since the scheme would raise revenue, how should the distributional effect be evaluated, since the distribution of the government saving is unknown? Here, for the purpose of illustration, the revenue raised is used to increase the pre-tax level of child benefit.

Lastly, how would this increase in child benefit be integrated with means-tested benefits: would the amounts allowed for children be increased in line with child benefit so that the pre-tax incomes of all families are increased? Or would they be frozen so that families living on means-tested benefits were not affected by the scheme at all? (Income support assessments take account of child benefit, but most families in receipt of income support do not contain income taxpayers). Here again for illustrative purposes, the latter option is chosen. Furthermore technical issues must also be resolved. For example, since April 1996 investment income has been treated as the 'top slice' of taxable income so that it may be taxed at a reduced rate within the standard rate band only; Saunders and Smailes (1996: 67) provide a further explanation. Whether child benefit is introduced into taxable income as earned income below this 'slice', or whether it is treated as the top slice needs to be considered. Here it is assumed to be treated as earned income.

Just two possibilities are considered here: the first is that child benefit is taxed as the income of the recipient – the mother (or lone father) – at their particular marginal rate. According to POLIMOD the revenue collected is estimated to be £520 million per year (in 1996/7 terms), made up of £550 million in additional tax offset by £30 million in increased entitlements to means-tested benefits, which depend on after-tax income. These estimates were obtained from the model by calculating the net effect for each element of income for each household in the sample, and by weighting them and adding them to arrive at the national revenue effect. Using this revenue allows child benefit to be raised by £1.20 per child per week. This calculation involved several iterations, adjusting the size of the increase in child benefit until the overall net revenue effect was zero. Each such run takes about two minutes on a desktop PC with a Pentium 100 processor.

The second possibility is to tax child benefit as the mother's income in the first instance but to transfer all or the remaining part of the income to the father for taxation as his income in all cases where the mother's income is too low to attract tax. This transferability option more than doubles the revenue raised to £1,120 million per year, made up of £1,190 million in tax, offset by an increase in means- tested benefits of £70 million. The increase in child benefit that can be financed in this case is £3.00 per child per week.

In choosing between the two options their distributional effects will be considered as will aspects which are not directly captured by the simulation. First, the modelling does not take account of changed administrative or compliance costs. The difference in these between the two schemes may be considerable. Transfer of child benefit between parents requires that their tax records be linked. This does not happen as a matter of course and would involve a substantial administrative cost. It also raises the issue of the treatment of non-cohabiting parents, cohabiting unmarried parents and step-parents. Complex family situations are not uncommon and the process of establishing to whom the taxable income should be transferred is likely to be unpopular for all concerned. This, and compliance costs in all but the simplest cases will make the scheme involving transfer seem relatively much less attractive than it does on revenue grounds alone. Sutherland (1994) considers these issues in more detail.

Many options are also available for assessing the distributional results. Again, the choice will affect the apparent relative advantages and disadvantages of the schemes. Figure 1 plots the frequency of gains and losses by household income level for the transferable scheme, the scheme that allowed child benefit to be increased by £3 per child. Households are ranked by household post-tax incomes, using the pre-reform levels. Household incomes are adjusted for differences in household size and composition (using the McClements (1977) equivalence scale) and divided into ten equal-sized groups, or deciles. The percentage of each group which gains from the scheme is plotted as upward-pointing light grey bars. The percentage of households losing is plotted as downward pointing darker bars. Note that most households are not affected. Only some 30 per cent of households in the UK contain children, and in this scheme those that are in receipt of income support will be insulated from change, and will neither gain nor lose. More households lose than gain. Losers are concentrated in the middle of the household income distribution, as are gainers, although about 13 per cent of the bottom decile are also gainers. Figure 2 shows an alternative way of looking at the same policy option. Here, instead of ranking by household income, individual adult incomes are used. Individual income is calculated when computing gain or loss, using a method developed by Sutherland (1996a). The impression given of the distributional effect of the change is now quite different. Gainers are concentrated at the low income end of the distribution. Losers again appear in the middle, but there are virtually no low-income losers. The reason for this is that women greatly outnumber men at the bottom of the individual income distribution. The enhanced child benefit is paid to mothers but for those with low individual incomes, most of the tax is paid by their (male) partners who are concentrated around the middle of the individual income distribution. The extreme no-sharing

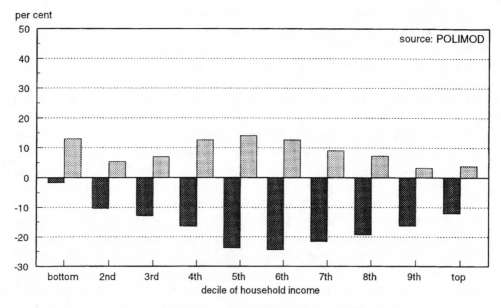

Fig. 1. Transferable taxation of child benefit by household income

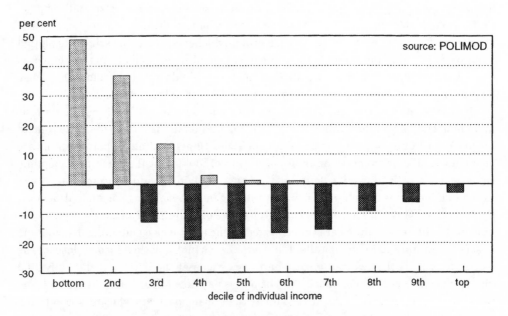

Fig. 2. Transferable taxation of child benefit by individual adult income

assumptions that have been built into the construction of the individual income distribution produce an impression that the transferable taxation scheme is most effective at distributing income from middle income people to the poor. However, a comparison of this picture with that displayed in Figure 1 shows that at least some of that redistribution is occurring *within* some households. According to some views, this may be considered to be a positive result. However, it is less clear that the mechanism that has been considered – the tax treatment of child benefit – is the most appropriate one to achieve this redistribution since it involves so much direct intervention within households and between parents.

As well as providing a flavour of the type of analysis that be undertaken using these models, this example was intended to demonstrate two points. First, that the the the use of computer models for the analysis of policy reforms offers enormous flexibility in the way that the modelling is done, as well as in the specific policy proposals that are modelled. It prompts the user to think about issues in a concrete fashion and illuminates the various trade-offs that exist between revenue, distribution and incentives.

However, the second point is that this flexibility can itself present problems. Two graphical outputs from the same simulation can make very different impressions, with only one difference in assumption. Very many other aspects could have been changed. Not only is there the possibility of producing misleading results, but it is also possible that results are in fact very difficult to replicate unless all the assumptions are documented. A typical academic economics paper does not have the space to do this.

At its worst, such a paper turns the model into a 'black box', producing results that are hard to replicate or subject to peer review, although strategies can be developed to make the black box transparent. This is necessary if debates about policy are not to be confused with purely technical issues. What is needed is extensive documentation, of both model assumptions and underlying data, explanations of the implications of choosing certain options and the development of *standards* for research involving comparisons, either over time or across countries. With such background information, microsimulation models can become educational tools in the broadest sense.

Limitations and prospects

IT thus provides the facility to carry out numerous model runs and to display results in graphical and accessible forms. A model such as POLIMOD is a stand-alone tool which is flexible and user-friendly and which provides a durable platform from which numerous analyses can be produced within minutes. It has great potential to change the terms under which debates about policy take place. Not only is a greater range of participants included at an informed level, but also the time taken to respond to new ideas and initiatives is reduced. Indeed, it is possible to foresee a further collapsing of all the processes involved in using microdata for the analysis of policy proposals. The use of interactive models reduces the distinction between the formulation of policy and its evaluation; the distinction between data collection and data checking is already blurred, data transfer between locations has ceased to be the major headache it once was; and transformation of microdata into model inputs can be increasingly automated. Enhancement of one dataset with information from another, matching and merging of data from many sources, or running data from many sources through a unified model are each developments which make the creation of the database the most research-intensive part of the whole process. The use of meso-data (microdata aggregated into small groups of similar observations) will further distinguish the notion of the model's database from any single raw data set. These developments and initiatives face two related problems. The first is the problem of lack of access to microdata. The second is the problem of identifying the physical and intellectual property of the various participants in the process: in the case of POLIMOD, these are the data providers, the model builders and the model users.

Typically, the microdata on which policy evaluations depend are collected by government departments. According to Lievesley (1996) the three main barriers to access to such data are copyright, confidentiality and commodification. Under each of these headings the situation differs greatly across countries and is not necessarily static. *Copyright* has become increasingly important as data providers understandably want to be able to control the use made of their products, and to take credit for the use that is made of them.

Rules concerning restrictions on data access and data use related to *confidentiality* may derive from national data protection legislation, from confidentiality clauses in national statistical laws or from freedom of information legislation. However, what happens in practice is a matter of how the laws are interpreted. Clearly there is a real need to protect the confidentiality of respondents. There is also a need to protect response rates from erosion that is due to individual fears – founded or unfounded – about how the data will be used. There is little hard evidence, however, that the level of restriction concerning access to data for academic research has any impact on response rates. Indeed, it has been possible to convince the authorities that damage would not be caused by allowing access to samples of census data, without changing the law (Marsh *et al.* 1991).

The *commercial* value of data has increasingly played a role, particularly as statistical agencies have needed to generate revenue to make up for cuts in other income. However, the balance between raising revenue and establishing a pricing policy needs to be found that does not inhibit the progress of academic inquiry or of research that is in the public interest. The pessimistic view is that access to data collected by governments or international statistical agencies will increasingly become restricted to research contracted by those organisations or undertaken by privileged people with 'intimate and individual links' with them (Rhind 1991). Innovative, speculative or critical research will not gain access, nor will unestablished researchers, graduate students or academics who want to use microdata for teaching find an easy way past the gatekeepers. The optimistic view is that the benefits of the widespread use of data will outweigh short-term financial considerations. In the words of the Director of Statistics Sweden:

> Statistics bureaus also need an intimate relationship with science both for improvement of statistical methods in various policy areas and to provide official statistics as an infrastructure for social and related science. (Johansson (1990), quoted in Lievesley (1996, 7).)

While access to survey data is clearly a fundamental component of a model like POLIMOD, other complications also arise when the model is designed to be widely disseminated. Clearly copyright concerns are legitimate and it is quite proper for data providers to want credit and acknowledgement for their part in the model. However, it is also the case that model builders should claim credit (and take responsibility) for the way in which they have made use of the data, often transforming them beyond recognition. Similarly, the model user should claim credit and responsibility for the use they make of the model. However, the division among the players of the intellectual property in the final results of the model remains an open question. It becomes all the more important to answer this question if consideration is given to the changes to microdata use and micro-modelling that are already taking place and which are likely to accelerate in the near future. Models will extend their scope by using multiple data sets and by making use of increasingly complex methods of data transformation. The use of complex transforma-tions and meso-data will intensify the need for clarification of the regulations concerning the use of microdata for research. At what stage does a transformed data set become the intellectual property of its creator? Old solutions which depended on the functions of data collection, data transport, data analysis and paper publication being separable are no longer appropriate if the tools that are developed in an academic environment are to exploit the opportunities being offered now and to be offered soon by IT. Increased integration of these functions, accompanied by the ability to develop them independently of geographical location, requires a new framework for regulating the use of microdata. It is this practical but complex issue that is the immediate major challenge.

Acknowledgements

I have benefitted from helpful correspondence and discussions with many people while writing this paper. I would particularly like to thank A. B. Atkinson, B. Henry, H. Neuburger, L. Osberg, G. Redmond and F. Wilkinson. However, I alone am responsible for the views expressed. Data from the Family Expenditure Survey, which are Crown Copyright, have been made available by the Office for National Statistics (ONS) through the Data Archive and are used by permission. Neither the ONS nor the Data Archive bears any responsibility for the analysis or interpretation of the data reported here.

References

Atkinson, A. B., Corlyon, J., Maynard, A. K., Sutherland, H. and Trinder, C. G. (1981), 'Poverty in York: a re-analysis of Rowntree's 1950 Survey', *Bulletin of Economic Research*, 33: 59–71.
—— Maynard, A. K. and Trinder, C. G. (1983), *Parents and Children: Incomes in Two Generations* (London).
—— and Sutherland, H. (1983), 'Hypothetical families in the DHSS tax-benefit model and families in the Family Expenditure Survey 1980', TIDI Research Note No. 1 (STICERD, London School of Economics).
Berndt, E. R. (1991), *The Practice of Econometrics: Classic and Contemporary* (Reading, Mass.).

Buck, N., Gershuny, J., Rose, D. and Scott, J. (1994), *Changing Households: The British Household Panel Survey 1990–1992*, ESRC Research Centre on Micro-social Change, University of Essex.

Cowell, F. A. (1992), 'INEQ', STICERD, London School of Economics (mimeo and software).

Giles, C. and McCrae, J. (1995), 'The IFS microsimulation tax and benefit model', Institute of Fiscal Studies working paper No. 95/19.

Johansson, S. (1990), 'Information needs for the market and for democracy', *Journal of Official Statistics* 6: 1.

Lievesley, D. (1996), 'Access to European data', ESRC Data Archive, University of Essex (mimeo).

Marsh, C., Skinner, C., Arber, S., Penhale, B., Oppenshaw, S., Hobcraft, J., Lievesley, D. and Walford, N. (1991), 'The case for samples of anonymised records from the 1991 census', *Journal of the Royal Statistical Society (A)*, 154(2): 305–40.

McClements, D. (1977), 'Equivalence scales for children', *Journal of Public Economics*, 8: 191–210.

Neuburger, H. (1996), 'How should National Accounts respond to the intangible economy?', Office of National Statistics (mimeo).

Phillips, P. (1986), 'The ET interview: James Durbin', *Econometric Theory* 4: 125–57.

Redmond, G., Sutherland, H. and Wilson, M. (1996), 'POLIMOD: an Outline, 2nd Edition', Microsimulation Research Note MU/RN/19, Department of Applied Economics (DAE), University of Cambridge.

Rhind, D. (1992), 'War and peace: GIS data as a commodity' *GIS Europe* 1(8): 24–6.

Rowntree, B. S. and Lavers, G. R. (1951), *Poverty and the Welfare State* (London).

Saunders, G. and Smailes, D. (1996), *Income Tax 1996–1997* (Croydon).

Sutherland, H. (1994), 'The Commission on Social Justice's proposals for child benefit: a comment', Microsimulation Unit Research Note MU/RN/8, Department of Applied Economics (DAE), University of Cambridge.

—— (1995), 'Static Microsimulation Models in Europe: A Survey', Microsimulation Unit Discussion Paper MU9503, DAE, University of Cambridge.

—— (1996a), 'Households, individuals and the re-distribution of income', Microsimulation Unit Discussion Paper MU9601, DAE, University of Cambridge.

—— (1996b), 'EUROMOD', Microsimulation Unit Research Note MU/RN/20, DAE, University of Cambridge.

Commentary

GUY JUDGE

Department of Economics
University of Portsmouth

Adopting a travelling metaphor, Sutherland's paper has demonstrated, in relation to the use of Information Technology in economics, how far we have come, new directions which have been opened up for us and certain difficulties which remain ahead. These comments reiterate Sutherland's message, supplementing it by drawing attention to some areas in economics not mentioned in her paper where Information Technology (IT) has had important effects.

How far we have come

It is undeniable that IT is now *integrated* into the everyday work of *all* applied economists. Today nearly all economists have a powerful desk top machine with a full range of user-friendly software for quantitative analysis and the production of charts and word processed reports and articles. Via the networks users of these machines have access to electronic databanks, bibliographical sources and on-line collections of working papers, as well as links by e-mail to colleagues all over the world. Things have changed considerably in the twenty-five years since I was a graduate student. Then, as the following extract from Greene's (1993) econometrics textbook described, only hardened researchers made use of computers, and some effort was required to obtain your results. 'Computers and computer software have come a long way from the days when one trudged across campus in the snow to hand a deck of cards to the operator of a hostile mainframe (only to find out the next day that the entire job had aborted because of a comma punched in the wrong column).'

New opportunities

Changes in IT and computers since the introduction of the microchip have meant that more people can more quickly and more easily undertake tasks that were once the province of only a minority of researchers. Furthermore, as the main part of Sutherland's paper illustrated, because we now have small portable computers with user-friendly interfaces and excellent graphics facilities, computers can be brought fully into the process of debate and policy formulation and not just turned to for number crunching exercises running out of sight in the backroom.

It was in the field of macroeconomic applications that computers first made their impact in economic analysis, forecasting and policy making. To begin with computers just meant that previous procedures could be carried out more efficiently in terms of speed and verified accuracy. However, more powerful computers and the software developed to go with them meant that models with more flexible functional forms, lag structures and expectations mechanisms become practicable and it became possible to view results in more visual form on screen as well as in tables and printouts.

Because modern IT permits the storage and analysis of massive cross-section databases, it has also been possible to change the focus of policy debates so that one can look not only at models of macroeconomic and highly aggregated quantities, but also at those which take a much more microeconomic and disaggregated view, permitting also consideration of distributional issues. Drawing upon examples based on the use of POLIMOD, the model developed by the Microsimulation Unit at Cambridge, Sutherland illustrated how the detailed effects of different tax and benefits proposals can be assessed, highlighting the advantages of visual representations of the results of the simulation experiments which 1990s IT makes possible.

Improvements in IT have also opened up new approaches in econometrics where Monte Carlo studies have become valuable tools for investigating the properties of models, estimators and test procedures. Advances in applied econometrics have also been greatly assisted by new generations of computer hardware and software. The General-to-Specific methodology, advocated by David Hendry and based on the early work of Denis Sargan at the London School of Economics, requires a thorough search through models nested within a general specification and this demands extensive estimation and testing. This is in marked contrast to earlier work which presumed a known model which was to be fitted to the available data, with the possibility of minor model adaptations if the regression diagnostics suggested any 'econometric problems'. Although it might have been feasible for a dedicated and patient researcher to follow the Hendry strategy on old slow cumbersome computers with unfriendly input-out devices, it is doubtful whether the approach could have gained such widespread acceptance under such conditions.

New challenges

Notwithstanding the benefits which IT has provided in opening up new approaches in applied quantitative research and making them accessible to wider groups of people, Sutherland is right to draw to our attention some of the new problems which we now face. She noted that, with computer-assisted interviewing and automated data collection, there is already a blur between data collection and data checking. She is concerned that a further blurring is now occurring between policy formulation and its evaluation. Perhaps we need an independent Microeconomic Modelling Bureau to parallel the Macroeconomic Modelling Bureau at Warwick?

As her experience with POLIMOD highlights, it is often hard to distinguish a model's database from that of any single raw data set. In combining data with other information or in making it more accessible one redefines it and adds value to it. Referring to the three main barriers to data access identified by Denise Lievesley, namely copyright, confidentiality and 'commodification', Sutherland raises questions about how we can reconcile the needs of statistical agencies to generate revenue to pay for their activities with the needs of researchers to gain access to the information. A pessimistic view is that we might find ourselves in a situation where only privileged 'insiders' can gain access to the data that are needed if restrictive pricing policies are adopted for data use. It is thus vital that economists, in addition to benefiting from some of the advances in IT in their work, contribute to the debate about appropriate mechanisms for pricing and investing in IT resources such as the Internet and the databases which can be attached to it.

Reference

Greene, W. H. (1993), *Econometric Analysis* (New York).

The impact of computational tools on time-series econometrics

DAVID F. HENDRY AND JURGEN A. DOORNIK

Nuffield College
Oxford

Abstract. The paper discusses the evolution of a software system, and its influence on econometric practice. The main trends are from essentially 'techniques' to primarily graphical tools; a formalization of the underlying econometric modelling methodology; and a greatly increased emphasis on the user interface. Software has not only enabled vast calculations to be made that previous researchers deemed infeasible and allowed graphical presentation to render the resulting mass of output comprehensible, it has also altered the way in which econometric modelling is practiced, substantially improving the quality of empirical research. The present software exploits the Windows operating system to show data, results, evaluations, and graphics simultaneously on screen, thereby further facilitating econometric analyses.

Introduction

In the course of this century, econometrics has become an increasingly important part of the economics discipline, developing and investigating the statistical tools needed to relate economic analysis to the available empirical observations. In the words of Frisch (1933:1), econometrics involves the 'mutual penetration of quantitative economic theory and statistical observation'. Because the economy is a complicated, dynamic, non-linear, high-dimensional and evolving entity, in which controlled experimentation is difficult, the procedures being used are often highly sophisticated and complex (some critics object that they are sometimes more so than the data would warrant: see Leontief 1971).

This paper is concerned with time-series econometrics. The aim of an empirical study could be to investigate the properties of, and interrelations between, a small set of macroeconomic variables (as later in this paper). Such an applied econometric analysis requires a computational tool to manage the economic database and develop models using economic data, both graphically and implementing econometric techniques. An example of such a tool is our suite of programs collectively called PcGive (see Doornik and Hendry 1996, and Hendry and Doornik 1996a).

A second important aspect of econometrics is studying the statistical properties of the procedures used in empirical modelling. Here the computer is important to simulate cases which are analytically intractable. An example of such a tool is the matrix programming language Ox (see Doornik 1996), whose object-oriented features, together with preprogrammed classes for Monte Carlo analysis, facilitate these tasks greatly. Menu-driven simulation modules such as PcNaive, which can output Ox code, create a powerful, flexible, yet easy to use, system (see Doornik and Hendry 1997b). Compare this to the classical Monte Carlo experiments of Student (1908) and Yule (1926), which had to be done entirely by hand. Programs such as GAUSS, RATS, Pc-TSP and PCNAIVE are now routinely used to simulate the behaviour of estimation, evaluation and forecasting tools in large systems fitted to data from complicated artificial processes.

Computational tools are a vital component of econometrics. They embody and provide easy access to current knowledge, and facilitate both theoretical and empirical research. Even more importantly, computational limitations have been a straitjacket, which, though looser now, still restricts current practice. Much research effort has been invested in devising techniques which circumvent contemporaneous restrictions, in large part obsolete now. For example, Bean (1929) reported that a single four-variable regression analysis for thirty observations would take about eight hours of work. At the end of 1996, our computer does about 30,000 per second (and much more accurately), an increase in speed of almost 10^9. Indeed, it has only recently become possible to apply routinely the influential work of the Cowles foundation (see Koopmans 1950). It can be no surprise that improved computational power has had a major impact on the discipline. Nevertheless, other aspects have also been profoundly affected. This paper illustrates that impact using our computer software system.

The interactions between the development of our computer software and advances in econometric modelling practice are first reviewed. Historically, each in turn has induced advances in the other. The need to design the menu structure of a menu-driven program, so that a convenient order is defined, with cognate operations closely linked, requires a clear view of how to implement empirical modelling: see, for example, the discussion in Hendry et al. (1988). Conversely, the formalization of the theory of reduction (see, e.g., Hendry 1995) clarified how the menus should be structured to facilitate practice, as well as which new menus were needed (such as those monitoring the progress of a reduction exercise, or testing for encompassing between rival models).

Next, the role of the user interface, which consumes the bulk of program development time, is considered. Our aims were: to allow econometrics to be undertaken and evaluated by applied economists; to improve teaching practices, especially by allowing live class-room empirical analyses; to implement the developing approach of the theory of reduction; and to provide access to frontier econometric methods. Thus, the interface must be as transparent as possible; require little human memory – particularly for intermittent users; yet provide as much flexibility as needed to support a wide range of potential uses.

The use of graphical presentation is then examined. Not only has this transformed the insights one can glean into data, it is essential to solve the problem of information overload when modelling dynamic economic systems, often referred to as infoglut.

Finally, the benefits deriving from a Windows-type environment are considered, which will further improve the quality of empirical research by allowing more penetrating analyses of data through linking numerical and graphical descriptions.

Historical development

The computer software is now known generically as PcGive. It began life in the late 1960s as a mainframe FORTRAN package, on punched cards, with complex job control commands that took some expertise to master (see the brief discussions in Hendry 1970, 1974). Such software enabled vast calculations to be undertaken that previous researchers had deemed infeasible (see the discussion in Phillips 1986). For example, although Eisenpress and Greenstadt (1966) worried greatly about numerical optimization, maximizing a non-linear function of several hundred parameters is now relatively routine, as is the computation of high-dimensional multivariate test statistics to check the quality of the resulting models.

The original aim was simply to make available the latest econometric estimators and tests: the rest, specifically how to apply such methods, was up to users. However, the ever-increasing demand for the suite led to a major effort to document and explain it, leading to an analysis of the role of such computer software in implementing implicit methodologies in Hendry and Srba (1980). The design of later vintages of the program, reincarnated as menu-driven PC software, explicitly acknowledged the formal methodology of econometric modelling, (see Hendry 1986, 1988, 1989; Doornik and Hendry 1992, 1994; and Hendry and Doornik 1996a). Thus, software development has altered the way in which econometric modelling is practiced, substantially improving the quality of empirical research.

Table 1 gives is a brief history of the important developments of PC versions. The mainframe versions were not concerned about user friendliness: just being able to do an analysis posed sufficiently difficult programming problems. Indeed, using the code library required a substantial effort, compounded by the fact that computer time was mainly available out of normal office hours. The PC version saw a major shift towards usability: econometric analysis is easier not only because the computer is faster, but also because the human effort required is substantially smaller. A second aspect which took off with the PC version was data visualization, which is an important part of an empirical

Table 1. Important developments in the versions of PcGive

1983–4		Port of mainframe Fortran version to PC-based Fortran.
1984	V2	Ordinary least squares (OLS) and instrumental variable (IV) estimation; character graphics.
1985	V3	First bitmap graphics, and menus with colours and defaults. (under MS-DOS: requiring to switch between text and graphics modes).
1986	V4	Recursive OLS (RLS); help system; graphics written in assembly language.
1987	V5	Recursive IV (RIV); dynamic analysis; expert mode; first version of PCFIML (simultaneous equations estimation).
1989	V6	Johansen (1988) procedure; higher resolution graphics (still one at a time).
1992	V7	PcGive code converted to the C language; pull-down menus with mouse support; up to 16 graphs at once; calculator; spreadsheet-type database, 32-bit version.
1994	V8	PcFiml converted to C; Non-linear least squares (NLS); Recursive FIML and NLS; multivariate tests; last version to have graphics in assembly.
1996	V9	Standard Windows interface (in separate module); vector graphics. up to 36 graphs; multiple graphics, data and text windows; mixture of C and C++.

analysis, and the summary shows that improvements were made with each version. Initially, under the multitide of graphics cards in MS-DOS, adding graphical features was fiendishly difficult. Nowadays, the operating system hides such complexities from the programmer.

The developments also show an alternation between efforts to improve the friendliness and flexibility of the user interface with implementing advances in econometric technology, in all comprising three completely new interfaces in just over a decade (versions 3, 7, and 9). Although there is some evidence of shortening interface cycles, it is impossible to forecast the next interface overhaul, as interface innovations are dictated by general developments in operating systems, as well as user demands. Figures 1–6 illustrate these differences in PcGive versions with some screen captures.

User interface

Experience with developing versions of PcGive, accumulated over nearly a decade, has shown that roughly 75 per cent of the development effort is invested in the user interface and graphics. Other interactive statistical programs must face a similar balance. Every time there is an interface shift, a program has to struggle for survival: development is usually done by a small number of individuals who need to invest an inordinate amount of time to learn new programming skills. A couple of years' delay could jeopardize the continuing existence of a program: the menu-selection procedures of versions 2–4 look hopelessly out of date today, despite being innovative at the time. Command-driven programs face these issues to a lesser extent, owing to the much simpler interface, although providing powerful graphics remains a potential problem.

As was discussed in Hendry and Doornik (1996b), the current aims are more general than those noted in the previous section, namely: to help non-professionals at their desk undertake graphically-based econometric analyses; to enhance the teaching of econometrics with software that can simultaneously portray all essential aspects of an analysis; to implement the general-to-specific modelling approach based on the theory of reduction; as well as to provide rigorously-tested algorithms implementing the latest econometric techniques (for a more detailed discussion of that last issue, see Doornik 1995). Less obviously, avoiding information overload is important, as stressed in Hendry and Doornik (1994). Finally, program operation must be straightforward to learn, and be memorable for occasional users.

From the outset of the PC versions, great effort was devoted to sustaining live presentations, both for classroom teaching and for empirical seminars, where substantive issues can be resolved in situ. Such analyses emphasize that empirical research cannot be conducted by mechanistic application of recipes that guarantee useful answers. Rather, it is an iterative process of sifting information from evidence. The final product published in an academic paper conveys a false impression of the certainty of the exercise because it is retrospective: in reality, the study was probably undertaken in a fog of partial understanding. To serve the aim of live demonstrations, the program has to be extremely reliable, robust (essentially uncrashable), and virtually error free, so others' findings can be replicated. At the same time, the program must be easy to use, so that attention during presentations can be focused on the substantive issues and not on program use – yet remain flexible, general and powerful enough for the tasks at hand. Such design issues have been investigated in depth over years of testing and user feedback, and Figure 6 records the latest development (see Doornik and Hendry 1996).

The documentation has also been transformed in a matching way: there is no longer any 'Manual' section in the latest book on PcFiml (Doornik and Hendry 1997*a*), whereas its tutorials seek to teach both the use of the software and the econometric theory and methods for a user who is expected to be seated at the computer using the package. An extensive, context-sensitive, hyptertext help system supports learning the system as well as providing on-line information about the econometrics procedures.

Graphics

Graphics have been one of the most salient improvements. Consider the typical screen graph of the 1970s and early 1980s for an equation from the US annual model in Klein (1950) produced using a PcGive version circa 1985 (Figure 7) (see Davidson *et al.* 1978, for similar printed examples, albeit somewhat improved by ruler and pen!). Even with such a small sample, it is difficult to perceive how well the equation performs, although the last forecast looks somewhat off.

The first colour graphs were an improvement as Figure 8 shows (this graph was actually saved using PcGive6 in low resolution, but is essentially identical to PcGive3; earlier methods of graph saving failed to function under Windows NT). Nevertheless, such graphs involved screen mode changes, hiding the related results, so Figure 6 is a further important advance. Another major role for graphs is discussed in the next section.

Avoiding infoglut

Time-series macro-econometric modelling often involves large numbers of variables in multi-equation systems where there may be several thousand statistics to contemplate. Graphical representation has long seemed the only feasible approach. As an example, Figure 9 shows eighteen histograms with non-parametric density approximants, and then eighteen correlograms for the levels, first and second differences of the six quarterly macroeconomic variables: real consumers' expenditure (LC), the real wage (LWP), the retail price index (LRPI), real exports (LX) (all four in logs denoted by the leading L), the 3-month interest rate (RLA), and the unemployment rate (U). The sample periods differ for these series, but are mainly over 1955(1)-1993(4), with the shortest being 1977(1)-1993(4).

The legends for identifying the variables and their transforms have been left in, although these rather clutter the graphs. Nevertheless, despite the large amount of information, a glance shows that the distributional and time-series correlations of the variables are vastly different. Consider the first three histograms for LC, as against those for LWP; and similarly the great differences in their correlograms. Then contrast these with the shapes of those six graphs for U.

Figure 10 shows the fitted and actual values, the scaled residuals, the forecasts over

```
             A C T I O N    M E N U
        1.FULL SAMPLE ESTIMATES
        2.TRANSFORM SOME OF THE REGRESSORS
        3.DELETE  A REGRESSOR
        4.ADD A VARIABLE TO THE MODEL
        5.ADD THE REGRESSION PREDICTIONS TO THE DATA SET
        6.RUN A MODEL MODIFIED IN THIS MENU
        7.SAVE THE MODEL DATA
        8.RUN THE MODEL FOR A DIFFERENT SAMPLE SIZE
        9.RETURN TO THE MINI-MENU
              CHOOSE AN OPTION:  ▪
```

Fig. 1. PcGive 2: action menu

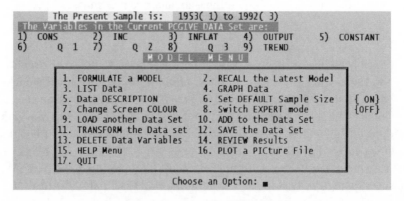

Fig. 2. PcGive 6: main menu

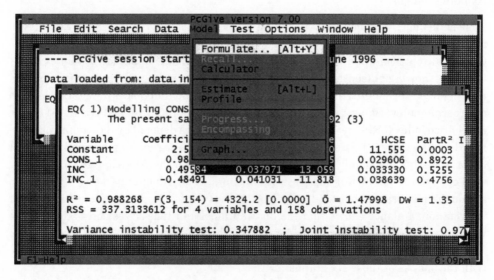

Fig. 3. PcGive 7: main menu

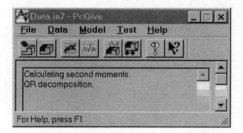

Fig. 4. PcGive 9: main menu

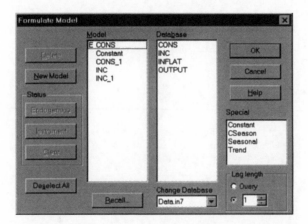

Fig. 5. PcGive 9: model formulation

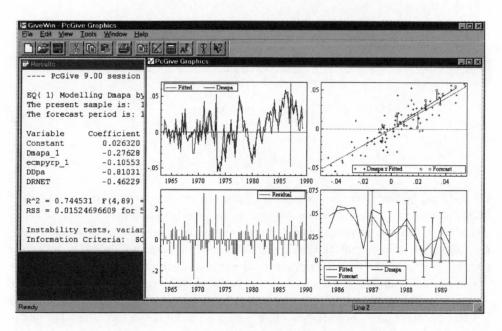

Fig. 6. GiveWin 1: main screen

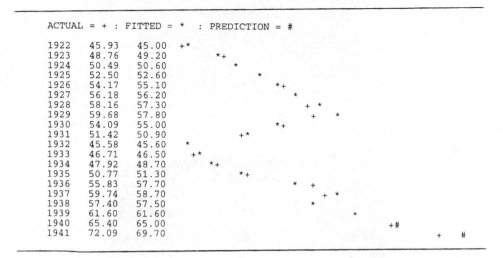

```
ACTUAL = + : FITTED = *  : PREDICTION = #

1922   45.93   45.00   +*
1923   48.76   49.20        *+
1924   50.49   50.60           *
1925   52.50   52.60              *
1926   54.17   55.10                *+
1927   56.18   56.20                  *
1928   58.16   57.30                    +  *
1929   59.68   57.80                      +    *
1930   54.09   55.00                *+
1931   51.42   50.90            +*
1932   45.58   45.60   *
1933   46.71   46.50   +*
1934   47.92   48.70        *+
1935   50.77   51.30          *+
1936   55.83   57.70                *    +
1937   59.74   58.70                    +  *
1938   57.40   57.50                  *
1939   61.60   61.60                        *
1940   65.40   65.00                          +#
1941   72.09   69.70                              +      #
```

Fig. 7. PcGive 2: Screen graph

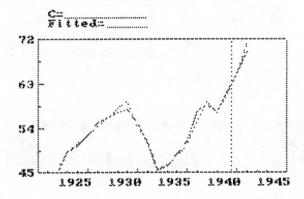

Fig. 8. PcGive 4: Colour graph

the last eight quarters, the residual correlograms, and the histograms of the residuals for all six equations. It takes a more practiced eye to absorb all this information, but it is again clear that the correlograms of the residuals are close to zero throughout, the densities are near to normal, and the forecasts close to the outcomes (the 95% confidence bars are shown centered on the forecasts). Closer inspection shows that there are some outliers in the residuals (mis-fits greater that two residual standard deviations). Such a mass of results would be totally incomprehensible if presented as numerical outcomes.

The problem simply overwhelms one's senses when statistics are calculated recursively, adding observations one at a time from an initial set, to attain the full sample.

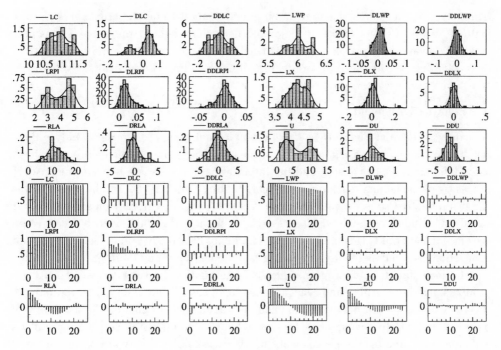

Fig. 9. PcGive: graphical statistics

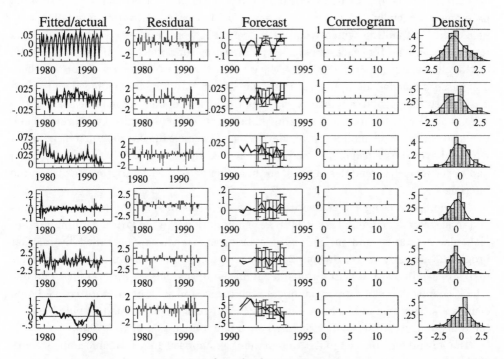

Fig. 10. PcFiml: graphical summary statistics

Graphical presentation is essential, and in practice, allows a quick perusal of the 'gross' features of an analysis to see if major problems lurk behind the usual full-sample estimates. Even non-linear estimation is feasible recursively, although a sound methodology for discovering the appropriate form of the non-linear links awaits development.

A Windows environment

As can be seen from Figure 6, a Windows-style environment lets users analyse data, results, text, and graphics simultaneously on screen, allowing intellectually and physically different ways of viewing and linking information. This is a boon to the creative processes of modelling, teaching and experimenting. Further, the graphics themselves can be interactive, so regression lines can be added to graphs already on screen, further variables included, or data revised and so on. Such facilities, which were a dream when the development of PC versions began, can highlight previously un-noticed features and connections, as well as greatly improving communication of the findings.

The look and feel of programs has become similar across a range of software products, making learning and remembering much easier, and enhancing productivity. Drop-down menus and dialogs are immediately familiar, and clicking on icons in tool bars is simple. Help systems can be comprehensive about both the program and its embodied tools and techniques, as well as being cross linked by hypertext to track and interrelate ideas.

One further important innovation occurred with version 9: a modular structure of the programs. Previously, there was one library for data input/output/manipulation, graphics, and text editing which was put in front of several econometric modules. This replicated the same interface across at least three programs (PcGive, PcFiml and STAMP: see Koopman *et al.* 1995). Now the interface called GiveWin – shown in Figure 6, where databases are loaded, data – transformed, and graphs and text are displayed and edited is an executable program which is separate from the econometric modules. The latter communicate with the former, requesting data, and sending text output and graphs back to the interface. This simplifies future development because the interface can be replaced without having any effect on the modules. Moreover, the interface between the front end and the econometric modules is open, so that others could develop programs using the interface.

OLE (object linking and embedding) is a set of procedures for compound documents and inter-process communication. OLE automation refers to the latter, defining a set of methods (functions) and properties of a program, which can be called by another program. Currently, GiveWin has 22 functions accessible from outside, 2 to receive text, 9 to send/accept data and provide database information, 13 for graphics, and one which enables the client to communicate the name, and whether it can receive batch commands. This communication is one way: it is always the client module which makes the function calls to GiveWin (except where a batch file is run in GiveWin).

The advantages of using OLE automation, as opposed to a Dynamic Link Library (DLL), are:

- complete separation of modules (each is in own address space; 32 bit DLLs also run in their own memory space, but this is mapped into the main process);
- easier access from other programs;
- could potentially use remote procedure calls;
- GiveWin can be used as a stand-alone program.

There are also some disadvantages:

- loss of speed;
- need to transfer all data;
- only one-way communication;
- complex, unless using compiler provided tools.

Speed is mainly a problem when too many calls are made. When a model is formulated in PcGive, it extracts a copy of all the relevant data from GiveWin. However, even in a single program, it is convenient to make a copy of the data, to ensure its integrity (i.e., transformations take effect onlywhen a model is formulated, but not during evaluation).

The OLE automation side will be documented in the hope that other developers will also create modules for GiveWin. The advantages are obvious: no need to create that part of the program which is tedious to develop, and which is tangential to the computational programming of the relevant econometric tools (albeit crucial to the usability of the program). There are several programs which are completely outdated in interface, but implement useful techniques, and these could be revived quickly in this way.

Recently, the Ox programming language (see Doornik 1996) has been developed to enhance the power, generality, and flexibility of the system, as a step towards an inference engine that will allow users to analyse the properties of their procedures for the data set under study. Under Windows, the functionality of Ox is in dynamic link library (DLL). Text output can appear on the console or in GiveWin, depending on the choice of executable to run the Ox code (Oxlw or Oxrun). When using GiveWin, graphs are also displayed. Figure 11 sketches the interactions.

Conclusions

Empirical econometrics is critically dependent on its computing platforms, their operating systems and the software written to support modelling. Earlier efforts were devoted to the enabling task, namely, providing access in some form to the computational tools. Computer power was a significant limiting factor in the subject's development. Next, considerable effort was devoted to the user interface to make programs more reliable and easier to use. Advances in screen graphics are important here. A further development was the attempt to embody explicit methodologies in the software to replace the previously implicit approaches. Finally, the reduction of infoglut has been a focus. Together, these advances have greatly improved the quality of empirical research, especially in conjunction with related advances in econometric methods and model classes.

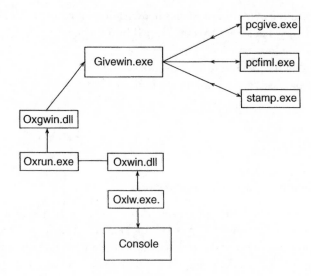

Fig. 11. GiveWin interaction

An environment such as Windows allows data, results and graphics to appear simultaneously on screen, enabling documenting of reports as modelling proceeds, as well as linking the main ingredients of empirical analyses. It is also a significant input into teaching, and has proved invaluable in relating theoretical concepts to their realization in practice.

Computing is a core aspect of econometrics, both to make the available methods operational and to develop new ways of thinking about modelling. In practice, PcGive has become an approach to econometrics as well as a computer program.

Acknowledgement

Financial support from the Economic and Social Research Council is gratefully acknowledged.

References

Bean, L. H. (1929), 'A simplified method of graphic curvilinear correlation'. *Journal of the American Statistical Association,* 24: 386–97.

Davidson, J. E. H., Hendry, D. F., Srba, F., and Yeo, J. (1978), 'Econometric modelling of the aggregate time-series relationship between consumers' expenditure and income in the United Kingdom'. *Economic Journal,* 88: 661–92. Reprinted in Hendry, D. F (1993), *Econometrics: Alchemy or Science?* (Oxford).

Doornik, J. A. (1995), *Econometric Computing.* Unpublished. Phd Thesis, University of Oxford.

—— (1996), *Object-Oriented Matrix Programming using Ox.* (London Oxford) http://www.nuf-f.ox.ac.uk/Users/Doornik/.

—— and Hendry, D. F., (1992), *PcGive 7. An Interactive Econometric Modelling System* (Oxford).

—— and Hendry, D. F., (1994), *PcGive 8: An Interactive Econometric Modelling System* (London and Belmont).

—— and Hendry, D. F., (1996), *GiveWin: an Interactive Empirical Modelling Program* (London).

—— and Hendry, D. F., (1997*a*), *Modelling Dynamics Systems using PcFiml 9 for Windows* (London).

—— and Hendry, D. F., (1997*b*), Monte Carlo sumilation using PCName for Windows unpublished typescript, Nuffield College, Oxford.

Eisenpress, H., and Greenstadt, J. (1966), 'The estimation of non-linear econometric systems'. *Econometrica*, 34: 851–61.

Frisch, R. (1933), Editorial. *Econometrica*, 1, 1–4.

Hendry, D. E (1970), 'The Estimation of Economic Models with Autoregressive Errors'. Unpublished Ph.D. thesis, London University.

—— (1974), 'Stochastic specification in an aggregate demand model of the United Kingdom. *Econometrica'*, 42: 559–78. Reprinted in Hendry, D. F. (1993), *Econometrics: Alchemy or Science?* (Oxford).

—— (1986), 'Using PC-GIVE in econometrics teaching'. *Oxford Bulletin of Economics and Statistics*, 48: 87–98.

—— (1988), 'Econometrics in action.' *Empirica*, 2/87: 135–56.

—— (1989), *PC-GIVE: An Interactive Econometric Modelling System* (Oxford).

—— (1995), *Dynamic Econometrics* (Oxford).

—— and Doornik, J. A. (1994), 'Modelling linear dynamic econometric systems'. *Scottish Journal of Political Economy*, 41: 1–33.

—— and Doornik, J. A. (1996*a*), *Empirical Econometric Modelling using PcGive for Windows* (London).

—— and Doornik, J. A. (1996*b*), 'A window on econometrics', *Cyprus Journal of Economics*, 8: 77–104.

—— Neale, A. J., and Srba, F. (1988), 'Econometric analysis of small linear systems using PC-FIML', *Journal of Econometrics*, 38: 203–26.

—— and Srba, F (1980), 'AUTOREG: A computer program library for dynamic econometric models with autoregressive errors'. *Journal of Econometrics*, 12: 85–102. Reprinted in Hendry, D. F. (1993), *Econometrics: Alchemy or Science?* (Oxford).

Johansen, S. (1988), 'Statistical analysis of cointegration vectors'. *Journal of Economic Dynamics and Control*, 12, 231–54.

Klein, L. R. *(1950)*, *Economic Fluctuations in the United States, 1921–41*. No.11. In Cowles Commission Monograph (New York).

Koopman, S. J., Harvey, A. C., Doornik, J. A., and Shephard, N. (1995), STAMP 5.0 *Structural Time Series Analyser Modeller and Predictor* (London).

Koopmans, T. C. *(1950) (ed)*, *Statistical Inference in Dynamic Economic Models*. No.10 in Cowles Commission Monograph (New York).

Leontief, W. (1971), 'Theoretical assumptions and nonobserved facts'. *American Economic Review*, 61: 1–7

Phillips, P. C. B. (1986), 'ET interview with Professor T.W Anderson'. *Econometric Theory*, 2: 249–88.

Student (1908), On the probable error of the mean. *Biometrika*, 6: 1–25.

Yule, G. U. (1926), 'Why do we sometimes get nonsense-correlations between time-series? A study in sampling and the nature of time series (with discussion)'. *Journal of the Royal Statistical Society*, 89: 1–64.

Supercomputing in Geographical Research

STAN OPENSHAW

School of Geography
University of Leeds

Abstract. The paper describes some of the ways by which High Performance Computing (HPC) hardware can be used in human geographical research. There is a discussion of the potential and also of the impediments facing the wider use of HPC in geography and the more generally in the social sciences. It is argued that supercomputing is now an extremely useful paradigm for geographical research and a new term, GeoComputation, has recently been invented to represent the adoption of a computationally intensive approach. The paper illustrates some of the possibilities via a number of case-studies based on use of the Cray T3D parallel supercomputer at Edinburgh.

Introduction

Currently there is considerable excitement in many traditional sciences about developments in supercomputing. Computation is now regarded as a scientific tool of equal importance to theory and experimentation as fast computers have stimulated new ways of doing science (see Hillis 1992). In this paper it is argued that a supercomputing based paradigm is equally relevant to many areas of human geography, with a potential that goes far beyond the narrow domain of quantitative geography and Geographical Information Systems. Moreover, the same paradigm is also relevant to many other disciplines in the social sciences and the humanities, particularly those with existing or potential large-scale computational problems. New HPC powered developments using Artificial Intelligence (AI) based technologies are now rapidly expanding the potential for computer applications into many new areas of geography and qualitative social science (Openshaw and Openshaw 1997). However, there are still significant impediments and historic HPC activities have been at a low level.

The terms High Performance Computing (HPC) and supercomputing are often used interchangeably with an increasing preference for the former. A High Performance Computer is defined as computer hardware based on vector or parallel processors (or some mixture) that offers an increase of at least one order of magnitude in computing power than is available from a workstation. This definition is perpetually changing in absolute terms as current personal computers (PCs) would almost certainly have been called HPCs less than a decade ago. In fact the gain in performance from using leading edge HPC hardware is now more likely to be at least two orders of magnitude as highly parallel processors take over from the earlier vector supercomputers. This whole area is now developing at a rapid rate with most new HPCs having a life cycle of only 2 to 3 years. The computing world has undergone a major technological change during the early 1990s and is now in a new era of highly parallel supercomputing. A highly or massively parallel processor (MPP) is a computing system with multiple central processing units (CPUs) that can work concurrently on a single task. In theory a parallel machine with 100 processors should be able to perform 100 times as much work as a single CPU *provided* the program is suitable for parallel computation. This is not a new idea but it is only in the last few years that the technology has matured sufficiently to become the dominant architecture of future HPC machines. Parallel hardware is destined to triumph over super computers with a vector single processor because of the inherent speed limitations of individual processors. Faster single processors merely mean an even faster multiple processor parallel machine built from them. Machines capable of sustained terraflop performances are expected by 2000 AD. (A terraflop is 1 million million floating point calculations per second – a single arithmetic addition is one floating point calculation – although current leading machines reach about one tenth of this level of performance.) It is this rapid speed up in HPC hardware that makes the notion of a supercomputer-based geography an increasingly viable proposition for the future.

An immediate technical obstacle to exploiting parallel machines is the need for a major change in programming technology. Parallelizing old serial code is seldom a trivial task unless the code is already in a parallel form. Thinking in parallel is important, but hard as it is , there is usually much more to parallel programming than putting serial code through an automatic parallelizing compiler. Often it involves an entirely new way of thinking about problems and how to solve them, requiring completely new algorithms. Parallelism is, of course, a natural phenomenon that is widely evident in the contemporary world. Learning to use it actually simplifies many modelling and analysis tasks once it is possible to escape from a serial thinking mentality that has been forced upon us by forty years of conventional single processor computing.

GeoComputation

HPC is a most significant technological development because, once computers became sufficiently fast and offered sufficiently large memories, it provided new ways of approaching human geography based on what can be termed a GeoComputational paradigm. GeoComputation is a relatively new term that is defined as the adoption of a large-scale computationally-intensive approach to the problems of geographical research, although it is more generally applicable. It involves porting current computationally intensive activities on to HPC platforms as well as the development of new computational techniques, algorithms, and paradigms that can take particular advantage of HPC.

The driving factors are three-fold: (1) developments in HPC stimulate the adoption of a computational paradigm to problem solving, analysis, and modelling supporting the development of new methodologies; (2) there is a need to create new ways of handling and using the increasingly large amounts of spatial information about the world; and (3) the increased availability of Artificial Intelligence (AI) tools and Computational Intelligent methods (Bezdek 1994) that are readily applicable to many areas of geography. GeoComputation also involves a fundamental change of style with the replacement of computationally minimizing technologies that reflect an era of hand calculation and all the simplifications this has engendered. It also comes with some grand ambitions about the potential usefulness that may well result from the fusion of virtually unlimited computing power with smart AI-based technologies that has the potential to open up entirely new perspectives on the ways in which geographical and, indeed, social science research is done. For instance, it is now possible to think about creating large-scale computing machine-based experiments in which the objects being modelled are artificial people living out their lives in computer-generated artificial worlds (Dibble 1996). HPC provides a laboratory within which many geographical and social systems can be simulated, studied, analysed, and modelled (see also Gilbert and Doran 1994, Gilbert and Conte 1995).

Whilst GeoComputation may initially appear to be technique dominated, it is much more than just supercomputing for its own sake. The driving force is in fact the Geo part with a focus on application. It can be regarded as the geographical analysis and modelling equivalent to Geographical Information Systems (GIS). Like GIS it is essentially applied in character but this emphasis should in no way diminish the need for solutions that rest on a strong theoretical understanding of how geographical systems work. The challenge is to create new computational tools that are able to suggest or discover new knowledge and new theories from an increasingly spatial data-rich world. GeoComputation is much more than just using computers in geography since it is simultaneously a tool, a paradigm and a way of thinking about solving problems.

There is an argument that GeoComputation would have developed sooner if the HPC technology had been more advanced. Indeed, until as recently as 1994 neither the power nor the memory capacities of the leading HPC machines were sufficient for many of problems of immediate geographical interest. What has changed is the maturity of massively-parallel computing, the continued speed-up of microprocessors, and the availability (after twenty years or so) of compilers that bring parallel computing within the existing skill domain of computationally-minded geographers. The recent standardization of Highly Parallel Fortran (HPF) and also of the Message Passing Interfaces (MPI) eases the task of using parallel supercomputers in many areas of geographical application as well as producing portable codes that are reasonably future-proof.

Raising HPC awareness

A major revolution in how geographical research can be undertaken is now underway; but many geographers have not yet either realized it is happening or understood the possible implications for their discipline. In common with many other social scientists most geographers have neglected the developments in the HPC world. There is no established supercomputing culture that can readily benefit from HPC and the absence of an Economic and Social Research Council (ESRC) Initiative in HPC has not helped. Three major reviews of supercomputing in the United Kingdom (UK) (SERC 1987, Catlow 1992, EPSRC 1995) made no reference to any significant social science or geographical applications, and in the last decade there have been very few geographers using any of the supercomputers in the UK. For example, in 1994, of the 28 early users on the latest, biggest and fastest parallel supercomputer (the Cray T3D at Edinburgh) there was only one geographer.

At present there is not a single funded grand challenge computational project that is explicitly geographical – a grand challenge project in science is one which is identified by a relevant peer group to be simultaneously of such critical importance and significance that it has to be tackled and yet presents such severe computational problems that it is on the edge of (or just beyond) what is computationally feasible with available hardware. Such a project is characterized by immense complexity, a strong link between the quality of the science and machine speed, and the use of computation as a substitute for experimentation that would otherwise be too expensive or impossible. The argument is that solving these very large and complex problems will produce enormous benefits. Examples are: weather forecasting, modelling global climatic change, the human genome, fluid turbulence, and quantum chromodynamics.

Are there really no grand challenge problems of a computational nature that are relevant to geography and the social sciences? Openshaw (1995a) argues that Human Systems Modelling is of equivalent (if not greater) importance and concern. Is it right that scientists can model virtually all the physical and environmental systems but none of the principal human systems? Historically, this neglect is understandable because of such features as complexity, chaotic and non-linear behaviours, lack of data, slow computers and the absence of tools. However, developments in IT, in the amount of data being collected, and the availability of supercomputers many thousands of times faster and bigger than even a decade ago all suggest that Human Systems Modelling is becoming feasible and that the relevant research councils should seriously consider how to tackle this important subject. The potential benefits in terms of better scientific understanding, improved planning and commerce would be equal to or greater than the payoff in other areas of science, e.g., from developing new drugs or new materials or new discoveries in physics. After all, people do matter!

The neglect of HPC is potentially disastrous if it continues. Openshaw (1994a) suggests that by 1999 it is quite likely that HPC hardware available for use by geographers will be 10^9 times faster (and bigger in memory) than what was available during the quantitative revolution in the 1960s, 10^8 times faster than that available during the mathematical modelling revolution of the early 1970s, 10^6 times since the GIS revolution of the mid 1980s, and at least a further 10^2 times faster than the current Edinburgh Cray T3D. One problem appears to be that most geographers have failed to appreciate what these developments in HPC mean. For instance, the Cray T3D has 512 processors and has a peak theoretical performance of 76.8 gigaflops (a gigaflop being 1000 million floating point operations per second) but what does this mean in a geographical context? One way of answering this question is to create a geography-based social science benchmark code that can be run on the widest possible range of computer hardware, ranging from PCs, through UNIX workstations, to massively-parallel machines. The widely-used science benchmark codes measure machine performance in terms of matrix algebra or problems in physics but it is not at all clear what relevance this has in a geographical context. Openshaw and Schmidt (1997) have developed a social science benchmark code based on the spatial interaction model which can be run on virtually any serial and parallel processor. The benchmark is freely available from the World Wide Web. Table 1 provides a preliminary assessment of the performance of some current HPC hardware in terms how many times faster it runs than on a humble 486 PC running at 66 MHz.

For small problems the best performance is the SGI Onyx, followed by the Fujitsu VPX240 vector processor. However, once the size of problems increases to reflect greater availability of data then soon there is no alternative to the massively parallel Cray T3D with gains of speed about 1,335 times for a 10,000 by 10,000 zone matrix (equivalent to the best resolution ward level journey to work or migration data for the whole of the UK from the 1991 census). This run took 2.4 seconds whilst the even larger 25,000 by 25,000 benchmark required 13 seconds. It should be noted that HPC is not just about speed; it is also about memory. The larger memory sizes required in these latter two runs reflect problems that previously were impossible to compute. One way of explaining what these

Table 1. Relative performance of a selection of available HPC hardware on a social science benchmark code in relation to 486 PC

Hardward	Number Processors	Problem Size: Numbers of Origin and Destinations				
		100 by 100	500 by 500	1000 by 1000	10000 by 10000	25000 by 25000
Massively Parallel						
Cray T3D	64	88				
	128		241	258		
	256			545	665	
	512				1335	1598
Parallel						
SGI Onyx	4	218	221	192	np	np
SGI Power Challenge	4	51	66	63	np	np
Vector Supercomputer						
VPX240	1	162	195	196	np	np
Cray J90	8	8	35	39	np	np
Workstations						
SGI Indy	1	10	10	9	np	np
HP9000	1	14	12	10	np	np
Sun Ultra 2	1	18	17	16	np	np
Personal Computers						
Pentium 133MHz	1	3	4	4	np	np

Note: Benchmark problem sizes greater than 1000 by 1000 cannot be run on a 486 PC. The times are estimated using linear interpolation which provides a good statistical fit to a range of smaller sized problems.

changes in HPC hardware mean is to ask how geographical research would be undertaken with a desk PC about 5,000 times faster and bigger than those currently available.

It is likely that some geographers would not know what to do with the extra speed, some would not want it, but some would spot major new possibilities for using it to do geographical research differently. It is this last type of researcher who will switch to GeoComputation and who will be best placed to benefit from the next two or three generations of HPC. However, merely identifying applications that are by their nature potentially suitable for parallel hardware is not sufficient justification to invest in the necessary effort in parallel programming. The applications also have to present a formidable computational challenge and some promise of significant 'extra benefit' that could not be realized without it. There should be some evidence of either new science or better science.

The opportunities are essentially four fold:

1 to speed up existing computing-bound activities so that more extensive experimentation can be performed;
2 to improve the quality of results by using computationally-intensive methods to reduce the number of assumptions and remove shortcuts and simplifications forced by computational restraints that are no longer relevant;
3 to permit larger databases to be analysed and or to obtain better results by being able to process finer resolution data; and
4 to develop new approaches and new methods based on computational technologies.

All are important although some are much more readily attainable than others. Indeed, in some applications there are almost instant benefits than can be gained with a minimal degree of effort.

Some examples of HPC applications in geography

Despite a widespread neglect of supercomputing within geography there have been some useful developments. The EPSRC's HPC Initiative (1994–7) funded a small geography project to port a selection of existing serial and vector codes on to the Cray T3D (Turton and Openshaw forthcoming). This small but diverse portfolio of applications may mark the beginnings of a HPC culture within geography. A key objective was to demonstrate some of the new science that can now be performed via case-studies using parallel supercomputing.

Parallel spatial interaction modelling of very large datasets

One of the earliest uses of parallel computing in geography has concerned the parallelization of the spatial interaction model (see Harris 1985, Openshaw 1987). This model is central to several important areas of regional science, urban and regional planning and spatial decision support (Wilson 1974, Birkin *et al.* 1996). For illustrative purpose the simplest spatial interaction model can be expressed as

$$T_{ij} = A_i \, O_i \, D_j \, B_j \, \exp(-b \, c_{ij}) \qquad (1)$$

where T_{ij} is the predicted flows from origin i to destination j, A_i is an origin constraint term, O_i is the size of origin zone i, D_j is the attractiveness of destination j, c_{ij} is the distance or cost of going from origin i to destination j, and b is a parameter that has to be estimated. The model was originally derived in a theoretically rigorous way by Wilson (1970) using an entropy maximizing method. Clearly this model is implicitly highly parallel since each T_{ij} value can be computed independently. Parallelization here is important because the model presents a computational challenge since computing times increase with the square of the number of zones (N). Small N values can be run on a PC but large N values need a supercomputer. The quality of the science reflects both the number of the zones (more zones provide better resolution than few) and the specification of the model.

Developments in IT over the last decade have dramatically increased the availability and sizes of spatial interaction data sets. The 1991 census provides journey to work and migration data that contain 10,764 origin and destination zones. A parallel version of equation (1) has been run on the KSR parallel supercomputer at Manchester. It had to use straight line distances because the storage of a 10,764 by 10,764 matrix of c_{ij} values was then infeasible. Openshaw and Sumner (1995) report that the calibration of a doubly-constrained spatial interaction model of all UK-wide journeys to work at the level of census wards took 29 minutes on the KSR1 64 processor parallel supercomputer, compared with 264 hours on a Sunsparc 10/41 workstation. The same code run on the 256 processor Cray T3D at Edinburgh required less than 3 minutes. A singly constrained model of the same data took 17.6 hours on the workstation compared with 8 minutes on the KSR1 and 40 seconds on the Cray T3D (Turton and Openshaw forthcoming). The parallelized code runs two orders of magnitude faster than the serial code and wall clock computing times diminish linearly with the numbers of processors being used (see Figure 1). Scaleability is a very desirable property in the world of parallel HPC as it opens

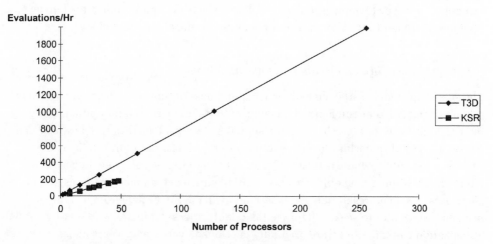

Fig. 1. Performance of a singly constrained spatial interaction model

up the possibility of being able to model the largest available spatial interaction data sets. When this model is used with network distances for the c_{ij} variable instead of straight-line distances then there is no longer any alternative other than the Cray T3D since the limiting factor is the need to store $10{,}764^2$ c_{ij} values. However, by current standards even this data set is small. For instance, in the UK there are 1.6 million postcodes and 27 million households for which interaction data sets probably already exist; for example, telephone traffic, and EFTPOS transactions. HPC now makes it possible to model the largest sets of flow data , a task of considerable practical value.

New methods of parameter estimation

Not all HPC applications require the use of large data sets. Diplock and Openshaw (1996) demonstrate some of the benefits of using genetic and evolutionary strategy-based methods of parameter estimation as a replacement for conventional non-linear optimization methods. Figure 2 shows that even for the simple spatial interaction model described in Equation 1 the function landscape is very complex because of arithmetic instabilities that are due to the exponential deterrence function which can generate very large and very small numbers depending on the parameter b. In fact the region where no arithmetic protection conditions are being generated is extremely small. The problems become worse when more parameters are used; for example, a two parameter competing destinations version is much more complex (Figure 3). Yet it is this function 'landscape' of flat regions, vertical cliffs, and narrow valleys leading to the optimal result that conventional methods of parameter optimization have to search. If they hit any of the barriers or the flat regions they tend to become stuck but have no way of indicating that this has happened. The new methods still work well on these problems as they are more robust. The implications are that virtually all statistical and mathematical models with exponential terms in them can very easily produce the 'wrong' result because there is no assurance that the conventional non-linear optimizers are safe to use. This is a good example of one type of application where HPC can have an almost immediate impact as a plug-in replacement for older conventional assumption-ridden technology.

Better spatial network and location optimization tools

The basic trip model is often embedded in a non-linear optimization framework that can require the model to be run many thousands of times in the search for optimal solutions; for example to determine the optimal spatial network of facilities. There are many different types of important location optimization problems in both public and private sectors; for example, where is the best location for a new clinic, or a new hypermarket; or which bank branches should be closed first with least impact on accessibility by customers. As finer resolution data become available, it becomes important both to use more zones and to seek to improve the quality of results being provided by spatial optimization methods that were originally developed over twenty years ago.

A collaborative project between Edinburgh Parallel Computing Centre (EPCC) and

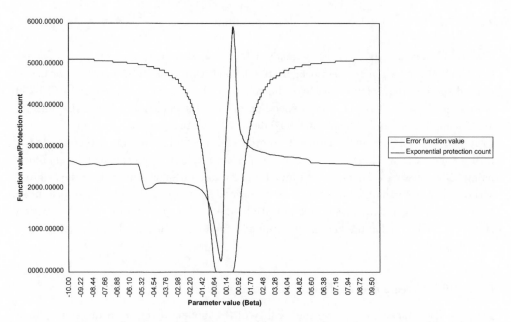

Fig. 2. Arithmetic instability plot for a singly constrained spatial interaction model

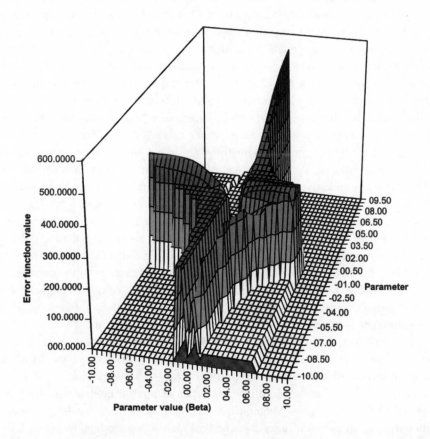

Fig. 3. Arithmetic stability map for a 2-parameter competing destinations spatial interaction model

GMAP Ltd (Leeds University) has already demonstrated some of the potential business benefits that can be gained. George *et al.* (1993), and Birkin *et al.* (1995) describe the use of a retail spatial interaction model to optimize a network of car dealers using the CM-200 parallel processor. They achieved a speed-up of 2260 times compared with the original serial code. Turton and Openshaw (1997) describe how they ported this model on to the Cray T3D and ran it using data for 822 shopping centres and 2755 origins. It computed at the rate of over 70 million model evaluations per hour, a computing speed of 7.6 gigaflops using 256 processors. This is an astonishingly 2.8 million times faster than the original serial code when run on a Sunsparc 1 workstation. The Cray T3D version also produced results twice as good as those previously attained. It is this type of application for which HPC is so well suited and where major applied benefits can be gained by becoming more HPC-minded.

Using HPC to create new models of geographic systems

There is also a need to improve the quality of the models being used in geographical research. The new computational technologies offer new ways of building models that either replace the existing models based on mathematical and statistical approaches or else can be viewed as complementing them. One approach is to create an automated modelling system that uses genetic algorithms and genetic programming techniques to suggest potentially useful new models. The Automated Modelling System (AMS) method of Openshaw (1988) used the Cray I vector supercomputer in an early attempt to define and then explore the universe of alternative spatial interaction models that could be built from the available pieces (e.g., variables, parameters, unary and binary operators, standard maths functions, and reverse polish rules for well-formed equations) by using evolutionary programming algorithms to 'breed' new forms of model. These methods are explicitly parallel (each member of a population of models is evaluated in parallel) and also implicitly parallel (the genetic algorithm's schemata theorem).

The problem with AMS was the use of fixed-length bit strings. Koza (1992, 1994) describes how this restriction can be removed by using what he terms Genetic Programming (GP). The AMS approach has now been re-developed in a GP format. Tests indicate that computing times of several weeks are needed on the Fujitsu VPX2400 and that GP is far more suitable for parallel rather than for vector supercomputers. The results from porting the genetic programming codes onto the Cray T3D suggest that not only can existing conventional models be 're-discovered' but also that new model forms with performance levels of two or three times better can be found (Turton *et al.* 1996, 1997; Diplock 1996). If the new methods work well, then they would constitute a means of extracting knowledge and theories from a world increasingly rich in geographical data. It is becoming increasingly possible to compute the way to better models.

Other new approaches to building new types of spatial models are described in Openshaw (1997). Table 2 gives a comparison of the performance of a selection of genetic, evolutionary, neural net, and fuzzy logic spatial interaction models. In general, perfor- mance improvements of over 200 per cent over conventional models are possible and this

Table 2. Comparison of the performance of different types of spatial interaction model

Model	Residual Standard Deviation	Index of Model Performance
Traditional Gravity Model	20.7	78
Entropy Maximising Model	16.3	100
Best Genetically Bred Model	12.7	128
Best Genetic Programming based	11.2	141
Best Neural Network Model	7.4	220
Best Fuzzy Logic Model	13.1	124
Best Hybrid partly Fuzzy Logic	11.6	141

Notes: All models are origin constrained. Entropy Maximising Model is that shown in Equation 1. The genetically bred model is based on four model pieces. The neural network model is a feed-forward perceptron with 50 neurons in a single hidden layer. The fuzzy logic model's fuzzy rules and membership functions was optimized by a genetic algorithm with 4 membership sets for each of the input variables and 8 fuzzy output sets. The hybrid partly fuzzy model uses fuzzy weights associated with each input to create a mixed distance decay, entropy, intervening and competing destination model.

may be more than sufficient to justify the 10,000 to 100,000 times more computation that they involve. Some of these new models are purely black boxes (e.g., the neural network models) but others are capable of expression in plain English (the fuzzy logic models) or are in equation form. The principal constraint on the further development of some of these computational modelling methods is slow HPC speeds. Some of GP runs reported in Turton *et al.* (1996, 1997) required over 8 hours on a 256 processor Cray T3D. It is likely that runs of two weeks on a 512 processor machine would yield even better results, but this is greater than the total ESRC allocation of Cray T3D time for 1996. In these complex search problems the quality of the results depends totally on the speed of the available HPC.

Flexible geographies under user control

A very common need of spatial data management is the development of better ways of partitioning map space. Many problems on spatial planning involve the design of zoning systems; for example, to create Parliamentary Constituencies that are of nearly equal size and of compact shape, the identification of sales areas and facility catchment areas to equalize accessibility by the population, and to design zones for reporting statistical information that are simultaneously safe, statistically comparable and meet user needs. GIS have created the prospect of flexible geographical aggregation of many spatial data sets that hitherto were reported only for arbitrary and fixed sets of areas. The problem is the lack of tools for engineering zoning systems and for coping with the fact that the same data aggregated to different sets of areas will often produce completely different results (see Openshaw 1976, 1978). Statisticians refer to this as the Modifiable Areal Unit Problem (Openshaw 1984). There is, therefore, an increasing need for automated zone design tools that will allow the use of the most appropriate zones for any given purpose.

Zone design is a special type of optimization problem;

$$\text{optimize } F(Z)$$

where $F(Z)$ is some user-defined function sensitive to the aggregation of zonal data specified by Z; and Z is an aggregation of N original zones into M regions ($M < N$) such that the members of each region are contiguous to other members of the same region and each of the N zones is assigned to only one region. There may be other constraints on the nature of the data generated by Z, e.g., that the regions have to have a minimal level of compactness in their shape or are above a minimum population size. This is a specialized and different type of optimization problem because Z is discrete (it is a zoning system) and $F(Z)$ is discontinuous, non-linear, non convex and probably has multi-optima. Various heuristic algorithms have been developed for solving this problem (Openshaw 1976, Openshaw and Rao 1995). Originally, only small problems could be handled but today the availability of digital boundary information for the 150,000 census enumeration districts used in the 1991 census of the UK have emphasized the importance of being able to handle hundreds of thousands of zones. It is likely that by 2001 there will be 1.6 million digital postcode boundaries available as basic spatial building blocks for flexible user-specific zoning systems. There is already talk of automating the design of census output areas for the 2001 census with a potential savings of tens of millions of pounds and the possible additional invisible benefits from the use of 'better' and more flexible spatial reporting frameworks.

The zone design problem can be solved using HPC. The best results require the use of a simulated annealing algorithm (Openshaw and Rao 1995) but computing times depend on the size of N. More complex constrained problems may take 1,000 times as long. Fortunately the zone design code has been re-developed in a parallel form (see Openshaw and Schmidt 1996; Turton and Openshaw forthcoming). The problem can be illustrated by an example. The current allocation of urban deprivation grants in the UK depends on the Department of the Environment's deprivation indicator computed at the census ward level. There is concern amongst local authorities that the use of wards under-represents the real situation in some areas. It may also exaggerate its extent in others. To investigate this problem , the census enumeration district data for Leeds-Bradford have been re-engineered to maximize the number of areas that would qualify for urban aid subject to the constraint that the areas should be compact, of a similar population size, and of the same number as the current wards. Figure 4 shows the ward-based results and Figure 5 the new results based on the re-engineered enumeration districts. Even better results would have been obtained if smaller building blocks (e.g., unit postcodes) had been used. In 1991 this was not possible and the cost was a potentially large misallocation of public funds. In 2001 it will be feasible. Potentially this ability to engineer purpose-specific geographical frameworks for reporting statistics is of considerable practical importance and would seem to be very relevant to many areas of spatial data management.

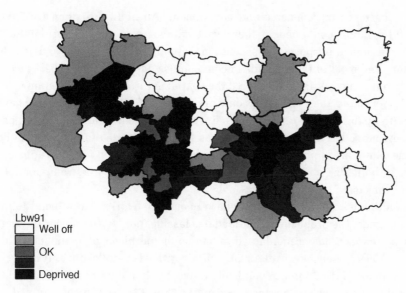

Fig. 4. Deprivation areas in Leeds/Bradford based on wards

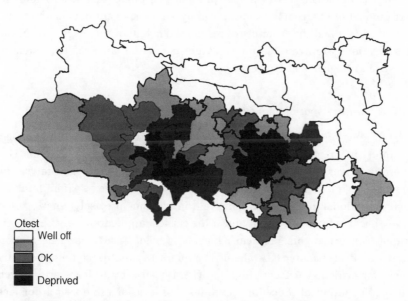

Fig. 5. Deprivation areas in Leeds/Bradford based on ward-like re-engineered areas

Improved spatial classification methods

The multivariate classification of spatial data is a very useful data reduction device. The spatial data explosion of the last two decades has increased the number of observations from a few tens (in the 1960s) to 150,000 census areas in 1991, to 1.6 million areas and 27 million households in 2001. Massive multigigabyte databases are an increasingly

common occurrence in commerce and government. An ability to summarize the geographic information contained in these vast databases is very important for many
research and applied purposes. Classification methods, such as cluster analysis, have a
long history and most of the methods in common use date from the 1960s. They can be
'scaled up' but in a geographical context, the spatial nature of the information is usually
ignored. For example, the 1991 census data are available for 150,000 small areas in Great
Britain, with up to 10,000 variables for each area. The data are a mixture of 100 per cent
and 10 per cent coded information, much has been randomized to preserve confidentiality, some values are suppressed, and the statistics are reported for geographical areas
that vary in both size and heterogeneity. Additionally, there are strong spatial auto-
correlation effects.

One solution is to develop classifier-based neural networks that attempt to include
rather than ignore the problems of spatial data classification. A Kohonen self-organizing
map-based approach has been adapted to handle the problems of spatial classification
(Openshaw 1994c; Openshaw et al. 1995). This algorithm is parallel but only at a very fine
level of granularity. It had to be completely re-written in a data parallel form so that it
would produce good levels of performance on the Cray T3D (see Openshaw and Turton
1996 for details). On the Cray T3D with 256 processors a single run takes 10 hours but the
results are quite different from those produced by a more conventional method and tell a
very different story about the structure of residential neighbourhoods in the UK. Some of
these classifications are available for research use in the GB Profiles system on the
MIDAS system at Manchester University.

Intelligent exploratory spatial analysis systems

A major by-product of the GIS revolution of the mid-1980s has been to add geographic
(x,y) coordinates in virtually all people-and property-related computer systems. Unfortunately there is as yet little appropriate technology for geographical analysis able to
explore efficiently and comprehensively these large and complex spatial databases for
patterns and relationships, without being told in advance precisely where, when, and
what to look for. It is interesting that one of the earliest applications of supercomputing
in geography concerned this problem. Openshaw et al. (1987) describe a prototype
geographical analysis machine (GAM) able to explore a spatially-referenced database on
child cancer for evidence of clustering. The GAM used a brute force grid search that
applied a simple statistical procedure to millions of locations in a search for localized
clustering. It was run on leukaemia data for Northern England and is credited with the
discovery of the Gateshead cancer cluster, a previously unknown problem (Openshaw et
al. 1987). The long computer run times of the later versions of GAM required the use of
supercomputers and reflected the importance of validating the results using large-scale
Monte Carlo simulation (see Openshaw and Craft 1991). A parallel version of the latest
GAM/K code is being developed for the Cray T3D.

The same basic GAM type of brute force approach has been used to search for spatial
relationships. The Geographical Correlates Exploration Machine (GCEM/1) of Open-

shaw *et al.* (1990) examines all 2^{m-1} permutations of m different thematic map layers obtained from a GIS in a search for localized spatial relationships. It too is massively parallel because each of the 2^{m-1} map permutations is independent and can be processed concurrently, but as yet no parallel version is available and this approach to spatial analysis needs further development. It is a good idea awaiting a faster HPC.

An important new need is to broaden the process of exploratory pattern search to include all aspects of spatial data (e.g., location in space, location in time, and attributes of the space-time event) as well as discover how to make the search more intelligent. Openshaw (1994d, 1995b) describes the development of space-time-attribute creatures, a form of artificial life that can roam around what he terms the geocyberspace in an endless hunt for pattern (Openshaw 1994b). The claim to being intelligent results from the genetic algorithm used to control the search process and the use of computational statistics to reduce the dangers of spurious results. It is strongly dependent on having sufficient parallel computational power to drive the entire process. Openshaw and Perree (1996) show how the addition of computer animation can help users to envisage and understand the geographical analysis. This type of highly-exploratory search technology is only just becoming feasible with recent developments in HPC and considerable research is still needed to perfect the technology. However, it promises a radically different and understandable approach to exploratory spatial analysis in GIS that is powered by supercomputers.

Using HPC to build geographical knowledge systems

GIS have provided a microspatial data rich world but there are no tools able to help identify either the more abstract recurrent patterns that exist at higher levels of generalization or new concepts from the wealth of data. Geography contains many theories about space that can be expressed as idealized two-and three-dimensional patterns that are supposedly recurrent. Traditionally, these concepts and theories have been tested using aspatial statistical methods that require much of the geography to be removed so that analysis can be performed. For example, if the question is asked whether the spatial social structure of Leeds as shown by the 1991 census conforms to a broadly concentric ring type of pattern, this hypothesis can be tested using statistical methods by first defining a central point, a series of rings of fixed width, and applying a statistic of some kind to census data to test the a priori hypothesized trends in social class. However, this clearly requires considerable precision and is not really an adequate test of the original hypothesis that did not specify ring widths, nor identify a central point nor define at what level of geographic scale the pattern exists. A possible solution is to use pattern recognition and robotic vision technology to see whether any evidence of a general concentric geographic structure exists in the census data for Leeds, after allowing for the distorting effects of scale, site and topography. If no idealized concentric patterns exist, then which of a library of different pattern types might be more appropriate? The HPC revolution of the mid 1990s provides an opportunity to become less precise and more general, by developing pattern recognition tools that can build up libraries of recurring map patterns of the many different types of recurrent idealized forms. Suppose the question is raised how many different spatial patterns do British cities exhibit. Currently it cannot be answered but at least the tools exist to allow geographers to start to find out. Openshaw (1994e) argues that a more generalized pattern recognition approach provides the basis for a new look at geographical information with a view to extracting useful new knowledge from it. However, this will become possible only as HPC enters the terraflop era and it becomes feasible to apply pattern templates to many millions of locations at many different levels of geographical resolution.

New results from old models

A related opportunity for a quick gain in benefit from HPC is the use of the bootstrap to estimate parameter variances. This is quite straightforward but needs a HPC to make it feasible. The model has merely to be run a few hundred or a few thousand times, a naturally parallel procedure because each run can be assigned to a different processor. No great effort at parallelization is needed and this strategy can be applied to many existing models in order to identify confidence intervals. Research with a multi-region population forecasting model used to make population forecasts for the European Union (EU) has identified the error limits in forecasts made for 2021 to 2051. The results are surprising as they suggest that currently there are no reliable long term forecasts for the EU as the confidence limits are extremely wide. The problem appears to be due to uncertainty in the forecasting of migration (see Turton and Openshaw 1998 for further details).

A GeoComputational future in geography

It is argued that many areas within geography could benefit from the adoption of HPC and a GeoComputational paradigm but there is unlikely to be a sudden HPC revolution that will suddenly sweep all before it. Instead, in those areas that need it and where a computational paradigm may be helpful, then there is a way forward. If the current HPC machines are too slow and access is restricted there will soon be much faster ones, but it is necessary to start developing the new approaches now and then safeguard the investment in software by using portable programming languages and conforming to emerging standards. Fortunately, access to the world's fastest HPC is not necessary to start the research. With modern parallel programming tools portable scaleable codes can now be written that can be developed and proven to work on low end HPC platforms (e.g., workstation farms) before moving on to more powerful multi-processor HPC platforms. The essential challenge is to discover how to use HPC to extend and expand researchers' abilities to model and analyse all types of geographical systems and not merely those which are already computerized. It would be a tragic waste if all they were used for was to make old legacy tools run faster resulting in a kind of HPC-based revival of old fashioned quantitative geography.

The opportunities are far broader than any backward-looking view would suggest. In some areas, almost instant benefits can be gained; for example, by switching to computationally intensive statistical methods to reduce reliance on untenable assumptions or to discover new information about the behaviour of models. In other areas entirely new GeoComputational applications can be expected to emerge. As HPC continues to develop it is likely that many subjects, not just geography, will have to undergo a major change in how they operate. The combination of large amounts of data from GIS, the availability of new AI tools and other types of computationally intensive analysis and modelling technologies, the increasing accessibility of HPC hardware, and emerging new needs for using geographic information all look set to create a new style of computational geography that, in the longer term, may well revolutionize many aspects of the subject by creating new ways of studying nearly all kinds of geography. The present is a very exciting time for supercomputer-minded geographers; it also a time when many future significant developments are likely to occur.

Acknowledgement

The research reported was supported by EPSRC Grant GK/K43933

References

Bezdek, J. C. (1994), 'What is computational intelligence?'. In Zurada, J. M., Marks, R. J., and Robinson, C. J. (1994) (eds.), *Computational Intelligence:Imitating Life* (IEEE, New York) 1–12.

Birkin, M., Clarke, M. and George, F. (1995), 'The use of parallel computers to solve non-linear spatial optimization problems', *Environment and Planning A* 27: 1049–68.

——— Clarke, G., Clarke M. and Wilson, A. G. (1996), *Intelligent GIS* (Cambridge).

Catlow, C. R. A. (1992), *Research Requirements for High Performance Computing.* Report of the Scientific Working Party. Science and Engineering Research Council SERC, (Swindon).

Dibble, C. (1996), 'Theory in a complex world: agent based simulation of geographical systems', *Proceedings of GeoComputation 1* (Leeds University, September), I: 210–13.

Diplock, G. J. (1996), *The application of evolutionary computing techniques to spatial interaction modelling.* (Unpublished Ph.D thesis, University of Leeds).

——— and Openshaw, S. (1996), 'Using simple genetic algorithms to calibrate spatial interaction models', *Geographical Analysis, 28:* 262–79

EPSRC. (1995), *A Review of Supercomputing 1994* Engineering and Physical Sciences Research Council (Swindon).

George, F. (1993), 'Spatial interaction modelling on parallel computers', EPCC-PAR-GMAP Report (Edinburgh University).

Gilbert, G. N. and Doran, J. (1994), *Simulating Societies: the Computer Simulation of Social Phenomena* (London.).

——— and Conte, R. (1995) (eds.), *Artificial Societies* (London).

Harris, B. (1985), 'Some notes on parallel computing with special reference to transportation and land use modelling', *Environment and Planning A,* 17: 1275–8.

Hillis, W. D. (1992), 'What is massively parallel computing and why is it important?'. In Metropolis, N. and Rota, G.C. (eds.) *A New Era in Computation.* (Cambridge Mass.) 1–15.

Koza, J. R. (1992), *Genetic Programming,* (Cambridge, Mass.).

——(1994), *Genetic Programming II: Automatic Discovery of Re-usable Programs* (Cambridge Mass.).

Openshaw, S. (1976), 'A geographical solution to scale and aggregation problems in region building, partitioning and spatial modelling', *Transactions of the Institute of British Geographers*, New Series, 2: 459–72.

—— (1978), 'An empirical study of some zone design criteria', *Environment and Planning A*, 10: 781–94.

—— (1984), 'Ecological fallacies and the analysis of areal census data', *'Environment and Planning A*, 16: 17–31.

—— (1987), 'Some applications of supercomputers in urban and regional analysis and modelling', *Environment and Planning A*, 19: 853–60.

—— (1988), 'Building an automated modelling system to explore a universe of spatial interaction models', *Geographical Analysis*, 20: 31–46.

—— (1994a), 'Computational human geography: towards a research agenda' *Environment and Planning A*, 26: 499–505.

—— (1994b), 'Computational Human Geography: exploring the geocyberspace' *Leeds Review* 37: 201–20.

—— (1994c), 'Neuroclasification of spatial data'. In Hewitson, B. and Crane, R. (eds.), *Neural Nets: Applications in Geography*, (Dordrecht) 53–70.

—— (1994d), 'Two exploratory space-time attribute pattern analysers relevant to GIS'. In Fotheringham, S. and Rogerson, P. (eds.), *Spatial Analysis and GIS* (London) 83–104.

—— (1994e), 'A concepts rich approach to spatial analysis, theory generation and scientific discovery in GIS using massively parallel computing'. In Worboys, M. (ed.), *Innovations in GIS*. (London) 123–38.

—— (1995a), 'Human systems modelling as a new grand challenge area in science', *Environment and Planning A*, 27: 159–64.

—— (1995b), 'Developing automated and smart spatial pattern exploration tools for GIS applications', *The Statistician*, 44: 3–16.

—— (1997), 'Neural network, genetic and fuzzy logic models of spatial interaction', *Working Paper*, School of Geography, University of Leeds.

—— Blake, M. and Wymer, C. (1995), 'Using neurocomputing methods to classify Britain's residential areas'. In Fisher, P. (ed.) *Innovations in GIS2* (London) 97–112.

—— Charlton, S., Wymer, C. M., and Craft, A. (1987), 'A mark I geographical analysis machine for the automated analysis of point data sets', *International Journal of Geographical Information Systems*, 1: 335–58.

—— and Craft, A. (1991), 'Using the geographical analysis machine to search for evidence of clusters and clustering in childhood leukaemia and non-Hodgkin lymphomas in Britain'. In Draper, G. (ed.) *The Geographical Epidemiology of Childhood Leukaemia and non-Hodgkin Lymphomas in Great Britain, 1966–83* (London) 109–22.

—— Cross, A. and Charlton, M. (1990), 'Building a prototype geographical correlates exploration machine', *International Journal of Geographical Information Systems*, 3: 297–312.

—— and Openshaw, C. A. (1997), *Artificial Intelligence in Geography* (London).

—— and Perree, T. (1996), 'User centered intelligent spatial analysis of point data'. In Parker, D. (ed.) *Innovations in GIS 3* (London) 119–34.

—— and Rao, L. (1995), 'Algorithms for re-engineering 1991 census geography', *Environment and Planning A*, 27: 425–46.

—— and Schmidt, J. (1996), 'Parallel simulated annealing and genetic algorithms for re-engineering zoning systems', *Geographical Systems*, 3: 201–20.

—— and Schmidt, J. (1997), 'A Social Science Benchmark (SSB/1) Code for serial, vector, and parallel supercomputers'. *Geographical and Environmental Modelling*, 1: 65–82.

—— and Sumner, R. (1995), 'Parallel spatial interaction modelling on the KSR1–64 super-computer'. *Working Paper 95/15*, School of Geography, University of Leeds.

—— and Turton, I. (1996), 'A parallel Kohonen algorithm for the classification of large spatial datasets', *Computers and Geosciences*, 22: 1019–26.

SERC (1987) *Forty Report*. Science and Engineering Research Council (Swindon).

Turton, I. and Openshaw, S. (1996), 'Modelling and optimising flows using parallel spatial interaction models', in Bouge, L., Fraigniaud P., Mignotte, A., Roberts, Y. (eds.) *Euro-Par'96 Parallel Processing* Vol 2, Lecture Notes in Computer Science 1124 (Berlin) 270–5.

—— and Openshaw (1997c), 'Parallel spatial interaction models.' *Geographical and Environmental Modelling*. 1: 179–97.

—— and Openshaw (1998), 'High performance computing and geography: developments, issues and case studies', *Environment and Planning A*, 30: 1839–56.

—— Openshaw, S. and Diplock, G. J. (1996), 'Some geographical applications of genetic programming on the Cray T3D supercomputer'. In Jesshope, C. and Shafarenko, A. (eds.) *UK Parallel'96*, (Berlin) 135–50.

—— Openshaw, S. and Diplock, G. J. (1997b), 'A genetic programming approach to building new spatial models relevant to GIS'. In Kemp, Z. (ed.) *Innovations in GIS 4* (London) 89–102.

Wilson, A. G. (1970), *Entropy in Urban and Regional Modelling* (London).

—— (1974), *Urban and Regional Models in Geography and Planning* (London).

Commentary

ANDREW CLIFF

Department of Georgraphy
University of Cambridge

As with any other discipline, the impact of High Performance Computing (HPCs) upon geographical research may be judged under three heads:

1. Does the increase in computing power permit old problems to be tackled in a more efficient way?
2. Will HPCs now permit long-standing problems, previously inaccessible because of an historic deficit of computing power, to be addressed?
3. Will HPCs lead to the identification of wholly new research problems or approaches?

In considering these questions, it is interesting to look back almost twenty years to a paper by Haggett (1969) which, like Professor Openshaw's, attempted to assess the impact of the then 'high-speed computers' upon geographical research. At that time, Haggett (p.499) argued:

> The main areas in which the use of computers appears most marked remains rather limited

and would seem to be (i) multivariate statistics, (ii) trend surface decomposition, (iii) computer graphics, and (iv) simulation.

Haggett's paper then goes on to discuss, *inter alia*, the need to make computers accessible to problem-solvers, and the temptations of apparently unlimited data-processing power. We are all too familiar throughout the social sciences and the humanities with number crunching exercises inadequately founded in either theory or experimental design (the Garbage In/Garbage Out syndrome). Finally, in concluding his paper, Haggett comments (p. 505):

> My own hunch would be that our problems will remain the traditional ones – areal differentiations, interregional comparison, regional analogues, spatial pattern environmental reactions – the computer may allow us to throw those problems farther forward in time from a concern with the past and present geographies to those of the future.

Many of the themes of Haggett's paper find their echo in Professor Openshaw's stimulating essay. So, for example, the computer graphics of history are mirrored in the display capabilities of Geographical Information Systems (GIS), simulation in the geographical analysis machine, and areal differentiation and interregional comparison in spatial classifications. Thus it appears that the answer to the first two questions posed at the outset is 'yes'. HPCs are being used to address many of the traditional themes of human geography, but with one fundamental difference highlighted in Professor Openshaw's paper – at levels of spatial detail and size of problem that simply could not have been contemplated in the past.

When we come to the third question, Professor Openshaw's search for the new 'Grand Challenge' problem(s) opened up by HPCs, the direction in which we are heading with the new technology is much less clear. In physical geography, such Grand Challenges have been found in attempts to model global climates, past, present and future, and in environmental modelling. When viewed as integrated systems, the processes shaping the physical world have already been shown, because of their size and complex interactions, to require the capacity of supercomputers to explore alternate solutions.

For human geography, Professor Openshaw's paper suggests a revitalized systems approach may be the HPC future for the analysis of geographical aspects of human behaviour. Such an approach helps us both to conceptualize a problem and to see the interlinking parts that go to make up the whole. But it also raises important questions. Under what circumstances will such models need to be solved in the round, rather than via smaller compartment models? How, in solving the human equivalents of global climate models, do we minimize specification risks and error propagation? How do we handle soft information?

Despite the quantity of data now pouring forth from international, and governmental and non-governmental agencies on all aspects of human activity, its reliability may make the adequate fitting of systems-based models extremely difficult. Much work will be required on appropriate robust ways of estimating our models if we are to avoid some of the worst excesses that beset early systems modelling in both physical and human geography. Yet the challenge must be faced. For it is likely to be in the solution of fully-integrated models that both the power of supercomputers will be needed and new insights into unforeseen interactions between the component parts are most likely to come to light.

A further consequence of the size and computational power unleashed by HPCs may be a shift of emphasis in human geography away from studies of group behaviour, often at rather coarse geographical scales, to models of individual behaviour. Such a move might then permit the age-old issue of the geographical scale of analysis to be tackled in a much more effective way than is presently possible to see how micro-scale models lead on to meso- and macro-level models and how scale levels mesh together. For, as the paper acknowledges, the end-judgement on the available power of HPCs will be the extent to which they enable us to address new problems or give fresh insights into existing problems rather than just increase the size of our existing analyses. If the latter occurs, there is a risk of squaring the circle back to Haggett's fear that we may drown in data and results without increasing the body of geographical theory on spatial processes.

A further issue relating to the use of HPCs highlighted in the paper is the need to make them accessible. Machines with large horsepower are of use to only a limited group of users unless appropriate software is available to exploit that power – appropriate in the sense of having canonical forms capable of being plugged into to solve a variety of problems, and with readily usable graphics user interfaces. Without these, the community of users will remain relatively small. The need for accessibility is also physical. If humanists and social scientists are to be able to evaluate the potential of these machines, an encouraging research environment is needed. Such machines are massively expensive in terms of both capital outlay and running costs; they are generally unavailable on-site to most users. Yet one of our main funding bodies, ESRC, has no supercomputer initiative in its current plans that will raise awareness of HPCs among social scientists and humanists, and their only firm commitment is to purchase just a one per cent share in the next public-domain machine.

Reference

Haggett, P. (1969). 'On geographical research in a computer environment'. *Geographical Journal*, 136: 497–507.

Social anthropology and information technology

MICHAEL BRAVO

Department of Social Anthropology
University of Manchester

Abstract. Social anthropologists are specialists in local culture, a task which has traditionally involved the study of communities in the field, generally in locations that are remote from the bases where the results will be analysed and described. The introduction of electronic techniques for collecting data has had several different effects on research techniques, although (as in other disciplines) developing these has been the work of a self-selected minority of dedicated individuals. Most changes have affected the anthropologist's 'toolbox' for collecting information in the field, in terms of what is recorded and in what form; others have worked to reduce the isolation of the individual researcher in the field. The impact of Information Technology (IT) has been greater in some fields, notably in visual anthropology, through the making of films, the use of multi-media techniques in both teaching and research, and the application of computing for the analysis of the material collected. At the same time, the impact of IT on global communications has affected the meaning of local culture in the communities being studied and in the approaches used by anthropologists to seek the cooperation of communities in securing the information they require; in particular, the development of IT skills within such communities has led some anthropologists to adopt a supporting role. All this has taken place against a background of debate among social anthropologists on their commitments to governments and to the communities being studied, which provides a context against which the impact of IT can be assessed.

Introduction

Social anthropology has a singular claim for demonstrating a self-conscious, critical and reflexive understanding of human experience and culture. It is the discipline which, more than others, has tried to understand the diversity of human social organization. To this end, anthropologists are specialists in describing local cultures. The term 'local' is worth examining more closely. It can refer to a single place or a limited, circumscribed area. However, few societies are actually as isolated as they have been portrayed in the romantic imagination. Most have extended relations with neighbours, for example, through trade, marriage, or travel. 'Local' in this sense might better be construed as a *locus* or prism in which wide-ranging, socio-economic forces converge and are visible as communities. The scale of these forces, their sources of power and their operation over large areas of the globe have been the subject of much debate in the social sciences. The opposition or tension between global and local phenomena has been at the forefront of anthropological debate in the 1980s and 1990s. It is therefore hardly surprising that the globalization of telecommunications systems, data recording, sampling, computing and networking technologies should be receiving the attention of anthropologists concerned with processes of local cultural change.

The aim in this paper is to show that the introduction of electronic information technologies (as opposed to the traditional notebook and pencil) has several different possible kinds of effect on the research practices of social anthropologists. This complexity is briefly illustrated by drawing upon a distinction in science studies between judging new technologies in terms of their *impact* on the one hand, and their *social shaping* on the other hand. The paper then examines the traditional British anthropological method, the journey into the field, and reflects upon how the long-standing use and presence of field technologies is affected by the advent of IT. First there is an obvious and pragmatic question: to what extent do anthropologists incorporate new IT developments into their practices (here referred to as the anthropologist's toolkit) to achieve traditional goals more effectively? A second, more complex question is how the very presence of IT in the field, either in the anthropologist's toolkit or in the everyday lives of the inhabitants of a given community, transforms what is actually being studied. The nature of evidence in the field may be changing as a result. New kinds of evidence may challenge the discipline's boundaries and understanding of its purpose. This issue is explored by conceptualizing the journey in terms of relations of time and space between the home institution (e.g., the university) and the field, and asking how information technologies are modifying these relations.

Most anthropologists have been reluctant to embrace IT with great enthusiasm. Although this may be in part technophobia, it also grows out of far-reaching anthropological debates about field technologies and the political implications of representing other peoples. In broad terms, two movements have been significant in this respect. Visual anthropologists, a diverse group which includes documentary film makers, theoreticians of visual representation and anthropologists of art, have been much more open and searching in facing up to important questions about the significance of innovative technologies of inscription or recording for generating visual languages capable of transforming the way images are read and culture is understood. The recent emphasis on digital modes of representation and analysis, at the expense of the verisimilitude associated with analog forms (which acquire their meaning through the process of inscription, and hence refer to some real physical process or measurable phenomenon), raises the serious prospect of a kind of visual revolution, whose outcome remains uncertain. Arguably a debate about the purpose of visual tools, whether their value lies in their capacity to make an objective record of ethnographic 'surfaces', or whether they can be used as a vehicle of exploration for deeper phenomena, has a complicated history going back to the use of photography and cinematic equipment by anthropological travellers and expeditions in the late nineteenth century. An excellent discussion of the issues and methods of visual anthropology has recently appeared in a collection of essays edited by Banks and Morphy (1997).

A different debate which emerged with the postmodern critique of anthropology over the past thirty years, made the process of writing itself an object of serious debate and reflection (Marcus and Clifford 1986, Clifford 1988): whether it has fundamentally been a bureaucratic instrument of colonial domination, and whether it enshrines an asymmetrical relationship between the observer and the observed. For all that only a minority of anthropologists consider themselves postmodernists, this debate has nevertheless changed the face of the discipline. Decolonization, together with growing investment in telecommunications infrastructures around the world, has resulted in many anthropologists adopting new working relationships with communities, placing more emphasis on self-representation, mutually beneficial research and the adoption of new codes of ethics. Visual anthropology and the crisis of representation in anthropology provide two useful contexts for discussing the reception of IT developments.

The local shape of global technologies

In order to study the significance of information technologies (the abbreviation IT is used to represent both information technology and technologies) on research in social anthropology, one can adopt a model of impact assessment. In this vein, IT is presumed to be an outside force acting upon anthropologists, updating their toolkits, and one therefore examines the ways that the modified toolkit has an impact upon canonical ways of conducting research. Another way to conceptualize the place of IT loosely derives from studies known as 'the social shaping of technology' (MacKenzie and Wajcman 1985). This recognizes that the value and use of changing information technologies are best understood by virtue of their presence, or social configuration, in the field. For example, if an anthropologist takes a digital audio tape recorder (DAT) into the field, the fidelity of the recording is not necessarily better than with a conventional reel-to-reel recorder, but the digital recorder is likely to be more portable, and the tapes will suffer less degradation over time, furnish unlimited perfect copies, and the contents can be easily stored on computer hard disks. Other technical possibilities include sharpening the audibility of the recording by applying digital signal processing techniques. To take a different example, suppose an anthropologist takes a video recorder into the field. The enhanced capacity of new models to record scenes in low light levels now means that cameras are being used more successfully indoors, giving access to more social spaces than was previously the case. In the first example, the additional technical capacity translated into enhanced capabilities for the fieldworker. In the second example, the increased versatility was also capable of creating new anthropological evidence.

The mere presence of IT often has a direct effect on the fieldworker's relations with members of the community. These socio-technical relations in turn shape the conditions as to when and how such technologies are used. The fieldworkers in the previous examples may, in the face of local opposition, find it more difficult to satisfy their recording goals, in spite of having technically superior equipment. However, these practical considerations reflect on a larger and ultimately more important question: how are technologies in general, and information technology in particular, perceived in the community in question? In some situations the presence of a recording device is perceived with hostility. It can reinforce the common prejudice that anthropologists take away knowledge for their own purposes, without reciprocating, or at the expense of the community. Keeping cameras out of the public eye initially and showing a willingness to be flexible can send the message that one has come to listen and to learn, rather than to impose some ideas gained prior to arrival.

In this respect field technologies play an important role in good anthropological practice. The reader may find it strange to learn that the business of recording should be perceived so politically (Ginsburg 1991). However, many indigenous groups have learned this from hard economic experience, as Michaels (1986) has discussed in the Australian case. To take a comparable example from the author's own fieldwork experience (1981–1988), the Inuit in Northern Canada are cautious when encountering 'high-tech' researchers because of an association with Greenpeace biologists who ostensibly came to study marine mammals, but actually used photographs of indigenous hunting to help secure a European ban on the importation of seal skins and to inflict irreparable damage on local Inuit economies (for which Greenpeace later formally apologized but paid no compensation). Because of situations like these, Inuit are very sceptical about researchers and their claims to objectivity. Moreover, Inuit have their own film makers, editing suites, and satellite television broadcasting facilities (Valaskakis 1982). The same anthropologist, now returning to the field with new digital video equipment, may discover that the young inhabitants of that community are now using PCs at school and are either surfing the Internet or using the television with playstations to play video games at home in the evenings.

While the anthropologist has been learning more about IT, so have the people in the community chosen for the study. The consequences can be quite varied, as the author discovered in his own fieldwork in Igloolik (Northern Canada). On the one hand, the anthropological interest of filming a child in front of a television screen has limited appeal for many audiences: it is far too familiar, and on a technical level, television screens ironically are difficult to record well on video. Likewise trying to record an interview in someone's home with the television blaring in the background is very disruptive. IT inevitably raises questions about the ownership of local knowledge. Visual images of Inuit culture are effectively an important source of local capital for the community, a central ingredient in local education, and have close connections to political interests. Although the issues of the ownership and politicization of research are too complex to discuss fully here, these examples suffice to show that an assessment of IT in anthropology must take account of the wide range of issues which govern the perception of the anthropologist's working practices.

Many anthropologists have recognized through their experiences of recording a need to adapt their working practices to the field. Some anthropologists like Badger and Nelson, who co-produced the Alaskan film series, *Make Prayers for the Raven* (Nelson 1983, Badger 1996), have stressed the value of collaboration with community leaders as a point of methodological principle. Besides consulting local elders about their wishes as to what should be recorded, Badger also gave up a substantial amount of control over the production process: how rituals should be framed, when they should be filmed, and so on. Because film production is dependent upon a large amount of cooperation, the relationship with the producer can be negotiated in a number of subtle ways rather than directly. On several occasions, Badger decided that working collaboratively required relinquishing the filmmaker's customary autonomy and methods (e.g., pre-planned storyboards), and listening to the local people who quietly insisted when, how and what content should be filmed. In retrospect, one can see that, rather than giving Badger more autonomy, his use of advanced film technology had quite the opposite effect. It increased his reliance upon the local community for many aspects of the production and even his sense of responsibility at the editing stage when he worked in their absence. Badger and Balikci (Badger, pers. comm. 1992) also organized a series of video work-shops in Siberia, where indigenous students chose their own topics, many of them cultural 'self-representations', and received technical training and assistance from the anthropologists. There are now similar examples of collaborative research, where both local communities and anthropologists benefit, particularly in the context of the United States, Canada and New Zealand. Increasingly anthropologists are translating this way of working into ideal practices and incorporating them into codes of ethics.

Even for those anthropologists who stick to the traditional tape recorder and SLR (single lens reflex) camera, many of the same issues are pertinent. The use of computer training in indigenous schools (e.g., throughout much of North America) raises the possibility of the formation of new technological elites, of pushing existing generation gaps between elders and 'youngers' to the point of schism, or of the erosion of traditional values in the face of new ones. That is a simplification, but it shows that the social structure of a community can be altered in a variety of ways by the introduction of new technologies. This in turn may affect which methods of study are adopted and, more generally, the attitude of communities towards the arrival of anthropologists, the perceived value of their presence and the opportunities of cooperation or collaboration necessary to create an insightful study. To gain an objective understanding of the role of IT in social anthropology is therefore a problem of more than one dimension. Such technologies affect anthropologists' range of tools, their relations with their chosen communities, their capacity to act autonomously (with the subtle implications that has for objectivity), and the very social structure they aim to describe.

The reception of IT in anthropological practice

To what extent do anthropologists actually make use of IT? In the absence of a comprehensive survey, this is in fact difficult to assess. This paper offers some personal impressions, gives some examples, and points out some uses and implications of IT for anthropology. Two lines of development are stressed here: first, visual anthropology in which the production of still and moving images has created fertile debates about the epistemological status of visual methods of observing and recording; second, the use of computing by anthropologists to enhance traditional forms of ethnography (i.e., the analytic description of a culture's structures) and in so doing, to raise new questions about computing and representation.

To begin with, one must recognize that the majority of anthropologists have received little systematic training in the use of IT. A self-selecting minority of researchers is responsible for the developments in this field. As in the other humanities disciplines, there is a fair measure of technophobia rooted in the 'two cultures' divide between those subjects which are bookish and those which are technical and mathematical. Anthropologists, like archaeologists and geographers, have tended to be somewhat more interdisciplinary in outlook than scholars in humanities subjects like history and philosophy, and therefore have tended to have a wider range of backgrounds, including some scientific or technical training. Curiously the image of the anthropologist roughing it in the field and participating in the local culture has rarely emphasized technical competence as a qualification. The propensity to study and learn another culture's techniques had precedents in the Victorian tradition of scientific travellers like Richard Burton, 'going native', adopting local and oftentimes exotic styles, moeurs and clothes.

Anthropologists have adopted a measure of this Bohemian sensibility in recent practices of 'participant-observation'. Hence learning a local or native skill gives a certain cachet (e.g., spearing fish), whereas bringing technical competence from one's own culture (e.g., craftwork like carpentry) goes largely unnoticed. Possessing literary talent or having artistic skills are exceptions to the rule as each has been seen as an important technical index of one's qualifications as an observer and an author. When postgraduate students undertake their fieldwork training today, their programme still consists primarily of reading and acquiring linguistic competence. Much less emphasis is placed on acquiring skills relevant or complementary to those to be encountered in the field. This large lacuna results partially from a misconception that the humanities and some social sciences in the universities should preclude technical training, together with a romantic belief that whatever needs to be learned for successful fieldwork will be learned courtesy of the local people. Once again the principal exception today is that some institutions provide training in recording methods for sound and image. This is especially true in programmes which specialise in visual anthropology.

The majority of anthropologists, like academics in other disciplines, are conversant with the use of standard word processors, but many experienced scholars are still being introduced to electronic mail. Increasingly, all manner of paperwork, including correspondence, conference notices, reading lists and so forth, is being moved to electronic formats. Learning to adapt to this is effectively compulsory. Again, anthropology is to that extent no different from other disciplines.

Some anthropological sub-groups or specialists have turned to IT for more specialist purposes. Makers of ethnographic film have benefitted most. The introduction of microprocessors in video recording is making affordable high quality video cameras at a fraction of their former price, so that something approaching broadcasting standards is now available for approximately £2000. The production and editing facilities are considerably more expensive. While film makers can afford their own basic editing equipment, it is more often an institution (e.g., a university) which will make the capital outlay necessary for a full production suite. Just as editing in the film industry as a whole has moved over to digital systems, the same trend is taking place in visual anthropology, albeit at a slower pace given the more limited operating budgets.

The Granada Centre for Visual Anthropology at Manchester University is a good example. It runs an MA course in the theory and practice of anthropological film-making, training approximately eight students per year. The films are usually an end in themselves, the equivalent of a textual publication for other scholars. Most students use 'hi-8' cameras, with digital cameras (DVCs) being gradually introduced. Digital, non-linear editing for video (e.g., Avid systems) and sound (e.g., Pro Tools software) is available under the guidance of professional editing staff, but only for the final 'on-line' edit. Within the next year, students may be able to use these digital techniques in working out their rough cuts as well. However, owing to high demand for the only digital suite, the preliminary 'off-line' editing still takes place on the less expensive analog suites, without the added digital advantages. Once again, falling prices mean that some of this software is now available for the lower price range of personal computers (PCs). The advantages of digital editing in video are threefold: it allows the editor much faster access to images by searching a hard disk instead of winding on a videotape, it allows the editor to experiment more freely and to simulate cuts, and it permits a wide range of possible alterations to the image (e.g., digital filters for enhancing edges, burning in details, colouring, special effects).

Visual anthropology refers not only to documentary film making, but also to the use of photography, video, computing and multimedia techniques as research tools. The term also seems to apply to the construction of databases of heterogeneous ethnographic information sources: film clips, still photographs, sound recordings, and texts. The Naga videodisc project carried out by Macfarlane, Jacobs, Harrison and Porter, was one of an interesting group of early examples. The videodisc and player provided access to an encyclopaedic range of sources collected over many years about Naga people and culture (Macfarlane 1990). The originality of the project owed much to the thought given to how users could move through the text and images. At the heart of the project was a versatile probabilistic search engine, which allowed the user to follow links based on a wide possible range of associations (now familiar to Internet users) rather than being restricted to the use of Boolean operators (OR, AND etc.) only.

Important work in computing and anthropology such as the Naga project has contributed to the recent synthesis of computing and visual documentary, but to some extent grew out of a separate tradition of enquiry from film making per se. Fischer (1998) has identified three phases of development in computing and anthropology: basic approaches to important problems with limited data in the 1960s; a shift towards more substantial ethnographic analysis (involving more elaborate statistical analysis in the mid-1970s and early-1980s); and a broadening of the ethnographic-based project in the 1990s to incorporate new goals and methods. In the 1960s, a number of explicit applications of computing for anthropological purposes emerged. For example, Coult and Randolph (1965) explored the use of computing methods in genealogy and kinship studies. Gilbert and Hammel (1966) showed that social processes could be analysed through modelling and computer simulation, as an alternative to direct long-term study, or to study a range of possible futures. Hymes's (1965) discussion of the use of computers in anthropology signalled anthropological computing to be a topic in its own right. The development of these studies between the 1960s and the present deserves a full study, but lies beyond the scope of this paper.

The institutionalization of anthropological computing in the United Kingdom (UK) took place at the University of Kent, where John Davis founded the Centre for Social Anthropology and Computing (CSAC) in 1985. The group's work has grown for it to become the primary centre of research for anthropological applications of computing in the UK. Its members have covered a wide spectrum of topics, but have tended to focus more on qualitative rather than quantitative forms of analysis. They have stressed the need for an awareness of the unique character of anthropological data, the dangers of being unreflective about computer-based analysis, and the need to interpret it with great care in each and every context. They have created a number of very useful on-line information sources such as a search engine for the *Journal of the Royal Anthropological Institute*, a bibliography with abstracts for research on anthropology and computing, software packages, student resources and sample projects.

Some of these on-line features provide reference information, whereas others are creating new techniques for research and teaching which would not otherwise exist. A development project to produce multimedia materials designed around the idea of 'experience-based teaching' will generate a wider range of teaching materials for anthropology departments (ref: http://lucy.ukc.ac.uk/Fdtl/). For example, computer simulation can guide a viewer through the virtual reality of a ritual, and convey a sense of movement that is often lost in textual descriptions. One of the key advantages afforded by multimedia is to rethink how different kinds of information are juxtaposed. Fischer (1998) has identified four models of computer-based media: computing as a channel of information flow; second, sequenced presentations of film, sound, graphics, text and video; third, emulation of pages or books; and fourth, layered multimedia. In the concept of *layering*, each layer corresponds to a different level or scale of representation, ranging from finished analysis down to raw data. As a researcher or student questions a given hierarchy or system of organizing information, this also invites a closer reflection on the relationship of movement to understanding. This creates subtly different possible 'tools' of fieldwork. Zeitlyn (pers. comm. March 1998) reports using digitized video clips in interviews, and thereafter linking them to make oral accounts more demonstrative and to make references visible. Furthermore, by making his transcripts and sound recordings available to readers, he chose to make his use of evidence more transparent or open. Just as Boast *et al.* (1997) used multimedia to create hypertext-based galleries, so Zeitlyn (1998) juxtaposed his own work with those of indigenous producers. On-line museum exhibitions like that in the Hunterian Museum in Glasgow have used multimedia to display Asante gold weights in such a way as to enable the viewer to see the back of them.

In other words, multimedia techniques of representation, juxtaposition and trans-formation can suggest different ways of seeing or reading anthropological information. As a result, students have the opportunity to peruse research projects, to play videoclips from the field, to enter interactive discussions online, and to learn by running simulations and carrying out problem-solving exercises. Already, authors can draw on the CSAC's expertise to publish electronically, or alternatively, to republish books which have gone out of print. In the longer run, CSAC has played a key role in contributing to the development of a wide range of computing projects in British universities beyond the domain of anthropology alone: for example, the JANET communications infrastructure, the BIDS citation indexes and electronic desktop publishing. (ref: CSAC's Ethnographics Gallery, http://lucy.ukc.ac.uk/CSAC, accessed 17 March, 1998).

Fischer (1998) and his colleagues, specializing in the use of computation for anthropology, have explored the practical relationships between IT, the structure of information, standards of recording and the changing conception of the archive. Their website demonstrates a variety of uses of computing in visual anthropology, including bibliographies, descriptions of research projects, and references to computing resources for anthropologists. The technical aspects of computing in anthropology fall outside the remit of this paper. Nevertheless, gains are derived from specific technical developments: for example, improved software for manipulating images, faster processing and drawing, and significantly larger and cheaper memory for storage. The fact that this equipment is increasingly rugged and so able to withstand being knocked about in the field makes it a more practical way of working. It is now quite common to take a portable computer into the field; add to this a video camera, together with the traditional notebook, stills camera, and tape recorder, and one has the basis of a multimedia archive.

Fischer (1994, 1995) emphasises the unification and integration of traditionally separate media. Combining diverse media into a common format is becoming significantly easier, as a result of the IT industries and governments establishing common digital standards which permit software to share or switch between these different kinds of data. Visual records need no longer be so static and resistant to documentation and comparative analysis. The application of a wide range of digital filtering techniques, to sharpen edges, to burn in details and to adjust colour balances, is the object of intensive research and development.

Whereas in the 1960s and early 1970s, anthropologists used computers to address a number of specific problems of structure in demographics, belief systems and navigation, Fischer (1996) argues that quantitative methods are now more oriented towards ethnographic projects, citing examples such as Goody's (1990) comparative study of the sexual division of labour, Rheubottom's (1994) simulation of historical kinship processes in Croatia, and Fischer's own (1998) study of constructed traditions in the Cook Islands. Because the underlying assumptions behind anthropological data are so vital to making sensible interpretations of such data, anthropologists inevitably have had to be creative, technically literate, and flexible in their use of quantitative methods.

The production of CD-ROMs is now a common, though still an expensive, component of anthropological projects. The effectiveness of delivering large amounts of ethnographic information is being augmented by a growing trend to use servers accessed through the Internet instead. Cost, size and ease of distribution make electronic dissemination a useful resource for teaching, provided that investment in IT infrastructure continues to support the growing volume of traffic. The degree to which users gain some measure of control over how they use the information depends in large part on the sophistication of the search engine (software), the multimedia architecture which accompanies the database, and the wider context in which the learning process takes place.

The concept of IT arose in part out of the conjunction of computing and communications. In the last ten years, the advent of solid-state, mobile, satellite communications has meant that fieldworkers with sufficient technical interest can establish a mobile field station for their work. In such situations, information can be transmitted directly from the field to a home institution. That means that the necessity of duplicating one's notebooks, sending them home in separate despatches, storing them for a long period until the fieldwork is complete, may no longer be so crucial. The use of mobile phones adds another dimension to the organization of fieldwork logistics. It enables the worker to have greater access to a wide range of information and to keep in touch with people and institutions who may offer various kinds of support.

The temptation to paint a picture of a technological panacea where the fieldworker is one node in perfect contact with other nodes of a worldwide information network should be resisted. This view is espoused with a surprising regularity by participants in serious discussion forums on the Internet as well as the more popular chat rooms like Lambda Moo, the first real-time, multiple-user dungeon (MUD), designed by Xerox's research establishment in Palo Alto. The ramifications of this for anthropologists in the field tend towards two extremes. Technologically determinist readings of the technology suggest that IT enables fieldworkers to transcend the locality of their field-sites by securing access to global information, while its impact on local indigenous culture is typically presented as a process of assimilation, or sometimes, cultural genocide. In contrast, the experience of anthropologists over the past century leads many to doubt that technological assimilation necessarily implies cultural assimilation. In order to find a perspective in between these two positions, a step back to place this problem in the context of the archetypal anthropological journey will be very helpful.

Reconstituting relations of distance in the field

Pedagogical systems in anthropology can tell us more about our own research traditions. This is especially true in British anthropology where training for fieldwork plays a fundamental role in the investiture of new recruits into the discipline. A truer picture might be that the experience of researchers and the socio-political situations in which they find themselves immersed may in fact be so varied, as to make generalization quite difficult. An unspoken understanding that field notes are effectively an anthropologist's private property reinforces this difficulty. Only through careful selection, quotation, and analysis do the notes become visible in the public realm. This selectivity might usefully be compared to the very protective attitudes of natural scientists who rarely permit competitors or outsiders to enter their laboratories. For these reasons, pedagogy becomes extremely important as a site where research practices are formalized and made visible. It provides a common idiom or platform for anthropologists whose work is so diverse and sometimes divergent to discuss methodological issues. It tends to reflect the discipline's idealized image of itself, a context in which to discuss changing disciplinary practices and boundaries, such as those brought about by IT.

Although many anthropologists will readily concede that their methods derive from a blend of philosophical traditions, social theory, history and economics, those who specifically stress traditions of empiricism, hold that *fieldwork* is the flagship of methodologies; visiting a remote field site, living there and participating in the life of the locals, so as to gain first-hand experience. However much of a caricature this may be – because many anthropologists now study urban environments, new social movements, or work 'at home' in their own country – it is still useful because it draws attention to the spatial separation between the sources of empirical evidence (the field) and the places of writing, publishing and debate. This tension creates certain problems which character- ize the history of anthropology and more generally, scientific travel, since the early modern period. The capacity to record one's observations, to render them objectively and to communicate them by helping the reader to imagine witnessing the observations, are essential ingredients in giving authenticity and power to an ethnographic narrative. Just as there are different traditions and ideals of fieldwork methodology, so too in the United Kingdom and the United States field-workers pay homage to their respective turn-of-the- century ancestors, Bronislaw Malinowski (1922) and Franz Boas (1940). Besides creating field-work schools, each was vitally concerned as to how the knowledge derived from the field should best be displayed, preserved or published for both specialist and popular audiences.

A programme of doctoral research today is organized, typically, as follows: in the first year students read secondary literature pertinent to their topic, participate in seminars, draw up a research plan, write an introductory chapter with a coherent theoretical frame, and make practical preparations for fieldwork; in the second or middle stage, the journey into the field, students undertake a predominantly *empirical* study of a community over an *extended* period, recording their observations and reflecting on their experience; in the third and final stage, students return to their home institutions to 'write up' their dissertations, which when complete, they submit to their degree board and defend against the criticisms of examiners.

In the fieldwork ritual, time and distance have traditionally been essential ingredi- ents in creating a boundary between the field and the metropolitan institution or university. The relative difficulty in travelling to many field sites also served to guarantee that the research experience would be relatively uninterrupted. The journey to the field and the heightened sense of arrival, the ensuing sense of isolation, and cultural immersion, created a space of contemplation and self-discovery in the Other's culture. These have been regarded as the minimum conditions for guaranteeing a full apprecia- tion of the 'local'. The experience of extended empirical study is under siege. Already the declining availability of research funds for students, and tighter rules governing completion dates, have meant that students now go to the field for nine to twelve months, whereas their supervisors might have had the opportunity to spend eighteen to twenty-four months. Taking into consideration the difficulty and importance of learning a local language and acquiring some local skills, this squeeze is widely perceived to threaten the integrity of the subject. The availability of IT for work in the field needs to be seen in this context, and not simply as something new.

The postmodernist contribution to anthropology, however one may evaluate it, has made anthropologists more conscious of their recording technologies. In the early twentieth century, the information technologies of fieldwork were the notebook, the sketchpad and the pencil, essentially the same as those of the Victorian field naturalist. The use of cameras (and more exceptionally, cinema cameras) on expeditions also became common in this period, and simultaneously a number of universities began to equip themselves with darkrooms. Less obvious, but equally important technologies, were the ocean-going vessels, the network of communications throughout European empires, and the local systems of transportation and exchange. These technologies, though they may now seem old-fashioned, were the globalizing technologies of the early twentieth century. Then, as now, anthropologists contemplated their position on the edge of political expansion, their relationship to institutional and technical vehicles of cultural assimilation and, in some regions, the genocide of indigenous peoples. In many respects, the technologies of travel and recording one hundred years ago were crucial in defining the anthropological journey, particularly its sense of time. Imperial and colonial networks, powered by European industrial and political expansion, created the conditions where networks of communication were sufficiently strong to support anthropological travel, and yet were sufficiently weak to enable anthropologists privileged access to 'their' communities.

This historical context provides a useful way to think about the complex and conflicting attitudes in anthropology to IT today. The marriage of telecommunications and computing implies for anthropology a fusion of representation (in the field) and translation (between the field and the home institution). The breakdown of traditional boundaries of time and space, which has almost acquired the status of a cliché in the academic world, holds some truth for anthropologists. The field is no longer so isolated and the source of the anthropologist's privileged access is not as certain. IT can be seen as contributing another feature to the ongoing debate about the place of anthropology in the wider world and the basis of its claims to authority.

The dialogical relationship between local and global phenomena has been mediated by IT most explicitly in the context of museums, which are thriving in a bid to interpret the diverse relationships between information as a manifestation of globalizing forces and local culture which continually makes the global its own and uniquely different. While ethnographic museums in the field (e.g., the U'mista Cultural Centre where Boas did his Northwest Coast fieldwork – see Clifford 1997) as well as in the metropolis, have not stopped collecting, preserving, classifying and researching, they have made considerable efforts to think about the relationship between anthropology and its audiences. Many members of the public still believe that local cultures lose everything unique about them when confronted by 'modern' technologies. This is so strongly ingrained in people's minds, as to be disorienting to think otherwise. One example of a museum which did this very successfully was the Museum of Mankind in London where IT often figures prominently. In the 'Living Arctic' exhibition (1987–88), for example, visitors could use electronic screens to navigate their way through various information sources salient to learning more about Inuit ways of life (Brody 1987). In one of the exhibition's rooms, an Inuit lounge where a hunter might come home to his family and watch television programmes received by satellite, was meant to induce a kind of vertigo and to encourage visitors to rethink relationships between tradition and modernity and the ways in which they can co-exist.

Although the public tends to see museums as sites of information, curiosity and entertainment, they also occupy an extremely important place in the research community. A wide range of contested issues at the heart of anthropology, such as the meaning of artifacts, the relationship of material culture to theory, the ownership of culture and the question of repatriating sacred objects, is being worked out by the curators and directors of museums (Clifford 1997, Prakash 1995). Many academic departments and museums are linked through universities, though these links are not adequately cultivated. A recent example is the Virtual Teaching Collection (Boast *et al.* 1997) where a team of researchers from Cambridge, Glasgow, Middlesex, and Oxford Universities and University College London has produced an object-oriented software package which allows users to combine text and images (using an object-oriented database) from museum collections placed on CD-Roms. Although it has been used successfully in a teaching pilot scheme, in general, attempts to use multimedia to encourage academic departments to make use of museum collections are still quite exceptional.

University managers have recognized the need for postgraduates to receive training in basic computing, such as word processing and statistics packages. While these may be of some general value, they do not cater to the specialist needs of anthropology students or address anthropological issues specifically. Visual anthropologists, on the other hand, have successfully engaged with the relationship between multimedia and the curriculum through intensive practical teaching, although their limited resources mean that their courses must be restricted to a small number of students. The lesson from these examples is that the integration of IT into the lecture theatre and seminar rooms has genuine potential, but not as a cost-saving mechanism.

Anthropology's politics of information

The globalization of the communications industries calls for anthropologists to rethink the discipline's traditional reliance on empiricism as its primary methodology. How does one study social relations when they are being negotiated electronically? The question is not only methodological. Some methods such as discourse analysis, appropriate for analysing transcriptions of sounds, are now used to study IT-intensive environments like the MUD chatrooms. However, a discussion of methodology also poses broader questions about the social and political meanings of information. While this is in some measure a question facing all humanities disciplines, anthropologists continue to reflect on its current practices specifically in the context of the discipline's history and its ethical commitments.

The idea that anthropologists have a political presence is hardly new. The foundation of the discipline of ethnology in the United Kingdom and France was riding the tide of the anti-slavery movement. The Aborgines Protection Society (founded 1837) was explicitly partisan and political, acting on behalf of abused aboriginal peoples, collectively and sometimes individually, when it petitioned the Colonial Office against the illegal excesses of colonial settlers (Bravo 1996, Stocking 1987). The acceptance of ethnology as a sub-section in the nascent British Association for the Advancement of Science was delayed for many years, precisely because of fears that its political content would endanger the credibility of the Association as a whole. The Ethnological Society of London (founded 1842) treads a fine line between carrying out its debates in objective terms while keeping the more obvious political implications of its members' work in the background. This tendency towards combining dissenting advocacy with objective research resurfaces again and again in the present day.

When the significance and use of IT surfaces in anthropological debate, the conversations are frequently couched in historical terms. Because the term 'information' is abstract and decontextualized from any particular culture, it raises the hackles of anthropologists for whom cultural difference is the key to the subject, and terms like the 'information society' smack of rhetoric. This caution or scepticism (however justified or unjustified) is typically discussed in terms of power relations and the history of the discipline. The complicity of anthropologists and the extent of this caution in late Victorian and Edwardian colonialism (Asad 1973, Grimshaw and Hart 1993) is still widely debated. The majority of anthropologists since the Second World War have been staunch, and even radical, critics of colonialism. The ethical practice of fieldwork today is reliant upon having kept the key ingredients of extensive empiricism, while extracting the whole enterprise from colonial contexts. This distance from institutions has been possible owing in part to the extent that the anthropologist's technologies of travel and recording have been globalized, democratized, and decolonized. Without wishing to enter this debate here, it nevertheless establishes a framework in which the use of IT in anthropology is likely to be evaluated within the discipline. Anthropologists do not believe that technologies are inherently politically neutral; they have values embedded in their constructions and their uses.

Arguments about anthropology's complicity with, and reliance upon, colonial infra-structures in the late nineteenth and early twentieth centuries, have also been widely discussed in the discipline. At various times in the past there is little doubt that anthropologists have been servants of colonial states and defenders of elitist evolu-tionary ideologies. The term 'intelligence', during late nineteenth century European colonization, acquired multiple meanings, referring alternatively to archives, state secrets and cognitive capacities (Richards 1993). Like other social sciences, anthropology has its dark side and its misuses. Anthropologists at different moments contributed to the imperial project as bureaucrats, as information collectors (and sometimes spies), and as the architects of theories of race and race improvement, advocates of eugenics and selective sterilization under the guise of objective science. Providing information to the state and legitimating ethnic relocations and reclassifications, anthropologists have taken on many different roles for the state. Across Europe they collected, collated, published and exhibited copious quantities of information about ethnic groups around the world. In some instances this information was obtained by the state to impose ethnic identities (e.g., Russia, Turkey) to satisfy wider nationalist or centralist aims. In Nazi Germany, the role of anthropologists as race specialists was especially pernicious. Any discussion of the place of information in the anthropological endeavour needs to be aware of its misuses and its inherent ideological content. For the historical reasons just mentioned, the use of IT in field practices has not been greeted with open arms.

The relationship of anthropology to information-gathering also has a more recent history. Drawing upon the development of operations research during the Second World War, national intelligence agencies in the United States harnessed the labour of anthropologists and information processing technologies for strategic Cold War purposes (Edwards 1996). The difficulties of coping with ever growing quantities of electronic information spurred institutions like the Rand Corporation to develop methods of modelling cultural variables using game theory, rationalist assumptions and anthropological data. Although some anthropologists sought practical solutions to the necessity of studying cultures 'at a distance' in politically sensitive or hostile regions, it is clear that they could be vulnerable to state manipulation (Edwards 1996).

It is generally accepted, however, that the crisis of anthropology which began in the 1960s – questioning the legitimacy of the whole enterprise, including the conditions of objectivity, the right to speak on behalf of other groups – had its roots in the political relations of colonialism, and subsequently, those of the Cold War. One key product of this crisis has been a much greater emphasis on the role of writing, technologies of visual representation, and narrative styles. This has sensitized anthropologists a great deal to the issues of using information technologies in their everyday field practices. Hence anthropologists are likely to ask how the possession of personal computers alters the power relations between anthropologists and informants. How does the acquisition of technical competence in IT assist the organization of anthropological material? Does it matter whether field notes are recorded in a traditionally bound notebook, or on a magnetic hard disk? If the latter is the case, how does present-day 'salvage anthropology', the project to record cultures before they disappear, differ from the approaches of our Edwardian predecessors? Do electronic information technologies significantly change the *local presence* of the anthropologist in the field?

Conclusions

The new information technologies associated with computing and telecommunications are significant for the field of anthropology today in four respects. The much vaunted globalization of culture, in part due to the globalization of IT, is itself an issue of central concern for anthropologists in comprehending the changing meaning of local culture. The impact of IT on anthropological practice is clearly more pronounced in some areas of anthropology than others. Those areas in which digital signal processing facilitates new kinds of practice will reap the most obvious rewards. Editing facilities for ethnographic filmmakers are becoming less expensive and considerably more powerful. In multimedia, common standards for integrating text with image and sound also display the benefits of applying IT. These developments in the research environment are visible in different areas of cultural debate: in on-line journals , in research seminars, in distance learning and teaching, at film festivals, and perhaps most importantly, in museums.

There is some evidence to suggest that IT itself is becoming a topic of research for anthropologists. In order to study its place in culture, some technical familiarity is very helpful, though not always necessary. Researchers who use the Internet to study on-line social relations are a good example of this. Some knowledge of computing is very important, both to understand the object of research, and to navigate and to record successfully what one is witnessing or observing.

The majority of anthropologists without such specialist interests are learning some basic computing skills in order to use word processors and to meet the expectations of institutions which are shifting much of their internal correspondence to electronic mail. At an intellectual level, IT is becoming of general interest in so far as it is becoming a powerful symbol of the 'information' age, post-industrial societies, another echelon of modernity, and a key industry in creating global markets. In this context, IT is not revolutionary and does not signal a paradigm shift in anthropology. It does, however, reinforce a number of existing concerns within the discipline about methodology. This debate has both a historical and an ethical dimension. The history of anthropology provides the most important context in which discussions about the significance of IT are taking place. Previous anthropological conceptualizations of information and technologies of representation create a backdrop against which new devices are received and compared.

No longer quite lone scholars in the tradition of the Malinowski myth, anthropologists have a much wider range of roles available to choose from. The adoption of IT by many indigenous groups for educational and political purposes means that their capacity to represent their own culture forces anthropologists to be responsive in studying those cultures. Better telecommunications allow some anthropologists to maintain a more regular, less costly, relationship with their informants in the field. However, this is no substitute for actually 'being there'. Many local cultures around the world are under threat. IT is a two-edged sword: it can be used for suppression and surveillance, and it can be used to resist and subvert and to represent in new ways. The declining costs of computing hardware and software and the development of common multimedia communications standards suggest that these will continue to be productive tensions in the field of anthropology.

Acknowledgements

The author would like to thank David Zeitlyn, Penny Harvey, the editor, and an anonymous referee for their useful comments and suggestions. A special word of thanks is owed to Michael Fischer, who made available a draft of a forthcoming article, 'Computer-aided Visual Anthropology'.

References

Asad, T., (1973) (ed.), *Anthropology & the Colonial Encounter* (London).

Badger, M. (1996), *Visual Ethnography and Representation: Two Case Studies in the Arctic*, unpublished PhD dissertation, Scott Polar Research Institute, (Cambridge).

Banks, M. & Morphy, H., (1997) (eds.), *Rethinking Visual Anthropology*. (New Haven).

Boas, F. (1940), *Race, Language and Culture* (New York).

Boast, R., Gere C., Lucy S., Thomas L. and Wintroub M. (1997), *The Virtual Teaching Collection CD: History of Science Collection*. Cambridge Museum of Archaeology and Anthropology.

Bravo, M. T. (1996), 'Ethnological Encounters'. In *Cultures of Natural History*. Secord J. A., Jardine N., and Spary E. C., (eds.) (Cambridge) 338–57.

Brody, H. (1987), *The Living Arctic: Hunters of the Canadian North*. Published in collaboration with the British Museum and Indigenous Survival International. (London).

Clifford, J. (1988), *The Predicament of Culture: Twentieth-Century Ethnography, Literature, and Art*. (Cambridge, Mass.).

—— (1997) *Routes: Travel and Translation in the Late Twentieth Century*. (Cambridge, Mass.).

Collier, Jr. J. and Collier, M. (1986), *Visual Anthropology: Photography as a Research Method* (Albuquerque).

Coult, A. D. and Randolph, R. R. (1968), 'Computer methods for analyzing genealogical space' *South-western Journal of Anthropology*, 24: 83–99.

Edwards, P. (1996), *The Closed World: Computers and the Politics of Discourse in Cold War America* (Cambridge, Mass. and London).

Fischer, M. (1994), *Applications in Computing for Social Anthropologists* (London).

—— (1996), 'Computer-aided visual anthropology in the field', unpublished paper.

—— (1998), *The Centre for Social Anthropology and Computing, University of Kent at Canterbury: CSAC's Ethnographic Gallery* website, http://lucy.ukc.ac.uk/index.html, accessed March 17, 1998.

Gilbert, J. P. and Hammel, E. A. (1966), 'Computer simulation and the analysis of problems in kinship and social structure' *American Anthropologist* 68: 71–93.

Ginsburg, F. (1991), 'Indigenous media: faustian contract or global village?' *Cultural Anthropology* 6(1): 92–112.

Goody, J. (1990), *The Oriental, the Ancient and the Primitive: Systems of Marriage and the Family in the Pre-Industrial Societies* (Cambridge).

Grimshaw, A. and Hart, K. (1993), *Anthropology and the Crisis of Intellectuals*. (Cambridge).

Hymes, D. (1965) (ed.), *Use of Computers in Anthropology* (The Hague).

Macfarlane, A. (1990), The Cambridge Experimental Videodisc Project: the Nagas of North East India. Discussed in 'The Cambridge Experimental Videodisc Project', *Anthropology Today*, 6(1).

MacKenzie, D. and Wajcman, J., (1985) (eds.), *The Social Shaping of Technology: How the Refrigerator got its Hum*. (Milton Keynes and Philadelphia).

Malinowski, B. (1922), *Argonauts of the Western Pacific: An Account of Native Enterprise and Adventure in the Archipelagoes of Melanesian New Guinea*, (New York).

Marcus, G. and Clifford, J., (1986) (eds.), *Writing Culture*. (Berkeley).

Michaels, E. (1986), *The Aboriginal Invention of Television in Central Australia, 1982–1986: Report of the Fellowship to Assess the Impact of Television in Remote Aboriginal Communities* Australian Institute of Aboriginal Studies (Canberra).

Nelson, R. K. (1983), *Make Prayers to the Raven: a Koyukon view of the Northern Forest* (Chicago).

Prakash, G. (1995) (ed.), *After Colonialism: Imperial Histories and Postcolonial Displacements* (Princeton).

Rheubottom, D. (1987), 'The Ragusa Project and its database', *Bulletin of Information on Computing and Anthropology* 5: 1–7.

—— (1994), 'Genealogical skewing and political support: patrician politics in fifteenth-century Ragusa (Dubrovnik)' *Continuity and Change* 9(3): 369-90.

Richards, T. (1993), *The Imperial Archive: Knowledge and the Fantasy of Empire*. (London & New York).

Stirling, P. (1998), *Forty-Five Years in the Turkish Village Project* website, (http://www.lucy.ukc.ac.uk/TVillage/notes.html, accessed March 20, 1998

Stocking, G. (1987), *Victorian Anthropology* (New York, Oxford, and Don Mills).

Valaskakis, G. G. (1982), 'Communication and control in the Canadian North: the potential of interactive satellites, *Etudes Inuit Studies*, Special Issue on 'Communications' 6(1): 19–28.

Zeitlyn, D. (1993), 'Reconstructing kinship or the pragmatics of Kin Talk', *Man* (later renamed *Journal of the Royal Anthropological Institute*) 28(2): 199–224

Preservation and networking in aid of research

SEAMUS ROSS

Director, Humanities Computing & Information Management
University of Glasgow

Abstract. Networked communication has become one of the dominant forces for change. This paper describes some of the impacts of networked communication on scholarship and draws attention to dangers that its rapid uptake may pose to scholarship. The long-term influence of networking on scholarship will depend in part on the increase in the quantity, diversity and quality of information resources available in digital form. The digital medium provides opportunities that print could never support, such as facilities to use a variety of data types and structures within a single scholarly work; new access and distribution models; and the capability to reanalyse dynamically data sets used in support of scholarly arguments. It poses institutional, sociological and technical obstacles. For example, the proliferation of resources in digital form requires that they be preserved, and doing so requires co-ordinated and comprehensive planning.

Introduction

The increasing use of electronic networks for communication, dissemination of information and access to resources is changing scholarship. It changes how scholars identify, select and access material, use resources, interrelate, write and publish. Research depends upon the accessibility and dissemination of information, and has traditionally relied upon the existence of a research infrastructure, including conferences, workshops, libraries, archives, museums and printed publications. Use of these services and resources has become subject to conventions and often requires the assistance and guidance of information specialists, such as librarians, archivists and colleagues. The Internet has rapidly evolved into a key facet of this infrastructure via the communications facilities it supports and the information resources provided on it. Increasingly holders of primary information resources, such as archives, museums and libraries, are investigating how they can make information about, and even digital versions of, their holdings accessible via the Internet (Information North 1998; MDA 1998; NCA 1998). British Academy projects, including the Lexicon of Greek Personal Names, the Beazley Archive, and the Corpus of Romanesque Sculpture in Britain and Ireland, illustrate the innovative ways in which humanists are making their research accessible on the net.

There is now widespread awareness that networking makes regular communication between distant scholars easier and that it enriches the kinds of data they can exchange as well as the consummate ease with which this can be achieved. It has, for example, changed the kinds of access users can have to catalogue information (http://portico.bl.uk/opac97or http://copac.ac.uk/copac) and altered the methods for distributing documents (e.g., websites, electronic journals). The role of Online Public Access Catalogues

(OPACs), databases, bibliographic resources, and text and image archives are services which the Internet can deliver to assist the research process. The development of networks for the academic sector was originally intended to support the sharing of limited computing resources. Their development as a fast and reliable communication medium between researchers and as a conduit for online information resources were not initially envisaged. Their use as a mechanism for scholarly communication evolved only gradually, even if our perception suggests this has happened relatively quickly. Electronic mail, or email, has become a significant mode of scholarly communication, although it no longer represents the most substantial component of network traffic. For instance, in 1998 Web traffic represented 70 per cent of the transatlantic bandwidth used by the University of Glasgow whereas email represented only 5 per cent. The transition to the use of digital content is occurring extremely rapidly, if we remember that the web was a new concept as recently as 1991. In order to ensure the future of scholarship we need to plan and fund the creation of digital content adequately, and vouchsafe the dissemination of the results of its study.

Access to networks

While Internet connectivity is fairly widely available in countries in North America and Western Europe, access is limited in much of the rest of the world (Press 1995:67; Pitkow & Kehoe 1996). It would be unwise to assume that access even in advantaged regions is anything like universal, but the picture is changing rapidly. For example, in 1995 only 2 per cent of personal computers (PCs) in the United Kingdom (UK) were equipped with modems (SCST 1996). By the beginning of 1997 a DTI study found that 39 per cent of homes had a PC and that 7 per cent of PC users had access to the web (DTI 1997). By April 1998 29 per cent of UK homes had access to the Internet and 14 per cent had regular Internet users. In the United States there are some 62 million Internet users, of whom 32 per cent first began using the Internet during 1997 (http://www.intelliquest.com/). Access to the Internet has become fairly universal in higher education institutions, but even here access to many services and information resources tends to be limited by the wealth of a scholar's home institution and sometimes even their department. Access to the Internet, however, does not bring genuine benefits without access to substantial quantities of content, adequate computing resources, and appropriate training (BLRDD/BA 1993).

Electronic mail is changing how scholars communicate, with whom they do so, the kinds of material they can exchange as part of a message, the speed of communication and expectations as to the length of time that will elapse between responses. Over time, scholarly use of such services as electronic mail, discussions lists and electronic conferencing and the amount of material exchanged will increase, network interaction will become less democratic, even, and especially, as access to the basic service becomes widely available. Of course, scholarly communication and access to resources have never been democratic. Babai (1990) has stressed that, as an instrument of scientific communication, email gives a well-chosen, sizeable, powerful elite the ability to make advances faster than others because it grants them access to information more quickly. The trend towards restricted virtual communities will accelerate as specialist electronic discussion groups attempt to avoid having their discussions polluted by contributions from non-specialists. The 'discussion group' often shows great variation in the quality and accuracy of the material exchanged. A closed discussion group or a moderator can prevent this tendency, but these either exclude access to knowledge from certain groups or allow a gatekeeper to control what information is disseminated. The essential problem here is the tension between the wide access to information and discussion made possible by networked communication, and *informed* discussion. Other factors, including the academic quality, frequency and topicality of contributions, all play a role in determining the impact and value of network-based communication.

Electronic mail is beginning to form a primary record of contemporary activity and scholarship (Bikson and Law 1993). In charting the development of ideas and the relative merits of the roles played by collaborators and discussants details of the exchanges themselves will form a resource of scholarship. As a result future researchers will need more than the printed journals and monographs. They will require access to the electronic messages and the data used by the scholars themselves.

At present anyone can make information available on the Internet. Indeed, the concern expressed in the 1993 report by the Royal Society/British Library working party on *The Scientific, Technical and Medical Information System in the UK* over the growth in this unstructured, non-refereed material with its capacity to overload the networks seems to be being borne out (RS/BL/ALPSP 1993: 7). Internet users must critically examine each document to discover whether its internal features provide clues which might verify its accuracy, authenticity, integrity and validity. In many respects there is nothing new about this; scholars have always been aware of the variation in the usefulness and validity of their sources. How does the user of the Internet Classics Archive establish the pedigree of an edition of Herodotus, Virgil's *Aeneid*, or any of the other classical texts which it makes available? If researchers are to benefit from the net-resources some quality control of the information will be essential. Currently, the textual resources available are of a variable quality and encoded to a variety of standards (e.g., variability in mark-up depth, metadata). Digital images are also created to variable standards and with only limited attention to metadata necessary for their access and preservation, which limits their scholarly applications. There is little object in creating digital resources if their quality, in terms of the accuracy, precision and comprehensiveness of the data they contain, is wanting.

Costs of networking

Academics frequently argue that access to information and network services should be free at point of use. Two cost factors are at play here: costs of the network itself and the costs of the services provided across it. The different network segments vary remarkably in costs; for example, high speed lines (TI) cost 30 times more in France than they do the US (Mannoni 1996: 102). Until recently network usage in the UK has been free to higher education (HE). The increase in usage has been unprecedented and this has been especially true on the transatlantic links. In order to control the demand and to generate income to fund a continued expansion of transatlantic bandwidth the UK Funding Councils have set a charge on all data which comes across the international links of about 2 pence per megabyte. Most HE institutions are absorbing the charges for the 1998/ 9 year, but many are exploring ways of passing them back to departments or to individual users. This is a very worrying trend, which will have an impact on research and teaching uses of online resources.

The Internet has made information available on demand, accessible from anywhere in the world, and capable of being provided in ways which makes its manipulation, recycling, integration with other materials, and its redistribution easily done. Researchers are concerned about the impact of charging on the use of digital resources. Observation suggests that charging discourages serendipity in information discovery and use. Charging for information on the Internet is becoming more common as mechanisms for secure handling of financial transactions become more readily available and as the sense of village life begins to diminish among the participants in 'networked culture'. From a scholarly vantage point there are already very valuable, if not essential, networked resources which are accessible only to those who have paid, can pay or are members of wealthy paying institutions (e.g., ISI citation databases such as an Arts and Humanities Index, Social Science Indices, RLIN or JSTOR). In the case of JSTOR only readers at member institutions can obtain access to the service, which by mid-1998 contained two million pages representing the contents of some 40 major scholarly print journals. Within three years it will include the runs of more than 100 scholarly journals. As the work of JSTOR makes evident digital information is expensive to create, maintain and preserve, and its future requires that it generate income to fund its long-term accessibility (Guthrie 1997).

Should scholars be concerned about the commercialisation of the Internet? Will commercial publishers change the fabric of networked communication? So long as the services that scholars wish to use are free at point of use, what difference does it make? Conventional economic wisdom suggests that commercialisation will, of course help to reduce the cost of access to the network itself. It will increase the user-base and expand the audience scholars can reach. It will also encourage the development of lower-cost, easier to use and longer-life hardware for accessing the network, as business attempts to increase the consumer base of network users. With commercialisation will come the spread of edutainment and the development of non-scholarly and scholarly resources in tandem.

Searching the network

An attempt to use the resources supposedly available on the Internet in preparing this paper revealed that much of the information lacked currency, some was redundant, most could not be verified by either standard measures of quality assurance or internal features of the documents themselves, some was no longer where the search tools believed it to be and others not what the index claimed it to be. None of the sites was indexed to the same standards. The same query submitted to five prominent browsers (i.e., AltaVista, Excite, HotBot, Infoseek, Lycos) produced different but sometimes overlapping results. Some of these indexes are formidable; in October 1996 Lycos had information about some 300,000 sites and 51 million of items in its database. How information on the Internet is indexed will need to change radically if it is to prove a viable resource for scholarship or a suitable way to disseminate results of scholarship. A study conducted by Lycos in 1996 found that the more than 50 per cent of Internet users spent time looking for information without finding it (http://www.lycos.com/press/Messy.html)

It is widely acknowledged that finding resources is a major problem. The Joint Information Systems Committee (JISC) and the British Library Research and Innovation Centre funded a study to examine the establishment of a UK-wide agency to ensure that resources needed by scholars were visible and accessible to them (Borphy 1997). The Agency would work to encourage the creation of collection level data and to ensure interoperability of access; moves to establish it are underway. This is a local solution to a global problem. Essentially a search across the network returns the trivial with the profound, the erroneous with the correct, the fundamental with the general, and the simple with the complex. If the medium is really to benefit scholarship much more attention needs to be given to the development of better tools for finding and retrieving resources (see, for example, Dempsey 1994). These range from browsers (e.g., Microsoft's Internet Explorer, Netscape), to search tools (e.g., AltaVista, Excite, Lycos), to discipline resource guides, to intelligent help facilities that ease the use of unfamiliar resources by providing guidance in response to how the user interacts with the service, to 'intelligent agents' that traverse the network looking for information that meets certain user-specified criteria (Etzioni and Weld 1995). Of these approaches to resource discovery 'intelligent agents' will become crucial tools. The agents themselves may come to be valued as scholarly resources. The success of all these search tools will depend upon better indexing and metadata.

Internet guides that provide a layer between users and subject arenas or discipline/based services give support to academics seeking resources on the net. A peer-reviewed directory (http://argos.evansville.edu) of networked resources for the study of the ancient and medieval world, is a good example as is a similar tool for biblical studies: http://www.hivolda.no/asf/kkf/rel-stud.html. Two other useful resource guides are SOSIG (http://www.sosig.ac.uk) and the American Arts and Letters Network (http://www.aal-n.org).

So far the use of the Internet has had only limited impact on how scholars use images and sound, although it has made an increasing amount of such materials available. It is worth remembering that, although network retrieval tools are essentially character-based, the resources on the network include still and moving images, and sound. Currently, these can be located only by means of textual descriptors. Icon-based disciplines, such as archaeology and art history, and sound-based subjects, such as music and oral history, require tools which can search for image or sound patterns with greater levels of subtlety and discrimination than are currently possible using text-searching tools in searching for text-based information. Developments, such as IBM's QBIC, a content-based image retrieval tool, for searching databases of images, which have shown promising results, are still at an early stage (Flickner *et al.* 1995; Okon 1995; Niblack and Flickner 1993).

The resources open to scholars and the ways of accessing them depend upon a powerful technical infrastructure (Davies 1995), at the national and international levels and at the level of the local institution. High-fidelity sound, high-resolution still and moving images, and interactive multimedia sessions can all effectively be distributed across those segments of the network supporting maximum bandwidth. What continues to be a problem for the academic community is the quality of the local services and services in poor countries. The World-Wide-Web, for instance, requires powerful personal computers, graphics terminals and access to high-speed network services (Bell *et al.* 1996). As an increasing number of World-Wide-Web sites, such as multimedia-based virtual museums, include still and moving images among their offerings, these kinds of local facilities will become a prerequisite for academic use.

Networking and publication

Network-based digital publications make it possible to produce articles which incorporate a great diversity of data types: images, sounds, charts, diagrams, text. These publications appear as websites, online monographs and digital journals. The numbers of electronic academic journals is mushrooming; they have grown in number since 1994 from 181 to 1093 in 1998 (Hearst 1998). http://www.edoc.com/ provides a comprehensive list of online humanities and social science journals. The social sciences and humanities have not yet fully exploited the medium because few of the several hundred journals do anything more than use the electronic medium to replicate paper-based journals (e.g., *Bryn Mawr Classical Review*). It would be unfortunate if this trend were to continue. Psychology, geography, music and archaeology are examples of disciplines where online journals make it possible to present material in support of hypotheses that could not be distributed in conventional publications. For example, an online journal within music could include sound clips, graphical representations of sound, scores and moving images in a single article, and an online journal in history of art might be based around extensive regular updated databases. Digital publication enables authors to use the data types most appropriate to their topic or argument and allows readers to interact with the original data or sources. These conclusions were borne out in the papers presented at the 1997 Conference on Electronic Publishing held in Stockholm (Butterworth 1998).

Work with *Internet Archaeology*, one of the journals funded under the JISC's Electronic Libraries (eLib) programme, suggests that the new digital environment should result in a radical rethink of what the results of scholarly endeavour might be and how they can be presented. The editors found, for instance, that the whole concept of a journal was redefined (http://intarch.ac.uk). Conventional printing constrains efforts to present archaeological evidence and its analysis (Heyworth, Ross and Richards 1996), but in a digital presentation archaeologists are able to distribute full excavation data and databases of archaeological information (e.g., archaeobotanical evidence), in addition to their interpretations, allowing other researchers to re-analyse the material to confirm conclusions or to draw new ones. Increasingly scholarship will depend on the mining and recycling of data created by other researchers and readers will expect that the base data on which conclusions are built are accessible.

In its first five issues (since September 1996) *Internet Archaeology* has demonstrated that photographs, drawings, databases, visualizations and dynamic or virtual reality reconstructions all have a role in the presentation of archaeological research. The concept of an article also changed and some articles were databases whereas others were the equivalent in size to monograph length studies. Of course, there are problems such as credibility, copyright, intellectual property rights, access, charging and preservation which need to be addressed as this technology is developed (Denning and Rous 1995; *Key Issues...* 1996). In the light of the experience of *Internet Archaeology* resolving these issues will be fraught with difficulties. Funding poses a major obstacle. *Internet Archaeology* examined four sources of funding: site-licensing, subscriptions, pay-per-view, and publication subventions. In archaeology because of the nature of excavation funding, supporting a journal through subventions is a very strong possibility; we do not believe that any of the other funding models alone will provide sufficient income to meet our costs.

A common temptation is to assume that, because the Internet makes it easy and fast to make the results of research available, that it is a good idea to do so. To paraphrase a axiom about driving: 'speed thrills, but speed kills'. There is nothing that will prove more dangerous to the process of scholarly endeavour than rapid but poorly executed publication of research. The notion expressed by colleagues of Harnard at Southampton that electronic journals should focus on rapid discussion and publication of ideas where time will be measured in days is scary (Hitchcock 1996). It will result in reactive rather than reflective scholarship. However, it is fair to say that this problem is merely an extension of recent trends in print publications. The network could initially endanger the peer-review process, but review-free publications will not last long. Electronic publication is also likely to change the process of review (http://www.u-koln.bath.ac.uk/ariadne/issue5/jime/). In the case of *Internet Archaeology* the project adopted the view that peer-review has two aspects: scholarship and presentation or content and concept.

Digital resources

The benefits which networked communication can bring to scholarship will depend upon the quality and quantity of the information it will make available. Reviews of higher education acknowledge the obstacles to research posed by the shortage of high-quality digital content (Dearing 1997). The creation of digital resources (whether new or retrospective conversions) is expensive. The scholarly community needs to address the question of how the costs for the creation, dissemination and preservation of information are to be distributed across the user community. Currently projects are funded in an *ad hoc* way, although in some countries such as the United Kingdom the higher education community has begun to address the issue of content creation in a concerted manner. Here significant efforts are being made to provide some focus to content creation and to the purchase of resources by planning support and building on consultation with the higher education community (CWG 1998).

There are substantial gaps between the demand for resources and those which already exist in digital form, as well as the available expertise and skills for their creation. This is reflected in the increasing emphasis which groups such as the JISC, through its eLib programme, the Library of Congress (http://www.loc.gov), the National Library of Australia (http://www.nla.gov.au/), the Public Record Office (http://www.pro.-gov.uk), and the Andrew W Mellon Foundation via projects such as JSTOR, have put on content creation. The huge push being orchestrated by the National Science Foundation towards the development of a digital library is one of the largest and best funded efforts. The Digital Library Federation, a consortium of the fifteen largest libraries and archives in the US, is co-operating to ensure that the content they digitise is accessible (http://www.lcweb.loc.gov/loc/ndlf). A great deal more mobilisation will be necessary if suitable funding and support activities are to be put in place to develop, an adequate information base. Other UK initiatives include the development of a Public Library Network (LIC 1997), and efforts to promote the development of an Archival Network (NCA 1998). These activities will result in an increase in the kinds and quantities of resources available to scholars and in the skills of students coming to university.

Converting the wealth of scholarly resource into digital form requires major financial investment. Estimates based on work done at Cornell University indicate that digitisation costs (excluding storage and access costs, see below) range between 18 and 21 cents a page (Berger 1997). These figures are far lower than those produced by other projects, but they provide a target costing. The actual costs will vary depending upon the kind of source material and the ways in which it can be handled. Projects, such as Internet Library of Early Journals (http://www.bodley.ox.ac.uk), have produced costs of upwards of £1.50 per page for digitisation, metadata and indexing. Retrospective conversion of print materials is a labour-intensive activity. With the exception of a few large projects, most activities in the field are small and fragmented and will only gradually have an impact on the vast amount of material which needs to be converted into digital form. The question of which criteria should be applied, and by whom, to the selection of material for digitisation and preservation ought to concern scholars. Criteria which might be used to govern the selection of material for digitisation include: where the information content is high; where significant research and teaching benefits would accrue from its conversion; where material is at risk; where the benefit of digitisation is greater than the risk to which it subjects the material being digitised; where the existing storage medium is no longer suitable (e.g., nitrate film, photographic prints); where digitisation would significantly increase resource accessibility; where clear (international) standards will be used to facilitate storage, retrieval and preservation; where 'rights' issues are not a bar to dissemination and reuse; and when it enhances the ways in which the content of collections can be studied, manipulated or accessed.

There are three main types of digital resources which have value to researchers: those which result from the retrospective conversion of analogue material into digital form; resources which are created solely in digital form; and resources created in digital form as a by-product of administrative and commercial activity. Examples of the first are The British Library's Beowulf Project (Kiernan 1994), The Archivo General de Indias (Gonzalez 1992), or the Bibliothèque de France (Fresko 1993). The Beowulf Project is creating a 'diplomatic edition' with transcription, translation and digital images to make this manuscript accessible to scholars in a way that will make it possible to develop a fuller understanding of it (Prescott 1998). The Archivo General de Indias project has digitised more than 11 million of the 86 million pages in the archives relating to the Spanish administration of their colonies in the Americas from Columbus to the end of the 19th century (Gladney *et al.* 1998, 50–51). The Bibliothèque de France is making 'digital images of every page in 100,000 volumes chosen as representative of the national heritage of French literature and works of reference in the humanities' (Fresko 1993: 13). There are numerous other kinds of retroconversion projects in areas such as moving image and sound. The work of Kurtz's team at the Beazley Archive has begun to add two hundred thousand images of Greek vases currently stored as photographic prints, to a text database of 50,000 entries (Kurtz 1993). 20th Century-Fox has some 10,000 hours of Fox-Movietone Newsreel film, much of which is of interest to twentieth-century visual and cultural historians, which is being digitised (Fox 1993: 19).

The second category of projects is creating electronic resources only, such as the British Academy's Corpus of Romanesque Sculpture in Britain and Ireland (CRSBI), the British National Corpus (BNC), the Scottish Cultural Resource Access Network (SCRAN), and Images of England Project run by the Royal Commission for Historical Monuments (England). CRSBI is creating a digital record with associated text-base of the surviving Romanesque Sculpture in Great Britain and Ireland and will eventually contain 60,000 images and 15,000 pages of text (Ross 1993: 20–21; 1994). The SCRAN Project, funded by the Millennium Commission, aims to create a digital record of holdings related to Scottish cultural heritage (http://www.scran.ac.uk). Each of these projects provides valuable material to scholars and students. In addition, they provide a bench-mark record and thereby preserve material to allow future researchers to identify and possibly to understand change. These resources shift how we conduct research. Scholar-ship is now data rich in ways that the use of analogue materials could never have made possible: rather than basing research on a small number of examples it can now be based on analysis of comprehensive data sets (Ross 1994). For instance, the 100 million words in the British National Corpus (BNC) provide a resource which changes how we study language (Rundell 1996). Its preservation is essential because it forms the raw material on which scholarly arguments and contemporary dictionary making will be based. The BNC also provides a benchmark to the state of the English language as we approach the millennium.

The third kind of digital resource results from the increasing dependence of contemporary society on information in digital form (Ross 1996). From credit card data to medical records, from airline passenger databases to tax records, from electronic mail to image and text databases, vast amounts of information about late twentieth-century society exist in electronic form. Although most transactions produce paper as their by-product (e.g., till receipts, credit card vouchers, tickets, prescription forms, invoices and statements), these paper records include only a fragment of the material captured in electronic form during a transaction. The sheer quantity, diversity and rich quality of the electronic information resources from which these records have been derived indicate that their preservation in electronic form could provide future scholars with a better opportunity to understand the present period than paper records alone could ever do. Medical historians may wish to integrate medical records with food retail sales data to study the relationship between diet and disease. Future researchers will wish to examine data in ways in which contemporary users do not need to and to analyse them in the context of other data sets. Electronic information is a cultural product, e-facts, and it forms an essential fragment of the cultural record of the contemporary world. Only a few substantial data sets of operational databases are accessible at present (e.g., http://ndad.ulcc.ac.uk).

Impact on scholarship

Scholarship could become more dynamic, more multidisciplinary and more co-operative than it has been in the past. It will become increasingly focused on sources and on a larger and more diverse number of types of sources. For example, scholars based in Rome, Berlin, Oxford, Boston and Tokyo could all examine the same suite of images of manuscripts drawn from multiple libraries simultaneously and engage in scholarly debate about them online. Sadly few users seem to engage in this sort of interactive discussion at present. The greatest problems facing these scholars are posed at the data capture and display ends and by variation in network bandwidth. These differences are crucial because, even if it is possible to move vast amounts of information, there is little value in doing so unless users have adequate tools for capturing and displaying materials. Research undertaken at the Getty Museum showed that image quality was of singular importance among art historians (Ester: 1995, 111–25). The issues which need to be addressed include: (1) quality of access (e.g., end-to-end bandwidth, network saturation, delivery benchmarks and levels of service); (2) end-user display technologies; (3) end-user image calibration (e.g., the configuration of end-user hardware and software can have a dramatic affect on what viewers see on their machines and the display may have little resemblance in areas such as colour fidelity or pixel depth to the image as delivered to the network by the museums, libraries, or archives); and, (4) at what resolutions will users by able to access images or sound.

What is evident from the work in the sciences is that networked communication fosters collaboration. Initially it breaks down isolated working as it makes sharing of information, effort and resources easier. Currently these exchanges are informal, *ad hoc* and not governed by established rules of behaviour which control more traditional kinds of collaborative ventures. This is because interaction of this kind is still a rarity and the processes are developing gradually. Even in the sciences, where there has been a tradition of laboratory work, such 'collaboratories' are still in their formative stage. Some issues are technical, such as shared computer display and whiteboard, shared electronic notebooks, online instrument display and web-browser synchronisation (Kouzes *et al.* 1996, 44). The psycho-social issues, which include such factors as 'autonomy, trust, sense of place, and attention to ritual' (ibid. 41) also need to be addressed if networked collaboration is to be successful as much more than a means of exchanging data at high-speeds.

To explain the complexity of the psycho-social problems involved in developing electronic laboratories it is useful to consider the issues posed by comparison between electronic and face-to-face communication. Most participants in face-to-face interaction come to understand over several meetings the subtle use of gesture, tone, facial expression and language by the other party and use this information to inform their interpretations of their interlocutor words; the linguistic element of the conversation is thus enriched by the non-linguistic component. At first glance electronic exchange appears to lack these cues (Lee 1994). Studying email messages, however, indicates that choice of words, syntactical and grammatical construction, length of sentences, para-graphing, and the use of space-filler words are all examples of variable characteristics which help us to sense the attitude and subtle meanings the author intends to imply. As email shifts from being solely textually-based to including graphics and sound, the non-linguistic elements will become ever richer. It is also likely that communication across the network, which has so far been informal, will become less so with increasing use. As users seek ways to differentiate between the significant and the insignificant, more formal styles and structures will naturally evolve. In a similar way protocols of behaviour will evolve for 'collaboratories'.

Preservation of networked resources

These developments pose a series of problems for scholars. Should networked commu-nications and resources be archived? How will networked resources, communications and digital scholarship be archived? Who should have access to the archive? What levels of documentation should be retained and how should it be generated? How will the vast quantities of digital content be secured? What standards of data encoding, compression, and storage media should be used? Who should finance the preservation? What criteria for selection should be used? How will net-resources, interconnected information units distributed across the network but linked together, be archived? The experience of *Internet Archaeology* shows that authors are concerned about the seemingly ephemeral nature of digital publications. Does the linking of bodies of information across the network constitute *scholarship* in the same way that seeing interconnections and relations might form the basic building block of scholarly research? If so, what strategies exist for preserving this information?

While legislation to protect individual rights (e.g., intellectual property rights, privacy, copyright), lack of awareness and lack of effort pose obstacles to preservation; hardware and software obsolescence, lack of standards and a lack of preservation methods or migration strategies act as further barriers (van Bogart 1997, RLG/CPA 1996, Ross and Gow 1999). Magnetic and optical media storage degrade naturally under optimal storage conditions (see http://www.nta.org/AboutNTA/ AboutNML/). They are left behind by technological developments, as has happened with paper tapes, punch cards, 8″ floppy disks, magnetic tape standards (i.e., storage densities) and low and high density 5.25″ floppy disks. Data encoding strategies are likewise superceded as developments in access technology increase the possible densities of media storage. The lesson of the last five decades of data storage and retrieval is that storage media and access technologies have limited life-spans. In some instances this is the result of the nature of the medium itself and in others it is because better technologies become available.

In many cases preservation of the data alone will not be sufficient. Specialised software used to store, manipulate and access certain categories of data (e.g., databases or proprietary image formats) may for certain purposes need to be preserved. Even where long-term access to the raw data can be guaranteed, such access is unlikely to be provided to future researchers in the same way as it has been supplied to contemporary users (Swade 1993, Rothenberg 1995). A problem with this is that valuable cultural data are contained in the record structures and in the software that is used to access the resources: to sever the message from its medium of provision debases the message. A judge in United States drew this conclusion in the case of Armstrong v. Executive Office of the President (1 F.3d 1274 (D.C.Cir 1993) when he ruled that there was information contained in the electronic records (e.g., in the case of email transmission and receipt data) that printouts did not include. This is particularly the case with virtual records. Without original software to process the data it will be impossible to determine what kinds of (or specific) virtual records users might have created. A similar state of affairs holds for software-dependent data objects produced by geographic information systems (GIS) and computer aided design (CAD) tools. Future generations of cultural and social historians or anthropologists will be interested not only in the information held in the records, but also in working practices and in the way that social behaviour was conditioned by the available equipment and the working environment in which it had been used. Just as medievalists study the functioning of scriptoria and monastic libraries, future scholars will investigate digital libraries.

Whereas the loss over time of small amounts of data, through say media degradation, might not be disastrous under some circumstances, the 'functional intactness' of software and some graphics formats is essential (Swade 1993: 96–7). Yet even if the software is retained on what hardware will it be run? Since the 1950s advances in hardware have become more frequent, and each has brought remarkable improvements in processing, storage and display capabilities. It is a utopian ideal to think that it would be possible to maintain computer hardware for use by future researchers. Swade (1993), Rothenberg (1995) and Ross and Gow (1999) have argued that it will be possible to emulate current software on new generations of hardware, much as Swade's colleagues simulated a 1958/9 Ferranti Pegasus computer on an IBM PC x486 and researchers at the University of Pennsylvania emulated the ENIAC-on-a-Chip (*Penn Printout* 1996). Such simulations and emulations demonstrate the feasibility of accessing earlier software. However, the experience of having seen the forty year old Pegasus machine run and perform the same data processing tasks provided an understanding of the process of work in the late 1950s that no simulation could do. It is at the digital borderline where the accessibility of a facsimile does not compensate for working with the original.

To ensure the long-term value not only must the electronic resources be kept but also details of their context. In the case of images, for instance, metadata are required about: how the image was captured; how many times removed the digital image is from the original object; whether the digital image has been modified; how many different formats it has been migrated through before it arrived in its current format; how colour was calibrated and re-calibrated. In the case of digital imaging, for example, the RLG Preservation Metadata Group has produced some guidelines (http://www.rlg.org.pre-serv/presmeta.html). Much more work in the area of metadata standards and guidelines needs to be undertaken. A broad range of other data is necessary and the essential metadata include information that allows users to identify the resources, details of their contents, terms of access, guidelines about how to open and read the material, assistance with its 'meaning', details of how, why, and when the resource was created, information about functionality, technical requirements and provenance – 'the nature of the process that produced and/or maintains the source'. Metadata are expensive to create and standards are just beginning to evolve (Bearman 1995, Meon 1995).

Mechanisms to aid the verification of the authenticity of electronic documents need to be developed. The ease with which digital information can be modified makes intellectual preservation of digital information problematic (Graham 1994). A variety of techniques from encryption to digital watermarking (Berghel 1997) could be used to protect against changes. Since electronic documents, whether composed of text, images, or sound, can so easily be copied, modified and redistributed, scholars are justifiably concerned that they may lose control of their material or that it may be modified in ways that may misrepresent them or their work.

This discussion raises an important issue of the role of and need for standards. Standards are crucial for the meaningful and intelligible exchange of information across space and time. They are also the key to the long-term viability of electronic information if data and information are to be accessible from a wide variety of hardware platforms and software packages for decades. The emphasis must be on 'portable standards' because no single standard will provide a vehicle for the preservation of data. Information will need to be migrated from each current standard to the next. Good standards are applicable across numerous computer systems, are widely used, are easily understood and applied by non-specialists, require no specialised hardware, are well documented, and are non-proprietary (Cargill 1989).

While standards are important for the exchange of information, the role of an individual standard in its preservation is more difficult to predict. The current generation of standards may not be those that will help to maintain current electronic information for the next decade, let alone the next century. Where standards will play an additional role here is by providing the correlation definitions needed to move data from its current format to a newer one. McLean and Cook examined the issue of standards for electronic publications on behalf of the Electronic Publishing Working Group of the Australian Vice-Chancellors' Committee and concluded that the success of net-based electronic publication depended upon the use of a limited range of standards (*Key Issues...* 1996, 61). The eLib programme in the UK has reached the same conclusion.

Considering all the pitfalls facing digital data, constant attention needs to be paid to the state of the digital archive (Conway 1996, Hedstrom 1995, 1991). The storage media give little clue to the presence, content or format of data and almost as little indication of what might be needed to access it. The resources must be monitored so that data are converted before software disappears or the file formats are replaced. It must be regularly used so that a large, indeed expanding, community is aware of its existence and value. A good preservation strategy involves technical approaches, good practices and marketing. It might have as its motto: 'publicize, distribute and migrate' (Ross 1995b). It is essential that as large a proportion of the research community as possible is aware of the opportunities provided by digital resources and that large numbers of projects reuse data sets as well as creating new ones.

Social scientists and humanists are right to be concerned about the long-term access to their online publications, the data resources on which they depend, and the online tools such as catalogues and museum documentation systems that assisted their research. Electronic resources require continual attention and, left unattended, quickly become inaccessible. To assume that material in electronic form will be available for future researchers is to underestimate the economic cost of migrating records from one environment to another, and the problems of suitably documenting them. There is also a danger of overestimating the benefits of preserving electronic resources. Where there is economic advantage in reusing information it will be easy to make a business case for the preservation of records. The future of scholarship depends upon preservation of digital resources. Activities such as the Arts and Humanities Data Service (Ross 1995b) and the social science Data Archive (Lievesley 1993) offer a home to the products of scholarly study. One of the most important developments for scholars will be the legal deposit of electronic publications. In some countries this has already happened, and in the UK this has become the focus of efforts led by the British Library to change copyright legislation.

Conclusions

While networks and the Internet in particular hold out much promise, and this holds true particularly in the area of informal communication, the benefits depend upon better and wider availability of network access: support and training in the use of network facilities; better navigational tools, finding aids, search engines; and more guides to resources (e.g., SOSIG and the American Arts and Letters Network); increased funding and recognition of the development of digital resources; and work to address the issues of copyright and intellectual property rights. Most importantly, concerted effort is needed to retroconvert the vast quantities of analogue materials into digital form and to create new digital information resources such as image and sound databases. More rationalised and structured plans to develop the digital libraries and to preserve the digital products and by-products of scholarship will be essential if the digital revolution is to benefit scholarly activity in a positive way. The growing discipline of humanities informatics and the increasing number of institutions such as the Humanities Advanced Technology and Information Institute at the University of Glasgow which are developing research and teaching programmes in this area should begin to provide the intellectual foundations, the necessary expertise, and the trained practitioners for these endeavours.

References

British Library Research and Development Department and the British Academy (BLRDD/BA) (1993), *Information Technology in Humanities Scholarship: Achievements, Prospects, and Barriers* (London: The British Academy and the British Library Research and Development Department (R&DD Report 6097)).

Babai, L. (1990), *E-mail and the Unexpected Power of Interaction*, University of Chicago Technical Report CS 90–15, (April 24, 1990).

Bearman, D. (1995), *Archival Strategies*, (Pittsburgh).

Bell, T. E., Adam, J. A., and Lower, S. J. (1996), 'Communications', *EE Spectrum* (January 1996), 30–41.

Berger, B. (1997), 'Digital Imaging Projects at Cornell University'. In *Preservation and Digitisation: Principles, Practice and Policies*. (London), 49–57.

Berghel, H. (1997), 'Watermarking Cyberspace', *Communications of the ACM*, 40(11): 19–24.

Bikson, T. K., and Law, S. A. (1993), 'Electronic mail use at the World Bank', *The Information Society* 9(2): 124–44.

Borphy, P. (1997), *Towards a National Agency for Resource Discovery*, (London). http://www.ukoln.ac.uk/services/papers/bl/blric058.

Bryant, P. (1997), *Making the Most of Our Libraries*, (London: British Library Research and Innovation Report 53).

Butterworth, I. (1998), *The Impact of Electronic Publishing on the Academic Community: An International Workshop Organized by the Academia Europaea and the Wenner-Gren Foundation.* (London).

Cargill, C. F. (1989), *Information Technology Standardization, Theory, Process and Organizations*, (Bedford).

Conway, P. (1996), *Preservation in the Digital World*, (Washington).

Content Working Group (CWG). (1998), *An Integrated Information Environment For Higher Education: Developing The Distributed, National Electronic Resource*. http://www.jisc.ac.uk/cei/dner_colpol.html.

Davies, H. E. (1995), 'EU networking projects in the humanities policy issues'. In Kenna, S. and Ross, S. (eds.), *Networking in the Humanities*, (Sevenoaks) 35–44.

Dearing, R. (1997), *Higher Education in the Learning Society. The National Committee of Inquiry into Higher Education.*

Dempsey, L. (1994), 'Network resource discovery: a European library perspective'. In Smith, N. (ed.) *Libraries, Networks and Europe: A European Networking Study*, British Library Research and Development Department, LIR Series 101 (London).

Denning, P. J. and Rous, B. (1995), 'The ACM Electronic Publishing Plan.' *Communications of the ACM* 38(4): 97–103.

Department of Trade and Industry (DTI). (1997), *Moving into the Information Society: An International Benchmarking Study*, Information Society Initiative, DTI.

Ester, M. (1995), 'Issues in the use of electronic images for scholarship in the arts and humanities. In: Kenna, S. and Ross, S. (eds.), *Networking in the Humanities,* (Sevenoaks) 111–25.

Etzioni, O. and Weld, D. (1995), 'Intelligent agents on the Internet: fact, fiction and forecast', *IEEE Expert* 10(4): 44–9.

Flickner, M., Sawney H., Niblack W., Ashley J., Huang, Q. Byron Monikai, B. D., Hafner J., Lee D., Dragutin P., Steele, D., Yanker, P. (1995), 'Query by image and video content: the QBIC system', *IEEE Computer,* 28(9): 23–32.

Fox, B. (1993), 'Old news acquires immortality on computer tapes', *New Scientist,* 25 September 1993, 19.

Fresko, M. (1993), *British Library Research Delegation Study Visit to Paris,* (British Library Research and Development Department, R&DD Report 6112), (London).

Gladney, H. M., Mintzer, F., Schiattarella, F., Bescós, J., and M. Treu. (1998), 'Digital access to antiquities', *Communications of the ACM,* 41(4): 49–57.

Gonzalez, P. (1992), 'Computerisation project for the Archivo General de Indias'. In Doorn, P., Kluts, C. and Leenarts, E. (eds.), *Data Computers and the Past* (Hilversum) 52–67.

Graham, P. S. (1994), *Intellectual Preservation: Electronic Preservation of the Third Kind* (Washington, D.C).

Guthrie, K. M. (1997), 'JSTOR: From Project to Independent Organization', *D-Lib Magazine* (July/August), http://www.dlib.org/dlib/july97/07guthrie.html.

Hearst, M. A. (1998), 'Innovations in electronic academic publishing', *IEEE Intelligent Systems and Their Applications,* 13(1): 6–7.

Hedstrom, M. (1995), 'Electronic archives: integrity and access in the network environment.' In Kenna, S. and Ross, S. (eds.) *Networking in the Humanities* (London).

—— (1991), 'Understanding electronic incunabula: a framework for research on electronic records.' *American Archivist* 54 (3): 334–4.

Heyworth, M., Ross, S., & Richards, J. (1996), 'Internet Archaeology: an electronic journal for archaeology', in H. Kammermanns (ed.), Interfacing the Past. Computer Applications and Quantitative Methods in Archaeology, CAA95, in *Analecta Praehistorica Leidensia,* no.28. (Leiden), 517–523.

Hitchcock, S. (1996) 'Web publishing: speed changes everything', *Computer* 29(8): 91–3.

Information North. (1998), *Virtually New: Creating the Digital Collection* (London: Library and Information Commission).

(Key Issues.) (1996), *Key Issues in Australian Electronic Publishing,* Collected Reports to the Australian Vice-Chancellors' Committee, *Key Issues,* (Canberra).

Kiernan, K. (1994), 'Digital preservation, restoration, and dissemination of medieval manuscripts'. In Oakerson, A. (ed.) *Scholarly Publishing on the Electronic Networks, Proceedings of the Third Symposium,* (Washington D.C).

Kouzes, R. T., Myers, J. D. and Wulf, W. A. (1996), ' "Collaboratories" doing science on the Internet', *Computer* 29(8): 40–6.

Kurtz, D. (1993), 'The Beazley Archive Database', *Archeologia e Calcolatori,* 4: 49–51.

Lee, A. S. (1994), 'Electronic mail as a medium for rich communication: an empirical investigation using hermeneutic interpretation', *MIS Quarterly,* 18(2): 143–7.

Lesk, M. (1998), 'How can we get high-quality electronic journals', *IEEE Intelligent Systems and Their Applications,* 13(1): 12–13.

Levy, D. M. and Marshall, C. C. (1995), 'Going digital: a look at assumptions underlying digital libraries.' *Communications of the ACM* 38(4): 77–83.

Library & Information Commission (LIC), (1997) *New Library: The People's Network.* http://www.ukoln.ac.uk/services/lic/newlibrary/.

Lievesley, D. (1993), 'Increasing the value of data'. In Ross, S. and Higgs E. (eds.), *Electronic Information Resources and Historians: European Perspectives,* (St Katharinen) 205–17.

Mannoni, B. (1996), 'Bringing museums online', *Communictions of the ACM,* 39(6): 100–105.

Michelson, A. and Rotherberg, J. (1992), 'Scholarly communication and information technology; exploring the impact of changes in the research process on archives'. *American Archivist,* 55 (Spring 1992): 236–315.

Moen, F. (1995), 'Metadata for network information discovery and retrieval', *Information Standards Quarterly* 7(2): 1–4.

Monk, P. (1993), 'The economic significance of infrastructural IT systems', *Journal of Information Technology,* 8(1): 14–21.

Museum Documentation Association (MDA). (1998), *Current and planned provisions of on-line digital learning resources from museums: a study for the Digital Content Task Group* (Cambridge).

National Council on Archives (NCA), (1998), *Archives On-line: The Establishment of a United Kingdom Archival Network* (London).

Niblack, W. and Flickner, M. (1993), 'Find me the pictures that look like this: IBM's Image Query Project', *Advanced Imaging,* (April).

Okon, C. (1995), 'IBM's image recognition technology for databases at work: QBIC or not QBIC?, *Advanced Imaging,* (May), 63 ff.

Prescott, A. (1998), 'Constructing *Electronic Beowulf,*' in: Carpenter, L., Shaw, S., and Prescott, A. (eds.), *Towards the Digital Library: The British Library's Initiatives of Access Programme* (London).

Pitkow, J. E., and Kehoe, C. M. (1996), 'Emerging trends in WWW user population', *Communications of the ACM,* 39(6): 106–8.

—— (1994), 'Commercialization of the Internet; *Communications of the ACM* 37(11): 17–21.

Press, L. (1995), 'Resources for networks in less-industrialized nations', *Computer* 28(6): 66–71.

Research Libraries Group and Commission on Preservation and Access. (RLG/CPA). (1996), *Preserving Digital Information: Report of the Task Force on Archiving of Digital Information* (Washington D.C.).

Ross, S. (1993), 'From conventional photographs to digital resources', *Archaeological Computing Newsletter,* 35: 14–21.

—— (1994), 'Designing a Tool for Research in Disciplines Using Multimedia Data: The Romanesque Sculpture Processor'. In Bocchi, F. and Denley, P. (eds.), *Storia & Multimedia,* Proceedings of the Seventh International Congress of the Association for History and Computing, Bologna 29.8–2.9.1992, (Bologna) 629–635.

—— (1995a), 'Intelligent Graphical User Interfaces: opportunities for the interface between the historian and the machine'. In Kropa, I., Teibenbacher, P., and Jaritz, G. (eds.), *The Art of Communication* (Graz: Akademische Druck- und Verlagsanstalt, 1995) 207–222.

—— (1995b), 'Preserving and maintaining electronic resources in the visual arts for the next century', *Information Services & Use* 15: 373–84.

—— (1996), 'Opportunities in electronic information'. In Brivati B., Buxton J. and Seldon, A. (eds.), *The Contemporary History Handbook,* (Manchester) 437–50.

—— and Gow, A. (1999) *Digital Archaelogy: Rescuing Neglected or Damaged Data Resources* (London).

Rothenberg, J. (1995), 'Ensuring the longevity of digital documents': *Scientific American,* 272(1): 24–9.

Royal Society (RS/BL/ALPSP) (1993), *The Scientific, Technical and Medical Information System in the UK: A Study on behalf of The Royal Society, The British Library and the Association of Learned and Professional Society Publishers,* BLR&DD, Report No. 6123, (London).

Rundell, M. (1996), 'Computer corpora and their impact on lexicography and language teaching'. In
    Mullings C., Deegan, M., Ross S. and Kenna S. (eds.) *New Technologies for the Humanities*,
    (London) 198–216.

(SCST), (1996), *Information Society: Agenda for Action in the UK, House of Lords Select Committee
    on Science and Technology*, Session 1995–96, 5th Report (London).

Swade, D. (1993), 'Collecting software: preserving information in an object-centred culture'. In
    Ross, S. and Higgs, E. (eds.), *Electronic Information Resources and Historians: European
    Perspective*, (St Katharinen) 93–104.

Van Bogart, J. W. C. (1997), 'Long-Term Preservation of Digital Materials', in *Preservation and
    Digitisation: Principles, Practice and Policies* (London).

Weber, H. and Dörr, M. (1997), *Digitisation as a Method of Preservation* (Amsterdam).

Commentary

EDWARD E. HIGGS

School of Historical, Political and Sociological Studies
University of Exeter

In his very interesting paper Seamus Ross raises numerous issues respecting the impact
of electronic preservation and networking on future research. The present contribution
will make a few comments on this paper, and then raise an additional issue with respect
to the possible impact of some suggested strategies for electronic archiving on future
research.

Dr Ross' paper needs to be placed in a rather broader context. Before scholars start to
panic about the implications of electronic media they should remember that many of the
issues which Dr Ross raises are not new, although they are certainly on a new scale.
Institutions with the most advanced telecommunications and computing infrastructures
may well become an elite, but has not this always been the case with libraries and
laboratories? Historians may worry about the criteria by which electronic records will be
selected for preservation but archivists have been grappling with these issues in paper-
based systems for decades. Scrolling on computer screens is a nuisance, but it will be
rather familiar to anyone who has used a medieval Chancery roll. It is necessary to place
contemporary developments in an historical perspective.

Secondly, one should note that many of the issues raised here are really about
'peoples systems' rather than technology. The problem with the amount of unscholarly
material which fills so many academic news groups is not technological, it reflects how
people currently use the technology. The real problems with network collaboration are
the same as with any collaboration – trust and the adherence to normal standards of
behaviour. The issues of privacy, copyright and intellectual property rights revolve
around human conventions, rather than hardware and software. How people relate to
each other as fellow human beings is in their own hands, or at least in those of Bill Gates,

and is not determined by technology. The issues here are of power and tact, not machinery.

Thirdly, one needs to be wary of the claim that the vast flows of information now available on electronic media will open up disciplines, and lead to multi-disciplinary work. The opposite is just as likely. Disciplines form around canonical texts, and within boundaries which can be policed – this is what gives them an identity, and thus an existence. The new information deluge may thus simply help to create smaller and more inward-looking specialities. The expansion of academic publishing since the Second World War and the proliferation of specialist journals do not seem to have broken down many barriers, and it is doubtful that the effects of the Internet will prove any different. In a broader context, it is interesting that information technology does not appear to be creating new disciplinary configurations – scholars using computers still refer to themselves as historians, geographers, lawyers and the like.

In conclusion, an issue that Dr Ross mentions only tangentially in his paper, that of custody, needs to be addressed. If electronic records need to be migrated, at some cost, across platforms, whilst they can be accessed anywhere from anywhere via networks, are central archives necessary? Records, some information managers now argue, should be maintained and migrated across computer platforms within organizations, rather than being transferred to central repositories. Records will be kept because they fulfil the business needs of such organizations. The role of the archivist would be, therefore, in ensuring that suitable archival principles are embedded in computer systems at their design stage, intellectual control, and the provision of gateways to electronic information (Bearman 1994). This model is already being put into practice by the Australian National Archives (Stuckey 1995). But if organizations become their own archives, will preservation for long-term cultural purposes survive? The history of paper archives in commercial organizations does not fill one with hope here. Will the historical record be sanitised in order to protect organizational interests? Will new barriers to access develop? All these issues may have just as great an impact on future scholarship as the technology of networking and electronic preservation itself.

References

Bearman, D (1994), *Electronic Evidence. Strategies for Managing Records in Contemporary Organizations* (Pittsburgh).

Stuckey, S. (1995), 'The Australian Archives policy on electronic records – the 'technical issues'. In Yorke (1995) 121–32.

Yorke, S. (1995) (ed.), *Playing for Keeps: the proceedings of an Electronic Records Management Conference hosted by the Australian Archives* (Canberra).

Overview

TERRY COPPOCK

Carnegie Trust for the Universities of Scotland
Dunfermline

This symposium provided a stimulating review of developments in the applications of information technology in research in the humanities and the social sciences, an opportunity that is only partially captured by the formal papers (which were given orally only in summary). Indeed, there was some indication in discussion that what was presented is only the tip of the iceberg and that much more activity is underway than is revealed in the printed word. The papers inevitably reflect what has happened, but this is likely to change as younger scholars, for whom computing is an accepted fact of life, replace their senior colleagues and as the application of information technology (IT) in teaching is given a high priority (Committee of Scottish University Principals 1992). A repeat symposium five years hence, for which this symposium may act as a benchmark, is therefore likely to convey a very different picture

There is no means of knowing how representative the seventeen views that have been presented above of the role of IT in research in a selection of disciplines within the humanities and the social sciences are of the situations in those disciplines, although a great deal of effort was devoted to making inquiries of knowledgeable individuals. Not all those approached agreed to participate and not all disciplines provided contributions; political science and languages, ancient and modern, are obvious absentees, although the first could have provided a case study of the monitoring of post-war British elections and the second is covered in part by Spärck Jones' contribution on linguistics (though she is the only scholar contributing as a computer specialist – and hence an onlooker rather than as a practitioner in one of the disciplines). Contributors also responded in different ways to the advice they were offered, some providing overviews on developments within their field, others presenting their own research, and others combining the two (the preferred approach). Yet it is doubtful if any other selection of speakers would have produced a very different over-all impression of great variability between and within disciplines – a view that receives some support from the commentators on the papers.

One feature that tends to be overlooked in any evaluation of the contribution of IT to research from a disciplinary perspective is the provision of common electronically-based facilities, which may properly be regarded as aids to scholarly research, whether the latter subsequently makes use of IT or not. Electronic versions of library catalogues, bibliographies, concordances, dictionaries and other such aids, whether centrally available in libraries or, increasingly as campus networks are created, in staff rooms, student workrooms and the like, and via modems in scholars' homes, are of increasing importance. Through the Internet, similar aids to research are accessible worldwide. These resources have greatly facilitated the tasks of finding what has been written on a subject or compiling bibliographies and list of references, time-consuming chores in setting up research projects, thereby releasing time – that most valuable of research resources – for the more creative aspects of research. They have also facilitated much more sophisticated searches than are possible with printed sources, linking several criteria to identify the information sought. Even word processing, probably the most widely used aspect of IT, plays its part in greatly facilitating the preparation and editing of research findings and obviating the need for unrewarding retyping (though unless a conscious effort is made to save earlier drafts, future generations of scholars are unlikely to discover how research actually proceeded or to find the equivalent of Beethoven's notebooks).

A further dimension has been added by the advent of email, probably used at present by a minority of academics, but where levels of use are rising rapidly and are likely to do so markedly if campus use for administrative purposes becomes widespread. Email may also become an important source in its own right in electronic archives, as is suggested by a decision of the Department of Defense in the early 1990s that it would no longer provide the National Archives in Washington with hard copy of correspondence, which would in future be available only in electronic form. Email is also helping the research process worldwide by providing links between scholars working in the same field.

Email is but one example of the ways in which the national and international application of IT is affecting scholarly research. The increasing importance of the global economy and of global communications, whether by cable, by television or by satellite, is generally recognized, but its importance in assessing the impact of IT seems understated. Two contributors explicitly recognize it. Thus Sutherland has drawn attention to the changes in in the nature of the economy and how it works, the increasing importance of information as a commodity, and the way in which accounting for stocks becomes less relevant and that for flows more important. Similarly, the information society with which politicians increasingly identify affects not only developed but also developing countries, and Bravo shows how some of the local communities that anthropologists have traditionally investigated as outside observers are being transformed by the acquisition of IT skills, with consequent effects on the way in which they must be studied. Advances in global communications have also created opportunities for an international division of labour in IT through the transfer of computing operations from developed to developing countries where skilled staff are relatively cheap and job opportunities poor, for examples, digital conversion in the Phillipines of entries in the *Dictionary of the Older Scottish Tongue.*

Information technology in the humanities and the social sciences

As Anthony Kenny makes clear in his introductory paper, there are differences in the degree to which disciplines in the humanities and in the social sciences have taken advantage of information technology in research, although the dichotomy is not clear-cut and, as the subsequent discussion shows, is becoming less marked in some fields. The humanities embrace a wider range of disciplines, in some of which there is little scope for IT (other than through the use of those general scholarly aids outlined above); others have little in common in terms of methodology, as the papers on music and theatre studies show. The range of disciplines in the social sciences is smaller and the more important tend to have much in common, using similar sorts of data and often applying the same research tools (Lee 1995). Moreover, a large part of research in the social sciences is applied rather than theoretical and this work tends to be better funded and to lend itself to applications of IT. It can also be claimed that the social sciences tend to be more eclectic and readier to draw on the experience, not only of each other, but also of the physical and biological sciences.

These differences are also reflected in the kinds of information available to researchers. It is not surprising, given that computing, with its pioneering role in the physical sciences, should lend itself to those disciplines in the social sciences that rely heavily on quantitative data, particularly those derived from governmental needs for information on people and resources. A large part of research in the social sciences is based on census-type data, collected by government agencies for their own purposes and usually available, since the 1960s at least, in digital form; and where such data are unavailable, for reasons of confidentiality, prejudice or cost, researchers can seek information through sample surveys, the nature of which can be specified and the methods tested in pilot studies, although the results will have to be digitized before advantage can be taken of IT. The quantity of numerical material in machine-readable form is vast and increasing rapidly, although what will/can be preserved for future research is an important issue discussed below. Few humanities disciplines make use of such material, although modern historians are increasingly likely to do so as contemporary records become historic, assuming that such sources, which are no longer required for official purposes, survive. It should be noted that such material is too often accepted at its face value, especially by those researchers who are more interested in techniques that in the data themselves, so that wrong conclusions can be drawn, especially where data from different sources are being related to each other. Although the situation is improving through the provision of metadata, describing the main characteristics of such digital data, there are still serious deficiencies, especially in respect of changes over time.

In contrast, many of the sources of interest to scholars in the humanities are textual and, until the 1950s, have been available only in printed or manuscript form. That situation has been transformed in recent years and it is reported that the volume of textual material in digital form is now larger than that of numerical data. The British National Corpus is said to contain over 100 million words and several major projects are underway to digitize the printed word, although the backlog of such printed material is vast and the process of retrospective conversion into digital form does not command any priority from national treasuries. As Kenny demonstrates, large quantities of classical writing are now available in machine-readable form, beginning with the *Thesaurus Linguae Graecae*. A similar situation exists in respect of graphical sources, as Vaughan shows in relation to art history. Publishers are also interested in such material where they can see commercial advantage in digitizing text and illustrations, a matter of concern to scholars because of the cost of obtaining such material and of the resulting problems of copyright. Yet this availability does not seem to have generated a correspondingly large body of research among the bodies that might use it, as Spärck Jones notes in respect of languages. It may be that early training, lack of skills and interest in IT applications, and even sheer technophobia may be responsible.

A further cause of differences between the two groups of disciplines may lie in their structure within the universities. Departments in the humanities are, for the most part, small – although sometimes, notably with history, several specialist fields have been linked in a federal structure. For reasons of economy and effective administration, some smaller humanities departments have been amalgamated, but characteristically each comprises a small number of scholars pursuing their individual research. Although there are exceptions, social science departments tend to be much larger (if rarely as large as science departments, which often have numerous research staff and postgraduate students) and increasing numbers tend to share common interests, especially where they are involved in and/or competing for research contracts or projects which require teams of full-time researchers. They are more likely to contain or be associated with research units consisting wholly of research staff, whether financed by the Economic and Social Research Council (ESRC) or other bodies or existing solely on the basis of their ability to raise funds. The existence of large communities of research-oriented staff, full-time researchers and postgraduates is often a stimulus to the use of IT in research. Larger departments are also more likely to afford specialist equipment and to recruit computer scientists or other IT specialists to provide advice; such appointees become increasingly valuable as they become familiar with the discipline and its research problems. A contributory factor may be the age structure of departments, as Fellowship of the Academy suggests, with proportionately more staff in humanities departments in older age groups, which are likely to be less receptive to new methods.

Associated with these differences in structure are differences in research style. Most scholars in the humanities work alone and group research is uncommon; many social scientists will be working in groups, and while there are numerous lone scholars, these are more likely to have contact with others working in the field, especially if they are studying the same sources. Social science research is also increasingly prescriptive, especially if it is publicly funded for work on applied problems. In contrast, much research by individual scholars is self-selected, self-funded and uncosted. The author, working on the agricultural censuses for England in the nineteenth century, had to travel to Lytham St Annes where the manuscript records were then housed and copy them by hand, a task taking several months in total; moreover, since computing facilities were then not available, he had to complete over half a million calculations by slide rule and desk calculator and to plot many hundreds of maps by hand (Coppock 1982). When computing facilities became available in the early 1960s, there was then the laborious task of converting the manuscript figures into machine-readable records. Only for this last stage was any funding available.

These differences do not necessarily imply that resolving them would lead to a beneficial application of IT. This can be illustrated by Darby's massive attempt to reconstruct the geography of eleventh century England (1952–77). Here, as in many research projects in the humanities, the difficult and time-consuming problems of interpreting the source were equally as demanding as (if not more so than) the main aim of the research. It is true that the research began in the mid-1930s and, interrupted by the war, was to last until the 1970s, so that it was well underway before the first computers began to be used in research. Darby relied on long division to calculate densities and the results were mapped by hand; even so, it is likely that the time taken would not have been greatly shortened had modern computing facilities been available. They would certainly have speeded up the calculation and mapping, but they would have had no effect on the time required for the careful evaluation of the source.

Lessening the contrasts between the humanities and the social sciences

As indicated earlier, the dichotomy in the application of IT in research in the humanities and social sciences was never absolute. Just as there are disciplines such as music that, in methodological terms, have little in common with other disciplines in the humanities, so there are increasingly similarities of approach between some disciplines in the humanities and some in the social sciences. In his application of computing to his work on medieval and sixteenth century political ideas in England, Genet noted that he necessarily had to acquire some of the skills of the archivist, of the social scientist and of the statistician, while retaining his core historical skills (although he also felt that many historians were fearful of losing their disciplinary identity in this way). There are also methodological links between numbers of disciplines in the humanities and in the social sciences. Thus, art history, archaeology and theatre studies share with architecture, human geography and, to a lesser extent, economic history, an interest in two- and three-dimensional graphics, and archaeology, economic history and geography have been increasingly involved in geographical information systems as a research tool, often as an improved way of graphic illustration but increasingly as a method of spatial analysis. Econometrics, geography and philosophy make extensive use of graphs to convey complex information and also as a research tool in their own right. This overlap of interest is reflected in the order of papers in this volume. Those by Smith and Morris, originally intended for the social science section, have in fact been included with the humanities. Smith applies a social science technique of simulation to historical data to reveal relationships that might not otherwise be suspected; Morris's paper also uses a social science approach in an historical setting and was included with the humanities in part because of the absence of a paper by a modern historian.

The preceding paragraph raises the question whether there might be a greater sharing of methodologies, not only between the humanities and the social sciences but also with other disciplines. For example, Scaltsas shows how approaches developed in chemistry and mathematics might be adapted for philosophical research, and it is noteworthy that several of the papers in the social sciences use the same technique of simulation both in studies looking forward and in those looking back. It may well be that those with a knowledge both of computing and of a discipline could identify approaches that might be more widely adopted, as the papers by Wilson and Knill show in the context of archaeology, and as the application of simulation in econometrics, history and sociology demonstrates. Indeed, Wilson argues explicitly that it is fruitful to search for *generic* technologies and theories.

The widespread acceptance that teaching in higher education will increasingly be based on information technology is also likely to lessen the distinction between the humanities and the social sciences, and several contributors find it difficult to draw a sharp line between the impact of IT on teaching and on research. Thus, while the use of multimedia has an important part to play in teaching, it can also serve the exploratory phases of research in bringing together a variety of sources. This emphasis on IT-based teaching is also helping to break down the distinction between the two set of disciplines in terms of equipment. When computing was undertaken only on mainframes, those wishing to use such facilities had to hand in a set of punched cards one day and collect the output on the next; at an even earlier stage, those with what were then regarded as large data sets might have to attend a computer centre during the night to feed punched paper tape manually into the machine, a disincentive for all but the most dedicated. Subsequently, the size of social science departments and the scale of funded research have led many to be relatively well-equipped, whereas even five years ago it was alleged that humanities departments were unfairly treated in the allocation of funds for equipment (British Library/British Academy 1993). The networking of campuses and the emphasis on teaching has lessened the contrast and there are certainly universities where every member of staff who wishes to do so has ready access to a personal computer (PC). Of course, the availability of equipment does not mean that it will necessarily be used, but little information seems to be available on levels of use, both in absolute terms and as between routine applications and its use in research.

Valuable work has already been undertaken under the Computing in Teaching Initiative (CTI 1997), under which twelve centres have been established to serve the humanities and the social sciences, with the aim of providing tools relevant to those disciplines, and such work will undoubtedly be developed further. In so far as this emphasis on IT in teaching encourages a much more exploratory mode of learning among undergraduates, this too is likely to have a beneficial effect upon the application of information technology to research, both generally and more especially in the humanities The greater the familiarity of staff with the computer for routine purposes, the greater the possibility of its being considered as a research tool. Since most staff will be devoting only a minor proportion of their time to research and hence be only intermittent users, it is important that both hardware and software be user friendly and that advice be available. It is possible that the availability of cheap software capable of direct input of continuous speech may help those (chiefly among older scholars) who lack keyboard skills, as will the increasing pressure for machines and software that operate across systems. Hendry has recognized the importance of user-friendly and easily memorable software for such intermittent users, though he also notes the heavy overhead that updating imposes on the time of skilled staff. Of course, there are risks attached to such a strategy. Attention has earlier been drawn to the danger that users of data sources, especially in the social sciences, may be unaware of the limitations of the materials they use, and similar problems have characterized the application of statistical packages to non-parametric data or to samples that are too small or non-random and hence will yield misleading results. The easier programs are to use and data to access, the greater the possibility that they may be misused.

Information technology and the time dimension

The concept of time is involved in a number of aspects of the application of IT in research in the humanities and the social sciences. In part, the limited use of IT in research in the humanities and, to a lesser extent, in the social sciences, reflects the increasing pressure on staff time, particularly in the last decade. Few university teachers can afford to take time out to learn the skills necessary to apply IT in a research context, even to the extent of acquiring keyboard skills. As noted earlier, any aspect of IT that has helped to eliminate laborious chores, e.g., by facilitating access to scholarly aids and by the provision of user-friendly hardware and software, has potentially released time for scholars keen to pursue research, but something might be learnt from experience in the United States in the quantitative revolution in the 1960s when the National Science Foundation funded summer courses to enable staff to acquire the necessary skills.

Equally important, as Genet demonstrates, is the effect of technological changes within IT and especially in computing, involving both hardware and software, especially if a project is conducted over a number of years or involves comparisons over time. The change to a new medium, from paper tape to punched cards and from cards to magnetic tapes and floppy disks, can have disastrous consequences for an individual researcher; the author possesses a large number of paper tapes, from which the data, laboriously converted into digital form, were not transferred at the end of the project to a new medium, and there appeared to be no machine in the country where these tapes could be read. Similar problems have occurred with punched cards and where the software designed to read the data will no longer operate on later machines; whether such software can be rewritten depends on how well it and the obsolete machines on which it ran have been documented. Problems likewise arise where programs have been superseded and are no longer supported, and the new versions of current popular programs which follow each other in quick succession present problems for less skilled users. Where such technological changes occur during a project, there will be a heavy overhead in the time required to effect an efficient transfer, often with little help for personal research projects. Of course, changes in the form of statistical data, in the boundaries of administrative units used for statistical purposes and the like are other complicating factors, although they cause problems whether the research is based on IT or not.

Judging by the rapid improvements in computing speeds and in storage capacity, the rate of technological changes is increasing. In respect of supercomputers, Openshaw suggests a 2-year cycle and emphasizes the importance of being prepared in terms of awareness of the possible opportunities and of mental acceptance of parallel processing in place of the serial processing characteristic of computing since it began. Even so, he stresses the need for a high level of competence in computing needed by those who wish to use these facilities, something which most academic researchers, existing and potential, are unlikely to have. The situation in this regard is improving, with staff in libraries and computing centres providing expert help to researchers, but such changes in hardware and software are a strong deterrent to those who are apprehensive about using IT in the first place.

There is also a time dimension in the adoption of computing in different disciplines, although such changes are poorly documented, both generally and by subject. They depend on a variety of factors which may appear to have been relevant only in hindsight, as Coppock and Rhind (1991) found in writing a history of geographical information systems, now a standard component in research tools. A dedicated charismatic figure may inspire others or be successful in raising funds, as Fisher did in the late 1960s in Northwestern and Harvard Universities with the development of SYMAP, a computer mapping program whose wide adoption was encouraged by the Laboratory for Computer Graphics (Chrisman 1988). In contrast, it has been suggested that some groups of individuals dedicated to the adoption of IT-based research have tended to talk only to each other, to preach to the converted and to constitute a ghetto within a department.

The early experiences of applications of IT in archaeology and social psychology present interesting contrasts. Acccording to Anderson, IT was immediately accepted in the latter and has grown from strength to strength from the 1950s, having an impact on virtually every aspect of the field, in part because the discipline already had a strong research arm. In archaeology, according to Shennan, the introduction of IT in the early 1960s was effected by a group whose practitioners sought to change the nature of archaeological research by the application of statistical techniques to archaeological finds; but their methods were shown to be flawed and there was a reaction in the profession away from computing and from science. Subsequently there was a revival of interest in the provision of archaeological information for planning purposes, although the scale was often too coarse for research needs, in making detailed records of archaeological excavations and, in conjunction with hypermedia, improving the quality of such records and their visualization. These applications apart, IT has primarily been represented by minor features of fieldwork techniques in archaeology that are universally accepted as routine, and hence not worthy of comment in research papers.

As Ross shows, the time dimension is an important, but neglected aspect of IT research in terms of the preservation of information in machine-readable form. A researcher's emphasis is very much on getting the research completed and published, with limited regard for what is to happen afterwards, particularly to the data that have so often been laboriously assembled. There have been major improvements in this regard with respect to data in machine-readable form with the creation of the ESRC Data Archive for social science data and, more recently, of the Arts and Humanities Data Service, but except where deposit is a requirement of funding, it is often an afterthought, if it is considered at all, and little attention is paid to the stability of the record and its migration to other media. In part this is because of cost; much individual research by academics in the humanities and the social sciences is inadequately funded, if it is funded at all, and whatever is available is used for the research itself. As Ross shows, the cost of creating, maintaining and accessing electronic archives is high, and involves a process of selection of what to conserve. Some idea of the scale of the problem is indicated by the fact that negative decisions on what to keep have been made on 95 per cent of government records before the remainder are sent to the Public Record Office, where even this five per cent occupies one mile of shelf space each year. Similar problems of selection affect electronic archives.

Such costs affect both non-standard and official sources. The trend is to provide numerical material in machine-readable form, but such material is increasingly available to researchers only at a cost. The difficulties can be illustrated by reference to the digital archive of basic-scale maps of the Ordnance Survey (OS). In the past, when maps were printed on paper, copies of each new edition were added to the collections in the legal deposit libraries where they could freely be used as research material. Such paper maps are no longer printed and, as an interim solution, aperture cards containing microfilm have been provided. The digital maps now cover the whole country, but while the OS has an obligation to maintain the present coverage, it is not funded to maintain an historic archive, nor are the legal deposit libraries currently equipped to handle maps in digital form. The issue was considered in 1992 at a meeting at the Royal Society (endorsed by the Society and by the Academy) and attended by a wide variety of users or potential users of such material – academic, governmental, private and professional (Board and Lawrence 1994). A case is being argued at governmental level that maintaining such an archive is a national obligation, which in any case will necessarily involve decisions on what to keep, especially as revision of the basic-scale maps is now a continuous process. Whatever the solution adopted, costs are involved, for the collectors of information, the institutions which hold it and the researchers that need to access it.

Improving the situation

The importance of full and proper documentation of data sources has already been stressed in relation to transfers resulting from changes in hardware, and it is equally important that those using such data in IT-based research techniques are aware of their strengths and weaknesses, especially those who are more interested in the IT techniques applied than in the data themselves. Moreover, there may be alterations in methods of collection which may affect the extent to which changes over time can be studied. Without understanding these, which may not be documented, wrong conclusions may be drawn, especially if data from a variety of sources are used. In the author's experience, those responsible for the collection of official data are often unaware of these limitations, especially those resulting from changes in the basis of collection where these are not essential for the purposes for which they are collected. This issue is particularly important for those academic researchers who are dependent on data collected by others. In the past, two sets of volumes on sources of official statistics have been produced, the more recent that published in the 1970s and 1980s under the auspices of the Social Science Research Council (as it then was) and the Royal Statistical Society (Maunder 1974–92); a revised version, in electronic form so that it could be easily updated, would be a valuable resource. A companion series covering the humanities would be much more difficult to achieve, given the diversity of both sources and users, but the concept is worth exploring.

Equally important, if not more so, is the need for scholars, particularly in the humanities, to articulate more precisely what their problems are, so that a dialogue can occur between IT specialists and those researchers in the discipline to see if there are ways in which research can be helped. Researchers unfamiliar with computing, which requires precise specifications, often express their needs in very general terms, if they perceive them at all. To the question 'What help with research would you like from IT?', the answer is often a counter question 'What can I have?' IT is likely to have a wider application in research only if the researchers see it as contributing something that justifies the time and effort.

A related issue is the plea for good examples, acceptable in scholarly terms, of the application of IT to real research problems. This is easier said than done. Research rarely proceeds in the logical way that published papers suggest. There are mistakes, failures and dead ends, so that in many ways it is as important to learn from failed applications as it is from those that succeed – unfortunately those who have this valuable experience are generally unwilling to admit to failure. The Association for Geographic Information at its annual conferences has held sessions in which examples of successful applications of IT are presented; but perhaps because of their commercial orientation they are of limited value. In eight years as founding editor of the International Journal of Geographical Information Systems, the author urged the submission of articles that would demonstrate the value of of applying Geographical Information Systems in real situations, but few were submited; indeed, many researches appear more interested in the technology that in its successful application to real problems.

Most of the computer software available for research is general-purpose software, which is often seen by scholars in the humanities as ill-adapted for the problems in hand. There is clearly a need for greater evaluation of existing programs from the perspective of the humanities and the social sciences (not least with the aim of making them more user-friendly), the identification of gaps and, once solutions have been found, a mechanism for ensuring that potential users are aware of their existence, perhaps through the publication of some form of newsletter analogous to a Which publication.

Most important of all is the need, identified above in the context of the Ordnance Survey, but common to all sources of information, whether numerical, textual or graphical, to safeguard such sources against destruction, both intentional (in the interests of economy or because the data are no longer regarded as useful for official purposes) and unintentional (through neglect or because of failure to transfer records to new media). The topic is vast and governments, which must provide the finance, are not sympathetic to the preservation of past records, which must compete for funds with present pressing needs (although, as with the legal requirement to identify contaminated land, past records may unexpectedly prove to be a vital source). Scholars in the humanities and the social sciences should collectively be mounting the strongest possible case for the preservation of such records, ideally in disaggregated form (subject to considerations over confidentiality until these are time-expired), so that their use in research is not unncessarily constrained.

Conclusion

This symposium set out to assess the extent to which the advent of Information Technology, and in particular computing, had affected the way in which research in the humanities and the social sciences was undertaken and the kind of research topic chosen, and asked whether there had been a paradigm shift in research in these disciplines. By its nature, the symposium was both selective and qualitative, and any assessment necessarily conditional. The application of IT falls under two heads, those developments that facilitate research, whether IT-based on not, and those in which IT is part of the research process sensu stricto. The way in which the symposium was organized and the papers structured placed the emphasis on the latter, but underpinning much of this work is that made possible by the conversion of library catalogues, bibliographies, concordances, dictionaries and the like into machine-readable form. Not only are these approaches complementary, but as Scaltsas suggests, with the huge increase in the flexibility of searching, such sources must increasingly be regarded as part of research sensu stricto. Thus, he sees concept searches and language manipulation as becoming central to many research projects in the humanities. The increasing availability of immense quantities of both numerical and non-numerical information in machine-readable form has created the potential for a wide range of research applications, although whether that potential is realized depends on awareness of its existence, the scope of IT for analysing it and its relevance to the research questions scholars wish to investigate.

While it is true that bibliographic searches have revealed very few studies that could not have been undertaken without IT, such searches undoubtedly understate the extent to which IT has played a part in the research. There are numerous projects which have been aided by IT at some stage in the research process, but there seems to be a tendency for application of IT not to be prominently reported (if at all) in the findings of such research; indeed some IT-based research aids have become so routine that their use in a particular study does not merit mention. What has been done by laborious manual effort can now be undertaken in a small fraction of the time and a wide range of alternatives explored; studies that were limited to small samples or to small and possibly unrepresentative areas can now be soundly based; and the rapid increase in the speed of computing in recent years has permitted approaches that could not be undertaken by manual means or even with the slower speeds and limited storage capacity of earlier computers. While most projects seem to have involved the application of IT to existing processes, there are others where entirely new approaches have been devised or conceptualized which could not be implemented until adequate computing power was available. The massive increase in such power available through supercomputing, particularly through parallel processing, appears to offer possibilities that could not previously have been contemplated. This development will primarily help research in the social sciences, but less-technically qualified researchers in both the humanities and the social sciences will also benefit from the greatly increased capacity of desk-top PCs.

One question which the symposium implicitly poses is whether the Academy should adopt a more pro-active role in encouraging the use of IT in research. Several problems have been identified – the need to promote greater awareness of developments and opportunities: for greater academic recognition of and funding for the development of better tools and applications: an updating/extension of critical information on available sources: the encouragement and publication of good examples of applications of IT in research: and the archiving of electronic data of relevance to the humanities and the social sciences. Advances on some of these fronts will require collaboration with the Economic and Social Research Council (ESRC) and the Acts and Humanities Research Board (AHRB), perhaps with the Academy taking the initiative; progress on others are for the Academy alone to consider. Under the first could the Academy, in collaboration with ESRC/AHRB, provide funds, on a competitive basis, for accounts of successful applications of IT to real research problems? Could they jointly, possibly in collaboration with the Royal Statistical Society, support an updated evaluation of statistical sources? Could awareness be promoted by the publication of summary accounts of developments in software that are likely to be of interest to researchers in fields covered by the Academy? Could the Academy take a leading role in policy and practice in the archiving of electronic records? Could it, again in collaboration with the ESRC, make the case to Government for funding as 'big science' of topics such as demographic modelling, public service provision and urban development, as advocated by Wilson, on the grounds that these are as complex and as important as those being supported in the physical and biological sciences? Lastly, is there a need for a better focus on such matters within the Academy, on the part of both staff and Fellows? Should there be an Assistant Secretary (IT) with responsibility for such matters and should there be some structure that brings together those in the different disciplines who see the research potential of IT, assuming (as the symposium suggests) that there is sufficient community of interest for such a structure to work and sufficient specific and problem-oriented topics to encourage busy people to devote time and effort to making it do so?

While the advent of IT has been a necessary condition for its application to research in the humanities and the social sciences, it is not a sufficient condition. Apart from the availability of material in machine-readable form, the culture of research in the different disciplines appears to have been a major factor. Indeed, IT can be applied only if scholars see it as relevant to their research needs and can specify, in consultation with IT specialists, what their needs are. That appreciation seems most lacking in some sectors of the humanities, although the contributions have suggested that a sharp distinction between humanities and social sciences is both inappropriate and declining. The increasing emphasis in higher education on the application of IT to teaching is likely to lead to a greater receptivity to its application in research, as will the advent of a generation of younger scholars for whom IT is not an innovation but part of modern living. What is important is that more thought should be given to the time dimension, particularly in so far as it affects the preservation of data; it would be a tragedy if the advent of greatly improved techniques for analysing data were to be accompanied by the progressive loss of what has been made machine-readable, whether through oversight or through the failure to recognize and meet the costs that the proper archiving of data impose.

Acknowledgments

The author is grateful to Professor P. Haggett, Professor A. Wilson, Dr T. Scaltsas and Dr N. Stuart for helpful comments on earlier drafts of this overview.

References

Board, C., and Lawrence, P. (1994) (eds.), *Recording our Changing Landscape: Problems and Prospects*. The Royal Society and the British Academy (London).

British Library and British Academy (1993), *Information Technology in Humanities Scholarship* (London).

Chrisman, N. (1988) 'The risks of software innovation: a case study of the Harvard Lab', *The American Cartographer*, 15: 263–75.

Committee of Scottish University Principals (1992), *Teaching and Learning in an Expanding Higher Education System*, Report of a Working Party under the chairmanship of A. J. G. MacFarlane (Glasgow).

Coppock, J. T. (1982), 'Mapping the agricultural returns; a neglected tool of historical geography'. In Reid, M. (ed.) *Discovering Past Landscapes* (London) 8–55.

——— and Rhind, D. W. (1991), 'The history of geographical information systems'. In Maguire, D. J., Rhind, D. W. and Goodchild, M. F. (eds.) *Geographical Information Systems: Principles and Applications* (London) 21–43.

CTI Support Services (1997), 'Centre Directory', *Active Learning*, 7: 69.

Darby, H.C. (1952–77), *The Domesday Geography of Eastern England – Domesday England*. Seven volumes, each with different titles (Cambridge).

Lee, R. M. (1995) (ed.), *Information Technology for the Social Scientist* (London).

Maunder, W. F. (1974–92) (ed.), *Reviews of United Kingdom Statistical Sources*. Various titles. The Royal Statistical Society and the Social Science Research Council (Oxford).